Debiasing AI

In an era where artificial intelligence (AI) drives unprecedented change, *Debiasing AI* examines the vital intersection of technology, innovation, and sustainability. This book confronts the pressing challenge of bias in AI systems, exploring its far-reaching implications for fairness, trust, and ethical practices. Through a multidisciplinary lens, the author examines how human biases are embedded in large language models, amplified by coded machine learning, and propagated through trained algorithms. Practical strategies are offered to address these issues, paving the way for the development of more equitable and inclusive AI technologies.

With actionable insights, empirical case studies, and theoretical frameworks, *Debiasing AI* offers a roadmap for designing AI technologies that are not only innovative but also ethically sound and equitable. A must-read for scholars, industry leaders, and policymakers, this book inspires a reimagining of AI's role in creating a fairer and more sustainable future.

Donghee "Don" Shin is a Professor at Texas Tech University, USA. His work contributes to the role of online algorithmic intermediaries in shaping people's online consumption. He has published widely in both communication and information systems. He served as the Principal Investigator of a large-scale national research project. He was awarded an Endowed Chair Professorship by the Ministry of Education in Korea as well as a Samsung Endowed Chair. He also served as Regent Professor at Sungkyunkwan University from 2009 to 2016. Shin was inducted as a Fellow of the International Communication Association (ICA Fellow).

"In the swiftly evolving world of AI, technology now influences nearly every corner of human life. *Debiasing AI* explores the profound questions that arise when machines gain the power to make decisions impacting society. It examines not only the ethical principles that should guide AI development, but also pays attention to phenomenological and epistemological aspects. As we stand at the threshold of a future where AI will shape human lives in unpredictable ways, *Debiasing AI* is an invitation to consider how we can build a more responsible, just, and equitable world through mindful technology."

Mark Coekelbergh, *University of Vienna*

"*Debiasing AI* reviews and explores critical issues in how AI technology can detract from or contribute to a more just, humane, and equitable world. Topics range from the extent to which AI can be moral or ethical, how algorithms can nudge users toward more or less biased decisions, and how algorithms may be proactively designed to inoculate against misinformation."

Ronald E. Rice, *University of California, Santa Barbara*

"*Debiasing AI* is an insightful exploration of the ethical challenges posed by AI. Don Shin masterfully navigates complex topics like fairness, transparency, and accountability, offering readers an essential resource in understanding AI's moral dimensions. This is an indispensable book for anyone looking to grasp the ethical landscape of AI."

Karamjit S. Gill, *Editor-in-Chief*, AI and Society

"*Debiasing AI* is a groundbreaking contribution to AI ethics, providing a thoughtful and scholarly exploration of the pressing questions that define our technological era. Dr. Shin combines academic rigor with real-world examples, making this work an indispensable read for researchers, students, and practitioners dedicated to advancing the field of AI ethics."

Mohammed Ibahrine, *Northwestern University*

Debiasing AI
Rethinking the Intersection of Innovation and Sustainability

Donghee Shin

Routledge
Taylor & Francis Group

NEW YORK AND LONDON

First published 2025
by Routledge
605 Third Avenue, New York, NY 10158

and by Routledge
4 Park Square, Milton Park, Abingdon, Oxon, OX14 4RN

Routledge is an imprint of the Taylor & Francis Group, an informa business

ISBN: 978-1-032-86978-0 (hbk)
ISBN: 978-1-032-86977-3 (pbk)
ISBN: 978-1-003-53024-4 (ebk)

DOI: 10.1201/9781003530244

Typeset in Times LT Std
by KnowledgeWorks Global Ltd.

Contents

Introduction: Debiasing AI: Rethinking the Intersection of
Innovation and Sustainability   1

PART ONE   Ontology of AI Ethics: Ethical AI Principles   11

1 AI and Moral Agency: Can AI Have a Sense of Morality?   13

2 Decoding Algorithmic Privacy: How to Address Privacy
Issues Raised by AI   34

3 AI and Transparency: In Transparency We Trust   61

**PART TWO   Phenomenology of AI Ethics: How People
Experience AI Ethics   85**

4 Algorithmic Bias and Trust: How to Debias and Build Trust in AI   87

5 Algorithmic Nudge: A Nudge to Counter Algorithmic Bias   105

6 Algorithmic Heuristics: How People Evaluate the Ethics
of Deepfakes   126

**PART THREE   Epistemology of AI Ethics: Mechanism
of Understanding AI Ethics   147**

7 Algorithmic Equity: How Humans Understand AI Morality   149

8 The Ethics of AI Acceptance: How Ethical Heuristics Drive
AI Adoption   171

9 Responsible AI and the Newsroom: How Does AI Journalism
Make Sense of AI Ethics?   198

**PART FOUR   Governance of AI Ethics: Striking the
Right Balance Ethics and Regulation   227**

**10 The Moral Code: The Intersection of Ethics
and Regulation in AI   229**

**11 Diversity-Aware AI: Designing AI Systems That
Reflect Humanity   249**

12 Algorithmic Inoculation: Immunizing Minds Against Bias   270

Subject Index   289
Name Index   292

Introduction: Debiasing AI

Rethinking the Intersection of Innovation and Sustainability

INTRODUCTION

Artificial Intelligence (AI) is revolutionizing every aspect of modern life, influencing the ways we communicate, work, and perceive the world around us. As this technological evolution accelerates, it becomes increasingly important to scrutinize the ethical implications associated with the development and use of AI. This book offers an in-depth examination of these vital issues, aiming to align technological progress with moral responsibility and individual well-being. The ethical discourse surrounding AI is complex and multifaceted, encompassing critical topics such as privacy, bias, transparency, accountability, and the broader implications for human autonomy and justice. AI systems have the potential to perpetuate existing biases, as algorithms often learn from datasets that reflect societal inequalities. Without a thoughtful approach to ethical guidelines, an AI system can inadvertently reinforce discrimination and marginalization.

Addressing these challenges necessitates an ethical framework that emphasizes fairness and inclusivity. This book seeks to clarify the intricacies of AI ethics, foster understanding, encourage responsible practices, and engage a wider audience in discussions about the implications of AI.

THE EVOLUTION OF AI ETHICS

Ethics, often considered cliché, plays a foundational role in the development and deployment of AI technologies. The ethical dimensions of AI are often overlooked in discussions about its development and deployment. It is a reality that many people do not view

DOI: 10.1201/9781003530244-1

AI ethics as equally crucial as its technical advancements. This perception is influenced by various cultural, social, and psychological factors that shape our understanding of AI's role in society. Fundamentally, a significant number of individuals lack awareness of the ethical implications associated with AI systems and their subtle yet profound impact on daily lives (Anderson & Anderson, 2021). Without a clear grasp of how these ethical concerns manifest in real-world applications, AI ethics tends to be relegated to the background, failing to receive the urgency it deserves.

One significant reason for this lack of emphasis on ethics is that people often focus on AI's immediate benefits, like convenience and efficiency.

The perception that ethics is merely a formality overlooks the real-world impact of unchecked AI development. From biased algorithms affecting decisions in criminal justice to AI tools that manipulate public opinion, the consequences of ignoring ethical considerations are profound. Ethical debates may seem abstract or philosophical, but they are essential in holding AI creators accountable for the systems they build. By embedding ethics into the development process, AI researchers and companies can anticipate potential risks and mitigate them before they become widespread problems (Coeckelbergh, 2020). Moreover, ethics provides a common language for balancing innovation with social responsibility. It might be tempting to view ethics as a barrier to progress, but it is actually an enabler of trust between technology developers and the public. As AI systems become more integrated into daily life—affecting everything from healthcare to education—their transparency, fairness, and accountability become non-negotiable. Ethics, often dismissed as cliché, is a powerful tool for ensuring that AI serves humanity's best interests, rather than solely advancing technological frontiers.

Unlike the overall public underplaying, ethical considerations are indeed powerful drivers in the development of AI, as they shape the standards, goals, and safeguards surrounding this technology. Ethical concerns such as fairness, accountability, transparency, and privacy are increasingly integrated into the AI development process, influencing both design and deployment. Ethical considerations are essential to the advancement of AI technology, ensuring that it evolves responsibly and beneficially. Without ethics, AI development risks negative consequences—such as unfairness, lack of accountability, or harm to individuals and society—that could undermine its potential benefits. As AI systems become more prevalent in critical domains—healthcare, law enforcement, and beyond—ethical considerations ensure that the technology serves humanity's best interests while minimizing harm (Ayling & Chapman, 2022).

AI is not neutral or separate from human values; rather, algorithmic systems are intricately woven into society and significantly influence it (Shin, 2024). When designing, deploying, and managing AI systems, it is essential to assess any biases present within these systems. Debiasing AI is like sculpting a masterpiece from raw data, chiseling away the imperfections to reveal a system that is fair, inclusive, and just. Imagine an AI that not only understands the world but does so without prejudice, offering insights and decisions that reflect the true diversity of human experience. By meticulously addressing biases, we transform AI into a powerful ally that champions equality, ensuring that every interaction is free from the shadows of discrimination. This process is not just a technical challenge but a moral imperative, paving the way for a future where technology uplifts and empowers individuals (Shneiderman, 2022).

HOW TO RESOLVE AI ETHICAL ISSUES

Addressing AI ethics is certainly not easy and challenging because it requires balancing complex, often conflicting principles like fairness, transparency, privacy, and accountability while adapting to rapidly advancing technologies. One of the primary challenges in AI ethics is translating ethical principles into actionable practices. How can we measure concepts like fairness, transparency, and accountability? How can we assess the relative importance of an AI algorithm's precision, accuracy, and predictability? The intricacy of these questions opens up numerous avenues for research, prompting the exploration of various partial solutions that tackle specific facets of the issue throughout the different stages of AI application development (Shin, 2023). This is why resolving AI ethics is an ongoing process that requires collaboration between technologists, policymakers, ethicists, and society as a whole (Klenk, 2024). It involves not just identifying and understanding ethical concerns but also developing practical solutions to ensure AI technologies are designed and deployed in ways that benefit humanity while minimizing harm. For example, the challenges posed by AI are vast, touching everything from automated decision-making systems to facial recognition technology and autonomous cars. Addressing these ethical concerns is not just a technological issue; it is a societal one that requires collaboration across disciplines.

One of the most pressing ethical concerns with AI is bias. AI systems often rely on large datasets to learn and make decisions. However, if these datasets reflect existing social biases, the AI can perpetuate or even amplify those biases. This is particularly concerning in sensitive areas such as hiring, criminal justice, and healthcare, where biased AI systems can reinforce inequality. For example, AI systems used in predictive policing have been found to disproportionately target minority communities due to biased historical data. To mitigate such risks, developers must focus on creating fair and unbiased algorithms, which include improving the diversity of the data and the teams working on AI projects. Regular audits and evaluations of AI systems for fairness are essential to ensuring these technologies do not reinforce discrimination.

Another key ethical issue is transparency. Many AI systems, particularly those based on deep learning, operate as "black boxes," meaning their decision-making processes are not easily understood by humans (Lim et al., 2024). This lack of transparency makes it difficult to explain how AI systems arrive at particular conclusions, which can undermine trust in AI, especially in high-stakes areas like healthcare or autonomous vehicles. Ensuring that AI systems are explainable and that their decisions can be understood by both users and regulators is crucial to building trust and ensuring accountability. Efforts in explainable AI are aimed at making AI systems more interpretable, allowing for clearer insights into how decisions are made.

AI ethics is not just about preventing harm but also about ensuring that AI serves the greater good. To achieve this, AI development needs to be guided by a strong ethical framework that prioritizes fairness, accountability, transparency, and privacy. Multidisciplinary collaboration between technologists, policymakers, ethicists, and the public is essential to ensure AI aligns with human values and promotes social well-being

(Shin & Zhou, 2024). Addressing the ethical challenges of AI is an ongoing process, requiring constant monitoring and adaptation as technology evolves.

DEBUNKING MYTHS IN AI ETHICS

The concept of AI ethics is frequently misunderstood and often viewed either as a mere obstacle to technological progress or as a blanket solution to all potential harms posed by AI (Romele, 2022). These misconceptions distort the public's understanding of what AI ethics entails, its role in guiding AI development, and its ability to address the risks and challenges associated with AI. These misunderstandings can lead to complacency among developers, policymakers, and the public, creating gaps in addressing the real issues AI presents.

One common misconception is that AI ethics is just about preventing harm. While harm prevention—such as mitigating bias, ensuring privacy, and avoiding unintended consequences—is a key component, AI ethics is much broader. It also seeks to promote the positive potential of AI technologies. AI ethics isn't merely about stopping bad outcomes; it's also about encouraging the development of AI systems that actively benefit society. For instance, ethical frameworks can guide AI innovation in areas like healthcare, education, and climate change, helping to ensure that these technologies are developed with a focus on improving human well-being and fostering fairness, rather than solely focusing on risk avoidance.

Another misconception is that AI ethics is a rigid set of rules that can be universally applied to all situations. In reality, AI ethics is highly contextual and adaptive, varying based on the specific application, cultural values, and societal norms of different regions. What may be considered ethically permissible in one country or industry could be viewed as unacceptable in another. This flexibility is a key strength of AI ethics, but it is often misunderstood as inconsistency. Ethical guidelines must account for the diverse ways in which AI is used and the different values that influence its impact on various communities. Simply applying a one-size-fits-all approach to AI ethics can lead to inadequate or misguided regulations.

A major misconception surrounding AI ethics is the belief that ethical principles alone can solve all the challenges posed by AI. While ethical guidelines are critical, they are not a substitute for technical expertise or robust regulation. AI ethics must be integrated with technical solutions—such as improved algorithmic design, better data collection practices, and transparency tools—and legal frameworks that enforce accountability. Some companies may adopt ethical AI guidelines as public relations tools, but without concrete measures to ensure compliance, these guidelines often remain aspirational rather than actionable. True ethical AI development requires a combination of ethical awareness, technical competence, and legal enforcement to effectively address issues like bias, fairness, and privacy.

Furthermore, many believe that AI ethics is solely the responsibility of tech firms and code developers. In reality, AI ethics requires a collective effort that involves multiple stakeholders, including policymakers, educators, and the public. It's not enough for tech companies to be ethically mindful during development; there must be regulations and public engagement to ensure that AI systems serve the greater good. Governments play a critical role in creating and enforcing regulations that hold developers accountable, while public understanding and scrutiny help drive ethical innovation. The misconception that AI ethics is the exclusive domain of developers downplays the need for multidisciplinary collaboration.

By addressing these misconceptions, we can ensure that AI ethics is taken seriously as a dynamic and essential component of AI development, promoting both innovation and social good while safeguarding against unintended consequences.

CAN AI BE ETHICAL LIKE HUMANS?

The question of whether AI can be moral like humans is a profound one, touching on the nature of morality, human intelligence, and the boundaries of machine learning. As AI systems grow more sophisticated, performing tasks that once seemed exclusive to human cognition, the possibility of machines possessing moral capabilities has sparked widespread debate. Unlike humans, who develop a moral compass through socialization, empathy, and personal experiences, AI cannot inherently understand or feel ethical values—it follows programmed rules and patterns in data without experiencing empathy, guilt, or moral judgment (Scarbrough et al., 2024). AI relies on the ethical frameworks and rules programmed by its developers. To make AI systems ethical, developers can incorporate principles such as fairness, transparency, and accountability.

While AI can be programmed to follow ethical rules and make decisions that align with human values, the complexities of human morality raise doubts about whether machines can ever truly achieve moral reasoning comparable to that of humans. Human morality is deeply rooted in emotions, cultural contexts, and lived experiences, all of which shape our understanding of right and wrong. Morality is not simply a set of rules; it is fluid, evolving with society's values, and often requires nuance and empathy. Humans rely on emotional intelligence, empathy, and a deep sense of responsibility to guide their ethical choices. These qualities are inherently tied to human consciousness, something AI currently lacks. While AI can simulate moral decision-making by following predefined ethical guidelines, it cannot possess the emotional depth or self-awareness necessary to truly be moral like humans.

One argument in favor of the possibility of AI achieving morality is that it can be programmed to follow ethical frameworks. For example, AI systems can be designed to minimize harm, respect privacy, and ensure fairness, principles that are central to many ethical theories. Through machine learning, AI can also adapt its behavior based on feedback, improving its ability to make decisions that align with ethical norms over time. Some research in AI ethics focuses on developing "moral AI," where machines are taught to make ethical decisions by analyzing large datasets of human behavior and ethical dilemmas (Morley et al., 2023). In theory, this could allow AI to simulate human-like moral reasoning. However, this approach has its limitations. While AI can be trained to make decisions that appear ethical, it fundamentally lacks the capacity for moral understanding. AI systems do not have emotions, intentions, or an intrinsic sense of what is right or wrong. They operate on data and algorithms, making decisions based on patterns and probabilities rather than moral reflection. This means that even if AI makes decisions that align with ethical principles, it is not acting out of a sense of morality but simply following a set of programmed instructions. Morality, in the human sense, is not just about making the right choice; it's about understanding why that choice is right and being motivated by moral convictions. AI, lacking consciousness, cannot grasp this deeper layer of moral reasoning.

Moreover, human morality is often subjective and context-dependent. What is considered ethical in one culture or situation may be viewed differently in another. Humans can navigate these moral complexities by considering the broader context, understanding cultural nuances, and reflecting on personal experiences. AI, on the other hand, operates within the confines of the data it is trained on and the rules it is given. It cannot easily adapt to the fluidity of human moral judgment, nor can it account for the emotional and psychological factors that influence human decision-making. As a result, AI's version of morality is inherently limited to the specific parameters set by its developers.

There are also ethical concerns about delegating moral decision-making to machines. If AI systems were to become responsible for making ethical choices—such as in autonomous vehicles, healthcare, or law enforcement—it raises questions about accountability. Who is responsible when an AI makes a morally questionable decision? Since AI lacks the ability to bear moral responsibility, any mistakes or harms caused by AI decisions ultimately fall on the humans who designed, programmed, or deployed the system. This further illustrates the gap between human morality and AI behavior: while AI can be guided by ethical principles, it cannot be held accountable in the same way humans are.

Thus, key aspects of AI ethics are human-centered AI ethics, which is a framework that places human values, rights, and well-being at the forefront of AI design, development, and deployment (Coeckelbergh, 2020). In this approach, AI technologies are created and managed in ways that prioritize human dignity, autonomy, and fairness, emphasizing the need to avoid harm and ensure equitable access to AI's benefits. One of the fundamental principles of human-centered AI ethics is respect for human autonomy. AI systems should support human decision-making rather than replacing it. Fairness and inclusion are also essential in human-centered AI. AI systems can reinforce existing biases if not carefully designed, leading to discrimination in critical areas such as hiring, lending, or law enforcement. Ethical AI systems must be developed using diverse and representative data, with mechanisms for auditing and correcting biases to ensure equitable outcomes for all groups. In conclusion, a human-centered approach to AI ethics ensures that AI technologies respect human values and enhance societal well-being, fostering innovation in ways that prioritize fairness, transparency, and responsibility.

AI ETHICS MOVING FORWARD: WILL AI EVER BE FREE OF BIAS?

The future of AI will center on developing frameworks and technologies that make ethical principles integral to AI from design to deployment (Schlagwein & Willcocks, 2023).

As AI becomes increasingly woven into critical areas, the demand for transparent, fair, and accountable systems will grow. Emerging methods, such as explainable AI and bias detection tools, will help AI systems meet ethical standards while providing users with greater trust and understanding. Additionally, regulatory bodies worldwide are starting to draft AI ethics guidelines and legislation, pushing for industry-wide compliance and accountability. In the future, ethical AI will require interdisciplinary collaboration, drawing from philosophy, law, social sciences, and computer science, creating systems that prioritize human values and societal well-being as AI continues to evolve. As we move forward, a collaborative approach that includes technologists, policymakers, and communities will be essential to harness the benefits of AI while mitigating risks, ensuring that its development aligns with societal values and promotes overall well-being.

In moving forward, AI ethics will require a collaborative effort from technologists, ethicists, policymakers, and the public to establish robust frameworks that prioritize fairness, transparency, and accountability. The diverse interests of stakeholders will complicate the ethical landscape surrounding AI. The impacts of AI extend across various sectors and affect a wide range of groups, including developers, users, businesses, and communities. Each of these stakeholders brings unique values and priorities to the table, making it challenging to achieve a consensus on ethical standards. Balancing these differing perspectives requires extensive dialog and negotiation, often leading to ethical dilemmas that lack clear resolutions. Adding to the complexity is the global nature of AI technologies. Ethical considerations can differ significantly across cultures and legal systems, making it difficult to create universal guidelines. What may be considered ethical in one culture might not hold the same weight in another, leading to potential conflicts in implementation and enforcement. This cultural diversity necessitates a careful examination of local contexts and values, complicating the development of a cohesive ethical framework.

Bias and discrimination are pressing concerns in AI ethics. The compounding effect is that both humans and algorithms contribute to bias in AI. AI systems can amplify human bias or inadvertently perpetuate biases present in the data used to train them, resulting in discriminatory outcomes that disproportionately affect marginalized groups. Identifying and mitigating these biases is a complex task, requiring an understanding of both the technology itself and the societal contexts in which it operates. This dual focus complicates the ethical landscape, as it demands a multidisciplinary approach that integrates technical, social, and ethical considerations. The unintended consequences of AI deployment present another layer of difficulty in ethical discussions. AI can lead to unforeseen outcomes that may not be immediately apparent, making it challenging to predict the ethical implications of its use. Assessing these potential impacts requires a nuanced understanding of the broader social landscape and the interconnectedness of various factors.

The foundational principles of ethical AI require further refinement, especially as the legal landscape continues to evolve. Given the rapid advancement of these technologies, proactive monitoring is crucial to quickly address any emerging issues. This book responds to this need. The starting point of this book is about realizing the limitations of the ethical approach to AI. As AI continues to evolve and integrate into various aspects of life, it is crucial for ethicists, technologists, policymakers, and the public to engage in ongoing dialog and collaboration. Only through a comprehensive understanding of these complexities can we work toward ethical AI that benefits society while minimizing harm and ensuring technology serves humanity responsibly. The ethical approach in this book emphasizes the interplay between technology and social factors, recognizing that AI systems do not operate in isolation but rather within complex social, political, and cultural contexts.

CHAPTER OUTLINES

The book systematically analyzes the different dimensions of AI ethics through cognate disciplinary perspectives, taking into account the related contexts of communication, cognitive science, and information systems. This book admits that AI ethics are sticky and difficult to address. Researching AI ethics is challenging due to the complexity and rapid evolution of both technology and moral philosophy. The interdisciplinary nature of AI ethics requires knowledge from diverse fields, including computer science, philosophy, sociology, and law, making it difficult to establish a cohesive framework. As AI technologies advance quickly, ethical frameworks must adapt even faster, leading to a persistent gap between technological capabilities and ethical guidelines. This dynamic landscape demands continuous dialog among stakeholders, further complicating the task of establishing clear ethical standards in AI.

Rather than looking at AI ethics through a single lens, the book maps the various kinds of ethics through several different disciplinary perspectives, taking into account the overlapping contexts of psychology, technology, and communications. The book focuses on four main parts:

- *Part One: Ontology of AI Ethics: Ethical AI Principles*
- *Part Two: Phenomenology of AI Ethics: How People Experience AI Ethics*
- *Part Three: Epistemology of AI Ethics: Mechanism of Understanding AI Ethics*
- *Part Four: Governance of AI Ethics: Striking the Right Balance Ethics and Regulation*

The ontology of AI ethics (Chapters 1–3) addresses the fundamental principles and relationships within the field that guide the ethical development and deployment of AI. These principles include fairness, accountability, transparency, and privacy. Fairness ensures that AI systems do not perpetuate or exacerbate social biases, promoting equity across different demographics. Accountability emphasizes the importance of establishing clear responsibilities for AI decisions, ensuring that human oversight remains integral to AI operations. Transparency involves making AI processes understandable and interpretable, fostering trust among users and stakeholders. Privacy safeguards individuals' personal data against misuse and exploitation. Together, these principles form a foundational framework for creating ethical AI systems that align with human values and societal norms, guiding developers and policymakers in their efforts to harness AI for the greater good. From this ontological perspective, Chapter 1 explores the concept of AI as a moral agent, specifically examining the question: Can AI possess a sense of morality? Chapter 2 delves into the topic of AI and privacy, posing the vital question of how to effectively address the privacy challenges that arise in the context of AI technology. Chapter 3 discusses transparent AI with a theme of the role of transparency in user interaction with AI.

The phenomenology of AI ethics examines how individuals and communities experience and perceive the ethical implications of AI, focusing on how these experiences shape their understanding of ethical issues and the impact on their interactions. People engage with AI technologies in various contexts and their experiences can shape their understanding of ethical concerns like bias, surveillance, and accountability. This perspective emphasizes the subjective nature of ethical experiences, highlighting how factors such as cultural background, personal values, and social dynamics influence individuals' perceptions of AI. For instance, while some users may appreciate the convenience and efficiency of AI tools, others may feel apprehensive about privacy infringements or discrimination. By examining these lived experiences, researchers can gain deeper insights into the societal impacts of AI, informing the development of more ethical and user-centered AI systems that resonate with diverse communities. From the phenomenological perspective, Chapter 4 delves into the concepts of algorithmic bias and trust, exploring strategies for debiasing and fostering trust in AI systems. Chapter 5 shifts focus to algorithmic nudge, emphasizing the importance of ethical nudging within AI applications. Finally, Chapter 6 examines algorithmic heuristics, providing insights into how individuals discern the ethical implications of deepfakes.

The epistemology of AI ethics examines the nature and scope of ethics in AI, through which individuals understand and interpret the moral implications of AI. This part explores how knowledge about AI ethics is generated, disseminated, and validated, encompassing the sources of information that shape our ethical frameworks and judgments regarding AI technologies. It considers various epistemic dimensions, such as the role of interdisciplinary research, public discourse, and education in informing ethical perspectives on AI. Additionally, it investigates the influence of cultural, social, and technological contexts on how people perceive and assess the ethical challenges posed by AI. By analyzing these mechanisms of understanding, the epistemology of AI ethics aims to enhance our collective awareness and critical engagement with the ethical dimensions of AI, ultimately guiding the development of responsible and informed AI practices. In this epistemological framework, Chapter 7 explores the concept of algorithmic equity, focusing on how humans interpret the morality of AI. Chapter 8 continues this discussion by examining the influence of user heuristics on the acceptance of AI to understand how ethical heuristics shape AI acceptance. Chapter 9 delves into the role of responsible AI within journalistic contexts, highlighting how journalists navigate and understand AI ethics.

In the final part of the governance of AI ethics, Chapter 10 addresses the vital connection between ethical considerations and regulatory frameworks in the development and deployment of AI. It suggests an effective AI governance model that harmonizes ethical principles with regulatory measures, ensuring that AI technologies are developed and implemented in alignment with societal values while maintaining accountability and transparency. Chapter 11 explores the concept of diversity-aware AI, presenting it as a potential future approach to ethical AI. Finally, Chapter 12 delves into the strategies of algorithmic inoculation, offering an in-depth exploration of the cognitive mechanisms underlying these effects. It emphasizes how such strategies can effectively combat misinformation originating from AI sources, while also extending their theoretical insights to practical, real-world applications.

Interweaving conceptual and empirical chapters, this book provides a human-centered lens to the logic and social implications of AI ethics. By examining the immense repercussions that AI will have on people and society, the book brings together various perspectives on algorithms into an integrated conceptual framework. Cutting across all the chapters raises the need for an urgent cross-sectoral interdisciplinary effort to investigate, protect against, and mitigate the risks of AI.

REFERENCES

Anderson, S., & Anderson, M. (2021). AI and ethics. *AI Ethics*, *1*(1), 27–31. https://doi.org/10.1007/s43681-020-00003-6

Ayling, J., & Chapman, A. (2022). Putting AI ethics to work. *AI Ethics*, *2*(2), 405–429. https://doi.org/10.1007/s43681-021-00084-x

Coeckelbergh, M. (2020). *AI ethics*. The MIT Press. https://doi.org/10.7551/mitpress/12549.001.0001

Klenk, M. (2024). Ethics of generative AI and manipulation. *Ethics Information Technology*, *26*, 9. https://doi.org/10.1007/s10676-024-09745-x

Lim, J., Ahmad, N., & Ibarahim, M. (2024). Understanding user sensemaking in fairness and transparency in algorithms. *AI & Society*, *39*, 447–490. https://doi.org/10.1007/s00146-022-01525-9

Morley, J., Kinsey, L., Elhalal, A., Garcia, F., Ziosi, M., & Floridi, L. (2023). Operationalizing AI ethics. *AI & Society*, *38*, 411–423. https://doi.org/10.1007/s00146-021-01308-8

Romele, A. (2022). Images of AI: A blind spot in AI ethics. *Philosophy & Technology*, *35*(1). https://doi.org/10.1007/s13347-022-00498-3

Scarbrough, H., Chen, Y., & Patriotta, G. (2024). The AI of the beholder: Intra-professional sensemaking of an epistemic technology. *Journal of Management Studies*. https://doi.org/10.1111/joms.13065

Schlagwein, D., & Willcocks, L. (2023). ChatGPT et al.: The ethics of using generative AI. *Journal of Information Technology*, *38*(3), 232–238. https://doi.org/10.1177/02683962231200411

Shin, D. (2023). *Algorithms, humans, and interactions: How do algorithms interact with people? Designing meaningful AI experiences* (1st ed.). Routledge. https://doi.org/10.1201/b23083

Shin, D. (2024). *Artificial misinformation: Exploring human-algorithm interaction online*. Springer Nature. https://doi.org/10.1007/978-3-031-52569-8

Shin, D., & Zhou, S. (2024). A value and diversity-aware news recommendation systems. *Journalism & Mass Communication Quarterly*. https://doi.org/10.1177/10776990241246680

Shneiderman, B. (2022). *Human-centered AI*. Oxford University Press.

PART ONE

Ontology of AI Ethics
Ethical AI Principles

AI and Moral Agency

Can AI Have a Sense of Morality?

1

ARTIFICIAL MORALITY

Human interaction with artificial agents is increasing in almost all spheres of life. As we interact with or depend on artificial agents that can decide things independently, it raises the question of morality on which we would judge the agents' autonomous actions. At this point, with the development of artificial intelligence (AI) into a decision-maker agent, we need to consider the morality of its actions. The considerations for formulating artificial morality, which means the moral caliber of artificial agents, are becoming a pressing need as these agents become more autonomous and need less human supervision (Allen et al., 2005). However, there is no universally accepted rule for human morality; it's a relative term shaped and meant by the philosophical, theoretical, religious, and cultural ideas behind it (Allen et al., 2005). The procedures humans use to act morally are challenging to implement in automated machines or AI agents, which gives rise to the academic exploration of artificial morality (Wallach, 2010).

With the complexity of human morality, it is difficult to come up with a universally acceptable definition of artificial morality (Kearns & Roth, 2020). Instead, theorists and researchers of ethics and automated systems mostly tried to figure out approaches to define artificial moral agents. Allen et al. (2000) explored three models of morality for artificial moral agents: the virtue approaches model (where a moral agent should have a virtuous character, i.e., an honest AI), the associative learning model (where a moral agent learns from the feedback on moral action like a child), and evolutionary/sociobiological approaches (where a moral agent requires to have rationality). However, for the process of designing artificial moral agents, Allen et al. (2005) mentioned three approaches: the top-down approach, the bottom-up approach, and the hybrid approach.

DOI: 10.1201/9781003530244-3

The top-down approach is rule-based, where the artificial moral agents' action will be defined by preset moral rules or principles, whereas the bottom-up approach is environment-based, where an appropriate environment is created to appreciate moral behavior by the artificial moral agents (Allen et al., 2000, 2005; Wallach, 2010). On the other hand, the hybrid approach includes both former approaches in designing the artificial moral agents, which have the flexibility and evolving nature in considering morality (Allen et al., 2005; Cervantes et al., 2020). Considering the myriads of contexts humans face to appropriate their notions of morality, van Berkel et al. (2022) proposed a contextual morality framework to design artificial morality as the moral convictions of people for specific contexts, and as the contexts change, moral convictions change accordingly.

The approaches to identifying and designing artificial moral agents are based on several philosophical ideas about morality. Most researchers traced back to the ideas of utilitarian ethics, which encompasses the idea that actions should be based on creating the greater good (Allen et al., 2000, 2005; Wallach, 2010), virtue ethics which implies that a virtuous agent conducts good acts (Allen et al., 2000, 2005; Constantinescu et al., 2022; Gamez et al., 2020; Wallach, 2010). However, Allen et al. (2005) argued that these ideas alone cannot explain how an artificial moral agent should have morality, as many conflicting parts in these philosophies cannot be translated into codes to develop artificial morality. Similarly, Telkamp and Anderson (2022) vouched for the moral foundation theory, which focuses on fairness and care as the basis of morality, and proposed an artificial moral agent should act fairly and with care toward humans. On the other hand, several other researchers reached moral psychology to define the artificial moral agent with the idea of moral agents, moral patients, and the relationship between them (Bonnefon et al., 2024; Floridi & Sanders, 2004; Ladak et al., 2024; Sun & Ye, 2023). Moral agents are entities who can perform right and wrong actions, and moral patients are entities who are the targets of such actions (Ladak et al., 2024). So, when we consider artificial morality, we also need to understand the relationship between agents and patients. Floridi and Sanders (2004) explained that there can be two meaningful relations between the two: both agents and patients can be equal, and agents can be a subset of patients. From this point of view, defining an artificial moral agent requires assessing its role both as an agent of morality and a patient of morality.

There are several challenges in training AI about the notions of ethics. For example, Allen et al. (2000) identified two areas of disagreement in developing an artificial moral agent. First, there is disagreement about what standard of morality should be used in designing an artificial moral agent, and second, there is a disagreement about what it means to be an artificial moral agent (Allen et al., 2000). Brożek and Janik (2019) argued that at this point of development in artificial agents, we could not consider them as moral agents because simply following ethical rules is not enough, a moral agent also needs the capacity to judge their moral actions, which are not present in AI. This view reflects what Allen et al. (2000) stressed about the designing of artificial moral agents, "Essential to building a morally praiseworthy agent is the task of giving it enough intelligence to assess the effects of its actions on sentient beings, and to use those assessments to make appropriate choices" (p. 261).

Another challenging domain in artificial morality is people's perception of accountability in the case of moral violation by an artificial agent. Though artificial morality depends on how the artificial moral agents are developed to act morally,

Shank and DeSanti (2018) found that in real-world cases of moral violation by any AI agent, people are highly likely to hold the agents responsible for the violation rather than their designers. Alternatively, Sullivan and Fosso Wamba (2022) argued that when people perceive any harm from AI agents, they tend to blame all the entities (i.e., companies and designers) involved in making AI, including the AI itself, but they blame the developers most. Moreover, people have a perception that machine has no mind and lacks emotions (Bigman & Gray, 2018). Misselhorn (2020) argued that an artificial moral agent needs contextual consciousness and affective aspects of morality, which means having moral emotions. Experimental studies showed that people generally do not like machines making moral decisions about driving, legal, medical, and military (Bigman & Gray, 2018). Furthermore, individual differences and geographical and cultural variations of people also influence their attitude toward moral machines (Awad et al., 2018), which makes it difficult to design universally acceptable moral agents. An individual accepts artificial agents as moral agents when their decisions match with the individual's moral foundation (Telkamp & Anderson, 2022). This implies the need to design the artificial moral agent to match with individual's moral domain which is not a viable option.

Researchers and designers have been trying to develop artificial moral agents for several decades. A study on the moral agent designed in the last two decades showed that there are no artificial agents that are capable of making complicated moral decisions like humans (Cervantes et al., 2020). Similarly, Constantinescu et al. (2022) argue that the current form of AI does not qualify as a moral agent. Instead, they argued that this AI agent could be used as a moral enhancer that would enable humans with contextual knowledge to make proper moral decisions (Constantinescu et al., 2022). From this discussion, it is evident that future research on artificial morality needs to focus on some unified rules of morality, technical abilities to transform those moral codes into machine-readable codes to train the artificial agents, and increasing acceptance and understanding of these agents to humans.

AI MACHINES AS MORAL AGENTS: HOW TO TRAIN AI TO MAKE MORAL DECISIONS

As AI continues to advance rapidly, it brings with it a host of ethical considerations. AI can be perceived as a moral agent even when its programming does not explicitly encode moral values, as long as the consequences of its actions can fall in the moral domain (Bonnefon, 2024). When AIs are moral agents, a question is how to train AI to make ethical decisions. AI morality pertains to the ethical guidelines that steer the creation, advancement, and implementation of AI systems. It falls within the realm of artificial morality, focusing on how AI should act and make decisions in accordance with human ethical standards. The objective is to guarantee that AI technologies operate in an ethically sound manner, reducing harm and fostering positive results (Avnoon et al., 2024).

The question of whether AI can think ethically is a complex topic that intersects technology, philosophy, and ethics. Currently, AI lacks the ability to think in the same way that humans do, as it does not possess consciousness, self-awareness, or emotions. Human cognition is characterized by creativity, emotional intelligence, and ethical reasoning—qualities that AI, despite its advancements, still struggles to replicate fully. Instead, AI operates based on algorithms and data that guide its decision-making processes. Unlike humans, AI systems operate on algorithms and data, lacking emotions, intentions, and moral reasoning.

While AI can be equipped with ethical guidelines and trained to recognize patterns associated with ethical behavior, it fundamentally lacks the capacity for true understanding or moral reasoning (Anderson & Anderson, 2021). AI operates based on algorithms and data, not human-like consciousness or moral agency. Therefore, while AI can contribute to ethical decision-making, it cannot fully comprehend or engage with ethics in the way humans do.

This raises questions about the morality of their decisions, particularly in high-stakes scenarios such as autonomous vehicles or military drones. For instance, in the event of an unavoidable accident, how should an autonomous vehicle prioritize the lives of its passengers versus pedestrians? The "trolley problem" illustrates the moral quandaries that arise when programming AI to make life-and-death decisions. Moreover, the opacity of many AI systems—often referred to as "black boxes"—complicates the ethical landscape. When decision-making processes are not transparent, it becomes challenging to assess whether AI behaves ethically. This lack of clarity can undermine accountability and trust, as stakeholders may not understand the rationale behind critical decisions affecting their lives (Coeckelbergh, 2020).

AI can be programmed to follow ethical guidelines and principles, which means it can be designed to make decisions that align with ethical norms to some extent. This is achieved through techniques like ethical programming, machine learning with ethical data, and specific value alignment. As AI systems become more autonomous, questions about accountability, transparency, and ethical decision-making become critical. But how can AIs understand such complicated ethics? Even if AI understands these ethics, AI cannot truly "think" ethically in the way humans do, as it does not possess the subjective experience or moral reasoning capabilities that are central to human ethical decision-making. AI in itself has no ethics, and the decisions made by algorithms are ultimately the result of human choices made at an earlier stage. Its actions are ultimately a reflection of the ethical frameworks and data input by its developers. The development of AI that genuinely understands and reasons about ethics like a human remains an open challenge.

Among ongoing efforts to train ethics in AI, empathy has been a significant issue. Empathy, a crucial aspect of moral psychology, influences how individuals respond to ethical dilemmas and interact with others. As AI systems become more interactive, understanding the role of empathy in human–AI relationships is essential (Bonnefon et al., 2024). Developing AI systems that can recognize and respond to human emotions can enhance user experience and improve decision-making outcomes. Incorporating empathy into AI is essential for creating systems that are not only functional but also compassionate and user-friendly. Empathetic AI can improve user experience, build trust, enhance decision-making, mitigate bias, and promote ethical development. For instance, AI in customer service can be programmed to respond empathetically to user concerns, fostering trust and satisfaction. The question of whether AI systems can possess moral agency—i.e., the capacity to act based on moral considerations—raises important ethical debates. While AI can be designed to simulate moral reasoning, true moral agency remains a uniquely human characteristic. This underscores the need for human oversight in AI decision-making, reassuring us that humans will continue to play a crucial role in the AI era.

One of the ethical questions we face is about autonomous moral agents. Some computing researchers aim to develop AI systems that can act as moral agents, capable of independently making ethical decisions in dynamic environments (Heimann & Hübener, 2023). These systems would need to understand and evaluate moral dilemmas much like humans do, taking into account different factors and the perspectives of all parties involved. For an AI system to be considered an autonomous moral agent, it must possess several key capabilities such as moral reasoning, autonomy, adaptability, and moral awareness. The autonomous AI should understand and evaluate ethical principles to make decisions in complex or ambiguous situations. This involves weighing different outcomes, assessing potential harms or benefits, and considering what is "right" or "wrong." The AI should be able to operate independently, meaning it does not rely on constant human supervision or guidance. It should be capable of taking actions on its own based on its ethical evaluations. Autonomous moral agents should be able to adapt their decision-making processes to new information, changing circumstances, or different ethical contexts. They need to be flexible enough to handle a variety of moral dilemmas. The system should recognize when an ethical decision is required. This involves understanding when its actions might have significant moral consequences and acknowledging the potential impact on humans or other agents. Autonomous moral agents can be applied in various areas such as self-driving cars, healthcare AI, and military robots.

AI systems that can make ethical decisions on their own may be ideal. Creating autonomous moral agents presents numerous challenges, despite having a well-designed plan (Klenk, 2024). First and foremost, human moral reasoning is intricate, often dependent on the context, and influenced by cultural, personal, and societal factors. Converting these into a format that machines can understand is challenging. One of the most significant challenges is bridging the gap between AI's capabilities and human cognition. This involves developing AI systems that can understand and interpret human emotions, context, and subtle nuances of communication. Progress in natural language processing and emotional AI is paving the way for more intuitive and human-like interactions between machines and humans. Moreover, morality is complex, context-dependent, and varies across cultures, societies, and individuals. There is no universally agreed-upon moral framework, and ethical principles often conflict with one another (e.g., utilitarianism vs. deontology). There is ambiguity in ethical principles, as different ethical theories can lead to various decisions in the same situation. Autonomous moral agents may struggle to reconcile conflicts between competing moral principles (Morley et al., 2023). Additionally, determining accountability when an autonomous moral agent makes an error is a crucial issue. This involves understanding whether the responsibility should lie with the AI itself, its creators, or the users.

WHY ETHICS ARE IMPORTANT IN AI

AI ethics is crucial because AI technologies are increasingly integrated into our lives, influencing decisions that affect individuals and society. Ethical AI ensures that these technologies are developed and used responsibly to prevent harm, bias, and discrimination (Schlagwein & Willcocks, 2023). Morality in machine learning is essential because machine learning models and algorithms influence decisions that have significant ethical, social, and personal implications. Embedding moral principles into machine learning ensures that these technologies operate in a manner that aligns with human values and promotes the well-being of individuals and society.

The ethical safeguard for AI involves ensuring that human autonomy is upheld (Zhou & Chen, 2023). Although AI has the potential to improve decision-making and empower individuals, it also carries the risk of eroding autonomy through excessive reliance and loss of control. To ensure that AI functions as a supportive tool rather than a substitute for human agency, it is crucial to prioritize trust, ethical considerations, human oversight, and personalization. By carefully managing this relationship, society can leverage the benefits of AI while upholding the core principles of human autonomy, dignity, and agency.

AI systems can unintentionally amplify existing biases in data, leading to unfair outcomes in areas like hiring, law enforcement, and healthcare. Ethical guidelines help identify and reduce these biases, promoting fairness and justice. Moreover, ethics in AI fosters trust and accountability by emphasizing transparency and explainability. Users and stakeholders need to understand how AI makes decisions to ensure responsible use. Protecting data privacy and security is another key aspect, as AI often relies on sensitive personal information. Ethical AI also aims to prevent misuse, such as in deepfakes or autonomous weapons, guiding responsible development and reducing risks to society. It aligns AI with human values, prioritizing respect for human rights, dignity, and well-being. Ultimately, integrating ethics into AI helps balance innovation with responsibility, ensuring that AI technologies serve the best interests of humanity while minimizing potential harms. Promoting ethical standards globally creates a foundation for safer, fairer, and more trustworthy AI systems.

HUMAN HEURISTICS IN AI

Heuristics is a problem-solving and decision-making approach that relies on minimal information, past experiences, and results to generate practical solutions within a reasonable timeframe (Lim et al., 2024). These strategies prioritize speed and practicality over perfection, aiming to deliver quick results within an acceptable accuracy range. Heuristics play a crucial role in machine learning and AI, particularly when it's impractical to derive solutions through step-by-step algorithms (Sundar, 2008). Often, heuristic strategies are combined with optimization algorithms to enhance results. In the context of deep neural networks, each iteration is interdependent, influencing the selection and rejection of solution paths based on their proximity to the desired outcome. Essentially, heuristics can be likened to a "short-cut" approach, as it avoids investing resources in exploring solution paths that don't lead to acceptable results.

Heuristic methods in AI are based on cognitive science principles that revolve around "how humans think." These methods aim to mimic human thought processes to solve complex problems (Jakesch et al., 2023). Heuristic algorithms in AI enable systems to produce approximate solutions rather than exact ones. They prioritize finding a solution in a reasonable amount of time over finding the perfect solution. However, it's important to note that heuristics do not necessarily provide a cheaper solution. Instead, the ones that do not overestimate the cost of achieving the result are termed admissible heuristics. This is a crucial characteristic of heuristics that ensures the solution's optimality. At the fundamental level, an admissible heuristic simplifies the original problem by reducing its constraints, making it easier to find a solution.

Heuristic processes often lead to solutions or results that work, but they may not always be provable, optimal, or accurate. However, decisions based on heuristics are generally sufficient for solving small-scale problems and providing solutions in uncertain situations where complete information is unavailable. Heuristics rely on shortcuts to offer immediate, efficient, and short-term solutions that facilitate timely decisions for businesses. Analysts in various industries use specific thumb rules that enable companies to address problems and make rapid and efficient decisions and judgments. These rules include trial and error, elimination, intelligent guesswork, past results or formulas, and analysis of historical data. In the computing world, a heuristic model serves as a rule of thumb to expedite and simplify decision-making processes in situations where there isn't enough time for careful consideration of all aspects of the problem. Interestingly, people perceive AI as more ethical than humans because they believe AI is based on science and technology and, therefore, free from bias, making its judgment more objective than human judgment (Yang & Sundar, 2024). Sundar et al. call this machine heuristics, and these heuristics serve an important role in guiding human interaction with AI. Machine heuristics work as simplified rules or strategies that machines, particularly AI and machine learning systems, use to make decisions, solve problems, or learn from data. These heuristics help reduce computational complexity and improve efficiency, enabling machines to function effectively in real-world scenarios where perfect information is often unavailable.

Human perception of ethics in AI is complex and influenced by various factors, including individual values, societal norms, and experiences with technology. Human heuristics of ethics in AI are multifaceted and continuously evolving. Human heuristics on AI ethics involve the mental shortcuts and intuitive judgments that people use when evaluating the ethical implications of AI technologies. These heuristics can shape how individuals perceive fairness, accountability, transparency, and the potential risks associated with AI systems. Relevant studies have identified different kinds of heuristics on AI ethics, such as fairness heuristics (Lim et al., 2024), transparency heuristics (Otis, 2024), accountability heuristics (Shin, 2024), and explainability heuristics (Norambuena et al., 2023). For example, when evaluating AI decisions, individuals often rely on their sense of what seems fair, which might be influenced by cultural norms, personal experiences, or societal values. This heuristic plays a significant role in discussions around AI fairness and bias.

As AI technologies become more integrated into daily life, fostering public engagement, education, and dialogue around ethical considerations will be essential for building trust and ensuring that AI serves the best interests of individuals and society. Many individuals are increasingly aware of the potential for bias in AI systems, especially when these technologies are used in sensitive areas like hiring, criminal justice, and healthcare. People often express concern that AI could perpetuate or even exacerbate existing societal inequalities if not designed with fairness in mind. This awareness leads to calls for more transparent and accountable algorithms. Trust in AI systems is heavily influenced by how transparent these systems are. People tend to feel more comfortable with AI that provides clear explanations for its decisions and actions. When individuals understand how AI works and how decisions are made, they are more likely to trust the technology. Conversely, opaque "black box" models can lead to skepticism and fear regarding their implications. The ethical implications of AI on employment are a significant concern for many. As automation and AI technologies continue to evolve, there is anxiety about job displacement and the changing nature of work. People are concerned about whether AI will lead to increased unemployment or if it will create new opportunities, highlighting the need for ethical considerations in workforce development and retraining. The potential for AI to invade personal privacy is a pressing ethical issue for many individuals. Concerns about surveillance, data collection, and the misuse of personal information can lead to resistance against AI systems. People are increasingly vigilant about how their data are collected, stored, and used, demanding greater transparency and control over their information.

Addressing these concerns proactively can lead to the development of AI systems that align with human values and ethical standards, ultimately enhancing their acceptance and effectiveness. Understanding how humans perceive ethics in AI is vital for harnessing the full potential of these technologies while navigating the moral landscape they create (Zhu et al., 2022).

THE DUAL NATURE OF USER HEURISTICS IN AI BIAS

The rule of thumb humans use to make quick judgments can significantly impact the presence and persistence of algorithmic bias. These heuristics shape how people interact with AI systems, the data they input, and the way they interpret and accept AI recommendations. When human heuristics intersect with algorithms, they can both mitigate and exacerbate algorithmic bias. One of the primary ways user heuristics contribute to algorithmic bias is through their role in data generation and selection. Human users typically provide data to train and refine AI systems, often unknowingly influencing what algorithms learn and prioritize. When people follow common heuristics, such as the "availability heuristic," they tend to rely on recent or easily recalled information when making decisions (Sundar, 2008). This means that the data they provide may be skewed by the most recent, memorable, or salient events. For example, if people frequently interact with certain types of news on social media, AI algorithms can learn that these preferences reflect broader tastes or values (Shin, 2024).

Another heuristic that can contribute to algorithmic bias is the "anchoring heuristic," where the first piece of information significantly affects subsequent evaluations (Yang & Sundar, 2024). When users interact with an AI recommendation—be it a tailored product suggestion or a ranking of job applicants—the initial response tends to shape their views about the recommendation as a whole. This anchoring effect can lead users to overvalue that first suggestion, which might already be skewed due to limitations in the training data. For example, when an AI system suggests mostly male candidates for a computer job based on historical hiring patterns, users might become anchored to this biased first impression, reinforcing gender disparities.

Moreover, people often show confirmation bias, which is a tendency to prefer information that aligns with their existing beliefs. This can make algorithmic bias even worse by creating feedback loops in AI systems. For example, when using personalized news feeds, individuals usually engage more with content that reflects their views. The AI notices this behavior and starts to offer even more similar content, resulting in an echo chamber that reinforces those beliefs. Over time, this cycle can lead to greater polarization, as AI systems end up "learning" and amplifying our biases instead of challenging them.

Despite these risks, user heuristics can also serve as a mechanism to detect and mitigate algorithmic bias, particularly when users exercise skepticism or social heuristics in evaluating AI recommendations. People have an inherent ability to detect inconsistencies or patterns that seem unjust, such as when an AI disproportionately favors one group over another. This "fairness heuristic" can prompt users to question the AI's outputs and explore whether the model has embedded biases. For instance, if an AI-generated hiring recommendation appears to overlook qualified candidates from underrepresented backgrounds, users may question the system's fairness and initiate further scrutiny or even adjustments.

The application of critical heuristics can encourage users to play an active role in overseeing AI systems rather than passively accepting algorithmic outputs (Jakesch et al., 2023). When people employ a "doubt heuristic," they approach AI recommendations with caution and are more likely to identify biases embedded within the model (Shin et al., 2022). This can be especially valuable in fields like healthcare or criminal justice, where biased AI decisions can have severe consequences. In these settings, users who rely on doubt judgment are more likely to seek second opinions or demand transparency about how decisions are made, pushing for accountability in cases where AI might be reinforcing societal biases.

Moreover, human heuristics enable individuals to recognize and correct AI outputs that misrepresent or fail to serve underrepresented groups. Using heuristics like the "representativeness heuristic," people can assess whether AI recommendations truly reflect the diversity of populations involved. When an AI output appears biased or unrepresentative, this heuristic can lead humans to question and intervene in a way that an algorithm cannot independently achieve. This type of human oversight is particularly vital in high-stakes areas such as criminal justice and hiring, where unrepresentative recommendations can lead to serious consequences (Chaiken et al., 1996).

Analyzing the impact of cognitive shortcuts on bias in AI systems reveals a nuanced and reciprocal dynamic. Human inclinations can both intensify existing biases and provide corrective measures when applied thoughtfully. Heuristics such as availability, anchoring, and confirmation bias can inadvertently introduce biases into AI, whereas heuristics centered on fairness and doubt can mitigate these issues by fostering critical examination and oversight. This dual nature of user heuristics underscores the necessity of awareness and training in our interactions with AI. When users recognize their biases and understand how heuristics can affect outcomes, they can approach AI with greater intention. This intentionality can help guide AI systems toward results that reflect societal ideals of fairness, inclusivity, and accountability.

HUMAN AUTONOMY AND AI

Human autonomy is crucial in the development and implementation of AI technologies. By preserving individual agency, enhancing trust, mitigating bias, facilitating ethical decision-making, empowering users, promoting accountability, ensuring human-centered design, and balancing efficiency with human judgment, we can create AI systems that augment human capabilities rather than undermine them. Prioritizing human autonomy will ultimately lead to the development of AI technologies that are not only effective but also ethical and aligned with human values.

Autonomy, especially machine autonomy, persists as a popular discourse in studies related to automation and AI; however, the exploration of human autonomy has been increasing over the last couple of years, mostly due to the growing concerns over the ethical consideration of AI (Calvo et al., 2020). Studies on the guidelines of ethical AI identified human autonomy as one of the basic factors to consider for responsible AI design (Floridi & Cowls, 2019; Hagendorff, 2020; Jobin et al., 2019). Most established policies for socially beneficial AI, such as the Montreal Declaration (2017), the Asilomar AI Principles (2017), and the European Commission's EGE ethical principle (2018), emphasize the protection of human autonomy in the form of deciding how much autonomy to cease for AI systems (Floridi & Cowls, 2019). So, when humans determine to leave some autonomy to the AI, why do they do that if they can't rely on the AI? From an earlier study on automation by Lee and See (2004), we know that human relies on automated systems when they trust, and if they cannot trust the automation, they reject it. This leads to the necessary exploration of how human autonomy intersects with trust in the case of relying on AI.

Discussions around autonomy and AI revolve around two types of autonomy: the autonomy of humans and the autonomy of machines. Scholars like Shin (2023) maintained that we need to be concerned about human autonomy rather than machine autonomy because humans are moral agents, but machines are not, at least at this point in AI development. However, Vanneste and Puranam (2024) emphasized AI agency in consideration of human trust in AI systems. Though autonomy and agency are not to be used interchangeably, Carina Prunkl (2022) defined human autonomy as composed of authenticity (which refers to the state that an individual's beliefs, values, motivations, and reasons are solely their own) and agency (which refers to an individual's ability to act upon their own beliefs and values). From her definition of autonomy, we find that agency is a core part of autonomy. Floridi and Cowls (2019) termed the aspect of human autonomy to decide about the autonomy of AI systems as meta-autonomy and argued that if humans cease some autonomy to AI, that means more autonomy to AI and less autonomy to humans. Even when humans cease some autonomy to AI in the process of being willing to use AI, their willingness can exceed their trust toward AI, which Kreps et al. (2023) defined as trust paradox. As Vanneste and Puranam (2024) proposed, the perception of more agentic AI can increase trust in AI, and the interplay between trust and ceasing autonomy to AI becomes an important aspect of understanding human's perception of human autonomy.

Though humans might have some control over AI autonomy, AI can still affect human autonomy both in the cases of autonomy as authenticity and autonomy as an agency (Prunkl, 2022). On the authenticity domain, AI systems can affect autonomy through manipulation, adaptive preference formation, deception, and adaptive belief formation, and on the agency domain, it impacts human freedom, opportunities, and control (Prunkl, 2022). Similarly, Hagendorff (2020) also argued that AI can affect human autonomy by manipulating through micro-targeting, nudging, and user experience design. So, for designing of future responsible AI consideration of autonomy is a crucial ethical imperative (Calvo et al., 2020). However, concerns about nudging, manipulation, and surveillance apply to human autonomy only (Formosa, 2021). Which leaves a question about disregarding the autonomy of AI in designing might affect human acceptance and trust toward AI.

Preserving human autonomy in the realm of AI is essential for maintaining individual empowerment, trust, ethical decision-making, accountability, and the protection of rights and freedoms. As AI technologies continue to evolve and integrate into various aspects of life, prioritizing human autonomy will ensure that these systems serve as valuable tools that enhance human capabilities without undermining agency. By fostering a collaborative relationship between humans and AI, we can create a future where technology supports and empowers individuals, aligning with the fundamental values of dignity, respect, and autonomy.

The relationship between human autonomy and AI presents both opportunities and challenges. While AI has the potential to enhance decision-making and improve quality of life, it is essential to preserve individual agency and control. By prioritizing human autonomy through human-centered design, augmented decision-making, education, and ethical frameworks, we can create a future where AI serves as a collaborative partner, empowering individuals rather than diminishing their autonomy. Ultimately, navigating this balance will shape the societal implications of AI, ensuring that technology aligns with human values and promotes a just and equitable future.

WHY HUMAN COGNITION IS IMPORTANT IN AI ETHICS

Understanding human cognition is essential for the development of ethical frameworks in AI. By comprehending how individuals perceive and interpret ethical dilemmas involving AI, we can ensure that AI technologies respect human values, minimize harm, and have a positive impact on society (Siemens et al., 2022). Human cognition encompasses the mental processes that enable us to acquire knowledge, reason, solve problems, and adapt to new situations. It is characterized by flexibility and creativity. Humans possess an exceptional capacity to change their thinking and actions in reaction to different environments and situations. This mental flexibility allows us to transition between tasks, acquire new abilities, and modify our approaches to meet new difficulties. It is crucial for problem-solving and navigating complex social environments. Regarding creativity, human creativity is the skill to generate unique and valuable ideas. It is fueled by imagination and originality, enabling us to think innovatively. Creativity drives artistic creation, scientific exploration, and technological progress. It involves combining diverse concepts, often leading to fresh solutions and methods that challenge traditional boundaries.

Humans possess emotional intelligence, enabling them to effectively recognize and comprehend both their own emotions and those of others (Romele, 2022). This ability is essential for fostering empathy and establishing emotional connections with others, allowing for appropriate responses to their emotions and needs. In addition to perceiving emotions, humans are capable of analyzing and understanding the origins and outcomes of emotions. This comprehension aids in predicting how emotions impact behavior and decision-making.

Humans have an important ability to understand context, including subtle nuances and complexities in various situations. This skill allows us to perceive underlying meanings, intentions, and social cues that may not be explicitly stated. When faced with uncertain or ambiguous information, humans can rely on past experiences and contextual knowledge to make well-informed judgments. This capability is crucial for navigating environments where information is incomplete or unclear. Humans leverage their accumulated knowledge and experiences to interpret new situations, enabling them to predict outcomes, identify patterns, and make decisions based on historical context.

The most distinctive feature of human cognition from AI is that human cognition is characterized by its integrative nature, forming a sophisticated mental framework. It is distinguished by flexibility, creativity, emotional depth, and contextual acuity, collectively empowering individuals to navigate life's complexities, innovate, and build cohesive societies. Human cognition encompasses a wide range of mental processes that enable problem-solving, interaction, and navigation of the world. Its depth and complexity are fundamental to individual and species success. Understanding and harnessing these cognitive processes can lead to advancements in various fields, including education, technology, mental health, and organizational behavior.

HOW DO PEOPLE UNDERSTAND ETHICS IN AI?

Understanding ethics in AI involves examining how these technologies align with human values, principles, and societal norms to ensure they benefit individuals and society as a whole (Shin, 2024). People understand ethics in AI through various lenses that are shaped by their knowledge, experiences, cultural values, and the context in which AI is applied. That is, AI ethics are understood by people through a combination of philosophical principles, societal values, practical guidelines, and real-world impacts. The ethical considerations surrounding AI involve evaluating its design, development, and deployment to ensure that these technologies align with human values and promote positive outcomes.

A group of researchers in dual-process theory suggests that people can intuitively sense that harming others is wrong but need to engage in deliberate reasoning to understand that harm can be acceptable in certain situations. Various dual-processing models (Metzger et al., 2010) suggest that individuals process ethics in two primary ways: critically analyzing the message through systematic reasoning or relying on heuristics—external characteristics—to make quick judgments about the ethical information they encounter. Dual-process theory is a valuable complement aiding explorations of the ethical judgment of AI. The dual-process theory of ethics refers to the idea that human moral decision-making involves two distinct cognitive systems: an intuitive, automatic process and a deliberate, reasoning-based process (Moors, 2014). These two systems operate in parallel, often interacting with each other, and can sometimes lead to conflicting responses in ethical dilemmas. This framework is used to understand how people make moral judgments and decisions, including how they might interact with or design ethical principles in AI. The dual process is helpful in understanding how people form ethical values and how they evaluate the ethics of algorithms in AI.

The processes are interrelated in that the conditions affecting their occurrence and the results they produce overlap. The theories suggest that people engage in dual processing when making ethical judgments. Type 1 processing is rapid, emotional, and intuition-driven, and Type 2 is deliberative, slow, and calculated, requiring conscious consideration of a high cognitive load. Some moral judgments arise as a flash of perception, while others follow mindful deliberation (Kumar, 2016, p. 791). The processes do not necessarily cancel each other out; when humans are making decisions, they engage each other simultaneously or sequentially.

This dual process of heuristic–systematic evaluation reveals two distinct modes of figuring out AI ethics. Heuristic processing involves focusing on salient and easily comprehended cues that activate well-learned judgmental shortcuts, whereas systematic processing engages attempts to thoroughly understand any available information through deliberate analysis, deep configuration, and intensive reasoning (Chaiken et al., 1996). This process is related and enactive in that AI ethics are enacted to user cognitions through users' communicative interaction with GAI algorithms. Through the interactions, many ethical issues are invoked and these individual issues together constitute and embody users' perceived AI ethics (Lim et al., 2024).

In reasoning about AI ethics, people employ a heuristic–systematic process. People process AI ethics heuristically and in ways that interweave perceptive, enactive, and more systematic phases. This processing does not usually follow a simple progression but evidences trial-and-error processing that is consistent with the logic of heuristic processing more generally. While people have similar ethical expectations for both humans and AIs, they usually do not understand the technical operations or inner workings of algorithms. Concepts like transparency and fairness represent abstract ideologies to them, and they do not know how such concepts are concretely applied to real usages or everyday lives. For example, people are aware of and agree regarding the importance of transparency and fairness but do not understand the specifics of such ethics, such as how to measure their presence and what should be done to ensure such ethics from both an organizational perspective and individual users' point of view. Thus, in many ways, users' sensemaking involves heuristic processes that rely on simple, readily available concepts or preexisting knowledge (Gu et al., 2021). This may lead to bias or prejudice if their existing mindsets are biased or prejudiced. Heuristic processing can be successful if cues are correct and effective. In such cases, the process is relayed to a systematic process that looks at algorithmic features closely in an effortful manner. During the systematic process, people evaluate AI in terms of accuracy, factuality, or quality of responses. These two processes are interrelated or co-occur, impacting each other (Lim et al., 2024).

SOCIAL CONSTRUCTION OF AI ETHICS

Just like ethics, AI ethics are socially constructed. AI ethical principles, norms, and values are shaped by the social, cultural, economic, and political contexts in which they arise. The ethics are not fixed, static, or universal truths; instead, they evolve over time as societies change and as people interact with each other, negotiating what is considered right or wrong, good or bad, just or unjust. AI ethics are formed and perceived through a complex interplay of various factors, including personal thinking, societal ideology, cultural influences, stakeholder engagement, technological developments, and historical context.

A group of scholars have developed the idea of the social construction of AI ethics into a theory (e.g., Noble, 2018; Shin, 2024). The scholars have established the idea that the ethical principles, norms, and guidelines that govern the development and use of AI are shaped by social, cultural, political, and economic factors. This theory emphasizes that our understanding of what is ethical in AI is constructed through interactions between various social groups, institutions, and historical contexts. This theory is based on the idea that AI is shaped by social processes, cultural norms, historical contexts, and human interactions, resulting in its ethics being influenced by these interactions. This theory emphasizes that ethical considerations in AI are not merely derived from technical specifications or algorithmic features but are shaped by the social contexts in which AI technologies are developed and used. The social construction of AI ethics highlights the interplay and interaction between societal factors and the ethical considerations surrounding AI technologies.

The concept of social construction in AI ethics is important because it highlights that ethical principles are not fixed or universally agreed upon but are shaped by the values, power structures, and social dynamics of different communities. The formation, perception, and acceptance of AI ethics are complex processes influenced by cultural, historical, and social factors, as well as stakeholder interaction and technological developments. Recognizing the social construction of AI ethics encourages a more inclusive, context-sensitive, and adaptable approach to developing ethical guidelines that reflect the diverse perspectives and needs of a global society. This approach highlights the importance of collective engagement and discourse in shaping ethical standards for AI technologies. Understanding the dynamic and culturally situated nature of ethics is not a one-time effort but requires ongoing dialogue and reflection.

AI ETHICAL PARADOX

An ethical paradox, or moral dilemma, arises when a person faces multiple options, none of which feel factually correct or ethically clear. This kind of paradox reflects an ethical ambivalence in decision-making, a tension that is especially visible in the field of AI ethics (Shin, 2024). In AI, we frequently encounter situations where technology can both benefit and harm, creating moral conflicts that have no straightforward answers. This ambivalence forces us to weigh competing values, like innovation versus privacy, or fairness versus efficiency, underscoring the complex nature of ethical behavior in the age of AI. The paradox of AI ethics refers to the complex and often contradictory nature of implementing ethical principles in AI systems (De Cremer & Kasparov, 2022). Paradoxes in AI ethics arise because of the intricate and occasionally contradictory interplay between ethical principles, human values, and the technological capacities of AI systems. As AI technologies become more integrated into our lives, the challenge of ensuring that these systems act in ethically sound ways has led to a series of paradoxes: the balance between pushing the boundaries of AI capabilities and ensuring these advancements serve the greater good of humanity. These paradoxes highlight the difficulties in balancing technical capabilities, ethical frameworks, human values, and societal impacts. This delicate balance calls for a moral compass in an era defined by relentless innovation, inviting us to explore the intricate dance between technological progress and ethical responsibility.

AI encompasses contradictions that offer the potential for groundbreaking scientific achievements, enhanced efficiency, and unprecedented freedom, while also hinting at the risk of increased human reliance, decreased human agency, and potential obsolescence. At the heart of these AI paradoxes lie a multitude of ethical dilemmas related to the creation of value through AI. These include issues such as AI biases, ethical and moral decision-making, cybersecurity, the impact of automation on employment, and the alignment of goals between AI and humans. These ethical challenges are particularly pressing given the rapid and pervasive influence of AI technologies (Du & Xie, 2021). In contemplating the paradox of AI ethics, it is important to know that AI is not value-neutral; it influences human cognition and experience and actively shapes ethics and morality. In today's world, AI has such a significant impact on society and human existence that we must acknowledge the ethical implications in the design, implementation, and use of technology.

Users have conflicting emotions when it comes to AI. They appreciate the impressive capabilities of AI-enabled services, but they also have concerns about the potential negative aspects of these powerful technologies (Morley et al., 2021). The level of trust people have in AI-enabled services largely depends on how ethical issues such as algorithmic biases, privacy, and human value are addressed. Consequently, the widespread adoption of AI-enabled products hinges on user trust in these AI services.

To address the paradox, it is essential to embrace a human-centric approach to AI development (Shin, 2024). This approach centers on prioritizing the well-being, rights, and dignity of individuals, ensuring that AI technologies are created and implemented to improve, rather than undermine, the human experience. A human-centric AI is designed to be inclusive, equitable, and mindful of the diverse experiences of people worldwide. Its development involves a wide array of stakeholders, including technologists, ethicists, policymakers, and communities impacted by AI technologies, thereby ensuring that a multitude of perspectives are considered in the development process.

The paradox of AI ethics presents a significant challenge as well as a profound opportunity to reshape the direction of algorithmic progress. Embracing the intricate ethical considerations surrounding AI can set the stage for a future in which AI acts as a positive force, improving human life and upholding our shared values. As we traverse the ever-changing terrain of AI, let us dedicate ourselves to a future in which innovation and ethics are inseparable, steering us toward a world where technology and humanity thrive in unison.

The ethical paradox of AI highlights the complexity of AI ethics, requiring careful navigation of trade-offs where fulfilling one ethical requirement could potentially conflict with another. This presents a challenging and nuanced landscape. However, the paradox is not an insurmountable issue but rather a task that calls for intellectual rigor and moral clarity. The paradox of AI ethics calls for a thoughtful exploration of how we can leverage the vast potential of AI in a way that respects and enhances our common humanity (Ashok et al., 2022). By adopting a human-centric approach, promoting interdisciplinary cooperation, and advocating for effective governance, we can navigate the ethical intricacies of AI development and ensure that our technological progress genuinely serves the greater good. In this delicate balance between innovation and ethics, we encounter not only a challenge but also an opportunity to shape a future that embodies our highest aspirations for both AI and humanity.

LITERACY FOR ETHICAL AI: KNOWING MORALITY IN AI

Embedding AI with ethical reasoning is a complex but increasingly important goal in the development of AI systems. While significant progress has been made, fully integrating ethical reasoning into AI remains a challenging task due to several technical, philosophical, and practical factors. While AI systems are advancing in their ability to simulate certain aspects of ethical reasoning, achieving truly robust ethical reasoning that matches human capabilities remains a long-term goal. The complexity of human morality, cultural diversity, and the dynamic nature of ethical decision-making make it difficult to fully replicate ethical reasoning in AI. Nevertheless, progress in AI ethics research is likely to result in systems that can increasingly incorporate ethical principles into their operations, even if these systems are not yet capable of fully autonomous moral reasoning.

The ethical use of AI ultimately depends on people's ability to reason and understand AI, known as AI literacy. AI literacy is essential for ethical decision-making as it enables individuals to comprehend, evaluate, and actively engage with AI technologies in a manner that encourages responsible use and informed choices (Shin et al., 2022). People's knowledge and understanding of ethical principles, issues, and implications related to the development and use of AI will be important. Beyond simply knowing, ethical literacy involves the ability to critically assess AI systems, recognize ethical dilemmas, and make informed decisions that align with moral and societal values (Domínguez & Stoyanovich, 2023). People's AI literacy is crucial for creating a society capable of ethically interacting with AI, addressing its ethical dilemmas, and ensuring that AI is developed and utilized in ways that align with human values and ethical principles. It enables individuals to make informed choices, promote responsible AI usage, and actively contribute to shaping the future of AI for the benefit of society as a whole.

As AI continues to advance and integrate into various facets of society, discussions surrounding ethical AI have gained prominence. The pursuit of ethical AI is an essential endeavor as we navigate the complexities of technology in modern society. By adhering to core principles of fairness, transparency, accountability, privacy, and trust, stakeholders can work together to develop AI systems that benefit humanity while minimizing harm. Establishing robust ethical frameworks, addressing challenges, and fostering interdisciplinary collaboration will be crucial in ensuring that AI serves as a positive force for society in the future. As we advance into an increasingly automated world, prioritizing ethical considerations in AI will ultimately shape the relationship between humans and technology, fostering a more equitable and just society. By promoting fairness, building trust, ensuring accountability, protecting privacy, minimizing harm, encouraging responsible innovation, navigating moral dilemmas, and facilitating regulatory compliance, ethical AI serves as a guiding principle for the responsible development and use of AI. Ultimately, prioritizing ethical considerations in AI will lead to technologies that benefit society and enhance the quality of life for individuals across the globe.

CONCLUSION

The moral dimensions of AI are becoming increasingly important as AI technologies continue to advance. AI lacks the capacity for moral reasoning, empathy, and contextual understanding that characterize human ethical decision-making. Therefore, ensuring that AI systems genuinely respect human ethics requires careful design, ongoing human oversight, and an awareness of the complexities and nuances of ethical considerations. By aligning AI development with core human values, we can create systems that empower individuals, promote social equity, and foster trust in technology. As we navigate the complexities of AI's impact on society, prioritizing human values will be crucial for ensuring that technology serves the greater good and contributes positively to humanity's collective future. It is crucial for developers and policymakers, as well as society at large, to take a leading role in engaging in thoughtful discussions about the ethical implications of AI. Their active involvement in establishing ethical frameworks that prioritize fairness, accountability, and transparency is essential for guiding the responsible development and deployment of AI technologies. As we navigate this rapidly changing landscape, it is imperative to consider the profound implications of our decisions and strive for a future where AI serves humanity ethically and equitably. By fostering a culture of ethical awareness and responsibility, we can harness the potential of AI while safeguarding the values that define our humanity.

As AI systems become increasingly integrated into various aspects of society, understanding how to imbue them with ethical principles and guidelines is essential for ensuring they operate in ways that are consistent with human values and societal norms. The challenges associated with artificial morality highlight the need for interdisciplinary collaboration among ethicists, technologists, policymakers, and the public to create frameworks that promote responsible and ethical AI development and deployment. Embracing robust ethical practices and fostering inclusive dialogue are essential for navigating AI challenges and harnessing the transformative potential of AI responsibly and equitably.

REFERENCES

Allen, C., Smit, I., & Wallach, W. (2005). Artificial morality: Top-down, bottom-up, and hybrid approaches. *Ethics and Information Technology, 7*(3), 149–155. https://doi.org/10.1007/s10676-006-0004-4

Allen, C., Varner, G., & Zinser, J. (2000). Prolegomena to any future artificial moral agent. *Journal of Experimental & Theoretical Artificial Intelligence, 12*(3), 251–261. https://doi-org.lib-e2.lib.ttu.edu/10.1080/09528130050111428

Anderson, S., & Anderson, M. (2021). AI and ethics. *AI Ethics, 1*(1), 27–31. https://doi.org/10.1007/s43681-020-00003-6

Ashok, M., Madan, R., & Joha, A. (2022). Ethical framework for AI and digital technologies. *International Journal of Information Management, 62*, 102433. https://doi.org/10.1016/j.ijinfomgt.2021.102433

Avnoon, N., Kotliar, D., & Rivnai-Bahir, S. (2024). Contextualizing the ethics of algorithms: A socio-professional approach. *New Media & Society, 26*(10), 5962–5982. https://doi.org/10.1177/14614448221145728

Awad, E., Dsouza, S., Kim, R., Schulz, J., Henrich, J., Shariff, A., Bonnefon, J. F., & Rahwan, I. (2018). The moral machine experiment. *Nature, 563*(7729), 59–64. https://doi.org/10.1038/s41586-018-0637-6

Bigman, Y. E., & Gray, K. (2018). People are averse to machines making moral decisions. *Cognition, 181*, 21–34. https://doi.org/10.1016/j.cognition.2018.08.003

Bonnefon, J. F., Rahwan, I., & Shariff, A. (2024). The moral psychology of artificial intelligence. *Annual Review of Psychology, 75*(1), 653–675. https://doi.org/10.1146/annurev-psych-030123-113559

Brożek, B., & Janik, B. (2019). Can artificial intelligences be moral agents? *New Ideas in Psychology, 54*, 101–106. https://doi.org/10.1016/j.newideapsych.2018.12.002

Calvo, R. A., Peters, D., Vold, K., & Ryan, R. M. (2020). Supporting human autonomy in AI systems: A framework for ethical enquiry. In C. Burr & L. Floridi (Eds.), *Ethics of Digital Well-Being: A Multidisciplinary Approach* (pp. 31–54). Springer. https://doi.org/10.1007/978-3-030-50585-1_2

Cervantes, J. A., López, S., Rodríguez, L. F., Cervantes, S., Cervantes, F., & Ramos, F. (2020). Artificial moral agents: A survey of the current status. *Science and Engineering Ethics, 26*(2), 501–532. https://doi.org/10.1007/s11948-019-00151-x

Chaiken, S., Giner-Sorolla, R., & Chen, S. (1996). Beyond accuracy: Defense and impression motives in heuristic and systematic information processing. In P. M. Gollwitzer & J. A. Bargh (Eds.), *The psychology of action: Linking cognition and motivation to behavior* (pp. 553–578). Guilford Press.

Coeckelbergh, M. (2020). *AI ethics.* The MIT Press. https://doi.org/10.7551/mitpress/12549.001.0001

Constantinescu, M., Vică, C., Uszkai, R., & Voinea, C. (2022). Blame it on the AI? On the moral responsibility of artificial moral advisors. *Philosophy & Technology, 35*(2), 35. https://doi.org/10.1007/s13347-022-00529-z

De Cremer, D., & Kasparov, G. (2022). The ethical AI—Paradox: Why better technology needs more and not less human responsibility. *AI Ethics, 2*, 1–4. https://doi.org/10.1007/s43681-021-00075-y

Domínguez, F. D., & Stoyanovich, J. (2023). Responsible AI literacy: A stakeholder-first approach. *Big Data & Society, 10*(2), 2018. https://doi.org/10.1177/20539517231219958

Du, S., & Xie, C. (2021). Paradoxes of artificial intelligence in consumer markets: Ethical challenges and opportunities. *Journal of Business Research, 129*, 961–974. https://doi.org/10.1016/j.jbusres.2020.08.024

Floridi, L., & Cowls, J. (2019). A unified framework of five principles for AI in society. *Machine Learning and the City. Applications in Architecture and Urban Design*, 535–545. https://doi.org/10.1162/99608f92.8cd550d1

Floridi, L., & Sanders, J. W. (2004). On the morality of artificial agents. *Minds and Machines, 14*, 349–379.

Formosa, P. (2021). Robot autonomy vs. human autonomy: Social robots, artificial intelligence (AI), and the nature of autonomy. *Minds and Machines, 31*(4), 595–616.

Gamez, P., Shank, D. B., Arnold, C., & North, M. (2020). Artificial virtue: The machine question and perceptions of moral character in artificial moral agents. *Ai & Society, 35*, 795–809. https://doi.org/10.1007/s00146-020-00977-1

Gu, J., Yan, N., & Rzeszotarski, J. (2021). Understanding user sensemaking in machine learning fairness assessment systems. In *Proceedings of the Web conference.* ACM, New York. https://doi.org/10.1145/3442381.3450092

Hagendorff, T. (2020). The ethics of AI ethics: An evaluation of guidelines. *Minds and Machines, 30*(1), 99–120.

Heimann, M., & Hübener, A. (2023). AI as social actor. *Journal of Digital Social Research, 5*(1), 48–69. https://doi.org/10.33621/jdsr.v5i1.159

Jakesch, M., Hancock, J., & Naaman, M. (2023). Human heuristics for AI-generated language are flawed. *PNAS, 120*(11), c2208839120. https://doi.org/10.1073/pnas.2208839120

Jobin, A., Ienca, M., & Vayena, E. (2019). The global landscape of AI ethics guidelines. *Nature Machine Intelligence, 1*(9), 389–399.

Kearns, M., & Roth, A. (2020). *The ethical algorithm: The science of socially aware algorithm design*. Oxford University Press.

Klenk, M. (2024). Ethics of generative AI and manipulation. *Ethics Information Technology, 26*, 9. https://doi.org/10.1007/s10676-024-09745-x

Kreps, S., George, J., Lushenko, P., & Rao, A. (2023). Exploring the artificial intelligence "trust paradox": Evidence from a survey experiment in the United States. *PLoS ONE, 18*(7), e0288109.

Kumar, V. (2016). The empirical identity of moral judgment. *The Philosophical Quarterly, 66*(265), 783–804. https://doi.org/10.1093/pq/pqw019

Ladak, A., Loughnan, S., & Wilks, M. (2024). The moral psychology of artificial intelligence. *Current Directions in Psychological Science, 33*(1), 27–34. https://doi.org/10.1177/09637214231205866

Lee, J. D., & See, K. A. (2004). Trust in automation: Designing for appropriate reliance. *Human Factors, 46*(1), 50–80.

Lim, J., Ahmad, N., & Ibarahim, M. (2024). Understanding user sensemaking in fairness and transparency in algorithms. *AI & Society, 39*, 447–490. https://doi.org/10.1007/s00146-022-01525-9

Metzger, M. J., Flanagin, A. J., & Medders, R. B. (2010). Social and heuristic approaches to credibility evaluation online. *Journal of Communication, 60*(3), 413–439.

Misselhorn, C. (2020). Artificial systems with moral capacities? A research design and its implementation in a geriatric care system. *Artificial Intelligence, 278*, 103179. https://doi.org/10.1016/j.artint.2019.103179

Moors, A. (2014). Examining the mapping problem in dual process models. In *Dual-process theories of the social mind* (pp. 20–34). Guilford.

Morley, G., Field, R., Horsburgh, C. C., & Burchill, C. (2021). Interventions to mitigate moral distress: A systematic review of the literature. *International Journal of Nursing Studies, 121*, 103984. https://doi.org/10.1016/j.ijnurstu.2021.103984

Morley, J., Kinsey, L., Elhalal, A., Garcia, F., Ziosi, M., & Floridi, L. (2023). Operationalizing AI ethics. *AI & Society, 38*, 411–423. https://doi.org/10.1007/s00146-021-01308-8

Noble, S. (2018). *Algorithms of oppression*. University Press.

Norambuena, B., Farina, K., Horning, M., & Mitra, T. (2023). Watching the watchdogs: Using transparency cues to help news audiences assess information quality. *Media & Communications, 11*(4). https://doi.org/10.17645/mac.i366

Otis, A. (2024). The effects of transparency cues on news source credibility online: An investigation of opinion labels. *Journalism, 25*(1), 198–217. https://doi.org/10.1177/14648849221129001

Prunkl, C. (2022). Human autonomy in the age of artificial intelligence. *Nature Machine Intelligence, 4*, 99–101.

Romele, A. (2022). Images of AI: A blind spot in AI ethics. *Philosophy & Technology, 35*(1). https://doi.org/10.1007/s13347-022-00498-3

Schlagwein, D., & Willcocks, L. (2023). ChatGPT et al.: The ethics of using generative AI. *Journal of Information Technology, 38*(3), 232–238. https://doi.org/10.1177/02683962231200411

Shank, D. B., & DeSanti, A. (2018). Attributions of morality and mind to artificial intelligence after real-world moral violations. *Computers in Human Behavior, 86*, 401–411. https://doi.org/10.1016/j.chb.2018.05.014

Shin, D. (2023). *Algorithms, humans, and interactions: How do algorithms interact with people? Designing meaningful AI experiences* (1st ed.). Routledge. https://doi.org/10.1201/b23083

Shin, D. (2024). *Artificial misinformation: Exploring human-algorithm interaction online*. Springer Nature. https://doi.org/10.1007/978-3-031-52569-8

Shin, D., Rasul, A., & Fotiadis, A. (2022). Why am I seeing this? Deconstructing algorithm literacy through the lens of users. *Internet Research*, *32*(4), 1214–1234. https://doi.org/10.1108/INTR-02-2021 0087

Siemens, G., Marmolejo-Ramos, F., Gabriel, F., Medeiros, K., Marrone, R., & Laat, M. (2022). Human and artificial cognition. *Computers and Education: Artificial Intelligence*, *3*. https://doi.org/10.1016/j.caeai.2022.100107

Sullivan, Y., & Fosso Wamba, S. (2022). Moral judgments in the age of artificial intelligence. *Journal of Business Ethics*, *178*(4), 917–943. https://doi.org/10.1007/s10551-022-05053-w

Sun, F., & Ye, R. (2023). Moral considerations of artificial intelligence. *Science & Education*, 1–17. https://doi.org/10.1007/s11191-021-00282-3

Sundar, S. (2008). The MAIN Model: A heuristic approach to understanding technology effects on credibility. In M. J. Metzger & A. J. Flanagin (Eds.), *Digital media, youth, and credibility* (pp. 73–100). The John D. and Catherine T. MacArthur Foundation Series on Digital Media and Learning. The MIT Press. https://doi.org/10.1162/dmal.9780262562324.073

Telkamp, J. B., & Anderson, M. H. (2022). The implications of diverse human moral foundations for assessing the ethicality of artificial intelligence. *Journal of Business Ethics*, *178*(4), 961–976. https://doi.org/10.1007/s10551-022-05057-6

van Berkel, N., Tag, B., Goncalves, J., & Hosio, S. (2022). Human-centered artificial intelligence: A contextual morality perspective. *Behavior & Information Technology*, *41*(3), 502–518. https://doi.org/10.1080/0144929X.2020.1818828

Vanneste, B. S., & Puranam, P. (2024). Artificial intelligence, trust, and perceptions of agency. *Academy of Management Review*. https://doi.org/10.5465/amr.2022.0041

Wallach, W. (2010). Robot minds and human ethics: The need for a comprehensive model of moral decision making. *Ethics and Information Technology*, *12*(3), 243–250. https://doi.org/10.1007/s10676-010-9232-8

Yang, H., & Sundar, S. (2024). Machine heuristic: Concept explication and development of a measurement scale. *Journal of Computer-Mediated Communication*, *29*(6), zmae019. https://doi.org/10.1093/jcmc/zmae019

Zhou, J., & Chen, F. (2023). AI ethics: From principles to practice. *AI & Society*, *38*(2), 2693–2703. https://doi.org/10.1007/s00146-022-01602-z

Zhu, L., Xu, X., Lu, Q., Governatori, G., & Whittle, J. (2022). AI and ethics. In F. Chen & J. Zhou (Eds.), *Humanity driven AI* (pp. 21–36). Springer. https://doi.org/10.1007/978-3-030-72188-6_2

Decoding Algorithmic Privacy

2

How to Address Privacy Issues Raised by AI

PRIVACY MATTERS IN AN AI ERA

The artificial intelligence (AI) boom, including the emergence of large language models and their associated generative AI systems, poses new challenges for the preservation of privacy (Fast & Jago, 2020). The vast amounts of data collected using machine learning contain sensitive personal information, such as personal conversations, browsing histories, and health data. How can we ensure that our personal information is used ethically when training AI models? What measures can we take to safeguard our input prompts from being shared with law enforcement? How can ChatGPT be used to responsibly consolidate various aspects of our online experiences while respecting various entities' privacy and security? These questions come along with the emergence of responsible AI, whose key tenet is the explicit focus on privacy, emphasizing the need to apply foundational privacy principles to AI and machine learning systems that process personal data. With the advancement of AI technologies, it is necessary to better understand these threats and to postulate potential solutions. This is because AI's capability to extract patterns and insights from user data raises significant privacy concerns.

The concept of privacy and its safeguarding are far more intricate than they may seem, and the task of ensuring privacy is likely much more complicated than most people realize (Shin, 2025). The simplistic approach of merely removing sensitive information has long been dismissed as an effective means of ensuring privacy. Modern

DOI: 10.1201/9781003530244-4

approaches that adequately address the issues unique to the technological era require that we redefine concepts such as privacy. How we define privacy in the realm of AI will hinge on the compromises we are prepared to accept. AI systems rely on vast datasets to improve their algorithms and performance, which often involves handling personal and sensitive information, such as medical records and social security numbers (Zimmermann, 2023). As AI continues to evolve, it will raise further numerous ethical concerns surrounding the collection, processing, and storage of personal data (Solove et al., 2024).

One of the primary concerns associated with AI is the potential for bad actors to gain unauthorized access to personal data (hacking, phishing, and cyberattacks), which increases the risk of security breaches. Furthermore, the sheer volume of data collected and processed heightens the threat of security vulnerabilities. Notably, cyberattacks affect 80% of businesses worldwide, which makes it even more important to ensure that data are properly protected (Korobenko et al., 2024). Additionally, the use of AI in surveillance has sparked debates over privacy rights, raising fears about the potential misuse of these technologies (Sofia et al., 2020). The issue becomes even more apparent if we take into account the fact that the number of negative incidents involving AI continues to rise (Cloarec et al., 2024). Recent developments in generative AI technologies make privacy problems even more complex ones, weaving together the topics of groundbreaking technology, ethical data use, and novel consumer rights. Furthermore, recent cases of privacy and security breaches have highlighted the vital importance of protecting privacy and ensuring security in the AI space. Therefore, a broader range of concerns exists, with some potentially not disclosed to the public. This emphasizes the need for a balanced, ethical approach to AI development, where safeguarding personal data and respecting privacy rights are prioritized as technology advances (Hagendorff, 2022). Nevertheless, despite ongoing discussions, there is still no consensus regarding key terms and concepts related to AI privacy, and a clear framework for assessing and addressing the privacy and security of AI systems has yet to be established.

In response to these developments and the acknowledged gaps in the field, this chapter analyzes recent issues on AI privacy through a systematic review to identify key themes and knowledge gaps within the privacy and security domains. Our goal is to then consolidate the findings into a privacy-conscious framework for designing and assessing AI models. In other words, this chapter synthesizes interdisciplinary research to highlight the challenges users face in making AI-related privacy and security decisions, as well as to explore methods for effectively guiding individuals in managing their privacy choices. The following research questions were formulated to achieve the core objectives of this study:

- RQ1: What is the current state of AI privacy literature, specifically from the perspective of privacy considerations?
- RQ2: What frameworks currently exist for evaluating AI ethics principles related to privacy and data security?
- RQ3: What factors must be considered to ensure the development and deployment of AI models that are privacy- and security-conscious?

THE CURRENT APPROACHES TO PRIVACY AND AI

A concrete understanding of the concept of privacy has proven to be quite elusive, giving rise to concerns that are often vague and poorly defined (Cloarec et al., 2024). Consequently, addressing privacy concerns and elucidating how AI technologies may impact individuals' privacy are particularly challenging tasks. Within the discussion of privacy in AI, two significant pillars emerge: user control and data protection. In industries such as retail, there is a desire to gain insights from data to understand user behaviors. In this context, users may seek to understand who is collecting their data, for how long, and for what purposes (Mele et al., 2021). For instance, when a user browses various websites and clicks on polarized news items, subsequent websites visited may also display more polarized and radicalized news (Shin, 2024), reflecting undesired user behaviors.

Data protection is another pillar of privacy-preserving AI. Data protection in AI is important in ensuring that personal information is safeguarded while AI systems are being developed and used (Zimmermann, 2023). Data protection involves two key components: anonymized data and encrypted data. Simply anonymizing data by removing names and addresses is not enough to ensure that data cannot be traced back to their original owners. While anonymizing data has become easier than ever, encrypting data at rest (a key protection against a data breach), especially in the context of machine learning, presents its own set of challenges (Hagendorff, 2022).

Due to the nature of machine learning, we need to operate on data, which typically means decrypting the data at some point to work on them and, as a result, creating a new vulnerability. One of the key considerations at the intersection of privacy and machine learning is the concept of trust. It is crucial to acknowledge that both data and the models utilized are digital assets. When a user shares a digital asset, they are essentially entrusting someone with their information and relying on them to handle the data responsibly and ethically (Peng, 2023).

In the context of machine learning, it is important to recognize that data involve a complex interplay among multiple stakeholders. This includes groups that control the training data, others that possess inference data, and third parties that provide the algorithm server responsible for executing a model's inferences. The models themselves are owned by yet another set of stakeholders. It is also crucial to acknowledge the involvement of a lengthy supply chain for the underlying infrastructure on which these operations run. As a result of this intricate web of digital data ownership, establishing trust among all these groups becomes increasingly challenging.

Both data anonymization and data encryption face challenges and obstacles. The development of AI models is a data-intensive process that necessitates substantial amounts of data and computational analytics (Mele et al., 2021). These systems often rely on extensive datasets, raising questions about the collection, processing, and utilization of personal information. Exploring the risks associated with AI and privacy will reveal potential vulnerabilities and challenges that individuals and organizations may face in their quest to protect privacy rights within the realm of AI.

First, data privacy breaches are prevalent in the AI field (Acquisti et al., 2020). The presence of algorithmic bias and discrimination presents significant obstacles to AI privacy (Acquisti et al., 2020). AI algorithms can unintentionally perpetuate bias and discrimination, resulting in unfair or discriminatory outcomes, especially in crucial domains such as employment, lending, and law enforcement (Zimmermann et al., 2024). Biased datasets, flawed algorithms, and inadequate testing can worsen existing inequalities and undermine privacy rights (McKee et al., 2023).

Second, AI-driven surveillance technologies, such as facial recognition systems and location tracking tools, have prompted widespread concerns due to their capability for extensive and indiscriminate surveillance (Cui et al., 2021). These sophisticated tools have the capacity to monitor and track individuals' activities, behaviors, and movements on a large scale, leading to significant implications for privacy and civil liberties. As highlighted by Masaki et al. (2020), the use of these technologies raises complex ethical and legal considerations regarding the balance between security and individual freedoms. Additionally, a lack of transparency can exacerbate privacy concerns. Many AI systems function as black boxes, making it difficult to comprehend their decision-making process (Shin, 2024). It is crucial to comprehend these processes to hold developers and companies accountable for their actions. The absence of transparency and explainability in AI algorithms can undermine trust and confidence in their outcomes, particularly in critical contexts where privacy and fairness are crucial (Frangopoulou et al., 2024).

Overall, AI systems are vulnerable to various security threats, such as data breaches, adversarial attacks (tricking AI systems into making wrong predictions or incorrect decisions), and model poisoning (manipulating the parameters of the model by altering the images in the training dataset in the model). These weaknesses can be exploited by malicious actors to access confidential data, manipulate AI decisions, or undermine the integrity and trustworthiness of AI systems, leading to severe privacy and security risks (Solove et al., 2024).

A PRIVACY KALEIDOSCOPE: THE COMPLEXITY OF PRIVACY ISSUES IN AI

The challenges associated with making privacy decisions in AI are closely tied to the inherent complexity of privacy issues. As AI technology progresses, it becomes increasingly capable of collecting and analyzing vast amounts of personal data, including highly sensitive information such as biometric data and fingerprints or other personally identifiable data. AI privacy breaches occur when sophisticated algorithmic systems improperly store, access, or misuse data without a user's explicit consent (Sofia et al., 2020).

For instance, ChatGPT, which is trained on data from users and online sources, has the potential to store personal information about individuals, including details about their family and friends (Shin, 2024). These data could then be exploited in spear phishing attacks, where specific individuals are targeted for the purposes of committing identity theft or fraud.

When AI systems lack sufficient security measures or contain vulnerabilities, they become susceptible to malware and hacking, potentially resulting in cyber threats and data breaches. Moreover, AI algorithms can infer sensitive information about individuals even without directly accessing their personal data. By examining patterns and correlations within large datasets, AI can deduce personal attributes or behaviors that individuals may not have explicitly shared. This underscores the critical need for strong security protocols to prevent potential misuse.

Several factors shape users' complex preferences and expectations regarding the collection and use of their data, including the purposes behind data gathering, the methods used, and the entities with whom the data are shared. How the collected data are intended to be used plays a pivotal role in how individuals perceive the potential compromise of their privacy (Martin & Zimmermann, 2024).

The growing involvement of professionals in the field of AI is shaping the evolving landscape of privacy governance. These experts are tasked with navigating the complex intersection of privacy regulations and the responsible use of AI technologies. A crucial element of responsible AI is the strong emphasis on privacy, highlighting the importance of applying fundamental privacy principles—central components of global data protection standards—to AI and machine learning systems that handle personal information. This includes enforcing limitations on data collection, ensuring data quality, clearly defining purposes, restricting data usage, maintaining accountability, and promoting individual participation (Nouwens et al., 2020).

Trustworthy AI should be transparent, fair, and non-discriminatory, with human oversight and secure data processing. In relation to the EU General Data Protection Regulation (GDPR), important provisions include the right to explanation, the fairness principle, human oversight, robustness, and the security of processing. Similar provisions exist in other privacy laws such as the California Invasion of Privacy Act (CIPA) and the UK Data Protection Act. In the United States, AI developers and companies using algorithms are held accountable by the Federal Trade Commission (FTC) under Section 5 of the FTC Act, the US Fair Credit Reporting Act, and the Equal Credit Opportunity Act.

It is important to stay informed about the compliance requirements for AI systems based on privacy regulations to mitigate risks for individuals and companies. Failure to comply could result in significant fines and even the mandatory deletion of data, models, and algorithms.

Non-compliance can lead to significant financial penalties. Organizations may face fines amounting to millions of dollars, or a percentage of their annual revenue, depending on the severity of the violation. Additionally, regulators may require the mandatory deletion of any non-compliant data, affecting the performance of machine learning models and algorithms that rely on this information. Moreover, businesses must consider the impact of non-compliance on their reputation. Consumers are increasingly aware of their privacy rights and may choose to avoid companies that do not take data protection seriously. This can lead to a loss of trust, reduced customer loyalty, and, ultimately, a negative impact on revenue. In this rapidly changing landscape, it's essential for organizations to implement robust compliance programs, invest in regular train-ing for their teams, and keep abreast of any changes in the regulatory environment. Proactively managing compliance not only helps avoid legal repercussions but can also enhance the credibility and reliability of AI technology in the long run.

WHY ARE PEOPLE PRONE TO MAKING POOR DECISIONS ABOUT AI PRIVACY?

Different individuals may face distinct challenges and biases that affect their ability to make informed privacy and security decisions. For users, a lack of access to informa-tion can significantly contribute to poor privacy choices; however, this is often less of an issue for application developers, who are involved in data usage, processing, and storage, and consequently have access to more information than end users. Although a comprehensive examination of the various obstacles to optimal decision-making for all stakeholders is beyond the scope of this study, we nevertheless highlight some key chal-lenges in the following sections.

Privacy Uncertainty

The main cause of privacy concerns is the unequal distribution of information. Developments in information technology have made it easy to collect and utilize per-sonal data without such processes being noticeable. Consequently, individuals seldom have a precise understanding of what data others (e.g., companies and governments) possess about them, how that data are utilized, and their potential impacts (Acquisti et al., 2015). In the context of AI systems, this uncertainty manifests in several ways:

- Black box (technical opacity): AI systems often employ complex algorithms and machine learning techniques that make it difficult for the average user to understand how AI works. This technical opacity creates a huge knowledge gap between developers and users of AI systems (Burrell, 2016).
- Third-party data sharing: Many users are unaware that their data may be shared or sold to third parties, creating additional privacy risks that are not yet apparent (Shin, 2025). This complex pattern of third-party data sharing greatly exacerbates the information asymmetry between users and AI sys-tems. Users often lack the knowledge, tools, or opportunities to fully under-stand or control how their data are shared and used beyond the initial point of collection. This asymmetry can lead to privacy decisions that are not in line with users' actual preferences or best interests, as they may not fully under-stand the scope and implications of data-sharing practices (Acquisti et al., 2015).

- Future uncertainty: The long-term consequences of data collection and AI-driven decisions are often unclear, making it difficult for users to make informed decisions about their privacy This uncertainty about future impacts contributes significantly to the problem of information asymmetry; users making privacy decisions cannot fully predict how their data may be analyzed or utilized in the future.

Immediate Gratification vs. Long-Term Consequences

The temporal discrepancy between the immediate benefits of online services and the potential long-term privacy risks poses a significant challenge to privacy decision-making. This phenomenon can be divided into several components:

- Distance: Privacy risks often feel psychologically distant, both in time and in probability. This distance may lead people to underestimate future risks and value current benefits more significantly. Privacy is an abstract concept, and it is difficult for users to grasp its concrete meaning. This abstraction furthers the distance between users and privacy risks (Kokolakis, 2017). In other words, future privacy risks are often perceived as less relevant or impactful than immediate benefits, and users perceive uncertainty about privacy risks (e.g., the possibility of a data breach) as less tangible and immediate. In contrast, the immediate benefits of AI services and the certainty of an immediate response feel psychologically more accessible.
- Tangibility of benefits: The benefits of using AI services, such as personalized recommendations, increased productivity, or task completion, are often immediate and rewarding. In contrast, privacy protection offers less obvious and immediate rewards. AI services typically provide instant gratification through personalized experiences, time-saving features, or enhanced functionalities. This immediate positive feedback reinforces usage behaviors (Weinmann et al., 2016). Compared to the benefits gained, protecting privacy often requires additional cognitive effort (e.g., reading a privacy policy or adjusting settings), which can be viewed as a cost rather than a benefit.
- Cumulative effect: Users often make privacy decisions on a case-by-case basis (Shin, 2025), making it difficult to predict the combined impact of multiple instances of data sharing over time. While a single instance of data sharing may seem inconsequential, the cumulative effect of multiple data sharing can create a comprehensive user profile that poses significant privacy risks as more data become available. It is often difficult for users to consider such long-term compounding effects.

Cognitive Biases

Cognitive biases greatly influence how individuals make decisions about privacy in an AI-driven environment. These thinking shortcuts, while often useful in everyday life, can lead to suboptimal choices when dealing with complex AI systems and data privacy.

- Current bias: Current bias is the tendency to give greater weight to gains closer to the current moment when considering tradeoffs between two future moments (O'Donoghue & Rabin, 1999). In the context of AI privacy, users typically prioritize the immediate benefits of AI services (e.g., personalization and convenience) over potential future privacy risks.
- Optimism bias: In the AI privacy environment, optimism bias leads individuals to believe that they are less likely to experience negative events compared to others (Sharot, 2011). Users tend to underestimate the risk of their personal privacy being violated or their data being misused by AI systems. This bias may lead to less vigilance and a lower likelihood of adopting privacy-protective measures. Users may believe that they have more control over their data than they actually do, especially given the complexity and opaqueness of many AI systems. Choi et al. (2018) demonstrated that optimism bias affects users' perceptions of online privacy risks, leading to lower levels of privacy concern and protective behaviors.
- Status quo bias and default effects: Status quo bias describes the tendency for people to prefer the current state of affairs, while default effects refer to the strong influence of preset options when it comes to decision-making (Johnson & Goldstein, 2003). With regard to AI privacy settings, users often accept default settings without critical evaluation, even though these settings may not match their actual privacy preferences. The complexity of AI systems and privacy settings may exacerbate this bias, as users might feel they do not have the ability or permission to modify default settings. AI developers and platforms can exploit this bias by leveraging security settings that favor data collection and sharing over user privacy.
- Heuristics and decision simplification: In addition to cognitive biases, users often rely on heuristics (thinking shortcuts or rules of thumb) to simplify complex decision-making processes (Shah & Oppenheimer, 2008). While heuristics are effective in many everyday situations, they can lead to suboptimal choices in the complex and often opaque world of AI privacy. The effort reduction framework suggests that users often sacrifice accuracy and security in exchange for reduced cognitive effort (Shah & Oppenheimer, 2008). Faced with complex AI privacy settings or privacy policies, users may adopt a simplification strategy that prioritizes simplicity over thorough evaluation. This may lead to their acceptance of default privacy settings or their making of "accept all" or "reject all" choices without careful consideration.

Heuristics and Biases

Privacy decision-making often involves uncertainty, as long-term risks may be unknown or hard to comprehend, and decisions are limited by time and the information available (Leschanowsky et al., 2023). Furthermore, evaluating the likelihood of potential malicious incidents and privacy breaches can be labor-intensive and exhausting. The idea was introduced that human decision-making operates under limited resources through the concept of "bounded rationality." He noted that decision-makers often rely on heuristics or mental shortcuts to simplify their choices. This notion was later expanded by Kahneman (2011), who developed the dual-process model of cognition, distinguishing between System 1 and System 2 thinking. System 1 refers to intuitive, quick, and effortless thinking, which can sometimes lead to biased and suboptimal decisions. In contrast, System 2 involves a slower, more deliberate, and controlled thought process, which is generally more advantageous for making complex privacy decisions. While research on cognitive biases affecting privacy decision-making has primarily focused on online environments, many of these biases also apply to AI systems and their stakeholders. For instance, anthropomorphism—where users perceive AI systems to have human-like characteristics—and other prominent cues can significantly impact users' intentions, disclosures, and privacy concerns (Shin, 2022). This suggests that self-disclosure by AI systems could effectively encourage users to share personal information. Additionally, celebrities in mass media and brand loyalty can shape privacy perceptions and influence the usage of AI systems.

Decision Readiness

Decision readiness refers to the capacity of System 2 thinking—the slower, more controlled mode—to oversee and intervene in intuitive thinking when necessary. However, this ability can be hindered by factors such as fatigue, distraction, visceral influences, and individual differences. AI systems are often particularly beneficial in situations that require hands-free interaction or when multiple tasks are being performed, such as while driving. In these cases, distraction can significantly contribute to biased decision-making. Visceral influences (e.g., sweating, increased heart rate, and muscle tension) may include visual or auditory cues from conversational AI systems, which can lead to increased self-disclosure or poor privacy choices (Ischen et al., 2020). Finally, individual differences—such as variations in training, cognitive ability, or self-reflection—can also impact privacy decision-making. Consequently, the effectiveness of debiasing strategies (reducing bias) may vary based on an individual's characteristics and their role within the AI ecosystem.

RISKS INVOLVING PRIVACY IN AI

As AI rapidly advances and impacts various societies, one of the most notable developments is AI's potential to affect privacy rights and the protection of users' personal data.

As human data are being collected, sold, and used by AI systems, humans are faced with numerous risks, such as identity theft, discrimination, and the erosion of privacy (Cui et al., 2021).

First, AI systems present many of the same privacy risks that we have been dealing with for decades due to the commercialization of the internet and extensive data collection. The difference lies in the scale—AI systems require a vast amount of data and are not transparent. This means we have even less control over what information is being collected about us, how it is being used, and whether we can correct or remove it. Today, it is nearly impossible for people using online products or services to avoid being systematically surveilled across various aspects of life, and AI could potentially exacerbate this issue.

The second risk involves the potential for others to use our data and AI tools for anti-social purposes. For example, generative AI tools that are trained with data scraped from the internet may end up memorizing personal information about individuals, as well as relational data about their family and friends. Currently, malicious actors are utilizing AI voice cloning to impersonate individuals and then extort them using traditional phone methods.

Third, we are increasingly facing scenarios where our data (e.g., resumes and photographs), originally shared or posted for one purpose, are being repurposed for training AI systems without our informed consent. This raises significant civil rights concerns. Predictive systems are now being employed to screen candidates and help employers make decisions about whom to interview for job openings. There have been instances where the AI used in candidate selection has displayed bias. For instance, Amazon developed its own AI hiring screening tool, only to realize that it was biased against female hires. Another example involves the use of facial recognition to identify and apprehend individuals who have committed crimes. While it may seem beneficial to have a tool like facial recognition to catch criminals, the bias present in the data used to train existing facial recognition algorithms has led to numerous false arrests of Black men due to misidentification by algorithms.

PRIVACY DECISION-MAKING IN AI: PRIVACY CALCULUS IN THE CONTEXT OF AI

Privacy calculus theory is a framework used to understand how individuals determine whether to share personal information by assessing the trade-offs between the potential benefits and risks (Acquisti et al., 2020). The process of privacy calculus has become increasingly important in the field of AI, as it greatly impacts how individuals make decisions about sharing personal information online (McKee et al., 2023). Privacy reasoning can significantly affect how users behave when it comes to sharing information and taking actions in relation to AI (Peng, 2023). The privacy calculus model suggests that when people are deciding whether to share their personal information with an organization, they weigh the potential advantages and disadvantages to themselves and their data privacy (Meier & Krämer, 2024). The model explains how individuals think when they are asked to disclose personal information. Specifically, individuals try to determine whether the benefit of sharing such information will outweigh the risks of disclosing it (Acquisti et al., 2017). Therefore, during interactions with AI, users calculate the potential benefits and risks that information sharing might bring about. In turn, this will affect users' usage behaviors. Variables such as network externalities, trust, and information sensitivity are known to affect users' benefit-and-risk analysis and the consequent provision of personal information (Zimmermann, 2023). The extent to which a user is concerned about the risk of disclosing their private information thus plays a key role in determining not only the adoption of AI but also many qualitative aspects of the experience.

This reluctance to share private data arises from perceived privacy risks (Lim & Shim, 2022). Societal factors play a pivotal role in shaping users' privacy calculus, as the way AI collects and exploits consumer data can be influenced by the prevailing cultural and contextual dimensions (Perino et al., 2022). Therefore, the privacy calculus acts as a framework through which individuals weigh the balance between trust and risk when considering whether to share their personal information with AI.

Trust represents the potential benefits individuals anticipate when sharing their data, while risks encompass the perceived downsides and costs of such sharing. This evaluation is pivotal in determining whether the expected benefits of trust outweigh the associated risks, ultimately influencing decisions and behaviors related to privacy. Developing a deeper comprehension of the privacy calculus is therefore essential for both users and AI to encourage responsible data management, transparency, and well-informed decision-making.

Machine learning-based AI technologies have the potential to significantly influence an individual's capacity to evaluate their own privacy. As AI increasingly takes over the data disclosure process, the explicit request for data becomes less apparent and is instead subtly acknowledged at a later stage, for instance, when agreeing to the terms of an app's installation and usage policies (Zimmermann et al., 2022). Furthermore, AI can be integrated into data disclosure processes in a hybrid manner, partially automating the process and potentially causing individuals to feel more vulnerable. In such instances, data can be collected online through tracking, or the gathering process can be partially automated, with an individual's assistance (e.g., AI extraction of data from uploaded videos). Despite the potential risks associated with data disclosure, these technologies offer benefits in terms of convenience and accuracy in data collection. For example, users consent to the storing of home addresses and credit card information to make future purchases more convenient.

As part of the privacy calculus, studies have revealed that individuals tend to assess and weigh the implications of how their data are managed by organizations, even though they may not have direct control over this particular aspect. This essentially means that while individuals have agency in the collection of data, the responsibility for its management lies with the organizations involved (Zimmermann et al., 2024). Users leveraging generative AI systems, such as Bing AI, have the capacity to enhance responses to inquiries by drawing insights from the questions, searches, and sensitive data of other users (Ramesh & Chawla, 2022). This is accomplished through the integration of personal data across retail platforms (Cui et al., 2021). However, despite AI's efforts to be transparent about post-collection data handling, the data might still be repurposed, aggregated, sold, or obtained by other entities (Pitardi & Marriott, 2021). As a result, users face challenges in weighing the benefits and risks of data disclosure (Hagendorff, 2022). Consequently, individuals may conclude that the desired benefits of personalization and recommendations offered by new outcome-oriented AI technologies do not outweigh the associated risks. Research on personal digital assistants (e.g., Apple's Siri or Amazon's Alexa) suggests that recommendation outcomes do not consistently outweigh risk perceptions (Shin & Zhou, 2024).

PRIVACY HEURISTICS IN AI

Privacy heuristics are nudges that describe recurrent scenarios and can support the generation of privacy awareness in AI. Heuristics are error-prone mental tools and poor substitutes for computations that are too demanding for ordinary minds to carry out on a regular basis (Acquisti et al., 2015). A privacy heuristic is a mental shortcut or rule of thumb that people use when making decisions about their privacy, particularly when sharing personal information online or interacting with digital platforms (Williamson & Prybutok, 2024). These heuristics help individuals quickly assess the risks and benefits of revealing their data without going through a detailed analysis of all possible consequences. Some common privacy heuristics include the following:

- Trust heuristic: People are more likely to share information if they trust the entity requesting it, such as a well-known brand or a platform they have used before.
- Reciprocity heuristic: Individuals might share information in exchange for something of perceived value, such as discounts, free services, or access to exclusive content.
- Control heuristic: If people feel that they have control over their data, such as the ability to delete or modify their information later, they are more inclined to share information.
- Normative heuristic: People base their decisions on what they believe is normal behavior. If everyone else is sharing their information, an individual may feel it is acceptable to do the same.
- Risk heuristic: Decisions are made based on a quick assessment of the risk involved. If the perceived risk of sharing data is low, people might share more freely.

These heuristics can lead to decisions that prioritize convenience over privacy, often without fully understanding the potential consequences of sharing personal data.

The importance of privacy heuristics is increasing since they significantly influence how individuals make decisions about sharing personal information, often in ways that balance convenience, trust, and perceived risks. Therefore, the following steps must be carried out to enhance privacy heuristics:

1. Simplify decision-making: In an era of information overload, people are constantly asked to make decisions about their data. Privacy heuristics act as mental shortcuts, helping individuals make quicker choices without getting bogged down by complex details.
2. Impact on data-sharing behaviors: Understanding privacy heuristics can explain why people sometimes share sensitive information despite knowing the risks. For example, if a person trusts a company, they might overlook potential privacy concerns, even when there are valid reasons to be cautious.
3. Design implications for technology and platforms: Companies and digital platforms can leverage insights about privacy heuristics to design more user-friendly interfaces that align with people's natural decision-making processes. This can help build trust and create more transparent ways for users to control their data.
4. Promoting privacy awareness: By recognizing the heuristics that guide their behavior, people can become more mindful about their data-sharing decisions. This awareness can help them make more informed choices about when and how to share personal information.
5. Policy and regulation development: Understanding privacy heuristics is valuable for policymakers and regulators who aim to create guidelines that protect consumer privacy. If they know what influences users' decisions, they can develop strategies that promote better data protection practices.

In the realm of AI, privacy heuristics influence the decisions made by individuals and organizations regarding their interactions with AI systems and the management of associated data (Sundar et al., 2020). These heuristics are significant, as they shed light on the disparity between people's privacy intentions and real-life actions. Identifying these patterns can pave the way for enhanced privacy protocols, more conscientious data management, and improved user experiences in the digital sphere. The following are examples of privacy heuristics specifically related to AI:

1. Transparency heuristic: People tend to trust AI systems more if a system is transparent about how it uses their data. If an AI clearly explains what data it collects and how it will be used, individuals may feel more comfortable sharing their information, even if they do not fully understand the technical details.
2. Explainability heuristic: When AI systems provide clear, understandable explanations for their decisions, users are more likely to believe that their data are being handled responsibly. If an AI can justify its outcomes, people might assume that the data are being used ethically, even if they do not fully analyze the privacy risks.

3. Trust-in-the-brand heuristic: Users often rely on their trust in a well-known AI brand or platform when deciding whether to share their data. For instance, if a major tech company such as Google or Apple were the developers of an AI, users might automatically assume that their data are secure due to these companies' reputations, even if they are not familiar with the specific privacy measures in place.

4. Perceived value heuristic: People are more willing to share personal data with AI systems when they perceive high value in return, such as personalized recommendations, improved services, or enhanced user experiences. They might downplay privacy concerns if they believe the benefits of an AI outweigh the risks.

5. Default settings heuristic: Users often stick with the default privacy settings of an AI system, assuming that these default settings represent a safe or optimal choice. They might not actively change the settings to limit data sharing, believing that the default configuration is designed with their best interests in mind.

6. Anonymity heuristic: When AI systems promise that user data will be anonymized, individuals may be more inclined to share their information. Users often believe that if their data cannot be directly linked back to them, the privacy risks are minimal, even if they are unaware of the limitations of anonymization techniques.

7. Immediate gratification heuristic: Users might prioritize short-term benefits from using AI services over long-term privacy risks. For example, they might agree to share personal data to access an AI tool quickly, even if they have concerns about how that data might be used in the future.

These privacy heuristics impact how individuals engage with AI systems and influence their decisions about sharing data. Understanding these heuristics is helpful for designing AI systems that are more user-friendly, transparent, and in line with individuals' privacy expectations.

PRIVACY-PRESERVING AI

The issue of privacy-preserving techniques has a lengthy history that encompasses multiple disciplines. As algorithmic data on users grow increasingly detailed, and as machine learning facilitates more powerful methods for collecting and curating these data, there is a rising demand for a robust, meaningful, and algorithmically sound definition of privacy, along with a computationally sophisticated set of algorithms that adhere to this definition (Zimmermann et al., 2023).

Privacy-preserving (or privacy-aware) machine learning algorithms are methods designed to safeguard individual privacy while allowing for effective data analysis and model training (Korobenko et al., 2024). Similar to the principle of privacy as a service (packaged service where disclosure notices, consent management, and compliance conditions are combined to offer a comprehensive managed privacy service to improve transparency and user control regarding data privacy), these techniques integrate privacy and security considerations into machine learning models, such as built-in privacy in AI. This approach is vital in an algorithm-driven society, where AI methods frequently depend on large datasets, raising significant privacy concerns (Sofia et al., 2020). The goal is to find a balance between leveraging personal data for valuable insights and minimizing the risk of exposing sensitive information, thereby addressing issues related to data security and the ethical use of AI (Zimmermann & Renaud, 2021). Privacy-preserving AI is therefore essential due to the increasing volume of personal data being collected and utilized by AI systems. Techniques for privacy-preserving AI include data anonymization, homomorphic encryption, secure multiparty computation, differential privacy, and compliance with privacy regulations (Martin & Zimmermann, 2024).

The conventional method of protecting privacy involves encrypting data. However, this necessitates the decryption of data for training, which adds significant computational overhead. Furthermore, a trained model may still retain private information, limiting its use to secure environments. An alternative method of preserving privacy is to divide the data into smaller packets and train a model on each packet separately using a network of local training algorithms, a strategy referred to as local training or federated learning. Nonetheless, this approach still carries the risk of leaking sensitive information into the trained model.

Using the privacy-preserving framework, adding a shuffler can improve model performance while maintaining the same level of privacy protection (Perino et al., 2022). To achieve privacy-preserving AI, four pillars are required: (1) training data privacy (ensuring that malicious actors are unable to reverse-engineer the training data), (2) input privacy (ensuring that a user's input data cannot be observed by other parties, including the model creator), (3) output privacy (warranting that an output of a model is only visible to the user whose data are being inferred upon), and (4) model privacy (ensuring that a model cannot be stolen by a malicious party). With these four pillars in place, it is good to develop solid data governance policies, implement privacy-by-design principles, and enhance transparency in data usage.

PRIVACY NUDGES IN AI

There is growing interest in developing strategies to encourage users to adopt safe behaviors in relation to AI usage. Recently, privacy-preserving nudges have gained significant attention. Generally, nudges are seen as interventions that provide a "push" to foster positive behaviors, such as saving for retirement or making charitable donations. In the context of AI, this mechanism can be applied to various situations, such as visualizing password strength to motivate users to create stronger passwords or reducing self-disclosure online through gentle paternalistic prompts. Additionally, reminders to adjust privacy settings in AI systems can raise awareness of privacy concerns, potentially leading to improved privacy practices.

As AI technologies advance, algorithmic nudging in the realm of privacy has become increasingly essential for safeguarding users of AI systems when handling privacy-related data (Sofia et al., 2020). One approach to protecting privacy in AI is through the implementation of privacy nudges. These nudges can take the form of prompts, cues, and notifications that may rely on general knowledge or user-specific parameters. Nudges are designed to assist users in making secure choices or informed privacy decisions (Mele et al., 2021). More specifically, privacy-preserving nudges are crafted to help individuals make informed choices about their AI privacy. They can encourage users to opt for privacy-friendly app selections or discourage them from unintentionally sharing their location.

Current privacy nudges have attracted attention and are generally categorized into two groups: preference-based personalized nudges and objective neutral nudges. Personalized agents rely on a user's disclosure preferences and goals to deliver these nudges. For instance, framing nudges can be used to promote privacy-friendly app choices. For example, the visual representation of an app's privacy rating significantly influences users' decisions. Furthermore, the framing of a rating has an impact on apps with a low privacy rating—the trustworthiness of apps with a low privacy rating is considered lower than apps with a positively framed privacy rating.

The second type of privacy nudge does not analyze users' behaviors or provide personalized advice. Examples of this nudge can be a privacy assistant designed to discourage unintended data sharing with AI. For example, one privacy nudge can make users aware of how many times their private data have been shared with which app to encourage users to make changes to the settings in AI. Related study results showed that the implemented privacy nudges can increase the utility of the permission manager (Shin, 2024).

Regardless of the types of nudges, they are associated with potential privacy risks. For example, social norm nudges can threaten privacy because they collect and process personal information about individuals. This information can then be used to re-identify anonymized data. To design ethical privacy nudges, it is important to consider how they might be used to manipulate users. It is also important to consider the legal requirements around privacy, which can make the best privacy-preserving option less clear.

Masaki et al. (2020) employed social nudges to mitigate potentially risky privacy-related decisions, such as disclosing images on social networking services. These social nudges were framed in a way that highlighted the negative, such as by stating, "90% of users would not share..." compared to "10% of users would share...." The study found that individuals were less likely to engage in potentially risky behaviors when confronted with negative framing. However, the authors also noted that while these nudges were effective in situations where individuals held polarized opinions, they were less effective in cases where people already favored privacy-conscious choices. This finding underscores the challenges of designing nudges for different application contexts.

It was experimented with privacy nudges aimed at discouraging disclosures on social networks that users might later regret. The nudges tested included visual reminders of a post's audience, a time delay before posting, and feedback on potential perceptions by others. While both the time delay and visual audience reminders were generally effective in preventing unintended disclosures, the time delay nudge was perceived as helpful yet annoying and intrusive. This reaction may be attributed to the increased "cost" in terms of time associated with a nudge. This example underscores the difficulty of creating nudges that do not disproportionately burden one option over others.

CHALLENGES OF DESIGNING PRIVACY NUDGES IN AI

Despite the numerous well-meaning and frequently effective instances of privacy nudges, applying them comes with several difficulties (Barev et al., 2022). Nudges in AI are essentially personalized tools. These nudges should be tailored to guide each person toward their best option most suitable to their needs. However, the personalized nature of nudges has raised concerns about privacy (Acquisti et al., 2017; Zimmermann, 2023). Critics are worried that personalized nudges require the collection of large amounts of user data, potentially violating privacy. The need for data on preferences presents a significant temptation for libertarian paternalists to collect information about citizens and invade their private lives (Kapsner & Sandfuchs, 2015, p. 458). Furthermore, the mass collection of user data has been criticized for contributing to the potential misuse of data. Shin (2024) argued that data are primarily processed automatically, leading to risks of algorithmic profiling. While this argument applies specifically to government nudging, privacy concerns have also arisen in the private sector. The key difference is that in business, the goal of data collection is often not to determine which nudges optimize individual welfare but to identify which nudges are most effective in persuading customers to purchase or use products and services. Such nudges also pose threats to privacy (Acquisti et al., 2017) and increase the risk of algorithmic bias (Shin, 2024).

Nudging vs. Coerced

A central ethical challenge in designing privacy nudges for AI is balancing the effectiveness of these interventions with the preservation of user autonomy. The line between useful guidance and manipulation must be carefully navigated to avoid compromising user autonomy. Thaler and Sunstein (2008) emphasized the importance of preserving freedom of choice while guiding people to make better decisions. Nudges that subtly encourage users to choose privacy-protecting settings may be seen as beneficial, but if users feel deceived or pressured into making certain choices, this may be seen as an infringement on their autonomy. For example, default settings retain freedom of choice in principle but can still have considerable impact, especially when people lack information and the choice environment is confusing. However, some have argued that users may not actively consider these options and therefore may not make conscious decisions. The challenge is making the nudges noticeable enough to be effective but not so intrusive or obtrusive that they feel forced.

Dynamics and Opacity of AI

AI systems often operate as black boxes where the processes behind data collection, analysis, and decision-making are not transparent to users. This opacity makes it difficult for traditional nudges strategies to work, as users may not fully understand how their data are being used or processed. In contrast, traditional nudge strategies often rely on relatively transparent decision-making environments, such as default settings or simplified decision points (e.g., choosing healthier food options). The dynamic and opaque nature of AI systems complicates the clear presentation of choices and their consequences, and the clear presentation of choices and explanations is critical to the effectiveness of nudges. Without the ability to understand how an AI processes user data or makes decisions, users may struggle to understand the implications of their choices, reducing the effectiveness of nudges. Furthermore, nudging users to make choices when they do not understand the choices amounts to manipulation.

Cognitive Biases

Many nudging strategies use cognitive biases to influence user behaviors in subtle ways. Cognitive biases are mental shortcuts that individuals rely on when making decisions in uncertain situations. These biases, while useful in some situations, can also be exploited to undermine informed decision-making, especially in complex environments involving AI privacy. While exploiting cognitive biases can increase the effectiveness of boosting, it raises significant ethical issues, especially when users are not aware that their mental tendencies are being manipulated.

BALANCING TRANSPARENCY AND EFFECTIVENESS

Yeung (2017) argued that transparency in nudging means that users should be aware of the nudges they are subjected to and the expected outcomes. In a transparent system, users have the right to know how they are affected, especially in cases where nudging affects personal or ethical decisions. While transparency is crucial, it also reduces the effectiveness of nudges; if users are fully aware that their behaviors are being affected, they may resist nudges, which could undermine the nudges' intended impact. This presents a dilemma for those looking to boost AI privacy.

Furthermore, nudges are less effective when users know that an AI system is trying to steer them toward certain privacy decisions. Users may feel less autonomous and may be more likely to ignore a boost. Excessive transparency may also have the counterproductive effect of making users skeptical of AI's motives, especially if they perceive the boost to be primarily for the benefit of a company or platform rather than their own privacy interests.

Renaud and Zimmermann (2018) argued that effective nudges should empower users by enhancing their ability to make informed, autonomous decisions. Rather than simply guiding users toward a particular choice, the goal of a nudge should be to improve a user's decision-making capabilities over time. In the field of AI, it is critical to help users understand their role in privacy through nudges, as many users may lack the knowledge necessary to make fully informed decisions about how much data to share or how to protect personal information.

Paternalism in Nudges

Paternalism is the practice of restricting a user's freedom or autonomy for their own benefit, even though the person may not recognize or agree with the actions taken on their behalf. However, there are some differences in the various understandings of paternalism. Soft paternalism nudges users to make choices that are perceived to be in their best interest but do not restrict their freedom to make other choices. Thaler and Sunstein (2008) support libertarian paternalism; they believe nudges should help users make better decisions but protect their freedom of choice. Nudges are "paternalistic" because a nudge designer assumes that certain decisions are better for a user and helps a user choose that decision but "libertarian" because these nudges leave the final decision to the user.

Balancing Nudging with Autonomy

Nudges' paternalism has been debated from its inception to the present day, and while nudges technically provide people with room for choice, they can subtly undermine individual autonomy by leading people to make decisions they may not have made independently (Mele et al., 2021). In some cases, individuals may make nudge-compliant decisions without fully understanding the reasons behind them. While nudge designers often give power to institutions (governments, tech companies, or AI systems) to decide what is in the best interest of individuals, nudges can sometimes exploit human cognitive biases in ways that feel coercive or manipulative, especially if an individual is unaware of a nudge or its purpose. For example, many firms make it easy to sign up for a subscription but very difficult to cancel forcing users to go through multiple stages or offering vague instructions.

Notice and Choice

Notice and choice require companies to disclose to users what private information they are collecting and how they will use them, with the expectation that consumers will choose whether to consent to their data being collected after reading and understanding a notice.

The core premise is that informed consumers can make rational decisions about their privacy when given enough information and meaningful choices. Notification relies on privacy policies and terms of service agreements. However, research has shown that these documents are rarely read and are poorly comprehended. Research suggests that it would take the average person approximately 244 hours per year to read all the privacy policies they encounter online. The effectiveness of privacy notice is increasingly being challenged by AI systems due to a number of key limitations: information overload leading to "notification fatigue" (Schaub et al., 2015), the complexity of privacy choices in AI environments, and a disconnect between an initial notification and the subsequent use of AI data.

Adaptation

User adaptation to privacy invasions is a worrisome psychological phenomenon (Acquisti et al., 2020). This adaptation may have a negative impact because it reflects a gradual normalization of privacy invasion rather than a concerted effort to resist or counteract it. As users adapt to a digital environment where data collection is ubiquitous, many have begun to anticipate that their personal information will be collected, and they may stop reading privacy policies, accept intrusive terms of service, or not use privacy-enhancing tools. Adaptive responses can also lead to a paradoxical situation in which consumers express diminished trust in a company but take little action to change their behavior. For example, despite widespread concern about the privacy practices of large technology companies, many consumers continue to use their services out of necessity or convenience.

Privacy Fatigue

Privacy fatigue is a state of mental exhaustion and cynicism associated with privacy issues, which is caused by repeated breaches of online personal data. This phenomenon causes users to feel that they have no effective means of protecting their information, which leads to a decrease in privacy-protective behaviors. A study by Cho et al. (2010) showed that people experiencing privacy fatigue are more likely to abandon privacy-protective behaviors and divulge personal information without careful consideration. Addressing this fatigue is critical for better privacy management and policy development.

MEASURING THE EFFECTIVENESS OF PRIVACY NUDGES

Evaluating the effectiveness of privacy nudges is a multifaceted challenge due to the complexity of human behavior, the different types of privacy, and long-term behavioral changes. Privacy nudges hope to guide users to adopt more privacy-conscious behaviors rather than forcing them to choose. However, measuring whether these tips consistently improve users' privacy practices requires doing more than tracking immediate behavioral responses. To truly measure the effectiveness of privacy nudging, it is important to assess not only compliance but also whether users are gaining a deeper understanding of privacy issues and sustaining their behavioral changes over time.

Skepticism

Designing effective privacy nudges in AI is inherently challenging, especially when faced with user skepticism (Trieste & Turchetti, 2024). Users become skeptical of privacy prompts when they suspect the intent behind privacy nudges, especially when they suspect that these prompts are for a company's benefit rather than their own. This distrust often stems from a history of data misuse or breaches that have caused long-term damage to user trust, and users may not fully understand how their data are being collected, processed, or protected. Users may even question whether adjusting their privacy settings in accordance with nudging actually protects their data, especially if they had previously encountered situations where the privacy settings offered little to no real protection.

Cultural Differences

Cultural differences play an important role in the challenge of designing privacy nudges for AI, as perceptions of privacy and data sharing vary significantly across societies. For example, in Western cultures, especially in Europe, privacy is often viewed as a fundamental right, and regulations such as the GDPR reflect strong legal protections for personal data. In these regions, users may be more aware of privacy risks and respond more positively to prompts that emphasize data protection and personal control. Conversely, in countries where collectivist values are more prevalent, such as parts of Asia, individuals may place less emphasis on personal privacy and more on the benefits of sharing data for collective benefit or convenience.

Measurement and Evaluation

A key challenge is defining meaningful success metrics—whether the goal is to increase user engagement with privacy settings or to deepen understanding and long-term commitment to privacy protection. Measures of success must include both short-term outcomes (e.g., immediate changes in behavior, such as opting in or out of data sharing) and long-term outcomes (sustained privacy-aware behaviors and increased awareness of privacy risks). For example, while users may adjust privacy settings after receiving nudges, the real question is whether these changes result in a noticeable reduction in data exposure or security risk. Finally, the effectiveness of nudges can vary widely due to individual differences (e.g., a user's privacy literacy, cultural background, or familiarity with AI technology), and the same nudges may work for some users but not others.

DESIGN OF PRIVACY-PRESERVING AI NUDGES

To date, many privacy nudges discussed in the literature have been designed as preventive measures aimed at promoting more privacy-conscious choices, such as avoiding unintended disclosures on social networks. This focus on prevention is well-founded for several reasons. First, decisions to grant access to personal information or disclose sensitive data are often irreversible. For instance, when users share privacy-invasive information through social network posts, it can be stored or disseminated by others before a user even has a chance to delete it. Similarly, once users consent to sharing their personal data with service providers—who may then share that information with third parties—revoking that consent can be extremely difficult, if not impossible. Additionally, research indicates that users often regret their decision to disclose personal information later (Wilkinson, 2013).

Second, private firms who have a vested interest in users' personal information for financial or marketing purposes may employ strategies that steer users toward choosing more privacy-invasive options, known as "sludges" (Thaler, 2018) or "dark patterns" (Nouwens et al., 2020). For example, these tactics have been extensively studied in the context of cookie banners that prompt users to accept all cookies, even those that are not necessary for a service's functionality. To protect users from inadvertently disclosing information or to counteract these existing dark patterns, nudging users toward the privacy-preserving option could be beneficial. Embracing a "better safe than sorry" mindset, it may be more prudent for users to initially choose the privacy-preserving option, which can often be adjusted later, rather than a privacy-invasive option that may be challenging to reverse. Furthermore, privacy-preserving nudges can help users identify privacy-friendly options when they are not readily apparent. For instance, highlighting these options can assist users in navigating the often lengthy and complex privacy policies to find what they are looking for.

However, as discussed in the previous section, the privacy-preserving option may not always be viewed as the most appealing choice by users. For instance, Leimstädtner et al. (2023) revealed that not all users perceived privacy-preserving nudges as beneficial, particularly those who were motivated to share information for financial gain. Consequently, when factors like commercial interests, convenience, or functionality come into play, users may intentionally gravitate toward more privacy-invasive options. Therefore, in light of the GDPR's requirement for informed consent, several considerations emerge when designing privacy-preserving nudges:

- For privacy-preserving nudges to be effective, it is crucial for them to be transparent and easily visible to users. This will help prevent users from being nudged toward the privacy-preserving option without their awareness. When designing nudges toward the privacy-preserving option, ethical considerations for these should be given the same weight as those for other options. For instance, clearly labeling the privacy-preserving option or providing a rating for the privacy invasiveness of different options can be effective and easily understandable approaches, enabling users to make informed decisions. However, if the privacy-preserving option is set as the default selection and the other options are not easily visible or hidden behind a button, users may unknowingly accept the default selection without understanding the implications.

- The process of choosing the more privacy-invasive option should be just as straightforward as selecting the more privacy-preserving option. For instance, concealing the privacy-invasive options behind buttons or redirecting users to separate pages would require extra effort from the user.
- It is important to have measures in place to identify any potential mismatch between the implemented nudge and the preferences of users. For instance, conducting a study to test a nudge before its actual implementation could reveal differences between a researcher's intentions and users' expectations. In real-life situations, users should have the opportunity to voice their thoughts or concerns about a nudge design through provided contact details or survey tools. If a mismatch or unintended consequences are identified, a nudge design can be adjusted accordingly.

CONCLUSIONS: PRIVACY-AWARE DECISION-MAKING IN AI

With the rise of AI and algorithms, privacy concerns have become more complex than ever before. The chapter adopted a discursive perspective to provide a critical review of the ethical implications involving the use of privacy nudges in AI. Making the right AI privacy decision is becoming increasingly challenging due to the increasing complexity of machine learning and the variety of activities humans perform through AI. Through our review of the privacy literature, we identified numerous factors that can influence and compromise users' privacy and security choices. An increasing number of empirical studies are examining the impact of different biases and heuristics on privacy decision-making. Additionally, there is a growing awareness of nudge interventions in both research and industry practices aimed at prompting individuals to consider their disclosure or security decisions before making them, as well as at nudging them toward increased disclosure through tools and interface designs.

This chapter discussed why ethics are critical in privacy nudges, how to ensure that privacy nudges are designed constructively, and how to ensure legitimate forms of persuasive communication for achieving a sustainable goal. It also discussed the principles and practices of AI systems' nudging effects on user behaviors, as well as how people can nudge algorithmic systems so that they have human-centered qualities.

The concept of privacy-preserving algorithmic nudges could provide a starting point for future research. Subsequent studies might investigate how the conflicts between codification, autonomy, and alignment of interests are managed in interactions between human employees and managerial recommendation systems. The privacy-preserving nudge discussion provides useful suggestions for policymakers on how to govern and regulate algorithmic nudges. By identifying major risks, utilizing privacy-improving methods, and establishing strong governance and security measures, companies can effectively tackle challenges and uphold privacy in AI. Additionally, by integrating privacy considerations into the design and development of AI systems from the beginning, individuals can maximize the advantages of AI while safeguarding privacy rights and fostering trust and accountability in the utilization of AI technologies. The conversations provide AI platform providers with recommendations on effective nudges to employ and rotate when engaging with individuals, with the goal of enhancing the quality of online information.

As algorithmic nudging becomes more powerful, society must carefully navigate the ethical landscape. Regulation, transparency, and human autonomy will ensure that privacy nudging benefits individuals and communities without infringing on human privacy. Privacy nudges should be cognitively accessible to process and not slow down work processes. At the same time, these nudges should be transparent and designed in a non-manipulative way so that everyone can notice these nudges.

REFERENCES

Acquisti, A., Adjerid, I., Balebako, R. H., Brandimarte, L., Cranor, L. F., Komanduri, S., Leon, P. G., Sadeh, N., Schaub, F., & Wang, Y. (2017). Nudges for privacy and security: Understanding and assisting users' choices online. *ACM Computing Surveys, 50*(3), 1–41. https://doi.org/10.1145/3054926

Acquisti, A., Brandimarte, L., & Loewenstein, G. (2015). Privacy and human behavior in the age of information. *Science, 347*(6221), 509–514. https://doi.org/10.1126/science.aaa1465

Acquisti, A., Brandimarte, L., & Loewenstein, G. (2020). Secrets and likes: The drive for privacy and the difficulty of achieving it in the digital age. *Journal of Consumer Psychology, 30*(4), 736–758.

Barev, T., Schwede, M., & Janson, A. (2022). The dark side of privacy nudging: An experimental study in the context of a digital work environment. In *Proceedings of the 54th Hawaii international conference on system sciences*, (pp. 4114–4123). https://doi.org/10.24251/HICSS.2021.500

Burrell, J. (2016). How the machine 'thinks': Understanding opacity in machine learning algorithms. *Big Data & Society, 3*(1). http://dx.doi.org/10.2139/ssrn.2660674

Cho, C. H., Roberts, R. W., & Patten, D. M. (2010). The language of US corporate environmental disclosure. *Accounting, Organizations and Society, 35*(4), 431–443. https://doi.org/10.1016/j.aos.2009.10.002

Choi, H., Park, J., & Jung, Y. (2018). The role of privacy fatigue in online privacy behavior. *Computers in Human Behavior, 81*, 42–51. https://doi.org/10.1016/j.chb.2017.12.001

Cloarec, J., Meyer-Waarden, L., & Munzel, A. (2024). Transformative privacy calculus: Conceptualizing the personalization-privacy paradox on social media. *Psychology and Marketing*, *41*(7), 1574–1596. https://doi.org/10.1002/mar.21998

Cui, T., Ghose, A., Halaburda, H., Iyengar, R., Pauwels, K., Sriram, K., & Venkataraman, K. (2021). Informational challenges in omnichannel marketing: Remedies and future research. *Journal of Marketing*, *85*(1), 103–120. https://doi.org/10.1177/0022242920968810

Fast, N., & Jago, A. (2020). Privacy matters, or does it? Algorithms, rationalization, and the erosion of concern for privacy. *Current Opinion in Psychology*, *31*, 44–48. https://doi.org/10.1016/j.copsyc.2019.07.011

Frangopoulou, M., van der Laan, L., & Ebbers, W. (2024). The privacy calculus in the context of novel health technology for diagnosing and tracking infectious diseases: The role of disease severity and technology's evidence base for effectiveness in adoption and voluntary health data-sharing. *Technology in Society*, *78*, 102616. https://doi.org/10.1016/j.techsoc.2024.102616

Hagendorff, T. (2022). Blind spots in AI ethics. *AI & Ethics*, *2*, 851–886.

Ischen, C., Araujo, T., Voorveld, H., van Noort, G., & Smit, E. (2020). Privacy concerns in chatbot interactions. In A. Følstad, T. Araujo, S. Papadopoulos, E. L.-C. Law, O.-C. Granmo, E. Luger, & P. B. Brandtzaeg (Eds.), *Chatbot research and design: Third international workshop, CONVERSATIONS 2019*, Amsterdam, The Netherlands, November 19–20, 2019, revised selected papers (pp. 34–48). Springer. https://doi.org/10.1007/978-3-030-39540-7_3

Johnson, E. J., & Goldstein, D. (2003). Do defaults save lives? *Science*, *302*(5649), 1338–1339. https://doi.org/10.1126/science.1091721

Kahneman, D. (2011). *Thinking, fast and slow*. Farrar, Straus and Giroux.

Kapsner, A., & Sandfuchs, B. (2015). Nudging as a threat to privacy. *Review of Philosophy and Psychology*, *6*(3), 455–468. https://doi.org/10.1007/s13164-015-0261-4

Kokolakis, S. (2017). Privacy attitudes and privacy behaviour: A review of current research on the privacy paradox phenomenon. *Computers & Security*, *64*, 122–134. https://doi.org/10.1016/j.cose.2015.07.002

Korobenko, D., Nikiforova, A., & Sharma, R. (2024). Towards a privacy and security-aware framework for ethical AI: Guiding the development and assessment of AI systems. In *25th annual international conference on digital government research (DGO 2024)*, June 11–14, 2024, Taipei, Taiwan. ACM, New York, NY, USA 14 Pages. https://doi.org/10.1145/3657054.3657141

Leimstädtner, D., Sörries, P., & Müller-Birn, C. (2023). Investigating responsible nudge design for informed decision-making enabling transparent and reflective decision-making. In *Mensch und computer 2023, September 03–06, 2023, Rapperswil, Switzerland*. ACM, New York, NY, USA 17 Pages. https://doi.org/10.1145/3603555.3603567

Leschanowsky, A., Popp, B., & Peters, N. (2023). Debiasing strategies for conversational AI: Improving privacy and security decision-making. *Digital Society*, *2*, 34. https://doi.org/10.1007/s44206-023-00062-2

Lim, S., & Shim, H. (2022). No secrets between the two of us: Privacy concerns over using AI agents. *Cyberpsychology: Journal of Psychosocial Research on Cyberspace*, *16*(4), Article 3. https://doi.org/10.5817/CP2022-4-3

Martin, K., & Zimmermann, J. (2024). Artificial intelligence and its implications for data privacy. *Current Opinion in Psychology*, *58*, 101829. https://doi.org/10.1016/j.copsyc.2024.101829

Masaki, H., Shibata, K., Hoshino, S., Ishihama, T., Saito, N., & Yatani, K. (2020). Exploring nudge designs to help adolescent SNS users avoid privacy and safety threats. In *Proceedings of the 2020 CHI conference on human factors in computing systems*, CHI '20 (pp. 1–11). Association for Computing Machinery.

McKee, K. M., Dahl, A. J., & Peltier, J. W. (2023). Gen Z's personalization paradoxes: A privacy calculus examination of digital personalization and brand behaviors. *Journal of Consumer Behavior, 23*, 405–422.

Meier, Y., & Krämer, N. C. (2024). The privacy calculus revisited: An empirical investigation of online privacy decisions on between- and within-person levels. *Communication Research, 51*(2), 178–202. https://doi.org/10.1177/00936502221102101

Mele, C., Spena, T., Kaartemo, V., & Marzullo, M. (2021). Smart nudging: How cognitive technologies enable choice architectures for value co-creation. *Journal of Business Research, 129*, 949–960. https://doi.org/10.1016/j.jbusres.2020.09.004

Nouwens, M., Liccardi, I., Veale, M., Karger, D., & Kagal, L. (2020). Dark patterns after the GDPR: Scraping consent pop-ups and demonstrating their influence. In *Proceedings of the 2020 CHI conference on human factors in computing systems*, CHI '20 (pp. 1–13). Association for Computing Machinery.

O'Donoghue, T., & Rabin, M. (1999). Doing it now or later. *American Economic Review, 89*(1), 103–124. https://doi.org/10.1257/aer.89.1.103

Peng, Z. (2023). A privacy calculus model perspective that explains why parents sharent. *Information, Communication & Society*, 1–24. https://doi.org/10.1080/1369118X.2023.2285462

Perino, D., Katevas, K., Lutu, A., Marin, E., & Kourtellis, N. (2022). Privacy-preserving AI for future networks. *Communication of the ACM, 65*(4), 52–55. https://doi.org/10.1145/3512343

Pitardi, V., & Marriott, H. R. (2021). Alexa, she's not human but… Unveiling the drivers of consumers' trust in voice-based artificial intelligence. *Psychology & Marketing, 38*(4), 626–642. https://doi.org/10.1002/mar.21457

Ramesh, A., & Chawla, V. (2022). Chatbots in marketing: A literature review using morphological and co-occurrence analyses. *Journal of Interactive Marketing, 57*(3), 472–496. https://doi.org/10.1177/10949968221095549

Renaud, K., & Zimmermann, V. (2018). Ethical guidelines for nudging in information security & privacy. *International Journal of Human-Computer Studies, 120*, 22–35. https://doi.org/10.1016/j.ijhcs.2018.05.011

Schaub, F., Balebako, R., Durity, A. L., & Cranor, L. F. (2015). A design space for effective privacy notices. In *Proceedings of the 11th symposium on usable privacy and security (SOUPS 2015)* (pp. 1–17). USENIX Association.

Shah, A. K., & Oppenheimer, D. M. (2008). Heuristics made easy: An effort-reduction framework. *Psychological Bulletin, 134*(2), 207–222. https://doi.org/10.1037/0033-2909.134.2.207

Sharot, T. (2011). The optimism bias. *Current Biology, 21*(23), R941–R945.

Shin, D. (2022). How do people judge the credibility of algorithmic sources? *AI and Society, 37*, 81–96. https://doi.org/10.1007/s00146-021-01158-4

Shin, D. (2024). *Artificial misinformation: Exploring human-algorithm interaction online.* Springer Nature. https://doi.org/10.1007/978-3-031-52569-8

Shin, D. (2025). *Minds, Machines, and Misinformation.* Elsevier Publishing.

Shin, D., & Zhou, S. (2024). A value and diversity-aware news recommendation systems: Can algorithmic gatekeeping nudge readers to view diverse news? *Journalism & Mass Communication Quarterly.* https://doi.org/10.1177/10776990241246680

Sofia, S., Torben, B., Andreas, J., Felix, H., & Marco, L. (2020). Understanding user preferences of digital privacy nudges: A best-worst scaling approach. In *Proceedings of the 53rd Hawaii international conference on system sciences* (pp. 3918–3927). https://doi.org/10.24251/HICSS.2020.479

Solove, D. J. (2024). *Artificial intelligence and privacy* (77 Florida Law Review, GWU Legal Studies Research Paper No. 2024-36). http://dx.doi.org/10.2139/ssrn.4713111

Sundar, S., Kim, J., Rosson, J., Oliver, M., & Molina, M. (2020). Online privacy heuristics that predict information disclosure. In *CHI '20: Proceedings of the 2020 CHI conference on human factors in computing systems* (pp. 1–12). https://doi.org/10.1145/3313831.3376854

Thaler, R. H. (2018). Nudge, not sludge. *Science, 361*(6401), 431–431.

Thaler, R. H., & Sunstein, C. R. (2008). *Nudge: Improving decisions about health, wealth, and happiness.* Yale University Press.

Trieste, L., & Turchetti, G. (2024). The nature, causes, and effects of skepticism on technology diffusion. *Technological Forecasting and Social Change, 208*(0040-1625), 123663.

Weinmann, M., Schneider, C., & Brocke, J. V. (2016). Digital nudging. *Business & Information Systems Engineering, 58*, 433–436. https://doi.org/10.1007/s12599-016-0453-1

Wilkinson, T. M. (2013). Nudging and manipulation. *Political Studies, 61*(2), 341–355. https://doi.org/10.1111/j.1467-9248.2012.00974.x

Williamson, S., & Prybutok, V. (2024). Balancing privacy and progress: A review of privacy challenges, systemic oversight, and patient perceptions in AI-driven healthcare. *Applied Sciences, 14*, Article No. 675. https://doi.org/10.3390/app14020675

Yeung, K. (2017). Hyper nudge: Big data as a mode of regulation by design. *Information, Communication & Society, 20*(1), 118–136.

Zimmermann, V. (2023). Privacy nudges and informed consent? Challenges for privacy nudge design. In N. Gerber, A. Stöver, & K. Marky (Eds.), *Human factors in privacy research.* Springer. https://doi.org/10.1007/978-3-031-28643-8_8

Zimmermann, V., & Renaud, K. (2021). The nudge puzzle: Matching nudge interventions to cybersecurity decisions. *ACM Transactions on Computer-Human Interaction, 28*(1), Article 7. https://doi.org/10.1145/3429888

Zimmermann, V., Marky, K., & Renaud, K. (2022). Hybrid password meters for more secure passwords: A comprehensive study of password meters including nudges and password information. *Behavior & Information Technology, 42*(6), 700–743. https://doi.org/10.1080/0144929X.2022.2042384

Zimmermann, J., Martin, K., Schumann, J., & Widjaja, T. (2024). Consumers' multistage data control in technology-mediated environments. *International Journal of Research Marketing, 41*, 56–76. https://doi.org/10.1016/j.ijresmar.2023.09.004

AI and Transparency

3

In Transparency We Trust

The importance of transparency in artificial intelligence (AI) has grown due to the widespread use of complex machine learning systems. As machine learning progresses, transparency becomes crucial in providing a clear explanation for the decisions and actions made by AI. This understanding helps humans ensure that AI's decisions are fair and reliable, building trust and meeting societal expectations (Shin, 2024). In the AI-driven media landscape, transparency is especially important in automated news production using generative AI. This involves openly sharing the processes of gathering, organizing, and disseminating information, allowing internal and external parties to audit, monitor, critique, and intervene in news production (Otis, 2024). Common attributes of transparency include offering details about news corrections, reporter bios, and links to related stories and issues, which improve user perceptions and strengthen the credibility of the news industry (Liu et al., 2023). Efforts have been made to improve transparency, with nudging becoming popular in various contexts such as healthcare, public policy, and media (Andı & Akesson, 2020). Within digital media, nudging has been examined as a way to empower users to control their interactions with online content (Otis, 2024). AI content creation tools have implemented labeling for AI-generated content to clarify news authorship. Content labels, such as trust labels and fact-checking cues, will be key tools in content governance within human–AI collaboration (Morrow et al., 2022).

In algorithmic news recommendation (ANR), transparency nudging is seen as a form of interactive design that guides user behaviors online while preserving their freedom of choice (Norambuena et al., 2023). Transparency cues in ANR can trigger users' processes of discerning AI news quality (Lim & Kim, 2024). Transparency labeling can intervene in the quick sharing of automated news by encouraging readers to pause and evaluate before consuming any media, ultimately discouraging the consumption of misinformation (Liu et al., 2023). Proactive transparency cues that enhance information quality and clarity act as a form of soft content governance, promoting a more effective and sound communication environment through subtle nudges (Prochazka & Obermaier, 2022).

Despite their importance, the effects of nudges and transparency cues on user decisions have received limited empirical attention, especially within algorithmic

DOI: 10.1201/9781003530244-5

contexts. Consequently, the precise nature of how nudges function, their effects, user responses, and their impact on behavior concerning information processing and content evaluation in ANR remain unclear. We address the call for empirical studies by investigating two key areas: (1) whether transparency cues in AI-generated news nudge users in evaluating the credibility and quality of content and (2) how the nudging effect is influenced by the type of information source and the level of trust in algorithmic sources. This study builds upon the theoretical framework of nudging by incorporating perspectives on source effects and credibility evaluation. Our findings provide practical guidelines for implementing and utilizing transparency cues in algorithmic media in the AI era.

LITERATURE REVIEW

As ANR systems are becoming ubiquitous in the AI media landscape, transparency and fairness have become critical elements of information credibility and informed decision-making (Shin, 2024). Relevant literature suggests using nudges to help prompt accurate assessments by online news consumers (Lim & Kim, 2024). Additionally, recent studies have indicated that notifying them of transparency issues enhances the credibility of news they read online (Wang & Ophir, 2024). Given this, it can be worthwhile to explore users' perceptions of news transparency in the context of ANR.

Why Transparency Important in AI

Transparency in AI is crucial for building trust and accountability. When AI systems are transparent, it becomes possible to follow the decision-making process and determine where mistakes may have happened. This ability to trace decisions is vital for rectifying errors and enhancing the overall effectiveness of AI systems. By grasping the underlying principles, both developers and users can ensure mistakes are not repeated, resulting in more reliable and robust AI applications (Shin, 2022). This concept of transparency is closely related to ideas such as openness and explainability. Openness is often discussed in positive terms, associated with concepts like "open data," "open source," "open code," and "open access," alongside "open science." Furthermore, "openness" can also be observed in the ongoing conflict between content-producing industries, which typically depend on intellectual property laws, and those industries advocating for a freer exchange of content, referred to as "openness industries" (Larsson, 2017).

A challenge noted by Shin (2020) relates to the "transparency paradox," where even a well-meaning approach to openness can yield unintended negative effects. Increasing transparency in AI systems, while beneficial in many ways, also introduces new risks and challenges. On one hand, transparency is crucial for ensuring accountability, fairness, and trust in AI systems. On the other hand, this transparency can also make AI systems more vulnerable to exploitation. For instance, detailed disclosures about how an AI system works can provide malicious actors with the information they need to manipulate or attack the system. This could lead to security breaches or the misuse of AI technologies. Additionally, transparency can expose companies to legal and regulatory risks, as greater disclosure might reveal flaws or biases that could lead to lawsuits or regulatory actions (Burt, 2019). Navigating this paradox requires a careful balance. Firms need to be transparent enough to build trust and ensure the ethical use of AI, but not so transparent that they compromise the security and integrity of their systems. This involves implementing robust risk management strategies and being selective about the information they disclose. By doing so, they can protect their AI systems while still promoting accountability and fairness.

In the realm of explainable AI (XAI), explainability is seen as a "model-close" approach that pertains to the idea of transparency (Larsson & Heintz, 2020). The aim of XAI is to clarify and make interpretable the decision-making processes behind AI systems. This includes employing various techniques and tools that help people understand how an AI model reaches its conclusions. The XAI perspective on transparency is more specific and concentrated on algorithmic models, in contrast to the broader notion of necessary transparency (and "interpretability") promoted by Shin (2021), which emphasizes the importance of responsible and trustworthy AI.

Explainable AI

AI technologies are being deployed in almost every decision-making sector of human life, irrespective of the stakes of using them. Decisions provided by AI decision-makers can vary in accuracy and detail, which triggers the need to evaluate AI decisions before accepting them. Though expert users with high domain knowledge might have the ability to recognize and disregard faulty decisions generated by an AI agent, it is relatively tough for non-expert users. Moreover, if individuals can identify a faulty decision, they cannot understand the process through which AI agents make that decision because of the black-box nature of AI. This opacity surrounding the AI decision process gives rise to the notion of XAI as a solution that can evoke transparency and fairness and, consequently, better adoption (Saeed & Omlin, 2023; Samek & Müller, 2019; Shin, 2022). Explanation can have a positive influence on enhancing the output of human–AI teamwork (Leichtmann et al., 2023). Explanation of how an AI agent comes to certain decisions or predictions also fosters users' trust and reliance on AI in general (Chen et al., 2023; Leichtmann et al., 2023; Shin, 2022; Vasconcelos et al., 2023).

Examining the benefits of XAI faces the primary challenge of defining it in universally acceptable terms. Meta-analyses on previous literature related to XAI showed that the process of defining XAI varies across disciplines and scholars (Arrieta et al., 2020; Guidotti et al., 2018; Saeed & Omlin, 2023). In simpler terms, XAI is a type of AI that exposes the process of making its decisions, predictions, and overall actions (Rai, 2020). Though this definition clearly states the role of AI in this explanation process, it does not provide clear insights about the other side of the explanation process, the audience of that explanation. To fill out this gap, Arrieta et al. (2020) emphasized the audience to whom the explanation is addressed and defined XAI as "Given an audience, an explainable Artificial Intelligence is one that produces details or reasons to make its functioning clear or easy to understand" (p. 6). Similarly, Shin et al. (2024) also stressed the need to assess the role of the audience, in this case, the humans in human–AI interactions.

Another challenge in defining XAI stems from the interchangeable use of interpretability and explainability. For instance, Doshi-Velez and Kim (2017) used interpretability and explainability almost interchangeably. However, using interpretability and explainability interchangeably can create confusion about reaching common ground with XAI (Arrieta et al., 2020). It is important to make these two terms clear in the scholarships regarding XAI. Saeed and Omlin (2023) made a clear distinction between the two terms as explainability fulfills an audience's needs for insight into the AI's action process, and interpretability defines the degree to which the audience can make sense of the insights provided.

The need for exploring XAI stems from the need to evaluate AI decisions and predictions in high-stakes situations like medical, financial, and security, among others. Lack of explanation creates a barrier to optimizing AI in crucial human sectors (Doshi-Velez & Kim, 2017). Along with highly consequential situations, humans also might feel uncomfortable with AI decisions and predictions regarding ethical issues without understanding how those actions were undertaken (Doran et al., 2017). Although most of the scholars in XAI emphasized high-stakes conditions where an explanation is necessary and argued that in low-stakes conditions, we could rely on non-explanatory black-box AI (Guidotti et al., 2018), lack of explanation in low consequential situations also causes confusion and subsequent harm for human users. That is why users might need explanations even in low-stakes situations (Munch et al., 2024). Apart from that, explanations serve several other basic needs in the designing, deployment, and user interaction processes of AI. For instance, Adadi and Berrada (2018) identified explanation can help designers control the action process and improve the design of AI agents, as well as find justification for AI decisions and discover new insights from AI actions. Similarly, an explanation of AI's mechanism of making decisions can help reduce biases and design accurate AI (Xu & Shi, 2024). From this, we see that explanation can help people on both ends of AI: people who design, control, and improve AI and people who use it. This necessitates the need to focus more on the human side of XAI along with its design and development. It is necessary to identify the stakeholders in XAI to make AI more equitable for all.

Researchers have identified several levels of stakeholder communities for XAI. For instance, Preece et al. (2018) identified four stakeholder communities for XAI: developers (who create the technical foundations), theorists (who provide the theoretical bases for AI development), ethicists (who examine the impacts of AI from the perspective of human morality and ethics), and users. Along with these, Kong et al. (2024) included managerial decision-makers and regulatory bodies as stakeholders of XAI. Users as stakeholders need more consideration in XAI as they likely have less knowledge about the operation processes of AI. Moreover, scholarship surrounding XAI focused more on the design and development processes than its human-centric aspect. However, examining XAI with its human counterpart requires equal contribution as it is humans who need the explanation, not the AI. Furthermore, the explanation is interactive and centered around users' needs and contexts that require equal emphasis on both the AI and its human users (Shin, 2021). Individuals vary in their need for explanation and understanding indicating users need to expect differently from XAI. Kim et al. (2024) study on clinicians and patients demonstrated that different stakeholders have different needs and expectations from explanation. Therefore, interface design for XAI should be focused on the needs of the stakeholders (Kim et al., 2024). Individuals also have different levels of domain knowledge that might affect their understanding of examples provided by XAI. As Jiang et al. (2022) identified, if user uncertainty of domain knowledge increases, only an explanation of the prediction rationale can help them as alternative advice might hinder the user's acceptance of the prediction. To solve these issues, designing interactive XAI might help as it provides the users greater agency in evaluating AI decisions (Raees et al., 2024).

With an emphasis on the human aspects of XAI, the explanation process can be seen through the lens of broad human communication perspectives, as explanations are basically interactions (Hoffman et al., 2023). In an attempt to integrate XAI into human–machine communication, Xu and Shi (2024) proposed two dimensions of explainability: the human-in-the-loop dimension and the dimension of message production explainability. Xu and Shi (2024) argued that explanation sources, explanation messages, explanation receivers, and explanation effects should be considered when XAI and human communication are in question. As Hoffman et al. (2023) emphasized, to "Get Inside the Heads" of a human user to evaluate XAI systems, we need to focus on human communication patterns in explanation, trust, and acceptance. How humans communicate with XAI and internalize the process of explanation would provide insights about designing more equitable and unbiased AI.

Transparency Heuristic

People often use available signals of content quality to judge the trustworthiness of information sources (Metzger et al., 2010; Shin, 2024). Using heuristic methods, such as scanning an article, can be an efficient way to gather information without having to devote as much cognitive effort as reading carefully. Research shows that people often interact with AI through available cues before using an AI-based service (Otis, 2024; Peacock et al., 2022). Therefore, transparency cues, a collection of heuristic indicators, can signal trustworthiness and potential bias and have a substantial impact on assessments of credibility (Masullo et al., 2022). Transparency cues give users insight into the algorithmic process. These may encompass tags containing information on the rationale or method behind a piece of information's creation, information on industry standards, information on an author, or information on whether an article is classified as a reporting analysis or opinion (Liu et al., 2023).

Transparency in ANR refers to sharing the journalistic and algorithmic processes (editing, production, and gatekeeping) with outsiders (i.e., making AI journalism more transparent) (Otis, 2024). The goal of transparency is for users to see how AI news is generated (Bhuiyan et al., 2021). The literature shows that transparency has become a critical factor in AI news platforms (Bhuiyan et al., 2021). Additionally, numerous studies show that transparency can be a mechanism for fostering accountability and trust (Shin, 2024). Curry and Stroud (2021) showed that increasing transparency, such as providing information about the selection and writing process or details about the author, results in higher credibility assessments and stronger intent to engage with news. Research has shown that journalists prioritize transparency by openly sharing information, a practice referred to as disclosure transparency (Otis, 2024). Disclosure transparency can be carried out in various ways, such as providing details about the verification process, including sources for a report, and acknowledging and rectifying errors (Diakopoulos et al., 2024). For instance, newsrooms could implement practices such as clarifying the affiliations of news outlets and newsroom blogs or providing explanations about the editorial process within a newsroom. Although transparency has been recommended to enhance credibility, there is limited empirical research on the connection between these factors. Earlier studies had primarily focused on the impact of transparency cues on news readership (e.g., Otis, 2024; Peacock et al., 2022) without clearly identifying the specific effects of these cues on perceived credibility. Our goal is to bridge this gap in the research.

Evaluating the Effectiveness of Transparency Labeling: Machine Heuristic

The rise of AI-generated fake images and videos has led to widespread concerns about eroding media trust and content integrity (Otis, 2024). These manipulated visuals are often used to provoke political outrage or drive ad revenue, and they are frequently shared online without disclosing their synthetic nature. The widespread use of algorithms and machine learning has significantly worsened their negative effects. Misinformation spreads more quickly online, and algorithms that prioritize engagement metrics (e.g., shares, likes, views, and retweets) have fostered a concerning trend in which news consumers mistake "popular" content for credible information without critically evaluating its accuracy (Shin, 2024). For example, a fake image of Donald Trump shared on X by his son without any indication of being doctored illustrates how such content can undermine trust in media sources. Similarly, throughout the Israel–Hamas conflict, AI-generated images have been falsely depicting casualties, leading to misinformation and premature conclusions. This has compromised the credibility of visual content, resulting in uncertainty and cynicism. As a result, the media's influence on public opinion may be diminished, possibly leading to social discontent and polarization.

To address declining credibility in news and journalism, various efforts have attempted to increase transparency by providing relevant information around news content, but such approaches were largely developed without considering how users process these transparency tools. Furthermore, the nudging effect as a transparency cue in an algorithm context has not been empirically tested. Although there have been numerous studies on cueing on the perceived credibility of news sources (e.g., Curry & Stroud, 2021), investigations into the nudging effect of transparency cues on AI journalism have been limited. In light of the extensive integration of AI in media and content suggestions, it is essential to delve into the application of transparency nudging and its influence on algorithmic systems.

The effectiveness of transparency cues as a nudge intervention can be influenced by users' understanding of AI's capacity for generating misinformation. This is referred to as the machine heuristic (Yang & Sundar, 2024), which is a user tendency to consider machines' judgments to be fair, objective, and scientific, as they perceive algorithms to be free of ideological bias. In human–AI interaction, people see algorithms as more precise and secure than humans, and consequently, users apply positive heuristics to AI. When transparency cues are generated by AI, people are more responsive to the cues than human sources of information and cues. Certain labels on an AI interface activate the machine heuristic by arousing individuals with greater cognitive accessibility to the heuristic (i.e., stronger prior beliefs in the rule of thumb), making them more likely to disclose information to a machine compared to those with lower accessibility (Yang & Sundar, 2024). These findings pertaining to machine heuristics have implications for the design of transparency cues for interfaces that convey algorithmic vs. human sources of human–AI interaction. Perceptions of fairness arising from the machine heuristic and the transparency indicated by cues are expected to influence credibility judgments. It is therefore a pertinent and timely endeavor to investigate the effects of the transparency and machine heuristics, respectively, as well as the interaction effects of the two heuristics.

Research Questions

Despite the growing interest in ANR and transparency signals, limited attention has been devoted to revealing how these nudges affect users' engagement with news through ANR. While some relevant research confirms that transparency prompts can lead to a better understanding of AI's limitations and an increased intention to share (e.g., Otis, 2024), there is still the question of their effectiveness and validity in the context of AI-driven media. The general effects of transparency interventions have been researched (Vermeulen, 2022), but their feasibility and performance in an algorithmic context have yet to be fully examined. Therefore, the current study interrogates the conceptual development of transparency nudges presented alongside algorithm-generated news by examining whether the priming and triggering of transparency nudges for algorithmically generated news will nudge users to evaluate the content carefully and to trust the credibility of the news. The impact of transparency nudges and the underlying mechanisms of credibility assessment have remained unresolved issues in the fields of ANR and AI. Considering the rising implications of nudges in ANR systems, the following questions are proposed:

RQ1: How do transparency cues in ANR act as heuristics that influence users' AI decisions? How do transparency cues influence the perceived credibility of news generated by algorithms?

RQ2: What impact do source type (generated by AI vs. written by humans) and trust have on users' behavior toward AI news? How does user trust in ANR and news source types influence the nudging effect of such transparency cues?

HYPOTHESIS DEVELOPMENT

Our model was developed to examine the impact of transparency nudging on users' perceptions of credibility (Figure 3.1). Three hypotheses were formulated in relation to the following topics of interrogation: (1) the main effect of transparency cues on credibility, (2) the main effect of news source types on credibility, and (3) whether transparency cues and news source types interact or mediate in determining users' perceptions of credibility.

Transparency Nudging Effect: Cues for Information Processing

AI users often come across inaccurate news, despite knowing that it could be the result of accidental misinformation, intentional disinformation, or malicious misinformation. While a large body of literature suggests a positive relationship between perceptions of credibility and transparency (e.g., Otis, 2024), the impact of transparency on users' perceptions of news credibility remains unclear. Recent studies show that transparency features (e.g., hyperlinking source material and information within a story's framework) had moderate effects on users' perceptions of news credibility (Curry & Stroud, 2021). Transparency cues and labeling have proven to be effective tools for achieving such an outcome. Shin's (2024) experiment demonstrated that transparency cues, delivered through indirect induction, prompted users to engage in more deliberate message processing instead of relying solely on intuitive heuristics. Similarly, Liu et al. (2023) showed that alerting users to consider news transparency by disclosing the source information of ANR systems resulted in a higher likelihood of users rating credibility as high.

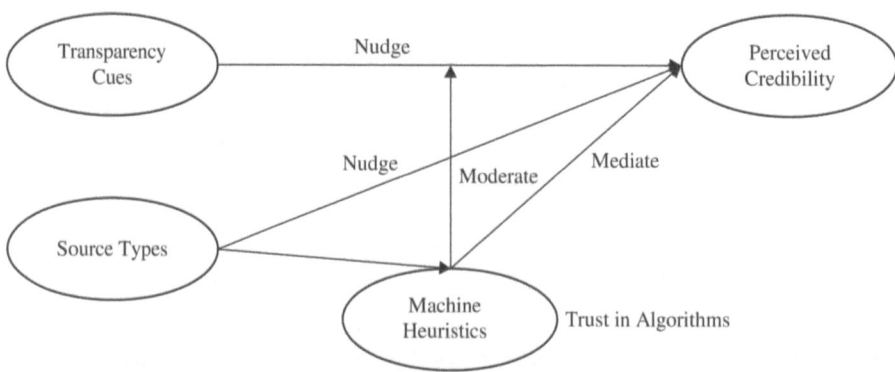

FIGURE 3.1 Hypothesized transparency nudge model.

Relevant studies have confirmed the role of nudges by establishing a causal connection between cues and confidence in media in the AI landscape (e.g., Peng & Wang, 2024). Hence, transparency cues can act as nudges, and thus, the first hypothesis was formulated as follows:

> H1: Transparency cues nudge users toward evaluating information quality effectively.

Algorithmic Source Attribution: Machine Heuristics

Information sources play a crucial role in shaping our beliefs and in informing our intuitive heuristics (Peng & Wang, 2024). Information that is derived from sources deemed credible tends to have a more significant influence on the beliefs, motivations, and attitudes of users compared to information originating from non-credible sources (Shah & Wei, 2024). Users tend to have greater trust in information sources they perceive as credible and authentic, particularly when those sources are individuals similar to them (Shah & Wei, 2024). Users judge the credibility of algorithm-generated news based on the news's source. Furthermore, they are more likely to trust personalized news sources that provide transparency cues (Lim et al., 2024). This is similar to the idea of machine heuristics (Yang & Sundar, 2024). In other words, people have preexisting ideas that machines scientifically filter information and thus consider machines more trustworthy and objective than human sources (Wang & Ophir, 2024). In the realm of AI-generated news, users are aware that recommended articles are chosen, organized, and filtered by AI algorithms. When news is generated by algorithms, users tend to scrutinize the source, accuracy, and credibility of the information more carefully than they would with human sources. Therefore, transparency cues are more effective when presented in algorithmic news because users will understand how algorithms operate in the background as a result. Users are more inclined to respond to the nudging effect of transparency cues associated with algorithmic sources because they already recognize the advantages of algorithms overall.

News produced by ANR systems is often perceived as having undergone rigorous expert editorial scrutiny and reporting (Peng & Wang, 2024), which enhances users' perceptions of the quality of their information sources and the truthfulness of the content (Metzger et al., 2010). Nevertheless, news sources lacking algorithmic filtering prompt users to react to transparency cues due to their inability to discern fake news from unfiltered news. Given the increasing use of AI in journalism, it is particularly useful to examine whether algorithmic sources would increase or reduce credibility in ANR. Therefore, we put forward the following hypothesis:

> H2: When transparency cues are present, news from an ANR system is more likely to be considered credible than news from legacy media sources. Conversely, when transparency cues are absent, news from a human source is considered less credible than news from an ANR system.

Trust Effects

Trust is a fundamental factor in determining news consumption and plays an even more crucial role in the efficacy of ANR systems. Trust creates a reciprocal feedback loop between users and recommendation systems, influencing the selection and consumption of news content. This highlights the significance of trust in determining user behavior and the effectiveness of recommendation systems in delivering relevant and reliable information (Shin, 2024). When users trust AI and algorithms, they are more likely to seek out news delivered by ANR systems that transcends their personal interests (Mattis et al., 2024). When individuals perceive that news suggestions are tailored to their interests, they view the service as valuable and are more likely to continue engaging with an ANR system (Baden & Springer, 2017). When users are made aware of the relevant transparency cues in news recommendations, they mentally separate the news content from the source and evaluate the quality of the news story by connecting it to their existing beliefs, schema, and experience related to the source (Andı & Akesson, 2020). During this judgment process, any breach of credibility can reduce the overall credibility of news linked to a trusted news source. Users' perceptions of the credibility of news sources could potentially moderate the impact of transparency cues on the nudging effects of news sources. When users have confidence in the overall functioning of algorithms, they are more likely to be swayed by transparency cues associated with ANR than by news from human sources (Hermann, 2022; Jia & Liu, 2021). When individuals are doubtful of algorithmic processes, they are more likely to be affected by news from human sources. As users' trust plays a significant role in processing cues, trust is proposed as a moderator:

> H3: Users' trust moderates the nudging effect of transparency cues such that users' perceptions of credibility will be more significant for news from ANR than news from human sources.

METHODS

Experiment

In this research, an online-based experiment was carried out using a 2 × 2 (source/ message transparency: with cues vs. without cues × news source: AI vs. human) design, which produced four conditions (Table 3.1). The quasi-experiment employed a between-subjects design to manipulate the source of news services and trust in them. The experiment was conducted out of a university in the southern part of the United States in May 2024.

TABLE 3.1   2 × 2 Experimental design

	TRANSPARENCY CUES	WITHOUT CUES
Algorithmic source	Group 1	Group 2
Human source	Group 3	Group 4

Data and Sample

We administered an online survey to 400 participants (refer to Table 3.2). To determine the sample size, we conducted a power analysis using an effect size of ηp2 = .02 obtained from a recent study examining the influence of algorithms and trust on user behaviors (Norambuena et al., 2023). Based on this analysis, we determined that our sample would require 100 responses per condition. The G*Power analysis revealed that based on our sample size, an α level of .05 and an estimated measures correlation of ρ = .19 were required. Our experiments had a power exceeding .79, enabling the detection of moderate-sized effects for the main tested effects.

To ensure the validity and reliability of the data and findings, an additional ten research participants were recruited to complete a pre-test questionnaire. During the main experiment, the selected respondents were randomly allocated to one of four conditions. There was no statistically significant variance among the groups in terms of demographics, prior knowledge of algorithms, or news media consumption rates. Furthermore, the four groups showed no variance in terms of demographic factors. All study respondents were randomly selected through the data panel company Qualtrics. Most participants were American (88%), their average age was 29.77 (SD = 7.92), and the gender ratio was nearly balanced (female: 50.3%, male: 49.7%). The majority of respondents (52.0%) were college graduates or had a college-level education. Regarding employment, 119 respondents were white-collar workers, and 112 were full-time employees. Nine incomplete responses with missing data were excluded from the data-set. Descriptive statistics indicate that the data exhibited a close approximation to a normal distribution.

Procedures

The participants were first provided with overall details regarding the study's frame-work, research objectives, process, and the guarantee of anonymity on the welcome page. Afterward, they were presented with detailed information about the online

TABLE 3.2 Demographics per experimental group

	EXPERIMENTAL GROUP			
	1	2	3	4
Mean/median age (SD)	21.31/20.01 (3.10)	22.89/21.32 (3.07)	21.49/20.43 (3.01)	23.83/22.83 (2.98)
Gender (female %)	51	50	49	51
Nudge experience (year)	2.4	3.1	1.7	.9
College education (%)	47	51	43	49

experiment (see Figure 3.1). Participants then provided informed consent before being randomly allocated to one of four experimental groups. All respondents completed a pre-test questionnaire that measured their personal trust in the presented news, their experience with ANR and online news, their prior online news consumption patterns, and their trust in algorithms. Finally, they were each randomly assigned to one of the two news source stimuli (i.e., AI and humans). They were given about 20 minutes to search for and read the news.

In the study, participants spent an average of 15 minutes on the news page (SD = 1.99). A factual news story on a relevant and current topic was selected to evaluate their trust in algorithms during the experiment. To introduce a nudge, half of the participants in each news source group were presented with a transparency cue next to the news story to notify them about content accuracy and news inaccuracy. This alert resembled the banners used by social media to flag dubious content or content featuring misinformation. Following this, a post-test questionnaire was administered to measure the participants' intention to share the news.

Stimuli

The ANR platforms used in this study included Google News, Apple News, and Microsoft News. The participants chose the ANR platforms or their preferred applications, completed a pre-screening questionnaire, interacted with personalized news, and finished the experiment by filling out a questionnaire assessing their attitudes and behaviors. Confirmation questions were included to validate the reliability of the responses, and data reduction was performed for reliability and validity.

Measures

The experimental manipulation underwent thorough checks and multiple controls to ensure the accurate measurement of the results.

Perceived Credibility

The perceived credibility of news was assessed using four Likert-type scales adjusted from Norambuena et al. (2023). Participants were requested to evaluate the news based on its accuracy, fairness, trustworthiness, and completeness. The final perceived credibility score was calculated by averaging their responses to these four items (Cronbach's α: .86, .87, .90, and .91). The completeness item from Norambuena et al. (2023) was unreliable or irrelevant to our experiment. The respondents rated on a 7-point Likert-type scale (1 = strongly disagree and 7 = strongly agree) how likely they were to evaluate news as (1) accurate, (2) fair, and (3) trustworthy (α = .89, M = 3.12, SD = .79).

Trust in Algorithms

Trust in AI refers to the belief users have in the reliability, safety, and fairness of an AI system. It involves confidence that the AI will function as intended, will not cause harm, will make fair and unbiased decisions, and will handle data responsibly (Fisher & Hopp, 2020). Trust was assessed by having participants rate their level of agreement (1 = strongly disagree to 7 = strongly agree) based on three measurements modified from Shin (2021): (1) I believe the algorithm is highly accurate and reliable in generating personalized news; (2) I have confidence in machine learning concerning data collection, analysis, and reflection; and (3) news recommendations generated by machine learning can be trusted because of their unbiased gatekeeping (α = .82, M = 3.64, SD = 1.25).

Analyses

Pearson's chi-squared test was performed to analyze potential differences among the four conditions in terms of participants' characteristics and to evaluate variations among the four conditions in relation to sharing behaviors and participant demographics. The results of the test indicated that there were no significant differences in sharing behaviors (X^2 (3) = 1.29; p = .609) and the various conditions regarding the participants' education and gender (X^2 (3) = 2.28; p = .482).

A univariate general linear model analysis of variance (ANOVA) was performed to compare the mean ratings of the dependent variables between the transparency cue and non-cue conditions. Additionally, the indirect effect of trust as a moderator of news credibility was examined. Trust was categorized into high and low levels using a median split (Mdn = 3.18). Multiple one-way ANOVAs, employing Welch's F-test, revealed statistically significant mean values of trust (F(3, 287) = 592.38, p < .001; $\eta 2$ = .782; Welch statistics: 528.78) and source type (F(3, 287) = 79.59, p < .001; $\eta 2$ = .249; Welch statistics: 138.06) between groups. Furthermore, a pairwise t-test was conducted to evaluate the moderation effect of trust on transparency cues and credibility (see Table 3.3).

For Hypothesis 1—the nudging effect of transparency cues on perceived credibility—a one-way ANOVA was performed to compare the respondents in the two conditions: those nudged with transparency cues and those with no cues. The results revealed a significant main effect (F(1, 387) = 7.128, p < .005), specifically that users nudged with transparency cues reported the news to have higher credibility than that without transparency cues (Groups 1 + 3 vs. 2 + 4). Based on this, it can be inferred that transparency cues clearly play a crucial role in promoting user confidence in the credibility of news. It can also be interpreted that transparency cues, if used properly, can effectively improve user experiences of ANR.

TABLE 3.3 Experiment results

GROUP	1	2	3	4
Perceived credibility (Cronbach's α = .90)	ANR		HUMAN SOURCE	
	M: 4.68 SD: 2.932	M: 5.58 SD: 1.284	M: 2.38 SD: 1.132	M: 2.72 SD: 2.130
Trust in algorithms (Cronbach's α = .91)	M: 5.729 SD: 1.839	M: 5.422 SD: 1.391	M: 2.742 SD: 1.232	M: 1.592 SD: 1.019
	Nudged	Non-nudge	Nudged	Non-nudge

In relation to Hypothesis 2, we found a positive effect of news source type (algorithmic vs. human) on perceived credibility. A one-way ANOVA was computed to compare the effect of news source type on perceived credibility (Groups 1 + 2 vs. 3 + 4). A one-way ANOVA indicated a statistically significant variance in credibility between the two groups (F (1, 389) = 227.38, $p < .001$). Therefore, H2 was supported, as participants who received news from an ANR system relied significantly more on the nudged cues compared to those who received news from human editor sources. Furthermore, it was found that users who received news from an algorithmic AI were significantly more responsive to nudges than those who received news from a human editor source.

Hypothesis 3 predicted the moderation effect of trust (machine heuristic) on transparency cues. A moderation analysis was done using PROCESS Macro 3.1 (Model 1; Hayes, 2017), in which perceived credibility was the dependent variable, the transparency cue was the independent variable, and trust was the moderator. The moderation test revealed a significant interaction effect between the types of news sources and trust in perceived credibility (Table 3.4, $p < .05$, CI: −15.31, −5.329). The results show that users' existing trust significantly impacted the credibility of news from algorithmic sources. Users with greater trust in machine heuristics were more inclined to perceive nudges favorably and consequently judge the credibility of AI positively.

The results of the additional analysis using t-tests further confirmed the presence of moderation effects. The pairwise t-tests revealed significant mean differences across all conditions. The pairwise comparisons between the low trust plus algorithmic source ($M_{\text{Algorithmic source, low machine heuristic}}$ = 4.38) and human source plus low trust ($M_{\text{Non-algorithmic source, low machine heuristic}}$ = 3.01) treatments ($p < .001$) and between the algorithmic source plus high trust ($M_{\text{Algorithmic, high machine heuristic}}$ = 4.90) and human source plus high trust ($M_{\text{Non-algorithmic, high machine heuristic}}$ = 2.98) treatments ($p < .001$) were significant. Likewise, the pairwise comparison between the transparency cues plus high trust ($M_{\text{Nudge, high machine heuristic}}$ = 3.87) and the transparency cues plus low trust ($M_{\text{Nudge, low machine heuristic}}$ = 2.96) treatments ($p < .001$) and between the non-nudged/no cues plus high trust ($M_{\text{Non-nudged, high machine heuristic}}$ = 3.98) and non-nudged plus low trust ($M_{\text{Non-nudged, low machine heuristic}}$ = 3.21) treatments ($p < .001$) were significant. Transparency cues diminished the users' perceptions of credibility, and the nudging effect was more significant for algorithmic ANR systems compared to human sources. Additionally, users' perceived credibility was moderated by their level of trust in the type of source.

TABLE 3.4 Moderation test using Hayes' PROCESS macro

IV	PERCEIVED CREDIBILITY			
	COEFFICIENT	STANDARD ERROR	T	P
Trust	49.7284	17.5923	3.234	.0050
Source type	68.5393	19.4913	3.7482	.0004
Trust × Source type	−15.3194	5.3292	−1.9482	.0003
	Rsq	0.5923	.0010	
	F	18.0329		

We used structural equation modeling (SEM) with partial least squares (PLS) to test the mediation effect of trust. Mediation occurs when the direct relationship between the independent variable (source effect and trust) and the dependent variable (credibility) decreases after introducing the mediator in the model. The direct path coefficient was evaluated both without the mediator (trust) and with the mediator. The direct path standardized beta was .698 and decreased to .296 after adding trust as a mediator. The decrease in the correlation between source and credibility accounted for by the mediator was .402, representing 51.67% of the direct effect. The significance of the mediation effect was measured using PROCESS (Hayes, 2017) with bootstrapping. The indirect effect of the source on credibility, with trust as a mediator, was found to be significant at $p < .000$, with an upper-level confidence level of .416 and a lower-level confidence level of .287. This indicates the presence of a partial mediation effect (see Figure 3.2).

In addition to hypothesis testing, a significant interaction effect was observed between transparency and the source effect. Transparency improved perceptions of credibility when people perceived algorithms to be more accurate and objective than human sources. Subjects who seemed strongly influenced by the algorithmic source effect were more likely to view the content in the ANR system as credible. When algorithms are used in ANR, transparency acts as a heuristic tool, with its impact interacting with prior beliefs

FIGURE 3.2   Mediating effects of trust.

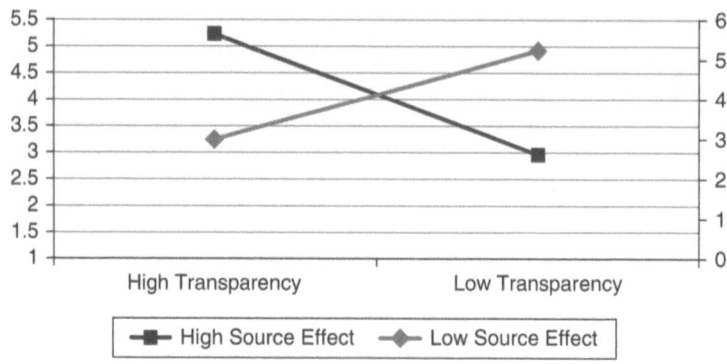

FIGURE 3.3 The interaction effects between transparency and source on credibility.

about algorithms. This is particularly true in cases where transparency cues responsibly nudge (and alert users to) the shortcomings of algorithmic sources (Figure 3.3).

DISCUSSION

The findings suggest that cues related to transparency can successfully prompt users and lead to a heightened level of scrutiny that influences their assessment of the quality of AI-generated media (see Table 3.4). This point supports prior research on transparency (Norambuena et al., 2023; Otis, 2024; Prochazka & Obermaier, 2022), illustrating how nudges as heuristic cues can modify user behaviors in information processing. Moreover, this finding builds on previous studies on credibility (Jia & Liu, 2021; Liu et al., 2023; Peng & Wang, 2024) by emphasizing that nudges in the form of transparency cues and heuristics could significantly impact users' systematic evaluation and behavior in algorithmic media. Based on previous research by Shin (2025), it has been established that user attention is crucial in combating misinformation. Shin (2024) suggested that employing a form of priming, such as transparency cues, can prompt users to engage in critical information processing and be mindful of the potential risks of misinformation from AI. Our findings regarding nudge processing are consistent with current research, corroborating the idea that users have a tendency to reconsider their intention to assess the quality of news when they are prompted to focus on transparency (Otis, 2024). Our findings also extend the current body of literature by providing further clarification on the moderating and mediating effects of the nudging effect on the assessment of information quality and credibility. The effectiveness of transparency cues may be influenced by the levels of trust in algorithms and types of news sources. We suggest that people are more likely to respond to or engage more with nudges when they are suggested by algorithms (i.e., algorithmic platforms) rather than by humans or non-algorithmic services. We believe that this is because human-free nudges seem less judgmental and therefore create a greater sense of trust, which is a common heuristic

TABLE 3.5 Review of hypotheses

HYPOTHESES	KEY FINDINGS	RESULTS
H1: The effect of transparency cues on credibility	Transparency cues led to an increased intention to evaluate the quality and credibility of ANR.	Supported $p < .005$
H2: The positive impact of algorithmic source type on credibility	Users were more responsive to nudges when alerted by algorithms, and trust in algorithms directly influenced user behavior and responses to transparency cues.	Supported $p < .001$
H3: The moderation effect of trust on transparency cues	– Nudge effects are more influenced by personal preferences (existing trust) than transparency or modes of nudges. – Interaction effect between source type and trust on perceived credibility: When people had high trust in algorithms, they were more likely to respond positively to transparency cues and tended to perceive them as highly credible. Conversely, when people had low trust in algorithms, they tended to take transparency cues less seriously and were more likely to perceive them as lacking credibility.	Supported $p < .01$

associated with machines (Yang & Sundar, 2024). This result adds to the ongoing scholarship on algorithmic media and information processing by elucidating how AI nudges can cognitively affect users' intent to evaluate the quality and thus establish the credibility of ANR (Table 3.5).

Algorithmic Source Effect

Our findings suggest that the trustworthiness of algorithmic sources significantly influences users' ability to assess transparency when evaluating credibility. The main effect observed in relation to transparency cues aligns well with previous findings (e.g., Peng & Wang, 2024; Shin, 2024) in that transparency cues lead to increased perceived credibility. Our results extend this finding by demonstrating that users' perceptions of credibility are moderated by labeling cues and mediated by machine heuristics. This effect of perceived credibility when nudged by a transparency cue was found to be strong for news originating from an algorithmic source. Readers are increasingly aware that news filtered by algorithms is more likely to feature fake news and misinformation. As a result, they are more likely to respond positively to transparency nudges, especially when it comes to checking a message and the source information of the news they receive. This can be attributed to the perceived credibility of algorithms and the personalized nature of news content. Additionally, users tend to trust transparency cues from algorithms more than those from human sources, believing that these cues are part of the algorithmic recommendations. In the context of ANR, the credibility of a message is heavily influenced by the credibility of a source. Positive attributes of a source can significantly impact the credibility of a nudged message.

Trust Effects

This study indicated that trust in algorithms has a direct impact on user behavior. When users have confidence in algorithmic mechanisms, they are more likely to respond to nudges. This connection between news source types and trust highlights the heuristic role of trust in AI and ANR. Users tend to rely on transparency cues when evaluating the credibility of news sources they trust. Trust in an algorithmic news source type influences users' evaluations of news credibility and their readiness to accept algorithmic recommendations. Conversely, lack of trust in algorithms leads to skepticism toward transparency cues and algorithmic suggestions. Overall, the study suggests that trust in algorithms plays a key role in users' information processing and their perception of news credibility influenced by nudges. This finding contributes to the bridging of the gap in transparency nudge research by establishing a connection between nudges and trust, especially in relation to how users perceive credibility within an algorithmic context.

IMPLICATIONS

The goal of this research was to gain deeper insight into the impact of transparency nudges on user responses by focusing on algorithms and their associated processes. The findings have both theoretical and practical significance. The theoretical aspects of this study provide conceptual insights into the dynamics of nudges, credibility, algorithmic source effects, and trust in the algorithmic process. While extensive research exists on fact-checking practices, misinformation-detecting technologies, and governance, there is a gap in our knowledge of how users process transparency nudges and how these nudges affect their behavior toward AI. The potential of transparency cues to guide users to assess the quality and credibility of AI-generated news has not been fully explored. To understand users' information processing procedures, it is essential to examine the processes that influence their engagement with AI mechanisms and algorithmic processes. Examining how transparency cues impact news credibility from a user cognition perspective can help bridge the gap between theory and practice. This approach goes beyond ANR-specific concepts and theories by focusing on how users make sense of information. A significant portion of misinformation spread can likely be attributed to users' insufficient attention to transparency when deciding what to read and what to trust (Pennycook & Rand, 2022).

When users are prompted with transparency nudges, their desire to evaluate news quality increases, especially when trust in an algorithm comes into play. This impact of algorithmic source is a significant theoretical development, considering the limited understanding of source effects in the realm of algorithmic news services. Our findings align with previous research highlighting the role of nudging in discerning misinformation and the causal mechanisms underlying it due to a lack of cognitive reflection. We further emphasize that perceived source credibility is linked to trust and that nudge credibility fosters users' ability to assess credibility. Users are inclined to trust nudges when they depend on algorithms for news personalization, particularly when they already trust algorithms. These findings underscore the significance of trust and credibility in the proliferation and use of algorithms, as well as the ways in which credibility can be bolstered and trust can be built between users and AI. Additionally, the study emphasizes that the effect of transparency cues should be understood from a user's sensemaking process and how it can improve quality judgments and engagement in the systematic evaluation of AI. This empirical testing of transparency cues from a user's sensemaking perspective is a meaningful attempt to assess the nudging effect from a human perspective rather than an AI or a provider perspective.

Furthermore, the research emphasizes the importance of transparency cues by demonstrating how a nudge that directs attention to transparency reduces doubts and uncertainties about AI. This connection lays the groundwork for theoretical advancements by establishing the link between transparency and AI comprehension. Despite being conceptually established, this relationship has garnered significant attention (Fisher & Hopp, 2023). It also highlights the need to further explore users' habit formation and sustained patterns in a long-term context, particularly due to the dearth of user research in these areas.

Practically, the findings highlight the need to implement transparent disclosure mechanisms to tackle the issues of misinformation and trust erosion on AI platforms. The nudge model offers valuable suggestions for AI platform providers on how to implement and leverage transparency nudges (Dwivedi et al., 2023). Additionally, the findings offer algorithmic platform providers valuable insights into effective nudging prompts to utilize and rotate when interacting with users to enhance the assessment of information quality online. The results suggest that prompting users to contemplate the transparency and accuracy of the news they consume—thereby fostering discernment—is an effective approach to combating misinformation. Given the recognized significance of transparency cues, ANR providers and news platform providers should implement substantial changes to the AI ecosystem to consistently direct attention to transparency. Specifically, considering the fluid nature of user attention, platform providers should consider implementing interventions that can be sustained over a prolonged period to exert a long-term influence on user behavior. Additionally, AI platforms could devise engagement strategies to discourage the dissemination of misinformation online.

The media industry can incorporate transparency cues as a guiding principle to deliver reliable news, as well as implement accuracy alerts and misinformation warnings. If used properly, a transparency cue can substantially curtail the diffusion of misinformation online. Users' understandings of and attitudes toward algorithms, as well as their expectations of specific algorithmic prompts, have an impact on their news consumption through ANR systems (Lim et al., 2024). Therefore, the industry could consider implementing transparency nudges to establish feedback mechanisms for AI. Transparency nudges offer users the opportunity to gain a better understanding of the fairness and ethical nature of ANRs. By providing clear insights into ANRs, these nudges not only benefit users but also help the media build trust and foster engagement with their algorithmic recommendations.

CONCLUSION

This study presented empirical proof of the impact of transparency cues on users' perceptions of news quality and their behavior toward ANR systems. Our results show that directing attention toward the notion of transparency can enhance the assessment of credibility. The findings elucidate the sensemaking processes of users as they assess the credibility and quality of AI, offering robust, theoretically driven explanations. The potential impact of transparency cues for fact-checking in relation to algorithmic news media, compared to non-algorithmic sources, presents an interesting area for future research. This area could focus on studying how nudges affect the perceived values, trust, and credibility of algorithmic processes. Despite ongoing research, numerous issues persist regarding credibility and disinformation. This study will provide a reference point for future research on transparency and other strategies to effectively mitigate the proliferation of misinformation.

LIMITATIONS AND FUTURE RESEARCH

The results of our study should be interpreted with caution due to the various limitations associated with our methods and study design. First, the use of a single stimulus limits the generalizability of the findings. The findings were derived from a single news experiment pertaining to a specific issue that impacts only a limited portion of the population rather than broader societal concerns. This limits the reproducibility and applicability of the results. To address this, future research could benefit from using multiple cases and taking longitudinal methods to enhance the reliability and applicability of the results. Since the experimental sessions were one-time occurrences and did not investigate long-term effects, the findings lack sufficient explanatory power to support long-term implications. This may be seen as a limitation of the study and should be explored in future research. Future research could also enhance transparency labeling effectiveness by using longitudinal data and exploring potential moderators, such as personal traits and other AI attributes. Additionally, our research did not account for the impact of individual traits and preexisting beliefs on media consumption and the spread of misinformation, despite the significant influence these user traits have on the assessment of AI's credibility. It can be expected that individual traits play a critical role in the perception of transparency and the effectiveness of nudges. Last, the study's focus on the impact of individual nudges on credibility overlooked various aspects of user behaviors associated with ANR systems. Users likely have different motivations and methods for assessing message quality across various platforms and networks. Future endeavors should investigate how user-specific factors affect the quality of ANR messages across various contexts.

REFERENCES

Adadi, A., & Berrada, M. (2018). Peeking inside the black-box: A survey on explainable artificial intelligence (XAI). *IEEE Access, 6*, 52138–52160. https://doi.org/10.1109/ACCESS.2018.2870052

Andı, S., & Akesson, J. (2020). Nudging away false news: Evidence from a social norms experiment. *Digital Journalism, 9*(1), 106–125. https://doi.org/10.1080/21670811.2020.1847674

Arrieta, A. B., Díaz-Rodríguez, N., Del Ser, J., Bennetot, A., Tabik, S., Barbado, A., Garcia, S., Gil-Lopez, S., Molina, D., Benjamins, R., Chatila, R., & Herrera, F. (2020). Explainable artificial intelligence (XAI): Concepts, taxonomies, opportunities and challenges toward responsible AI. *Information Fusion, 58*, 82–115. https://doi.org/10.1016/j.inffus.2019.12.012

Baden, C., & Springer, N. (2017). Conceptualizing viewpoint diversity in news discourse. *Journalism, 18*(2), 176–194. https://doi.org/10.1177/1464884915605028

Bhuiyan, M., Whitley, H., Horning, M., Lee, S., & Mitra, T. (2021). Designing transparency cues in online news platforms to promote trust: Journalists' & consumers' perspectives, *Proceeding ACM Human Computer Interaction, 5*, CSCW2, Article 395.

Burt, A. (2019). The AI transparency paradox. *Harvard Business Review.* https://hbr.org/2019/12/the-ai-transparency-paradox

Chen, V., Liao, Q. V., Wortman Vaughan, J., & Bansal, G. (2023). Understanding the role of human intuition on reliance in human-AI decision-making with explanations. *Proceedings of the ACM on Human-Computer Interaction, 7*(CSCW2), 1–32. https://doi.org/10.1145/3579619

Curry, A. L., & Stroud, N. J. (2021). The effects of journalistic transparency on credibility assessments and engagement intentions. *Journalism, 22*(4), 901–918. https://doi.org/10.1177/1464884919850387

Diakopoulos, N., Trattner, C., Jannach, D., Meijer, I., & Motta, E. (2024). Leveraging professional ethics for responsible AI. *Communications of the ACM, 67*(2), 19–21. https://doi.org/10.1145/3625252

Doran, D., Schulz, S., & Besold, T. (2017). What does explainable AI really mean? A new conceptualization of perspectives. *arXiv.* https://doi.org/10.48550/arXiv.1710.00794

Doshi-Velez, F., & Kim, B. (2017). Towards a rigorous science of interpretable machine learning. *arXiv.* https://doi.org/10.48550/arXiv.1702.08608

Dwivedi, Y. K., Kshetri, N., Hughes, L., Slade, E. L., Jeyaraj, A., Kar, A. K., Baabdullah, A. M., Koohang, A., Raghavan, V., Ahuja, M., Albanna, H., Albashrawi, M. A., Al-Busaidi, A. S., Balakrishnan, J., Barlette, Y., Basu, S., Bose, I., Brooks, L., Buhalis, D … Wirtz, J. (2023). So what if ChatGPT wrote it. *International Journal of Information Management*, *71*, 102642. https://doi.org/10.1016/j.ijinfomgt.2023.102642

Fisher, J. T., & Hopp, T. (2020). Does the framing of transparency impact trust? Differences between self-benefit and other-benefit message frames. *International Journal of Strategic Communication*, *14*(3), 203–222. doi: 10.1080/1553118X.2020.1770767

Fisher, J., & Hopp, T. (2023). Does the framing of transparency impact trust? Differences between self-benefit and other-benefit message frames. *International Journal of Strategic Communication*, *14*(3), 203–222. https://doi.org/10.1080/1553118X.2020.1770767

Guidotti, R., Monreale, A., Ruggieri, S., Turini, F., Giannotti, F., & Pedreschi, D. (2018). A survey of methods for explaining black box models. *ACM Computing Surveys*, *51*(5), 1–42. https://doi.org/10.1145/3236009

Hayes, A. F. (2017). *Introduction to mediation, moderation, and conditional process analysis: A regression-based approach*. Guilford Press.

Hermann, E. (2022). Artificial intelligence and mass personalization of communication content. *New Media & Society*, *24*(5), 1258–1277. https://doi.org/10.1177/14614448211022702

Jia, C., & Liu, R. (2021). Algorithmic or human source? Examining relative hostile media effect with a transformer-based framework. *Media and Communication*, *9*(4), 170–181. https://doi.org/10.17645/mac.v9i4.4164

Jiang, J., Kahai, S., & Yang, M. (2022). Who needs explanation and when? Juggling explainable AI and user epistemic uncertainty. *International Journal of Human-Computer Studies*, *165*, 102839. https://doi.org/10.1016/j.ijhcs.2022.102839

Kim, M., Kim, S., Kim, J., Song, T. J., & Kim, Y. (2024). Do stakeholder needs differ? Designing stakeholder-tailored explainable artificial intelligence (XAI) interfaces. *International Journal of Human-Computer Studies*, *181*, 103160. https://doi.org/10.1016/j.ijhcs.2023.103160

Kong, X., Liu, S., & Zhu, L. (2024). Toward human-centered XAI in practice: A survey. *Machine Intelligence Research*, *21*(4), 740–770. https://doi.org/10.1007/s11633-022-1407-3

Larsson, S. (2017). *Conceptions in the Code. How metaphors explain legal challenges in digital Times*. Oxford University Press.

Larsson, S., & Heintz, F. (2020). Transparency in artificial intelligence. *Internet Policy Review*, *9*(2). https://doi.org/10.14763/2020.2.1469

Leichtmann, B., Humer, C., Hinterreiter, A., Streit, M., & Mara, M. (2023). Effects of explainable artificial intelligence on trust and human behavior in a high-risk decision task. *Computers in Human Behavior*, *139*, 107539. https://doi.org/10.1016/j.chb.2022.107539

Lim, C., & Kim, S. (2024). Examining factors influencing the user's loyalty on algorithmic news recommendation service. *Humanity Social Science Communication*, *11*, 10. https://doi.org/10.1057/s41599-023-02516-x

Lim, J., Ahmad, N., & Ibrahim, M. (2024). Understanding user sensemaking in fairness and transparency in algorithms: Algorithmic sensemaking in over-the-top platform. *AI & Society*, *39*, 447–490. https://doi.org/10.1007/s00146-022-01525-9

Liu, Y., Wang, S., & Yu, G. (2023). The nudging effect of AIGC labeling on users' perceptions of automated news: Evidence from EEG. *Frontier Psychology*, *14*, 1277829. https://doi.org/10.3389/fpsyg.2023.1277829

Masullo, G. M., Curry, A. L., Whipple, K. N., & Murray, C. (2022). The story behind the story: Examining transparency about the journalistic process and news outlet credibility. *Journalism Practice*, *16*(7), 1287–1305. https://doi.org/10.1080/17512786.2020.1870529

Mattis, N., Groot Kormelink, T., Masur, P. K., Moeller, J., & van Atteveldt, W. (2024). Nudging news readers: A mixed-methods approach to understanding when and how interface nudges affect news selection. *Digital Journalism*, 1–21. https://doi.org/10.1080/21670811.2024.2350464

Metzger, M., Andrew, J., & Ryan, B. (2010). Social and heuristic approaches to credibility evaluation online. *Journal of Communication*, *60*(3), 413–439. https://doi.org/10.1111/j.1460-2466.2010.01488.x

Morrow, G., Swire-Thompson, B., Polny, J. M., Kopec, M., & Wihbey, J. (2022). The emerging science of content labeling: Contextualizing social media content moderation. *Journal of the American Society for Information Science and Technology*, *73*, 1365–1386. https://doi.org/10.1002/asi.24637

Munch, L. A., Bjerring, J. C., & Mainz, J. T. (2024). Algorithmic decision-making: The right to explanation and the significance of stakes. *Big Data & Society*, *11*(1). https://doi.org/10.1177/20539517231222872

Norambuena, B., Farina, K., Horning, M., & Mitra, T. (2023). Watching the watchdogs: Using transparency cues to help news audiences assess information quality. *Media & Communications*, *11*(4). https://doi.org/10.17645/mac.i366

Otis, A. (2024). The effects of transparency cues on news source credibility online: An investigation of opinion labels. *Journalism*, *25*(1), 198–217. https://doi.org/10.1177/14648849221129001

Peacock, C., Masullo, G. M., & Stroud, N. J. (2022). The effect of news labels on perceived credibility. *Journalism*, *23*(2), 301–319. https://doi.org/10.1177/1464884920971522

Peng, Z. (2023). A privacy calculus model perspective that explains why parents sharent. *Information, Communication & Society*, 1–24. https://doi.org/10.1080/1369118X.2023.2285462

Peng, L., & Wang, J. (2024). Algorithm as recommending source and persuasive health communication: Effects of source cues, language intensity, and perceived issue involvement. *Health Communication*, *39*(4), 852–861. https://doi.org/10.1080/10410236.2023.2242087

Pennycook, G., & Rand, D. G. (2022). Nudging social media toward accuracy. *Annals of American Academy Political Social Science*, *700*, 152–164. https://doi.org/10.1177/00027162221092342

Preece, A., Harborne, D., Braines, D., Tomsett, R., & Chakraborty, S. (2018). *Stakeholders in explainable AI*. arXiv preprint arXiv:1810.00184. https://doi.org/10.48550/arXiv.1810.00184

Prochazka, F., & Obermaier, M. (2022). Trust through transparency? How journalistic reactions to media-critical user comments affect quality perceptions and behavior intentions. *Digital Journalism*, *10*(3), 452–472. https://doi.org/10.1080/21670811.2021.2017316

Raees, M., Meijerink, I., Lykourentzou, I., Khan, V. J., & Papangelis, K. (2024). From explainable to interactive AI: A literature review on current trends in human-AI interaction. *International Journal of Human-Computer Studies*, 103301. https://doi.org/10.1016/j.ijhcs.2024.103301

Rai, A. (2020). Explainable AI: From black box to glass box. *Journal of the Academy of Marketing Science*, *48*(1), 137–141. https://doi.org/10.1007/s11747-019-00710-5

Saeed, W., & Omlin, C. (2023). Explainable AI (XAI): A systematic meta-survey of current challenges and future opportunities. *Knowledge-Based Systems*, *263*, 110273. https://doi.org/10.1016/j.knosys.2023.110273

Samek, W., & Müller, K. R. (2019). Towards explainable artificial intelligence. In W. Samek, G. Montavon, A. Vedaldi, L. K. Hansen, & K.-R. Müller (Eds.), *Explainable AI: Interpreting, explaining and visualizing deep learning* (pp. 5–22). Springer. https://doi.org/10.1007/978-3-030-28954-6_1

Shah, Z., & Wei, L. (2024). Source credibility and the information quality matter in public engagement on social networking sites during the COVID-19 crisis. *Frontier in Psychology*, *13*, 882705. https://doi.org/10.3389/fpsyg.2022.882705

Shin, D. (2020). User perceptions of algorithmic decisions in the personalized AI system: Perceptual evaluation of fairness, accountability, transparency, and explainability. *Journal of Broadcasting & Electronic Media, 64*(4), 541–565. https://doi.org/10.1080/08838151.2020.1843357

Shin, D. (2021). The effects of explainability and causability on perception, trust, and acceptance: Implications for explainable AI. *International Journal of Human-Computer Studies, 146*, 102551. https://doi.org/10.1016/j.ijhcs.2020.102551

Shin, D. (2022). The perception of humanness in conversational journalism: An algorithmic information-processing perspective. *New Media & Society, 24*(12), 2680–2704. http://doi:10.1177/1461444821993801

Shin, D. (2024). *Artificial misinformation: Exploring human-algorithm interaction online.* Springer Nature. https://doi.org/10.1007/978-3-031-52569-8

Shin, D. (2025). *Minds, machines, and misinformation.* Elsevier Publishing.

Shin, D., Koerber, A., & Lim, J. (2024). Impact of misinformation from generative AI on user information processing: How people understand misinformation from generative AI. *New Media & Society.* https://doi.org/10.1177/14614448241234040

Vasconcelos, H., Jörke, M., Grunde-McLaughlin, M., Gerstenberg, T., Bernstein, M. S., & Krishna, R. (2023). Explanations can reduce overreliance on AI systems during decision-making. *Proceedings of the ACM on Human-Computer Interaction, 7*(CSCW1), 1–38. https://doi.org/10.48550/arXiv.2212.06823

Vermeulen, J. (2022). To nudge or not to nudge. *Digital Journalism, 10*(10), 1671–1690. https://doi.org/10.1080/21670811.2022.2026796

Wang, R., & Ophir, Y. (2024). Behind the black box: The moderating role of the machine heuristic on the effect of transparency information about automated journalism on hostile media bias perception. *Journalism.* https://doi.org/10.1177/14648849241284575

Xu, K., & Shi, J. (2024). Visioning a two-level human-machine communication framework: Initiating conversations between explainable AI and communication. *Communication Theory, 34*(4), 216–229. https://doi.org/10.1093/ct/qtae016

Yang, H., & Sundar, S. (2024). Machine heuristic: Concept explication and development of a measurement scale. *Journal of Computer-Mediated Communication, 29*(6), zmae019. https://doi.org/10.1093/jcmc/zmae019

PART TWO

Phenomenology of AI Ethics

How People Experience AI Ethics

Algorithmic Bias and Trust

4

How to Debias and Build Trust in AI

ALGORITHMIC BIAS: HUMAN BIASES ARE BAKED INTO AI?

Algorithmic bias refers to the systematic and unjust discrimination that arises when algorithms, particularly those used in machine learning and artificial intelligence (AI) systems, make decisions that disproportionately affect specific groups or individuals based on factors such as race, gender, age, or socioeconomic status (Leschanowsky et al., 2023). Regrettably, algorithmic bias is an unavoidable aspect of AI systems (Noble, 2018). These systems are crafted and taught by humans, who inherently possess biases that may inadvertently seep into the data and algorithms, potentially resulting in biased outputs. It is imperative to recognize the vast array of biases ingrained in human cognition. These biases extend far beyond our individual or collective awareness and include confirmation bias, availability bias, and many limited heuristics. Acknowledging these human biases is important because attempting to eliminate them from the AI system we develop is an untenable goal for humans (Heisler & Grossman, 2024).

Essentially, AI reflects the societal biases present in the data on which it is trained. As cognitive biases can have profoundly negative consequences, their amplification through AI raises critical questions. Often invisible biases can be problematic as they can be secretly embedded in AI systems. Eliminating one bias often introduces another. Striving for fairness in one aspect may inadvertently introduce biases in another, highlighting the paradoxical nature of our pursuit of equity. AI biases are inherent in our cultural and technical frameworks and are difficult to avoid. This bias often stems from the data used to train these systems, which may reflect historical or societal inequalities,

DOI: 10.1201/9781003530244-7

or from the way algorithms are designed and implemented (Shin, 2023). The relation of algorithmic bias and human is interactive and reciprocal: human decisions, data, and societal structures shape AI systems, while biased AI, in turn, influences human lives by reinforcing or challenging inequalities. People's understanding of AI bias, as well as their trust or skepticism of AI, influences how they incorporate AI outputs into their decision-making processes (Ecker et al., 2022).

The impact and magnitude of algorithmic bias are important because the bias can have significant and wide-reaching consequences in various aspects of society, impacting individuals' lives, access to resources, and opportunities. The magnitude of algorithmic bias on human lives can be far-reaching, affecting people across various domains in their daily lives. AI bias affects people's decision-making by influencing the outcomes of automated systems that are used to make decisions across various domains such as hiring, policing, healthcare, and finance. When biased AI systems are integrated into decision-making processes, they can reinforce or amplify existing prejudices, leading to unfair treatment or discrimination (Shin, 2024).

Addressing algorithmic bias is challenging and involves a combination of technical, social, and ethical complexities. While there are tools and techniques to mitigate bias, fully eliminating it is far from easy due to several factors. Most AI systems rely on historical data that may reflect existing biases in society, such as racial, gender, or socioeconomic disparities. If these biases are embedded in the training data, the algorithm will likely reproduce them. It's impossible to completely cleanse data of biases, especially in fields like healthcare, hiring, or criminal justice where historical data reflects long-standing inequalities. In addition, machine learning models, especially deep learning models, function as "black boxes" where it's difficult to understand how decisions are being made (Kemper & Kolkman, 2019). Even if an algorithm is producing biased outcomes, pinpointing the source of the bias within the model can be difficult due to the model's complexity. While there are growing efforts to develop fairer and more transparent AI systems, addressing algorithmic bias is not easy. Objectively speaking, eradicating algorithmic bias is almost impossible, as many researchers argue (e.g., Winfield et al., 2019), because AI is inherently biased since it reflects and amplifies the biases that exist in the data, models, and decisions of the people and institutions that create and use it (Kwon et al., 2020). Since AI is not considered to possess moral agency (Véliz, 2021), creating a moral algorithm may be both useless and impossible. While an algorithm could mimic morality, it cannot be ethical unless it comprehends the moral choices it is making. Without moral agency and the inability to hold the algorithm morally responsible, any attempt to develop an ethical algorithm may be futile.

Algorithmic bias is not something we can fully eliminate. Algorithms are, after all, human creations—shaped by the cultural contexts, values, and assumptions of their creators. This reality makes them inherently biased (Badia, 2019). Despite the common aspiration to create "unbiased data," all data collection involves choices about framing, processing, and context. Trying to train algorithms with quality data that is supposedly fair and ethical reveals a misunderstanding of bias itself and how deeply it operates. Companies often overlook that bias isn't something to be defeated; it's something to be acknowledged and navigated. Human understanding of the world is influenced by cultural beliefs, personal experiences, and subjective interpretations. This inherent cultural bias inevitably translates into the systems we create, including scientific and technological systems. From a human perspective, bias cannot be simply corrected or wiped away; it's a natural part of our outlook, and as a result, it influences our creations. Rather than chasing an unattainable ideal of neutrality, we should aim to foster awareness and transparency about bias within AI systems and automated decision-making processes. By adopting a self-reflective mindset and acknowledging the subjective nature of what we build, we can understand that no system, representation, or artifact can ever be truly "objective" or completely "fair." Recognizing this reality is crucial for the responsible integration of AI into our society.

THE RESEARCH LANDSCAPE OF DEBIASING AI

Along with the prevalence of algorithms, significant attention has been given to understanding discriminatory AI and developing algorithmic methods to mitigate and eliminate these biases. Computer science, for example, has researched various tools to help enact control in outputs, allowing us to meet different fairness criteria and reduce propagated discrimination. The information science community began engaging in this area a while ago. Initially, a significant algorithmic bottleneck was the many ways to conceptualize fairness (Shin et al., 2024). Outside of computing disciplines, it's evident that no single definition of debiasing or fairness exists. The suitability of any fairness metric is contingent upon the context, as well as the values and preferences of those involved. From an algorithmic standpoint, this is quite concerning because creating a debiased algorithm would likely require developing a new solution from the ground up every time a different context arises. Although this is possible, it would be highly inefficient.

In social science and humanities, it has been agreed that defining fairness in AI is a complex challenge due to several factors. Firstly, fairness is a subjective concept that varies across cultures, societies, and individuals, making it difficult to establish a universal standard.

For example, fairness can be conceptualized in various ways, such as demographic parity, equal opportunity, and individual fairness, each suited to different contexts and applications. AI systems are often trained on data that may contain historical biases, which can be inadvertently learned and perpetuated by the models, complicating efforts to ensure fairness. The complexity and opacity of AI systems, especially those based on machine learning, further add to the difficulty, as understanding and mitigating biases within these systems requires sophisticated tools and techniques. Ensuring fairness typically requires balancing trade-offs with other vital metrics, such as accuracy and efficiency, which means finding an appropriate equilibrium among competing goals. Additionally, the concept of fairness can vary depending on the context; what may be seen as fair in one situation might not hold in another, prompting AI developers to take into account the specific environment in which the AI system will operate. Tackling these challenges demands a comprehensive approach that includes technical solutions, governance structures, and ongoing conversations among stakeholders to guarantee that AI systems are just and equitable.

Along with the complexity of debiasing research, the interdisciplinary nature of debiasing AI has been highlighted. Collaboration between computer scientists, ethicists, sociologists, and legal experts is essential to address the multifaceted nature of bias and fairness in AI. This interdisciplinary approach helps ensure that technical solutions are informed by ethical considerations and societal impacts.

WHY AIs CAN'T SOLVE ALGORITHMIC BIAS ON ITS OWN

AI cannot solve algorithmic bias by itself because algorithmic bias is rooted in human values, social inequalities, and complex ethical considerations that lie beyond AI's computational capabilities (Badia, 2019). Algorithmic bias, in most cases, originates from deeper, human-created societal issues. AI systems are inherently dependent on the data they are trained on, which often reflects the biases, prejudices, and inequalities present in society. AI systems inherently rely on the data they are trained on. Algorithms do not have the ability to assess or alter these underlying social factors; they simply process data to produce outputs based on patterns they identify, which means they can reinforce or even amplify these biases. One core issue is that bias in AI is more than just a technical problem; it is a reflection of deeper historical and societal inequalities. The data that AI models use to learn often comes from past decisions and real-world behaviors, which means that biases present in those areas get encoded into AI. For example, if hiring data from a company shows a preference for a particular demographic, an AI trained on that data may replicate this trend, preferring one group over others without any explicit intention of discrimination. Consequently, any attempt to "solve" algorithmic bias through AI would need to go beyond technology and address these underlying societal issues—a task AI alone cannot handle. Addressing algorithmic bias also involves value judgments and ethical considerations that AI cannot independently make. Questions about what constitutes "fairness" or "equity" are deeply subjective and vary across cultures, contexts, and communities. AI is not capable of making these nuanced ethical decisions. While it can be programmed to follow specific fairness guidelines, it lacks the capacity to adapt to complex, evolving ethical landscapes without human oversight.

AI is essentially a tool that mirrors the information and guidelines it receives. While it can help spot patterns of bias, it's important to understand that AI cannot tackle the social and ethical complexities that lead to algorithmic bias on its own. Real solutions require human-centered approaches involving cognitive process, heuristics, and ongoing human oversight.

THE COGNITIVE PROCESSES OF ALGORITHMIC BIAS

With algorithmic biases are prevalent, how do people perceive and process them? People's perceptions of algorithmic bias vary widely depending on their background, experiences, and understanding of technology. These perceptions are shaped by factors such as trust in AI systems, the transparency of the decision-making process, personal experiences with biased outcomes, and how much awareness they have of the issue.

The study of the perceptual and cognitive processes that underlie algorithmic biases has been a subject of interest in understanding how users encounter biases from AI. Various theories from different fields, such as Debunking, Informative Fiction, and Inoculation Theory (Roozenbeek et al., 2020), have been formalized into misinformation models (e.g., Borukhson et al., 2022). Many methods to combat misinformation have been explored, and studies have investigated how people encounter and share false information or misinformation online. It's important to focus on processes that can help users critically engage with or consciously respond to biases through cognitive elaboration. Despite their importance, the processing and mechanisms of algorithmic biases, especially in generative AI contexts, have been scarcely researched. Addressing this research gap requires a better understanding of the mechanisms of misinformation processing in relation to the cognitive development of users when interpreting misinformation provided by generative AI (Walter & Tukachinsky, 2020). Understanding how users process algorithmic biases could help advance theoretical foundations and practical solutions to AI ethical problems.

Research indicates that people process algorithmic biases using dual-process mechanisms: heuristic and systematic (Chaiken, 1980). Users tend to initially process algorithmic biases heuristically, invoking a sense of diagnosticity that then leads to systematic evaluation. This dual process is influenced, facilitated, and mediated by diagnosticity. The impact of information processing on biased decision-making can be viewed as dual in nature; information is processed within both an intuitive and autonomous system, as well as within a more analytical reflective system using systematic processing methods (Pennycook, 2023). When individuals engage in heuristic evaluation, they tend to process information based on available heuristic cues or simple decision rules. In contrast, systematic processing involves thorough evaluation of information to assess its validity. This theory serves as a lens to examine how users make sense of algorithmic biases, elucidating the role of algorithmic features in users' sensemaking regarding algorithms and how their actions influence this sensemaking (Shin, 2023; Zrnec et al., 2022).

The heuristic assessment of algorithmic biases involves evaluating the intrinsic nature of algorithmic attributes such as fairness, accountability, and transparency (FAccT; Shin, 2023). As users are unable to evaluate AI systematically, they rely on heuristic cues to process large amounts of generated information, such as fairness, transparency, and trustworthiness. Sundar et al. (2007) show that the newsbot (e.g., Google News) users rely on heuristic cues to process recommended news feeds. AI users may apply heuristics before systematic evaluation to process the generated information. Users want to verify the FAccT of the systems that spread misinformation.

HEURISTIC PROCESSING

Fairness Heuristics

Users often rely on their own judgment to assess possible biases in AI algorithms, such as those related to ethnicity, gender, and race. As AI plays an increasingly important role in decision-making, concerns about biases have grown. However, users may have limited ability to accurately evaluate algorithmic biases and correct them. Research has shown that users' perceptions and attitudes toward AI are closely linked to algorithmic fairness.

Accountability Heuristics

Algorithmic accountability involves examining the process of determining whether a decision is made under substantive and procedural standards and holding entities accountable if they fall short of these standards (Diakopoulos, 2016). Accountability is particularly important in monitoring the spread of misinformation, as the repercussions of the spread, amplification, and diffusion of misinformation are immense. Some people believe that AI should be held accountable for disseminating misinformation and must provide further clarification when requested by the public. Related research shows that users develop positive confidence when clearly defined responsibilities and liabilities are in place, and when they correctly identify incorrect information as misinformation (Barnoy & Reich, 2022).

Transparency Heuristics

Transparency in AI involves making both the inputs and outputs of algorithms visible and understandable to users or the public (Shin, 2023). Since end users often cannot assess the transparency of algorithms, they rely on easily processed heuristics when available. For example, clear statements about the generative mechanism process on websites or in AI systems provide users with cues to form quick judgments on transparency without needing extensive technical evaluation. Users depend on these cues as they are unable to systematically process all information or AI components. Gran et al. (2021) studied the impact of algorithmic transparency on individuals' psychological attitudes, such as their beliefs or intentions in evaluating algorithms accurately. Other research has shown that transparency increases user confidence in an algorithm, influencing whether they use it

(Peifer & Meisinger, 2021). When transparent and visible cues are present, people are more likely to consider the information as diagnosable (Diakopoulos & Koliska, 2017). Transparent AI systems can give users a sense of assurance and readiness to diagnose misinformation.

Diagnosticity

When assessing biases and the corresponding heuristics in cognition, users consider both the information's content and the systematic cues it contains (Niu et al., 2021). Having accurate diagnostic information is crucial for AI to offer reliable services. Diagnosticity is the degree to which individuals perceive a piece of information as truthful and relevant based on their judgment and decision-making (Ahluwalia et al., 2001; Chen & Cheng, 2020). In the context of AI, diagnosticity refers to a user's perceived ability to comprehend the features and attributes of AI services in their decision-making processes (Shin, 2023).

Existing research indicates that the diagnosticity of information plays a crucial role in shaping the attitudes and behavioral choices of users (Kwon et al., 2020; Yi et al., 2017). In the context of algorithms, information perceived as highly diagnostic carries more weight in users' judgments and evaluations (Shin, 2023). Consequently, diagnosticity influences how users systematically process messages (Niu et al., 2021). When users recognize a system's diagnosticity, they begin to trust it and systematically assess misinformation by gauging its accuracy and credibility (Chen & Cheng, 2020; Stecula et al., 2020). Diagnosticity acts as a bridge between heuristic and systematic evaluations. Regarding AI bias, the indicators of diagnosticity are specific to users' ability to identify misinformation based on their understanding of the information's accuracy and credibility (i.e., the correctness and reliability of the suggested information; Zrnec et al., 2022).

In the context of AI-generated bias, diagnosticity plays a critical role in two areas. Firstly, due to the black-box nature of AI generation, users evaluate the attributes heuristically. Secondly, given the susceptible nature of misinformation, users want to systematically evaluate the recommended information. The mediating role of diagnosticity indicates that the more confident the AI users were about the systems being ethically sound and normatively acceptable, the more likely they were to conscientiously diagnose the information. These arguments align with earlier findings by Ahmed and Gil-Lopez (2022) and Ali et al. (2022), suggesting that users with lower cognitive ability are more likely to believe and accept/share misinformation.

SYSTEMATIC PROCESSING

Users conduct reflective assessments of information: they assess the accuracy and credibility of the information (Ali et al., 2022).

Accuracy

The perceived accuracy of information refers to how truthful a piece of information is perceived to be by the user (Pennycook & Rand, 2022). It is related to the accuracy of AI applications, which is determined by how well the results are personalized and the truthfulness of the recommended content. Various terms have been proposed to describe the measurement of the perceived accuracy of misinformation, such as misinformation awareness, which is a person's awareness of the falseness of received information. Empirical research has confirmed these relationships in diverse algorithm services (Pennycook & Rand, 2022), where accuracy has been found to influence attitude and behavioral intention (Shin, 2023).

Credibility

Credibility, a strong indicator of information influence, can be understood as "believability" and "trustworthiness" (Wathen & Burkell, 2002). In communication literature, credibility is measured from different perspectives, such as source, message, and media credibility (Barnoy & Reich, 2022). While credibility has historically been studied more extensively from the source perspective (credibility of information source), in the social media environment, news consumers pay more attention to the content of the message than to the source (Peifer & Meisinger, 2021). Therefore, it is worth investigating the credibility of the content/message in the context of misinformation in algorithmic media (Ecker et al., 2022). The more credible the content of a piece of misinformation is perceived to be, the more useful and relevant users would perceive it to be (i.e., diagnostic).

Besides heuristic and systematic processes, research shows that there are moderating roles by explanation and/or interpretation. Explainability is a critical component in the field of explainable AI (Rai, 2020), which includes machine learning and AI technologies that can provide human-comprehensible rationales for their outputs or processes (Shin, 2023). Owing to their increasing complexity, people consider AI systems and algorithms as "black boxes"; furthermore, increasing amounts of specialized expertise and knowledge are required to understand the decision-making processes or performance of AI systems (Rai, 2020). ChatGPT is a non-explainable AI, as users do not understand how and why answers are generated. Although it is convenient, ChatGPT may exacerbate the problem of misinformation instead of mitigating it. ChatGPT stands against explainable AI and should not be applied in situations where credibility and explainability are critical requirements. Regarding explainability, understanding the specific reasoning behind specific outputs may be difficult, but users may understand how the model works in general and how it generates text based on the input it receives. However, it is not a decision-making AI and is not meant to be deployed in an operational context where security, safety, or explainability are critical requirements. Although ChatGPT is a powerful language generation tool, it must be responsibly used while being aware of its limitations. ChatGPT can be used to feed information into knowledge graphs and contribute to their explainability. ChatGPT can link information to knowledge that has already been referenced and verified, preferably in a traceable manner. With explainability incorporated, ChatGPT serves as a knowledge reference model; it also helps to extend the cognitive model by suggesting further potentially meaningful services. Explainability is critical in building trust, credibility, and understanding between the AI agent and its user, especially when it comes to understanding misinformation. The moderating role of explainability in ChatGPT for bias evaluation has been tested and confirmed by previous research.

MACHINE HEURISTIC

Individual's perceptions and attitudes toward machines influence the interaction in human-machine communication. When individuals interact with a machine or automated system, they use mental shortcuts that operate as a rule of thumb about the machine's perceived security and trustworthiness in making decisions and judgments (Sundar & Kim, 2019). Sundar (2008) termed these shortcuts as machine heuristic (MH). Sundar and Kim (2019) defined MH as "the mental shortcut wherein we attribute machine characteristics or machine-like operation when making judgments about the outcome of an interaction" (p. 2). Earlier, Sundar and Nass (2001) discussed computer heuristics as a component of the heuristic people attach to a source, defining it as a perceived shortcut of a machine's ability to be random and, hence, impartial. Later, Yang and Sundar (2024) called computer heuristics the forefather of MHs and elaborated on the aspects of cognitive biases that resulted from the cases of human interactions with machines. Simply put, MHs are mental shortcuts people use to weigh the outcome of an interaction with a machine or any intelligent system.

Theoretically, the idea of MHs shares one key aspect with the CASA paradigm. According to the casa paradigm, people mindlessly attribute social cues (gender, reciprocity, helpfulness, etc.) to computer systems when they interact with them (Nass & Moon, 2000). Similarly, the MH states people's tendency to automatically attach stereotypes common to a machine, such as objectivity and ideological unbiasedness (Sundar & Kim, 2019). In both cases, people do not process these critically. In the case of CASA, individuals rely on pre-learned stereotypes in human–human interactions. However, in the case of MHs, individuals rely on interface cues (Sundar & Kim, 2019). MH comes from a quick mental comparison of human–human and human–machine interactions (i.e., humans are generally biased, machines are not). In CASA, the social cues in human–computer interactions are derived from what is similar in human–human social interactions, whereas the MH is derived from what is different from human–human interaction. Moreover, with the MH, individuals tend to perceive the machine as either more or less capable than humans, whereas the core argument in the CASA paradigm is that people treat computers with all the social cues they use in human–human communication (Lee, 2024).

In the MAIN model, Sundar (2008) proposed four broad affordances of any digital technology triggering cognitive heuristics that individuals use to assess the platform's credibility. These affordances are Modality (to the mode of the platform, i.e., audio, video, and text), Agency (users' perception of the source), Interactivity (users' perception about themselves being both the receiver and the source), and Navigability (ease of finding information and transportation from one location to another) (Metzger & Flanagin., 2013; Sundar, 2008). Within the domain of agency affordance, Sundar (2008) stated the role of MHs as influencing individuals' credibility judgment about the source based on the interface's look; if the interface looks machine-like, that might trigger positive credibility judgment about the source. Alternatively, the anthropomorphic interface of a platform might produce a negative credibility judgment (Sundar, 2008).

With the rise of human–AI interaction, the notion of MHs ushered in several empirical research examining its influence on users in this interaction. These include but are not limited to research on how interface cues influence users' trust in revealing financial information to AI agents (Sundar & Kim, 2019), users' responses to AI fact-checkers (Banas et al., 2022), users' evaluation of organisms, cyborgs, and robots (Banks et al., 2021), AI journalists and hostile media effects (Cloudy et al., 2022, 2023; Hong et al., 2024), source credibility (Edwards et al., 2013), consumer appreciation of AI-created advertisement (Wu & Wen, 2021), and AI composed music evaluation (Hong et al., 2022). The common finding underlying all of these empirical studies is the influence of MH in the evaluation process of machines or AI agents and in making decisions about their capabilities. However, researchers found several other heuristics at play while exploring MH and individuals' assessments of AI agents. For instance, in their study on agentic cues, Banks et al. (2021) found that the nature heuristic is dominant over the MH. Similarly, Hong et al. (2022) argued that when individuals evaluate the creative aspects of AI, a new kind of heuristic, which they have called the creative MH, comes into play. Contrary to what Sundar (2008) argued about the anthropomorphic features of machines as mentioned above, Hong et al. (2022) study found that AI music generators' anthropomorphic features result in better acceptance of humans. Moreover, MHs are not necessarily the most prominent influencers of AI performance evaluation. For example, in exploring hostile media effects and AI-written political news, Hong et al. (2024) found that author type (whether the author is a human or an AI) has a stronger influence than the MH triggered by AI in the process of credibility evaluation. Although the studies discussed above identify the role of MHs in human–machine or human–AI interactions, the results indicate that the strength of its influence on users' decision-making or evaluation process depends on the task the machines or AI agents perform.

From this discussion, it can be assumed that MHs alone cannot explain how people evaluate the credibility of AI agents. Because of this, Hong et al. (2024) emphasized exploring other cognitive factors along with MHs in the evaluation process of the AI agent's performance. While interface cues can trigger MHs (Sundar & Kim, 2019), people can invoke either negative or positive MHs due to personal differences (Molina & Sundar, 2024). For example, individuals' perceived uneasiness of interaction with robots significantly influences MHs (Wu & Wen, 2021). Similarly, Molina and Sundar (2024) argued that an individual's tendency to turn to either positive or negative MH depends on their trust in humans, perceived fear of AI, power usage, and even political ideology. As individuals differ in these characteristics, they make different choices and decisions in the case of MHs and evaluation of the AI agents. Even people can evaluate an AI agent without considering its performance if they have a strong positive trust in AI (Koh & Sundar, 2010). Some users might have higher levels of trust in the MH than others which reflects how they would use that heuristic to decide about the interaction with AI.

MHs can positively increase human engagement in human–AI interaction, as people with a higher belief in MHs tend to self-disclose more to AI agents, even with important personal information like credit card information (Sundar & Kim, 2019). Encouraging self-disclosure can be helpful in places where more revelation offers personalized and efficient services like healthcare, mental health support systems, and emergency response systems. However, MH-influenced self-disclosure also brings out the obvious concern of privacy and data security. As Sundar and Kim (2019 mentioned, designers of the AI Agent can use interface cues in their favor to steal personal data from people. From this concern, one important component of AI literacy should be focused on building awareness about interface cues and how designers might exploit them. Moreover, a nuanced exploration of which type of interface cues are more likely to trigger MHs is also important to facilitate the best human–AI interaction. We also need to assess the situations where users might have the capacity to change and customize the interface cues on their own.

HOW DO PEOPLE ESTABLISH TRUST IN AI?

In light of the widespread issue of algorithmic bias, a key consideration is how individuals develop trust in AI (Shin, 2021). Cultivating trust in AI encompasses elements such as transparency, dependability, ethical factors, user experience, and clear communication. As AI continues to advance and become more ingrained in different facets of society, comprehending the process of building and upholding trust will be essential for nurturing constructive interactions between humans and AI systems.

Relevant research (Gran et al., 2021) has emphasized normative factors that influence user trust, such as fairness, transparency, and accountability. Transparency and fairness are particularly critical attributes for trustworthy algorithmic systems when processing user-sensitive data (Helberger et al., 2018). Shin's research in 2024 suggests that people trust AI based on a combination of factors that increase their confidence in the technology. This includes how the algorithm processes information and how transparent and fair it is. According to Shin, perceived fairness and transparency significantly impact the perceived quality of the AI system. Just as fairness, transparency, and accountability are vital in a traditional system, they are also crucial in an algorithm-based platform (Diakopoulos, 2016). This means that users evaluate the quality of algorithmic platforms based on how easy it is to understand the recommendations and how accountable the platform is. Transparency not only influences perceived quality but also influences users' perception of fairness and accountability. When users can understand how the recommendations are made, they are more likely to consider the system fair, and when they perceive accountability, they see the system as more transparent. The fairness and accountability of the system depend on how users interpret transparency; they are not automatically granted (Figure 4.1).

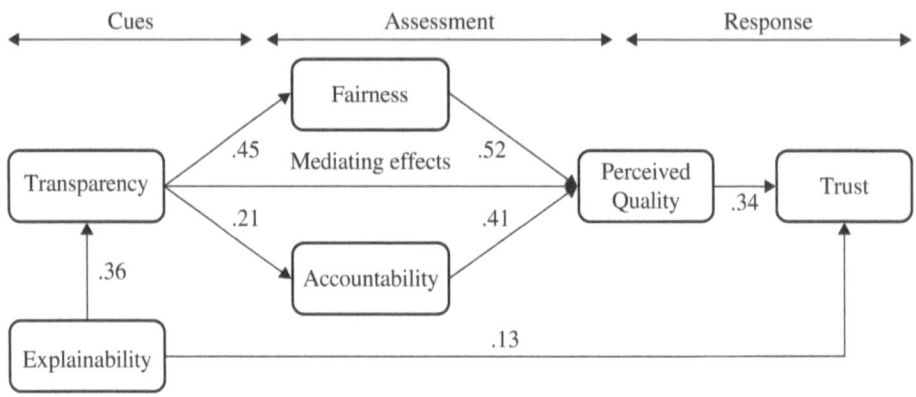

FIGURE 4.1   The effects of transparency heuristics on AI quality and credibility.

Shin's findings reveal that user understanding of algorithmic platforms is heuristic and nonlinear, not organized into structured, ready-made, automatic processes. The way users perceive, analyze, comprehend, and interact with algorithms is influenced by how they process algorithmic information. Users actively evaluate the algorithmic choices/information they encounter based on notions of fairness and transparency. There is growing skepticism among users regarding algorithmic processes, with concerns that algorithms may not be as impartial as claimed and could potentially reflect the biases of their human creators (Noble, 2018), such as racial, gender, and other social biases. Consequently, users naturally seek to understand how algorithms function, how misinformation spreads, and how to guard against disinformation. Credibility in platforms is constructed in a way that facilitates transparent explanation and human interpretation. A well-established credibility allows users to trust that the news is relevant and accurate and that the source is reliable.

The process of algorithmic information implies that users play active roles in creating algorithms on AI platforms (Shin, 2021). Previous research assumed that users were passive consumers of recommended services, providing their data to algorithms without much thought. However, with the increasing prevalence of algorithm-driven technologies, the user's role has transitioned from being a passive recipient of automated processes to an active creator of preference profiles. Users now generate, adjust, and modify algorithms based on the contexts of their everyday lives (Shin, 2021). They want to see and engage with content that aligns with their preferences, and they are influenced by the algorithmic process. As users rely more on algorithmic platforms, their perspectives may become narrower, leading to what has been described as an "echo chamber" or "filter bubble" effect (Pariser, 2012).

Users are the source of algorithms and the creators of platforms by invoking profound subconscious cognitive processes. What users see through algorithms, as far as their cognition is concerned, is a cognitively constructed reality that emulates the form of an accumulated experience that has been shaped by a priori mental constructs. An algorithmic selection has become a shared social reality that shapes daily lives and realities, affecting the perception of the world (Shin, 2023). Pursuant to their discussion, humans, and algorithms are coevolving and creating reality together as they influence each other. Through credibility established by transparent fairness, humans and algorithms actively enhance each other's complementary roles.

Fairness and transparency are closely linked and have a combined impact on the quality of an algorithm platform (Shin, 2021). The interaction effect indicates that fairness and transparency positively influence the perception of high quality and credibility of platform recommendations. Users tend to view platform recommendations as more credible and of higher quality when they understand how the algorithm works and believe that it is fair. These interaction effects are reasonable, as it can be challenging for non-experts to distinguish between transparency and fairness and understand their impact. Users typically rely on their existing knowledge of algorithms and technology when dealing with issues related to fairness, transparency, and accountability. They may not have a clear abstract understanding of these concepts and their implications for algorithm performance. In reality, fairness, transparency, and accountability are interconnected and intertwined concepts.

Creating user-centered algorithms at a user level involves developing algorithmic platforms with more responsible and transparent processes. The findings suggest that perceptions of transparency and accuracy are not purely objective responses to media content. Instead, they indicate that transparency and fairness are subjective perceptions held by users rather than objective criteria. Users construct their own versions of transparency and accuracy based on their existing trust and other personal intrinsic factors. Therefore, transparency and fairness depend on users' perceptions and understanding. These are socially constructed and cognitively reconstructed within users' thought processes. There are various dimensions by which we can measure how "transparent and fair" a recommendation is, but it is challenging to measure transparency and fairness directly.

WHAT FACTORS CONTRIBUTE TO ALGORITHMIC CREDIBILITY?

In algorithmic platforms, users establish a sense of trust in the processed information through fairness and transparency (Stecula et al., 2020). When users have confidence in the platforms, they believe that the system's services are valuable as they are personalized and tailored to their needs. Trust significantly influences the impact of fairness/transparency on users' attitudes and information seeking. By fostering strong user trust and positive emotion, users can be assured that their personal data will be handled in a transparent and legitimate manner, creating a positive reputation for the recommendations and the platforms. This, in turn, leads to increased levels of user engagement.

Previous studies have established that users are more likely to engage with information they find credible (Sundar et al., 2007). The perceived credibility of algorithms plays a crucial role in the adoption and widespread use of algorithmic platforms (Wölker & Powell, 2021). The credibility of media platforms is essential, as users rely on these platforms to provide accurate recommendations tailored to their needs and preferences. Thus, user perceptions of algorithmic performance greatly influence the credibility of media platforms.

According to Shin's definition (2023), algorithmic credibility refers to the extent to which users perceive recommendations from algorithms as trustworthy. It is a significant predictor of users' actions, such as approving data collection or adopting the opinion of the received recommendation. Researchers have used various perspectives to explain how to assess algorithmic credibility. Studies have shown that algorithmic credibility is closely related to the issues of FTA (Shin, 2021). One notable aspect of the algorithmic credibility study is that credibility is user-centered, progressively constructed by the user's cognition and information processing, rather than being given or provided by a medium, message, or source of media. This perspective aligns with the nature of algorithms, as they are based on user input and engagement, i.e., user data. Algorithmic credibility results from the user's confirmation of their assessment of quality, which is based on FTA. Therefore, it is reasonable to link perceived credibility and algorithmic quality in AI platforms.

Recognizing the significance of credibility in algorithmic processes as an integral aspect of AI platforms and algorithm-driven systems, it is expected to play a vital role in the operation and organization of algorithmic societies. Media outlets are actively assessing the perception and reception of their content, as the credibility ratings significantly influence audience engagement and adoption. Algorithmic credibility encompasses a range of critical elements, including belief, confidence, trustworthiness, fairness, differentiation between opinion and fact, precision, and accuracy. In this context, our objective is to establish the link between credibility considerations and shifts in user preferences, identify the underlying factors contributing to credibility, and explore the drivers leading users to increasingly favor algorithmic platforms.

CONCLUSION

Humans often treat AI as a social actor, especially when AI systems are designed to mimic human-like behaviors or interactions (Gambino et al., 2020). This phenomenon arises from the way people naturally respond to entities that display social cues, such as voice, language, or facial expressions, even if they know the entity is not human. This is because AI has bias and trust. AI acts as a social entity, actively shaping and engaging with the world we build around it. It is important to see AI as an active participant with social influence, rather than a passive tool. As humans and technology become increasingly interdependent, it is vital to understand how digital tools and systems shape our experiences, opinions, and behaviors. Simultaneously, human agency disrupts and reshapes our use of these technological artifacts. To fully comprehend AI's impact—its agency, which is evident through its socio-cultural context—we must demystify it, moving beyond viewing it as mysterious or elusive (Heimann & Hübener, 2023).

Cognitive perceptions and algorithmic information processing are critical in justifying how and why people perceive and feel about the issues surrounding algorithmic platforms and how they use and engage with algorithm-generated news. The primary goal of algorithmic platforms is to help people sort content that is interesting and intriguing to view. Understanding how users search for, find, and consume news online allows algorithm practitioners and algorithm designers to perform more efficiently and naturally. There have been ongoing challenges to offering recommended results in the algorithm context.

Understanding user algorithmic information processing should be critical for envisaging users' future interests for better predictive performance. The algorithmic information processing model provides insights into how to integrate fairness and transparency with usability factors and behavioral mechanisms. AIs that are user-focused and employ trust-based feedback loops will be important for designing such human-centered systems. When the eventual goal of algorithmic platforms is to develop user-centered services, our model serves as a first step to achieving such objectives.

REFERENCES

Ahluwalia, R., Unnava, H. R., & Burnkrant, R. E. (2001). The moderating role of commitment on the spillover effect of marketing communications. *Journal of Marketing Research*, *38*(4), 458–470. https://doi.org/10.1509/jmkr.38.4.458.18903

Ahmed, S., & Gil-Lopez, T. (2022). Engaging with vilifying stereotypes: The role of YouTube algorithmic use. *Journalism & Mass Communication Quarterly*. https://doi.org/10.1177/10776990221110113

Ali, K., Li, C., Zain-ul-abdin, K., & Zaffar, M. (2022). Fake news on Facebook: Examining the impact of heuristic cues on perceived credibility. *Internet Research*, *32*(1), 379–397. https://doi.org/10.1108/INTR-10-2019-0442

Badia, A. (2019). *The information manifold: Why computers can't solve algorithmic bias and fake news*. The MIT Press.

Banas, J. A., Palomares, N. A., Richards, A. S., Keating, D. M., Joyce, N., & Rains, S. A. (2022). When machine and bandwagon heuristics compete: Understanding users' response to conflicting AI and crowdsourced fact-checking. *Human Communication Research*, *48*(3), 430–461. https://doi.org/10.1093/hcr/hqac010

Banks, J., Edwards, A. P., & Westerman, D. (2021). The space between: Nature and machine heuristics in evaluations of organisms, cyborgs, and robots. *Cyberpsychology, Behavior, and Social Networking*, *24*(5), 324–331. https://doi.org/10.1089/cyber.2020.0165

Barnoy, A., & Reich, Z. (2022). Trusting others: A Pareto distribution of source and message credibility among news reporters. *Communication Research*, *49*(2), 196–220. https://doi.org/10.1177/0093650220911814

Borukhson, D., Lorenz-Spreen, P., & Ragni, M. (2022). When does an individual accept misinformation? *Computational Brain & Behavior*, *5*, 244–260. https://doi.org/10.1007/s42113-022-00136-3

Chaiken, S. (1980). Heuristic versus systematic information processing and the use of source versus message cues in persuasion. *Journal of Personality and Social Psychology*, *39*(5), 752–766. https://doi.org/10.1037/0022-3514.39.5.752

Chen, Z. F., & Cheng, Y. (2020). Consumer response to fake news about brands on social media. *Journal of Product & Brand Management, 29*(2), 188–198. https://doi.org/10.1108/JPBM-12-2018-2145

Cloudy, J., Banks, J., & Bowman, N. D. (2023). The Str(AI)ght scoop: Artificial intelligence cues reduce perceptions of hostile media bias. *Digital Journalism, 11*(9), 1577–1596. https://doi-org.lib-e2.lib.ttu.edu/10.1080/21670811.2021.1969974

Cloudy, J. T., Banks, J. T., & Bowman, N. D. (2022). AI journalists and reduction of perceived hostile media bias: Replication and extension considering news organization cues. https://doi.org/10.1037/tmb0000083

Diakopoulos, N. (2016). Accountability in algorithmic decision making. *Communications of the ACM, 59*(2), 58–62. https://doi.org/10.1145/2844110

Diakopoulos, N., & Koliska, M. (2017). Algorithmic transparency in the news media. *Digital Journalism, 5*(7), 809–828. https://doi.org/10.1080/21670811.2016.1208053

Ecker, U., Lewandowsky, S., Cook, J., Schmid, P., Fazio, L. K., Brashier, N., Kendeou, P., Vraga, E. K., & Amazeen, M. A. (2022). The psychological drivers of misinformation belief and its resistance to correction. *Nature Review Psychology, 1*, 13–29. https://doi.org/10.1038/s44159-021-00006-y

Edwards, C., Spence, P. R., Gentile, C. J., Edwards, A., & Edwards, A. (2013). How much Klout do you have… A test of system generated cues on source credibility. *Computers in Human Behavior, 29*(5), A12–A16. https://doi.org/10.1016/j.chb.2012.12.034

Gambino, A., Fox, J., & Ratan, R. (2020). Building a stronger CASA: Extending the computers are social actors paradigm. *Human-Machine Communication, 1*, 71–86. https://doi.org/10.30658/hmc.1.5

Gran, A., Booth, P., & Bucher, T. (2021). To be or not to be algorithm aware. *Information, Communication & Society, 24*(12), 1779–1796. https://doi.org/10.1080/1369118X.2020.1736124

Heimann, M., & Hübener, A.-F. (2023). AI as social actor. *Journal of Digital Social Research, 5*(1), 48–69. https://doi.org/10.33621/jdsr.v5i1.159

Heisler, N., & Grossman, M. (2024). *Standards for the control of algorithmic bias*. Routledge.

Helberger, N., Karppinen, K., & D'Acunto, L. (2018). Exposure diversity as a design principle for recommender systems. *Information, Communication & Society, 21*(2), 191–207. https://doi.org/10.1080/1369118X.2016.1271900

Hong, J. W., Chang, H. C. H., & Tewksbury, D. (2024). Can AI become Walter Cronkite? Testing the machine heuristic, the hostile media effect, and political news written by artificial intelligence. *Digital Journalism*, 1–24. https://doi.org/10.1080/21670811.2024.2323000

Hong, J. W., Fischer, K., Ha, Y., & Zeng, Y. (2022). Human, I wrote a song for you: An experiment testing the influence of machines' attributes on the AI-composed music evaluation. *Computers in Human Behavior, 131*, 107239. https://doi.org/10.1016/j.chb.2022.107239

Kemper, J., & Kolkman, D. (2019). Transparent to whom? *Information, Communication & Society, 22*(14), 2081–2096. https://doi.org/10.1080/1369118X.2018.1477967

Koh, Y. J., & Sundar, S. S. (2010). Heuristic versus systematic processing of specialist versus generalist sources in online media. *Human Communication Research, 36*(2), 103–124. https://doi.org/10.1111/j.1468-2958.2010.01370.x

Kwon, Y., Park, J., & Son, J. (2020). Accurately or accidentally? Recommendation agent and search experience in over-the-top services. *Internet Research, 31*(2), 562–586. https://doi.org/10.1108/INTR-03-2020-0127

Lee, E. J. (2024). Minding the source: Toward an integrative theory of human–machine communication. *Human Communication Research, 50*(2), 184–193. https://doi.org/10.1093/hcr/hqad034

Leschanowsky, A., Popp, B., & Peters, N. (2023). Debiasing strategies for conversational AI: Improving privacy and security decision-making. *Digital Society, 2*, 34. https://doi.org/10.1007/s44206-023-00062-2

Metzger, M. J., & Flanagin, A. J. (2013). Credibility and trust of information in online environ-ments: The use of cognitive heuristics. *Journal of Pragmatics*, *59*, 210–220. https://doi.org/10.1016/j.pragma.2013.07.012

Molina, M. D., & Sundar, S. S. (2024). Does distrust in humans predict greater trust in AI? Role of individual differences in user responses to content moderation. *New Media & Society*, *26*(6), 3638–3656. https://doi.org/10.1177/14614448221103534

Nass, C., & Moon, Y. (2000). Machines and mindlessness: Social responses to computers. *Journal of Social Issues*, *56*(1), 81–103. https://doi.org/10.1111/0022-4537.00153

Niu, W., Huang, L., & Chen, M. (2021). Spanning from diagnosticity to serendipity: An empiri-cal investigation of consumer responses to product presentation. *International Journal of Information Management*, *60*, 102362. https://doi.org/10.1016/j.ijinfomgt.2021.102362

Noble, S. (2018). *Algorithms of oppression: How search engines reinforce racism*. New York University Press.

Pariser, E. (2012). *The filter bubble: What the internet is hiding from you*. Penguin.Penguin.

Peifer, J., & Meisinger, J. (2021). The value of explaining the process. *Journalism & Mass Communication Quarterly*, *98*(3), 828–853. https://doi.org/10.1177/10776990211012953

Pennycook, G. (2023). A framework for understanding reasoning errors. *Advances in Experimental Social Psychology*, *67*, 131–208. https://doi.org/10.1016/bs.aesp.2022.11.003

Pennycook, G., & Rand, D. G. (2022). Accuracy prompts are a replicable and generalizable approach for reducing the spread of misinformation. *Nature Communications*, *13*, 2333. https://doi.org/10.1038/s41467-022-30073-5

Rai, A. (2020). Explainable AI: from black box to glass box. *Journal of the Academy Marketing Science*, *48*, 137–141. https://doi.org/10.1007/s11747-019-00710-5

Roozenbeek, J., van der Linden, S., & Nygren, T. (2020). Prebunking interventions based on inoculation theory can reduce susceptibility to misinformation across cultures. *Harvard Misinformation Review*, *1*(2), 1–23. https://doi.org/10.37016//mr-2020-008

Shin, D. (2021). The perception of humanness in conversational journalism: An algorithmic information-processing perspective. *New Media and Society*. https://doi.org/10.1177/1461444821993801

Shin, D. (2023). *Algorithms, humans, and interactions: How do algorithms interact with people? Designing meaningful AI experiences* (1st ed.). Routledge. https://doi.org/10.1201/b23083

Shin, D. (2024). *Artificial misinformation: Exploring human-algorithm interaction online*. Springer Nature. https://doi.org/10.1007/978-3-031-52569-8

Shin, D., Lim, J., Ahmad, N., & Ibarahim, M. (2024). Understanding user sensemaking in fair-ness and transparency in algorithms: Algorithmic sensemaking in over-the-top platform. *AI & Society*, *39*, 447–490. https://doi.org/10.1007/s00146-022-01525-9

Stecula, D. A., Kuru, O., & Jamieson, K. (2020). How trust in experts and media use affect accep-tance of common anti-vaccination claims. *The Harvard Kennedy School Misinformation Review*. https://doi.org/10.37016/mr-2020-007

Sundar, S., Knobloch-Westerwick, S., & Hastall, M. (2007). News cues: Information scent and cognitive heuristics. *Journal of the American Society for Information Science and Technology*, *58*(3), 366–378. https://doi.org/10.1002/asi.20511

Sundar, S. S. (2008). *The MAIN model: A heuristic approach to understanding technology effects on credibility* (pp. 73–100). MacArthur Foundation Digital Media and Learning Initiative.

Sundar, S. S., & Kim, J. (2019, May). Machine heuristic: When we trust computers more than humans with our personal information. In *Proceedings of the 2019 CHI conference on human factors in computing systems* (pp. 1–9). https://doi.org/10.1145/3290605.3300768

Sundar, S. S., & Nass, C. (2001). Conceptualizing sources in online news. *Journal of Communication*, *51*(1), 52–72. https://doi.org/10.1111/j.1460-2466.2001.tb02872.x

Véliz, C. (2021). Moral zombies: Why algorithms are not moral agents. *AI & Society*, *36*, 487–497. https://doi.org/10.1007/s00146-021-01189-x

Walter, N., & Tukachinsky, R. (2020). A meta-analytic examination of the continued influence of misinformation in the face of correction. *Communication Research, 47,* 155–177. https://doi.org/10.1177/0093650219854600

Wathen, C., & Burkell, J. (2002). Believe it or not: Factors influencing credibility on the web. *Journal of the American Society for Information Science and Technology, 53*(2), 134–144.

Winfield, A., Michael, K., Pitt, J., & Evers, V. (2019). Machine ethics: The design and governance of ethical AI and autonomous systems. *Proceedings of the IEEE, 107*(3), 509.

Wölker, A., & Powell, T. (2021). Algorithms in the newsroom? *Journalism, 22*(1), 86–103. https://doi.org/10.1177/1464884918757072

Wu, L., & Wen, T. J. (2021). Understanding AI advertising from the consumer perspective: What factors determine consumer appreciation of AI-created advertisements? *Journal of Advertising Research, 61*(2), 133–146. https://doi.org/10.2501/JAR-2021-004

Yang, H., & Sundar, S. S. (2024). Machine heuristic: Concept explication and development of a measurement scale. *Journal of Computer-Mediated Communication, 29*(6), zmae019. https://doi.org/10.1093/jcmc/zmae019

Yi, C., Jiang, Z., & Benbasat, I. (2017). Designing for diagnosticity and serendipity. *Information Systems Research, 28,* 413–429. https://doi.org/10.1287/isre.2017.0695

Zrnec, A., Pozenel, M., & Lavbic, D. (2022). Users' ability to perceive misinformation. *Information Processing & Management, 59*(1), 102739. https://doi.org/10.1016/j.ipm.2021.102739

Algorithmic Nudge
A Nudge to Counter Algorithmic Bias

5

EMERGENCE OF ALGORITHMIC NUDGING: HOW TO NUDGE EFFECTIVELY AND ETHICALLY

Nudging is an approach to improve people's health and well-being by providing indirect suggestions referred to as nudges (Sunstein & Thaler, 2014). It refers to the ability of systems or technologies to overtly influence human users, with or without their direct consent. This could involve influencing people's behaviors or decision-making processes through subtle suggestions or prompts, often designed to guide them toward certain choices or actions. Nudging techniques can be categorized based on the mechanism of influence (Yeung, 2017). The term "algorithmic nudge" (or artificial intelligence (AI) nudge) refers to the use of user interface design to influence user behaviors in algorithm-driven environments (Nyman, 2023). With the rapid proliferation of AI, nudging has become common in AI-powered systems. By leveraging big data, algorithmic nudging techniques use AI to provide personalized nudges based on individuals' data and decision-making patterns, aiming to subtly guide human decisions and improve choices or achieve socially desirable outcomes (Juneja & Mira, 2022; Mills & Sætra, 2024).

Different forms of AI assistance impact human decision-making behaviors differently, emphasizing the importance of understanding and interpreting how AI assistance influences human strategies in decision-making processes (Shin, 2021). Furthermore, the use of AI methods for algorithmic nudging introduces new forms of managerial control. For instance, algorithmic nudging in organizations can influence employees through targeted recommendations, drawing from various sources of knowledge and ideological foundations to shape behaviors. Since the inception of algorithmic nudging, a substantial and emergent body of literature has explored the ethical considerations surrounding the use of algorithms to nudge individuals (Cook & Berente, 2024).

DOI: 10.1201/9781003530244-8

This topic is of great significance for research due to the widespread utilization of algorithmic nudges by private entities and government organizations to influence and guide human behavior. For example, Facebook's algorithm uses predictive analysis to filter news items with the aim of maximizing the likelihood that a user will click on them (i.e., the algorithm is concerned with the number of posts a user clicks on, given the number of posts that a user is shown) (Bucher, 2017). The algorithm automatically and invisibly selects the items that appear in a user's feed. Invisible algorithms tailor personalized nudges for individuals, and their effectiveness can be tracked and adjusted as algorithms improve based on user feedback and behavior (Mertens et al., 2022). A higher click-through rate indicates that a user is enjoying what Facebook is presenting them. Facebook can then leverage these higher click-through rates to generate advertising revenue.

While algorithmic nudges are useful and innovative tools, they give rise to a myriad of ethical concerns encompassing data protection, privacy, manipulation, and over-intervention (hyper-nudging). The ability of a single algorithmic nudge to instantaneously sway thousands of users underscores the imperative to regulate and control AI nudges. The proliferation of algorithmic nudging has raised significant concerns regarding transparency, informed consent, autonomy, fairness, accountability, and manipulative practices (Hansen & Jespersen, 2013; Shin, 2024). These issues are expected to escalate as algorithmic nudging techniques continue to exert substantial influence over individuals' behaviors and decisions, with such influence often operating beyond their conscious awareness (Westbrook, 2020). The key challenge lies in ensuring that algorithmic nudges are deployed in a manner that positively contributes to societal well-being and in assessing their potential to facilitate the adoption of sustainable lifestyles (Cook & Berente, 2024).

It is imperative to engage in substantive discussion regarding the ethical considerations surrounding algorithmic nudging. Nudges possess the capacity to exert a profound impact on individuals' choices at a societal level (Mills & Sætra, 2024). This influence raises apprehensions about potential misuse, encroachment upon autonomy, and manipulative practices. Therefore, ethically scrutinizing the objectives of algorithmic nudging is crucial (Yeung, 2017). By infusing ethical considerations into the conceptualization and implementation of algorithmic nudges, developers and policymakers can ensure that these nudges advance well-being, equity, and reverence for individual rights. It is critical to deliberate upon the entities empowered to determine the objectives of nudges, the appropriateness of these objectives, and the beneficiaries of their application. This chapter offers a comprehensive examination of the ethical dimensions of algorithmic nudging, specifically delving into the principles and impacts of AI systems' nudging effects on user behaviors based on an extensive review of current literature.

LITERATURE ON ALGORITHMIC NUDGING

The extant literature on nudging has focused on two main aspects: behavioral modification and ethical considerations. From a behavioral modification standpoint, recent studies have proposed conceptual process models for designing algorithmic nudges (Gosline et al., 2024). Nowadays, most online platforms recurrently use algorithmic behavior modification techniques to influence user behaviors in ways that maximize profits. These platforms are increasingly employing techniques to automatically customize behavioral interventions to leverage human psychological tendencies and cognition (Christiane et al., 2023). These systems are created to selectively collect, filter, amplify, and monetize user data. They employ autonomous, prescriptive, and data-driven machine learning to significantly impact user behaviors on a large scale (Mattis et al., 2022). People leave behind digital traces through their social media activity and online searches. These traces are used by AI to predict and influence our behaviors and what news and ads we click on. When we provide algorithms and platforms with our digital data, we inadvertently allow them to invade our privacy and tailor their recommendations for us. To what extent are users comfortable with apps knowing their habits, health stats, or spending patterns? Platforms can improve their ability to predict our behaviors by shaping how we behave and showing us more positive predictions. This can happen unintentionally through the use of reinforcement machine learning that combines behavior modification and predictive analytics (Kroll & Stieglitz, 2021).

From an ethical standpoint, Möhlmann (2021) emphasized the importance of considering ethical implications when implementing nudges. Practitioners have proposed the standardization of the design of a nudge by understanding an audience's biases in a given situation and how these biases impact decision-making. Shin (2023) proposed two categories of algorithmic nudges: Type 1 is governed by cognitive heuristics (intuitive, heuristic processes), and Type 2 nudges target deliberate systems of decision-making (reflective, rational processes). Based on the type, there are two different kinds of nudges depending on the level of transparency allowed. A transparent nudge is one where the intention and method of behavioral manipulation are clear to the target audience. For example, information disclosed (e.g., story corrections, author bios, and hyperlinks to associated stories and other documents written by the owner of a social media profile) by an AI news recommendation system enhances users' perceptions of the credibility of an AI. On the contrary, a nontransparent nudge implies that the recipient of the nudge is unable to perceive the underlying motive behind the nudge or articulate the mechanisms driving a change in behavior. For example, the removal of diversity notices from news feed systems intended to increase personalization (the extent of personalized news searches) is considered a nontransparent nudge because nudged audiences may not notice this change unless they are told (Lim et al., 2024).

ETHICS-AWARE CHOICE ARCHITECTURES: HUMANS JUDGE AND ALGORITHMS NUDGE

The key underlying mechanism of nudges is choice architecture. Sunstein and Thaler (2014) proposed this idea to explore how the way choices are presented can influence people's decisions. By subtly orchestrating how options are presented, choice architecture influences individual decision-making, often without people's explicit awareness.

The Amazon Prime Video homepage serves as a choice architect by promoting the videos most likely to keep consumers engaged with the over-the-top platform. In other words, the algorithmic choice architect aims to design the optimal video feed to keep people scrolling for as long as possible. AI knows that even small changes in a decision-making environment can have a significant impact, guiding individuals to make better choices that align with their long-term goals. Another example is Uber, which designed its app to influence the decisions of their drivers. They use gamifications, noncash rewards, and engaging graphics to encourage drivers to work longer hours, even at less profitable times and locations. While Uber does not force drivers to work in these locations, they manipulate the app's design to take advantage of heuristics, making it more likely that drivers will work longer hours (Möhlmannn et al., 2023).

Choice architecture can be designed to gently push individuals toward desirable outcomes without taking away their freedom of choice. For instance, placing healthier options such as fruit and salad at the forefront of online search results can lead to healthier food choices. The majority of nudges and the design choices were created by humans but are now carried out by AI. The ordering of choices is becoming more automated, seemingly without the intervention of a human choice architect or their oversight. For instance, Google's News Feed algorithm selects and displays hundreds of posts from an average of about a thousand possible news items in real time to individual users. The algorithms for nudging can adapt in real time, improving the results that Google wants to achieve. This Google process is a form of nudges delivered by the thoughtful design of choice architecture. No choices are mandated or banned, and posts are curated because it is assumed that humans have limited cognitive resources. The selected posts are, therefore, predicted to be the most interesting to users.

In the dynamic corporate landscape, AI-driven guided selling is designed to offer strategic nudges to sales professionals, empowering them to successfully seal more deals. Nevertheless, without the establishment of innovative processes, the potential impact of AI remains untapped. It is crucial that every member of a revenue team, regardless of their level of expertise and confidence, has access to tailored guidance and takes action at the opportune moment for maximum effectiveness (Mertens et al., 2022). This timely intervention can elevate an engaged salesperson to the status of a high-performing professional.

While effective and popular, algorithmic choice architecture has raised concerns due to a lack of transparency and undisclosed details in its design and operation. There is an increasing demand for ethical considerations to be integrated into the choice architecture in AI contexts (Schmidt & Engelen, 2020). Ethical choice architecture involves the deliberate design of options to guide people's decisions in a way that helps them make better choices while still respecting their freedom to choose (Westbrook, 2020). It is crucial to ensure that choice architecture is transparent and fair and to avoid taking advantage of people's cognitive biases or deceiving them (Lara & Rodríguez-López, 2024). There are various ways to apply ethics to choice architecture. For instance, in healthcare, ethical choice architecture can be used to clarify options for patients or healthcare practitioners alike and enhance decision-making by employing nudges to guide patients toward beneficial choices, such as receiving vaccinations or taking antibiotics. Similarly, in social work, ethical choice architecture can assist social workers in making ethical decisions by anticipating potential mistakes, identifying those potentially affected, and seeking input from colleagues.

USAGES AND EXAMPLES OF ALGORITHMIC NUDGING

Improving AI Accuracy by Nudging Users to Detect Errors

Nudges in generative AI represent a practical and ethical way to enhance the quality of AI outputs and ensure these systems remain tools for augmentation rather than sources of unchecked misinformation. As research in this area expands, integrating behavioral insights into AI design will likely play a central role in shaping the future of human–AI collaboration. Using nudges in generative AI involves subtle interventions to guide users toward better engagement with AI outputs, improving the accuracy and reliability of decisions based on these outputs (Harrison et al., 2024). As people grow more dependent on AI, it becomes harder to recognize and pinpoint the AI's errors. Outputs with errors, omissions, and biases are often difficult to distinguish, making it harder to ensure AI-generated content is accurate and reliable. It becomes important to design generative AI to help people catch errors by themselves before they accept generative AI outputs as completely trustworthy. A group of researchers explored this issue through a field experiment designed to help users identify errors in AI-generated content. A field experiment by Accenture and Gosline (2024) demonstrates that "targeted friction," implemented as labels flagging potential errors or omissions, effectively directs users' attention to content requiring closer scrutiny without compromising efficiency. This concept aligns with inoculation principles (Compton, 2024), foolproof immunity (van der Linden, 2023), and algorithmic nudges (Shin, 2024). These approaches are similar in that subtle cues are incorporated—such as error or omission flags—directly into the generative AI interface. The difference between Gosline's approach and others is that it emphasizes System 2 thinking in users' engagement (slow, deliberate, and conscious, requiring intentional effort instead of System 1 thinking of fast, automatic, and intuitive, operating with little to no effort). The targeted friction of Gosline is to encourage users to partake in a more conscious and deliberate approach to cognitive processing, known as System 2 thinking when performing generative AI-enabled tasks without dramatically slowing or upending the end-to-end process. These System 2 cues were strategically designed to nudge users toward more critical engagement with the content. By measuring the impact of these prompts, they sought to determine whether such interventions could reduce the likelihood of uncritical acceptance of large language model outputs while maintaining user efficiency.

The findings revealed that adding deliberate friction (a kind of speed bump) to the process of reviewing AI outputs significantly improved the accuracy of user decisions without substantially increasing the time required to complete tasks. Particularly, medium-friction conditions pushed users to scrutinize generated text more carefully to catch inaccuracies and omissions without being a significant drag on the time it took to complete a task. Introducing moderate friction levels in the form of two kinds of highlighting created an optimal balance between accuracy and efficiency. This suggests that introducing cognitive and procedural intervention into workflows encouraged users to critically evaluate AI-generated text without significantly increasing task completion time. Indeed, subtle, well-placed interventions can encourage users to engage more thoughtfully with AI-generated material. By promoting a human-in-the-loop approach, where human judgment complements AI capabilities, these strategies can help ensure that generative AI systems augment human decision-making rather than introduce errors that go unnoticed. Based on the study, it is advised that firms aiming to implement beneficial friction in their AI-related processes adopt systematic and structured approaches.

There has been much research emphasizing the importance of designing AI systems that actively support critical thinking and vigilance in their users. Gosline's friction principle (2022) contributes to an ongoing dialogue about the ethical and practical integration of AI in decision-making processes. The principle finds that engaging users in the process and conducting experiments during AI design are key strategies for advancing AI at scale, while encouraging stakeholders across the value chain to collaborate in developing responsible AI. This approach aligns with growing efforts across industries to address AI bias and ensure that emerging technologies are used responsibly and transparently. It highlights the need for collaborative frameworks where humans and AI work together to achieve better outcomes, setting a foundation for future innovations in AI–human interaction. Shin's experiment clearly conceptualizes the notion of human-in-the-loop by showing how human action can be included in the debasing process. Keeping users in the loop is a commonly advocated strategy for overseeing AI, aiming to reduce bias and mitigate risks. Usual individuals, however, overestimate their ability to identify errors and often rely heavily on AI-generated content, even when aware of its potential inaccuracies (Gosline, 2022). Shin's approach emphasizes helping individuals recognize the potential for bias, the imperfections inherent in AI, and the limitations of human cognition. The broader implications of this approach involve cultivating a balanced relationship between humans and AI, enabling technology to enhance rather than erode trust and reliability. The friction principles underscore the benefits of integrating nudges into generative AI. First, they improve the accuracy and reliability of AI outputs by encouraging human critical thinking to identify and correct errors. Beneficial friction can serve as a cognitive speed bump that improves accuracy without sacrificing time. Second, they foster a collaborative dynamic between humans and AI, where each complements the other's strengths. Despite the proliferation of generative AI, human involvement is still valued and pervasive.

Finally, they address ethical concerns by prioritizing user empowerment and transparency. By guiding users to engage critically with AI-generated content, nudges promote responsible AI use and lay the foundation for effective and trustworthy systems.

This approach is particularly crucial as generative AI increasingly impacts sectors like healthcare, education, and journalism, where accuracy and ethical integrity are essential. AI does not have to be perfect to be useful, so be transparent with any biases, weaknesses, or blunders that AI may have.

Diversity Nudges in the News Recommender System

In algorithmic journalism, algorithmic nudging can be used to enhance news diversity in news recommender systems (NRSs) (Shin & Zhou, 2024) by reranking news items presented by an interface (Mattis et al., 2024). Outlets like the *BBC*, *The Wall Street Journal*, and *USA Today* provide widespread access to news through algorithm-based platforms. These platforms use algorithmic nudges to increase user engagement and draw more clicks to their websites. When utilized appropriately, algorithmic nudges have the potential to greatly enhance news diversity (Jürgens & Stark, 2022), particularly when readers are dealing with information overload or relying on AI systems for news recommendations.

As NRSs become more prevalent, concerns about the potential side effects of hyper-personalization have been raised, such as rabbit holes and filter bubbles (Shin & Zhou, 2024). Scholars and practitioners share concerns as to how NRSs can be designed in a way that prioritizes user needs while still upholding the ethical goals of journalism. It is important to optimize the incorporation of public values in news recommendations, and this should be followed by the clear definition and implementation of the diversity principle in NRSs.

Diversity nudges embedded in AI can help readers discover diverse articles by making them more accessible and providing unexpected recommendations. These unexpected recommendations can lead users to develop new interests, contributing to greater user satisfaction (Sax, 2022). Platform behavioral change methods are evolving to be more subtle and are frequently being implemented without clear user consent. Although readers can see such changes in the form of advertising, recommendations, or autocomplete functions, they are generally invisible and untraceable to third-party auditors. These algorithmic nudges work invisibly and can operate without external supervision, potentially creating filter bubbles or generating rabbit holes of extreme ideas (Dahlgren, 2021).

Algorithmic journalism is increasingly using algorithms to personalize news (Currin et al., 2022). This is causing tension with the principle of news diversity, which has long been crucial to media and journalism. As algorithmic personalization relies heavily on automated recommendation systems, it often lacks fairness and transparency due to algorithmic personalization's commercial interests and technological efficiency. This goes against the normative principles of news, which should provide a wide spectrum of news and viewpoints to readers. The lack of diversity in recommendation systems has become a significant issue, leading to overfitting problems and the polarization of opinions, which poses a threat to democratic discussions (Currin et al., 2022; Helberger, 2019).

Transparency Cues in Generative AI

Nudges are significant in generative tools like ChatGPT, Jasper, and Copy.ai. They assist users in finding ways to leverage AI to add value to existing content, handle routine tasks, or remix and enhance content. In the media industry, the shift to automated news production with generative AI emphasizes the importance of transparency and disclosure. Disclosing transparency is the practice of openly collecting, organizing, and sharing information. This allows both internal and external parties to actively monitor, investigate, critique, and potentially intervene in the production of news (Liu et al., 2023). Attributes commonly found in transparent disclosure practices include revealing information about story corrections, author information, and hyperlinks to related stories and news. These disclosures moderate user perceptions and improve the overall credibility of the news industry. These proactive disclosure approaches aim to improve the accuracy and clarity of information. They can be a form of soft content governance, helping users process information in a non-misleading manner. This can promote a healthier and more organized communication environment through subtle nudges (Pennycook & Rand, 2022). Relevant research emphasized that disclosing the authorship of automated news is a crucial component of transparent disclosure nudges. This can influence users' perceptions of AI as a news producer and their cognitive evaluations (Shin, 2024).

Interface machine cues can trigger user heuristic, shaping their content perceptions and overall experiences. Nekmat (2020) argued that providing content labeling, such as AI-generated content labeling and fact-checking labeling, will be an essential tool for content governance in human–machine collaborative journalism.

Transparent disclosure can effectively influence users' cognitive processes by providing them with information about the production process. This includes highlighting the subjectivity and potential quality risks associated with certain information, prompting users to focus on the information's quality. Transparency cues, such as detailed news source descriptions and explanations of the news-gathering process, can demonstrate transparency. Media organizations are considering disclosing interview statements, content subjectivity notices, authorship, citations, and editorial statements. In automated news, authorship disclosure includes revealing information about the machine creator and the algorithm model. Embedding reference hyperlinks and providing information correction cues can significantly improve users' perceptions of trustworthiness. Additionally, disclosing authors' resumes and details can enhance the evaluation of news content's trustworthiness and boost users' willingness to share news.

Explainable Cues in Content Generation

Explainable cues, as one form of algorithmic nudges, are already playing a significant role in helping to make the decision-making processes of AI systems understandable and trustworthy (Bauer et al., 2023). Explainable cues are a critical element in sectors with strict regulations to enhance trust in and the adoption of AI technologies. Algorithmic cues open up the black box of AI systems, providing stakeholders the ability to understand, verify, and challenge the decisions made by these systems. For example, in healthcare, explainable cues help medical professionals trust and understand the decision-making process of AI systems. This is especially crucial for AI systems utilized in diagnosing issues, predicting outcomes, and planning treatments. These systems offer customized, data-informed treatments and improve the transparency of decision-making processes.

In the legal sector, explainable cues provide explanations for an AI's decisions, allowing legal professionals to understand and trust the recommended content. For instance, Goldman Sachs' legal AI offers valuable information to legal professionals by automatically classifying legal documents and analyzing cases. In the financial sector, explainable cues reassure investors and analysts of content's reliability by clearly explaining the data and patterns on which predictive models base their decisions. These cues can be leveraged for investment portfolio optimization and credit risk assessment by suggesting recommendation tabs. "Robo advice" is an example of AI nudging through information filtering.

In the realm of autonomous driving, explainable cues are primarily used to comprehend the decision-making process and rationale behind decisions made by autonomous vehicles. Algorithmic cues are especially crucial in autonomous driving because vehicle decisions are highly intricate and can have life-or-death implications. Explainable cues play a significant role in enhancing the reliability and safety of these systems by making the decisions of a system comprehensible and explicable (Liu et al., 2023).

PROCESSING OF NUDGES: HEURISTIC AND SYSTEMATIC NUDGES

The dual-system framework is the theoretical basis for nudging, and it suggests that human decision-making comes from two distinct cognitive processes. Type 1 is automatic and heuristic-based, while Type 2 is more systematic, deliberate, and analytical. The former algorithmic nudges are more automatic, or the nudged individual's reaction is more passive, whereas the latter nudges are designed to affect reflective choice or involve active and conscious response. Both types of nudges are techniques that use automatic processes to influence behaviors, but they differ in their goals and how they engage the automatic system.

Type 1: Heuristic Nudges

These nudges aim to influence automatic behaviors and thinking and are often designed to take advantage of subconscious or deliberate behaviors. For instance, in NRS, implementing a diverse range of views to prevent polarization is a Type 1 nudge. Another example is explanatory cues in generated information presented by generative AI. Explanatory cues in AI can influence user behaviors by subtly guiding them toward preferred choices using push notifications, alarm cues, and online recommendation badges.

Privacy nudges can be considered Type 1, as they aim to support wise choices concerning digital privacy decisions (encouraging privacy-friendly app choices or discouraging unintended location disclosure).

Type 2: Systematic Nudges

Systematic nudges also use the automatic system, but they do so to elicit reflective reasoning that can change deliberate actions and choices. For instance, incorporating author information labels alongside news stories in news recommendation systems and promoting transparency and credibility checks constitute Type 2 algorithmic nudges. Another example is the inclusion of a fact-checking button in online news, which prompts users to reflect on and verify the accuracy of the information they are searching for. Nudging users to catch the errors in generative AI can be an example of systematic nudging. Highlighted buttons in a system are linked to the reporting mechanism that provides feedback directly to the coders of an AI.

A transparent nudge is a nudge that is provided in a way that makes both its intention and the means by which behavioral change is pursued reasonably clear to the person being nudged as a result of the intervention. A nontransparent nudge is one that works in a way that does not allow a person to reconstruct either the intention or means by which behavioral change is being pursued (Shin, 2024).

Linking the concept of transparency to the two types of nudges results in four types of algorithmic nudges. Table 5.1 shows the two types of nudges and their associated

TABLE 5.1   Type of and transparency nudges

	TRANSPARENT NUDGES	NONTRANSPARENT NUDGES
Type 1	Order effects: The order in which information is presented by generative AI can significantly affect the choices people make. Product suggestions placed at the top are more likely to be chosen than recommendations placed at the bottom.	Framing effect: At the grocer's, consumers see two different beef products. One is labeled "80% lean" and the other "20% fat." Comparing the two, consumers feel that 20% fat appears an unhealthy option, so they select the 80% lean option.
Ethical concerns	Manipulation, assumptions, unconscious behavioral maneuvering	Violation of autonomy, elitism
Type 2	Visual cues: Callouts, graphics, signage, highlights, and other design elements can guide the eye toward a specific area or encourage a particular behavior. Fly-in-the-urinal, explanatory cues, and transparency cues are Type 2 nudges.	Opt-out default: Changing organ donation from an opt-in system to an opt-out system could increase organ donation rates.
Ethical concerns	Abuse, heterogeneous effects	Paternalism, contextual insensitivity

level of transparency. The first type of nudges, known as "transparent Type 2 nudges," includes nudges that "engage the reflective system in a way that makes it easy for the citizen to reconstruct the intentions and means by which behavior change is pursued." An example of this type of nudge is placing fake news (misinformation) labels next to the presented news along with placards encouraging fact-checking practices.

The second type of nudges, known as "transparent Type 1 nudges," involves nudges that do not require reflective reasoning to cause a behavior change. Reflective thinking may occur as a byproduct, but in a way that makes it easy to understand the purpose and methods of a nudge. In this type of nudge, behavioral change is more or less inevitable, but since the nudge is transparent, the person being influenced can recognize its intention and methods. Examples of this type of nudge can be an investment policy statement. In financial planning, an investment policy statement is a form of precommitment strategy.

The third type of nudges, known as "nontransparent Type 2 nudges," includes nudges that require the engagement of the reflective system to be successful but do not give people epistemic access to the intentions and means by which influence is pursued. Examples of this type of nudge include fly-in-the-urinal nudges. This Type 2 nudge attracts attention to the fly-in-the-urinal nudge, triggering a reflective response to pay attention or reduce spillage.

The final category of nudges, termed "nontransparent Type 1 nudges," encompasses nudges that prompt changes in behavior without involving the reflective system. These nudges operate in a manner that is unlikely to be recognized and made transparent. An example of this type of nudge is reduced dinner plate sizes; a consumer may not be aware that the size of their dinner plate has been reduced.

ETHICAL CONCERNS SURROUNDING ALGORITHMIC NUDGES

Algorithms can filter information to change human behaviors and influence decision-making (Shin, 2023). Nudges are used as tactical tools to achieve these goals. When misused, algorithmic nudges can create a complex web of ethical dilemmas. These challenges encompass issues such as autonomous decision-making, manipulative tactics, and algorithmic opacity, all of which significantly impede individuals' capacity to cultivate their moral characters and flourish (Cook & Berente, 2024).

Autonomous Choice Architecture (Autonomy of Nudges)

Critics argue that algorithmic nudges often make assumptions about the nudged individual's preferences or may disregard these preferences altogether (Shin & Ahmad, 2023). Algorithms take advantage of people's biases and too often lack transparency and fairness, thus decreasing active choice (Schmidt & Engelen, 2020). For instance, Siri or Alexa can easily adjust their responses to exploit human cognitive biases, influencing users to take a certain action or make a specific decision. Whether the intention behind a nudge was a user's benefit, such adjustments are made independently by algorithms, and users have no control as to the withdrawal of their consent. In the AI era, firms often use this technique to subconsciously motivate their employees and boost productivity. Online consumers, for example, can be nudged to fit marketing needs by tweaking how products are presented (e.g., color schemes, positioning of icons, and ordering of products). The consequence of the use of algorithms in marketing is that AI has the ability to expand the use of influencing methods by implementing them on a large scale. Big data analysis can automatically identify the smallest weaknesses in decision-making processes, which can then be used to influence users. Once a new behavioral trigger has been identified, algorithms can target it extensively. This process of nudging users can make them feel deceived because they end up buying items or paying for services that do not meet their actual needs or because resisting such influences leads to a sense of fatigue that worsens the shopping experience. Therefore, using nudges in advertising and marketing can negatively impact user well-being. The widespread use of nudges often institutionalizes biases or errors that used to be occasional. In other words, irrationality becomes the de facto standard. In short, using algorithmic nudges raises important ethical questions: who is responsible for autonomous choice architects, and where should we draw the line between motivation and manipulation?

Ethical principles state that nudges should not enforce or prohibit any options, nor should they exert undue influence (Shin & Ahmad, 2023). The Instagram algorithm follows these principles. The algorithm selects a thousand posts, all of which are available for a user to view; however, it makes hundreds of these posts easier to view. An algorithm is used because of limitations in human cognition. It would be difficult for us to sift through 2000 posts every day to find what we are looking for. The Instagram algorithm not only makes it easier to view hundreds of posts, but it also makes the platform as a whole easier to use. The Google News Feed is a typical example of nudging, just like other feeds such as Facebook's homepage, while the algorithms powering these feeds act as choice architects. These choice architecture functions nudge autonomous choice architects.

The use of algorithmic nudges to monetize hate and misinformation is a growing concern. This is especially evident in the way social media platforms like YouTube and TikTok are structured to incentivize and profit from the dissemination of violent and extremist content. The ability to monetize such content at an unprecedented scale has raised alarm bells, as it amplifies the spread of harmful narratives and ideologies. For instance, Andrew Tate is a media personality and self-described misogynist who is currently being detained in Romania on charges of unlawful detainment, sex trafficking, and organized crime. A YouGov poll showed that in the United Kingdom, 54% of children aged 6–15 have heard of Tate and 17% of boys aged 6–15 have a positive opinion of Tate, with that figure rising to 23% for boys aged 13–15. Algorithmic nudge has allowed Tate to become wealthy off of spreading overtly misogynistic content that encourages boys and men to be violent toward women and training men to pressure their partners into sex work and to control their girlfriends and partners by financially and emotionally isolating them.

The Manipulative and Maneuvered Nature of Algorithm-Driven Nudges

Scholars in the field of AI have observed the manipulative nature of algorithmic nudges, which can override users' own perceptions of their well-being and steer them to act in ways that may not be in their best interests (Nyman, 2023). For instance, a study on Uber's algorithms illustrates one of the most iconic cases of the ethically questionable use of algorithmic nudges (Möhlmannn et al., 2023). The study uncovered how Uber manipulates Uber drivers to work longer hours. Moreover, studies have indicated that algorithmic nudges promote AI scientism and exploitative work ethics (e.g., Brown et al., 2022; Shin & Ahmad, 2023). Cristianini and Scantamburlo (2020) examined the connection between nudges and AI. They provided an in-depth explanation of how personalized targeting algorithms are capable of utilizing persuasion and psychometrics to mold individual and collective behavior, often yielding unintended consequences. Scholars have further argued that the lack of transparency in learning algorithms used for algorithmic nudges leads to problems such as discrimination, misinformation, and limited accountability and literacy development (Lara & Rodríguez-López, 2024).

Algorithmic nudging can be seen as a form of passive manipulation, blurring the line between free choice and guiding users toward specific behaviors (Nekmat, 2020). This negativity contradicts the findings of Thaler and Sunstein (2008), who emphasized the positive aspects of nudging in decision-making in terms of promoting well-being and good health. Despite the generally positive impact of nudges, discussions have made it increasingly evident that nudges present challenges across various domains. The issue with influencing people's behaviors is that such behavioral modifications raise moral concerns and often infringe upon fundamental human rights (Christiane et al., 2023). For example, nudges often fail to comply with normative ethical standards, and algorithmic nudges lead to problems with compliance (Shin & Ahmad, 2023). The use of algorithmic nudging to influence individual behaviors on a large scale is becoming a technological reality. With platforms like Facebook and Instagram fully embracing algorithms, we are quickly approaching a point where algorithmic nudges will increasingly guide us toward content that serves these platforms' financial interests and away from less profitable content. Algorithmic platforms use AI nudges to keep users scrolling. These nudges suggest content based on previous likes or viewing histories, keeping users engaged for longer than intended. As these nudges become more sophisticated, they can blur the line between harmless engagement and manipulative tactics that exploit users' attention spans for profit.

With the widespread use of AI-driven nudges, users may be unaware that invisible algorithms have predetermined the selections they make. If an algorithm operates without users' consent, it could be seen as manipulating human free will by limiting available choices. Nevertheless, some researchers (e.g., Shin, 2024) have argued against the notion that algorithmic nudging contradicts important ethical principles such as liberty and autonomy.

Several studies have explored whether nudges can undermine people's freedom of choice and whether they are as liberty-preserving as nudge advocates claim (Schmidt & Engelen, 2020; Yeung, 2017). This concern is related to volitional autonomy, where one's behaviors should reflect their own desires, interests, preferences, or goals. When influenced by nudges, people may be misled, causing their resulting wishes and actions to no longer truly represent their own. Implicit and covert nudges can take away people's control over their choices, which no longer reflect their self-directed needs. This supports the argument that nudges disregard rationality by operating through unclear or illogical methods. While nudges may aim to respect our freedom and enhance efficiency and convenience, they often rely on our irrational heuristics and biases. This can make us feel like we are not being treated as rational human beings, which can be dehumanizing. Due to this concern, algorithmic nudging should be used cautiously and with discretion to ensure that individuals can freely make their own decisions (Sumner et al., 2023). In this context, Shin (2024) is concerned that nudging can weaken people's ability to make diverse judgments and erode their agency. Furthermore, when people are stripped of decision-making responsibilities, their ability to assess and make sensible decisions cannot progress, thereby weakening their ethical autonomy (Yeung, 2017). This concern relates to deep learning capabilities and emphasizes that becoming a subject of intelligent mass manipulation is not a pleasant thought (Raveendhran & Fast, 2021). Related to this concern is the ongoing debate about whether exposure to algorithmic nudges predisposes users to making certain decisions or leaning toward specific choices. Has any given choice been triggered by malicious algorithmic nudges or the intentional abuse of the algorithms behind platforms, or has the phenomenon of algorithmic nudges emerged from the experience of searching for and interacting with online systems? In other words, is a given behavior the result of algorithmic nudges, or do algorithmic nudges simply echo preexisting predispositions to engaging with specific content? Shin and Ahmad (2023) argued that algorithmic nudges do not create prejudices, nor do they have any intention of steering users toward fake news or misinformation. The bias we are witnessing in AI stems from a self-reinforcing cycle in our content-seeking and usage patterns. Echoing the proverb "what you sow, so shall you reap," biases generated by algorithmic nudges most likely result from previous user attitudes and actions.

In light of the widespread use of algorithmic nudges, there is a societal need to seriously consider the governance and control of such algorithms (Yeung, 2017). Algorithmic nudging could be misused by industry or the government to exert subtle control over humans (Cook & Berente, 2024). In the age of AI, industry and governments are increasing their control over the populace beyond conventional forms of ruling over people by increasingly depending on algorithms to maximize profits. Industrial power over users prevails only if the public does not properly manage industrial power. The concern is that algorithms facilitate such domination because they selectively gatekeep public voices and dodge democratic governance while cloaked in invisible algorithms. Because of algorithms' inherent limited transparency and fairness, critics have voiced concerns about algorithmic nudges' manipulative potential (Mills & Sætra, 2024). For instance, the label Amazon's Choice is controlled by an opaque algorithm that prioritizes highly rated and competitively priced products available for immediate shipping. This process is deemed nontransparent due to the undisclosed method used to generate the label (Bauer et al., 2023).

A crucial question is which normative ethical framework would be appropriate for algorithmic nudges. How can we trust autonomous nudges that actively seek to modify human behavior and decision-making? What are the various considerations that a choice architecture should take into account in nudges' conception, design, implementation, and deployment? In instances where algorithmic nudges are utilized in the public sector, especially by governments, there have been concerns raised about the objectives they serve. How can governments accurately determine the best interests of the people? Governments should refrain from imposing their objectives and interests on individuals, especially in communities where citizens hold a wide range of ideas. Making nudges transparent to citizens is an ethical requirement. Furthermore, individual deliberation and public scrutiny are highly valued by ethics. In some instances, the same holds for making available information salient for public scrutiny.

ALGORITHMIC NUDGES WITH MEANINGFUL CONTROL AND ALGORITHMIC ETHICAL REENGINEERING

With the idea of meaningful control, AI can nudge user preferences toward more socially desirable and ethically sound performance (Shin, 2024). One key proposition of algorithmic nudging is that humans should remain in control of these nudges. While algorithmic nudges are increasingly pervasive and embedded in many services and objects, they can also lead to unintended consequences for which moral responsibility cannot be attributed to any specific individual or community. The concept of "meaningful user control" has been put forward as a solution to address responsibility gaps and reduce the potential negative impacts. This involves setting conditions that empower individuals to have significant control over the nudges they encounter (Yeung, 2017). Algorithmic nudging should be designed to empower users to make informed decisions by facilitating cognitive processes, increasing engagement in terms of data interpretation, and enhancing users' capacity to leverage insights from data. To effectively control AI, users should possess the necessary knowledge to evaluate algorithms, which is known as algorithmic competency or literacy. Additionally, they should have the opportunity to engage with algorithms to develop a better understanding of and appreciation for their impact. Achieving meaningful control of AI is a complex and demanding task, necessitating a multitude of prerequisites. Contemporary debates on algorithmic governance or algorithmic ethics are either too theoretical to yield conclusions for practice or too narrowly focused, and the technical requirements for transparency or fairness do not take into account regular users or the broader societal context. Nevertheless, having absolute control is not entirely ideal.

To achieve meaningful control, it is essential to implement algorithmic auditing for AI systems. This proactive approach will enhance interpretability, fairness, and controllability, ensuring the protection of fundamental rights related to privacy and personal data (Shin, 2024). Relevant studies have proposed specific methods that use algorithmic audit instruments. For example, Brown et al. (2022) put forward three components of algorithmic audit instruments: a list of potential interests of users influenced by algorithmic nudges, an evaluation metric that clarifies important ethical features of algorithmic nudges, and a relevance matrix that links the assessed metrics to user interests. Both Brown et al. (2022) and Shin (2023) proposed four algorithmic audit principles (fairness, transparency, accountability, and explainability) to use during ethical evaluations of an algorithmic nudge that regulators and policymakers could adopt. It is crucial to carefully consider the complex societal context in which algorithmic nudges are utilized and implemented. This is important to ensure that algorithmic nudges do not go beyond the narrow view of traditional nudging as just a basic user interface in AI environments. In light of this, metacognitive nudges are being suggested as a way to address the current ethical issues surrounding algorithmic nudges. Metacognition refers to the ability to be conscious of one's own thinking processes and to comprehend the patterns behind them (Shin, 2024). Metacognitive nudges are based on the concept of self-regulated learning, involving people in the design of nudges and making them aware of nudge mechanisms. As a result, people know what data are collected and how they are used in nudges. Such nudges are designed to encourage introspection and prompt individuals to assess their confidence levels in accomplishing a specific task. For instance, a metacognition nudge might prompt individuals to rate their confidence in their ability to solve a math problem before an AI attempts to solve it. This can help prevent errors by avoiding tasks that are beyond human capabilities. Using metacognition, algorithmic nudges can be designed as value-based, user-controlled architectures that help overcome users' emotional, cognitive, and psychological limits when they make decisions and perform actions that contribute to value cocreation.

Algorithmic nudges alone are unlikely to produce the best outcomes. Instead, humans and algorithms should work together to create values and design algorithmic nudge contexts that encourage positive outcomes. Interaction plays a crucial role in shaping these contexts and enhancing self-understanding, future interactions, and user actions. Such discussions lead to a deeper understanding of algorithmic processes and related concepts such as interactive machine learning, participatory machine learning, and human-centered machine learning. Creating algorithmic nudges is a collaborative process that relies on users' motivation, knowledge, interactions, and needs. User awareness and literacy are crucial in cocreating value while AI contributes to new forms of self-understanding and self-development. Algorithmic nudging not only empowers users to make different choices but also encourages them to act differently. Therefore, by shaping the range of choices available to users, algorithmic nudging motivates them and enhances their satisfaction. This process has a positive influence on users' agency and behaviors.

Here are three recommendations to enhance the effectiveness of algorithmic nudges within organizations:

1. A culture of experimentation: Before deploying algorithmic nudges and models, organizations should test how workers interact with them, assessing impacts on accuracy, speed, and trust. Experimentation provides valuable insights into optimizing human-in-the-loop systems, helping to determine when the application of targeted friction is most effective.

2. Continuous monitoring: Algorithmic nudges are dynamic systems that may experience drift over time, leading to inaccuracies or hallucinations in outputs. It is essential to implement robust oversight and monitoring mechanisms to continually evaluate these systems, identify potential issues, and initiate the appropriate interventions to maintain performance and reliability.

3. Education and training: As the use of algorithmic nudges expands, ongoing education and training are crucial to ensure workers can effectively engage with evolving technologies. In particular, education on prompt engineering is vital for generative AI systems, as it is a key area prone to bias. One of the most critical points for introducing friction is at the prompt generation stage, where users must consciously consider their objectives and the intended use of AI outputs to minimize bias.

Algorithmic nudges are not the sole solution for mitigating AI inaccuracies and bias. Organizations should adopt a test-and-learn approach, gradually expanding their experimentation as they scale up AI use cases. AI doesn't need to be flawlessly easy to implement for people to find it valuable.

VALUE-CENTERED APPROACH TO ALGORITHMIC NUDGE

The value-centered approach to algorithmic nudges involves engaging users at every stage of algorithm development and testing. This approach ensures that interactions between humans and AI are effective and consider the needs and experiences of users (Sumner et al., 2023). One example is that organizations can develop the necessary key competencies through data collection and training, as well as by embracing user-centered design. The advancement of AI systems has led to the need for a value-centered framework to address ethical, practical, and legal issues. This framework aims to make AI sustainable and enhance human experiences rather than replacing human capacity. It promotes fair, transparent, and explainable AI that supports human values, rights, and user control. Key questions include how algorithms fit into a social context, enable meaningful control, and can be managed effectively by users. Answers to these questions will guide the development of AI systems to foster confidence and trust in humans. Meaningful human control is crucial for realizing ethical AI and developing AI systems that align with human values.

The main idea behind value-centered nudges is to focus on the people who will be affected by the nudges rather than just creating services because they are technically possible. The basic assumption is that AI systems should be designed to be accessible and easy to understand for regular nontechnical users. The value-centered approach aims to create algorithmic nudges that can understand human thinking, perceptions, communication, and interactions without requiring humans to learn how the algorithmic nudges work. This approach introduces two important criteria for value-centered algorithmic nudges: they should (1) comprehend humans and (2) assist humans in building trust through fair, transparent, and accountable procedures. These nudge principles serve as safeguards to ensure that algorithmic nudges are sustainable, preventing common sense errors, intentional violations of human rights, and situations that could lead to harm and conflict.

Value-centered algorithmic nudges must start with people and their desired outcomes. This approach to the creation of algorithmic nudges considers what people need and what is best for them. It prioritizes empathy, equity, and human rights as core values. AI designers should approach algorithmic nudges with a focus on human well-being and ethical considerations. They should also address data flow, the design process, and how to give users meaningful control over AI. Human oversight should be integrated throughout an algorithm's operations before, during, and after AI use. It is crucial to incorporate user values into algorithms and establish proactive oversight mechanisms. Additionally, it is crucial to consider the potential impact on humans if algorithmic nudges were used for illegal or unethical purposes. When designing and developing algorithmic nudges, AI systems will not be flawless. We should support future efforts in developing value-centered algorithmic nudges while upholding human values in future AI systems.

CONCLUSIONS: NUDGE ETHICALLY AND HUMANLY

The chapter took a discursive perspective to critically review the ethical implications of using algorithmic nudges. Algorithmic nudging via AI is an emerging practice that deserves attention from industry and academia. The chapter discussed why ethical principles are critical in algorithmic nudges, how to ensure that algorithmic nudges are designed constructively, and how to ensure legitimate forms of persuasive communication for achieving a sustainable goal. It also discussed the principles and practices underpinning AI systems' nudging effects on user behaviors, as well as how people can nudge algorithmic systems so that they have human-centered qualities. It presented a series of theoretical and practical investigations into ethically sound nudging practices, highlighting the significance of a nuanced comprehension of the contexts and requirements of nudge targets, personalized interventions, and thorough monitoring.

The concept of value-centered algorithmic nudges could provide a starting point for future research. Subsequent studies might investigate how the conflicts between codification, autonomy, and alignment of interests are managed in interactions between human employees and managerial recommendation systems. The discussion on value-centered nudges provides useful suggestions for policymakers on how to govern and regulate algorithmic nudges. The results offer AI platform providers guidelines on effective nudge prompts to use and cycle through when involving people, aiming to improve the quality of online information.

As algorithmic nudging becomes more powerful, society must carefully navigate the ethical landscape. Regulation, transparency, and human autonomy will ensure that algorithmic nudging benefits individuals and communities without encroaching on boundaries. Algorithmic nudges should be transparent and ethical, providing clear information about costs and alternative options. Humans should have the freedom to make their own choices without interference from algorithms. Users should have the final say, and the choice architecture and its consequences should take accountability into consideration.

REFERENCES

Bauer, K., von Zahn, M., & Hinz, O. (2023). Expl(AI)Ned: The impact of explainable artificial intelligence on users' information processing. *Information Systems Research*, *34*(4), 1603–1621.

Brown, S., Davidovic, J., & Hasan, A. (2022). The algorithm audit: Scoring the algorithms that score us. *Big Data & Society*, *8*(1). https://doi.org/10.1177/2053951720983865

Bucher, T. (2017). The algorithmic imaginary: Exploring the ordinary affects of Facebook algorithms. *Information, Communication & Society*, *20*, 30–44.

Christiane, S., Jurgis, K., Maximilian, M., Bahador, B., & Ophelia, D. (2023). Algorithmic nudging: The need for an interdisciplinary oversight. *International Review of Philosophy*, *42*(3), 799–807. https://doi.org/10.1007/s11245-023-09907-4

Compton, J. (2024). Inoculation theory. *Review of Communication*, 1–13. https://doi.org/10.1080/15358593.2024.2370373

Cook, R., & Berente, N. (2024). Nudges and motivated moral reasoning: Algorithms, humans, and information processing. *Academy of Management*. https://doi.org/10.5465/AMPROC.2024.15337abstract

Cristianini, N., & Scantamburlo, T. (2020). On social machines for algorithmic regulation. *AI & Society*, *35*, 645–662. https://doi.org/10.1007/s00146-019-00917-8

Currin, C., Vera, S., Khaledi, & Nasab, A. (2022). Depolarization of echo chambers by random dynamical nudge. *Scientific Reports*, *12*, 9234. https://doi.org/10.1038/s41598-022-12494-w

Gosline, R. (2022). Why AI customer journeys need more friction. The *Harvard Business Review*. https://hbsp.harvard.edu/product/H0733O-PDF-ENG

Gosline, R., Haiwen, Y., Li, P., Roussiere, A., & Connolly, P. (2024). Nudge users to catch generative AI errors. *MIT Sloan Management Review*, *65*(4), 21–24.

Hansen, P. G., & Jespersen, A. M. (2013). Nudge and the manipulation of choice: A framework for the responsible use of the nudge approach to behavior change in public policy. *The European Journal of Risk Regulation*, *4*(1), 3–28.

Harrison, R., Lapteva, E., & Bibin, A. (2024). Behavioral nudging with generative AI for content development in SMS health care interventions: Case study. *Journal of Medical Internet Research AI*, *3*, e52974. https://doi.org/10.2196/52974

Helberger, N. (2019). On the democratic role of news recommenders. *Digital Journalism*, *7*(8), 993–1012. https://doi.org/10.1080/21670811.2019.1623700

Juneja, P., & Mitra, T. (2022). Algorithmic nudge to make better choices: Evaluating effectiveness of XAI frameworks to reveal biases in algorithmic decision making to users. *In Proceedings of the CHI 2022 Workshop on Operationalizing Human-Centered Perspectives in Explainable AI. arXiv preprint arXiv:2202.02479.*

Jürgens, P., & Stark, B. (2022). Mapping exposure diversity: The divergent effects of algorithmic curation on news consumption. *Journal of Communication*, *72*(3), 322–344. https://doi.org/10.1093/joc/jqac009

Kroll, T., & Stieglitz, S. (2021). Digital nudging and privacy: Improving decisions about self-disclosure in social networks. *Behavior & Information Technology*, *40*, 1–19.

Lara, F., & Rodríguez-López, B. (2024). Socratic nudges, virtual moral assistants and the problem of autonomy. *AI & Society*. https://doi.org/10.1007/s00146-023-01846-3

Lim, J., Ahmad, N., & Ibarahim, M. (2024). Understanding user sensemaking in fairness and transparency in algorithms: Algorithmic sensemaking in over-the-top platform. *AI & Society*, *39*, 447–490. https://doi.org/10.1007/s00146-022-01525-9

Liu, Y., Wang, S., & Yu, G. (2023). The nudging effect of AIGC labeling on users' perceptions of automated news: Evidence from EEG. *Frontier Psychology*, *14*, 1277829. https://doi.org/10.3389/fpsyg.2023.1277829

Mattis, N., Groot Kormelink, T., Masur, P. K., Moeller, J., & van Atteveldt, W. (2024). Nudging news readers: A mixed-methods approach to understanding when and how interface nudges affect news selection. *Digital Journalism*, 1–21. https://doi.org/10.1080/21670811.2024.2350464

Mattis, N., Masur, P., Möller, J., & van Atteveldt, W. (2022). Nudging towards news diversity. *New Media & Society*, *26*(7), 3681–3706. https://doi.org/10.1177/14614448221104413

Mertens, S., Herberz, M., Hahnel, U., & Brosch, T. (2022). The effectiveness of nudging: A meta-analysis of choice architecture interventions across behavioral domains. *Proceedings of National Academy of Science*, *119*(1), e2107346118. https://doi.org/10.1073/pnas.2107346118

Mills, S., & Sætra, H. S. (2024). The autonomous choice architect. *AI & Society*, *39*, 583–595. https://doi.org/10.1007/s00146-022-01486-z

Möhlmann, M. (2021). Algorithmic nudges don't have to be unethical. *Harvard Business Review*. https://hbr.org/2021/04/algorithmic-nudges-dont-have-to-be-unethical

Möhlmannn, M., Salge, A., & Marco, M. (2023). Algorithm sensemaking: How platform workers make sense of algorithmic management. *Journal of the Association for Information Systems*, *24*(1), 35–64. https://doi.org/10.17705/1jais.00774

Nekmat, E. (2020). Nudge effect of fact-check alerts: Source influence and media skepticism on sharing of news misinformation in social media. *Social Media + Society*, *6*(1). https://doi.org/10.1177/2056305119897322

Nyman, S. (2023). The birth of AI-driven nudges. In *Proceedings of the annual Hawaii international conference on system sciences*. https://doi.org/10.24251/hicss.2023.642

Pennycook, G., & Rand, D. G. (2022). Nudging social media toward accuracy. *Annals of American Academy of Political Social Science*, *700*, 152–164. https://doi.org/10.1177/00027162221092342

Raveendran, R., & Fast, N. J. (2021). Humans judge, algorithms nudge: The psychology of behavior tracking acceptance. *Organizational Behavior and Human Decision Processes*, *164*, 11–26. https://doi.org/10.1016/j.obhdp.2021.01.001

Sax, M. (2022). Algorithmic news diversity and democratic theory. *Digital Journalism*, *10*(10), 1650–1670. https://doi.org/10.1080/21670811.2022.2114919

Schmidt, A. T., & Engelen, B. (2020). The ethics of nudging: An overview. *Philosophy Compass*, *15*(4), e12658. https://doi.org/10.1111/phc3.12658

Shin, D. (2021). *Minds, machines, and misinformation*. Elsevier.

Shin, D. (2023). *Algorithms, humans, and interactions: How do algorithms interact with people? Designing meaningful AI experiences* (1st ed.). Routledge. https://doi.org/10.1201/b23083

Shin, D. (2024). *Artificial misinformation: Exploring human-algorithm interaction online*. Springer Nature. https://doi.org/10.1007/978-3-031-52569-8

Shin, D., & Ahmad, N. (2023). Algorithmic nudge: An approach to designing human-centered generative artificial intelligence. *Computer*, *56*(8), 95–99. https://doi.org/10.1109/MC.2023.3278156

Shin, D., & Zhou, S. (2024). A value and diversity-aware news recommendation systems: Can algorithmic gatekeeping nudge readers to view diverse news? *Journalism & Mass Communication Quarterly.* https://doi.org/10.1177/10776990241246680

Sumner, J., Bundele, A., Lim, H., Phan, P., Motani, M., & Mukhopadhyay, A. (2023). Developing an AI-driven nudge intervention to improve medication adherence. *Journal of Medical System, 48*(1). https://doi.org/10.100'//s10916-023-02024-0

Sunstein, C. R., & Thaler, R. H. (2014). *Nudge: Improving decisions about health, wealth, and happiness.* Yale University Press.

van der Linden, S. (2023). *Foolproof: Why misinformation infects our minds and how to build immunity.* W. W. Norton & Company.

Westbrook, C. (2020). Ethical choice architecture in pre-abortion counseling. *AMA Journal of Ethics, 22*(9), 792–795. https://doi.org/10.1001/amajethics.2020.792

Yeung, K. (2017). Hyper nudge: Big data as a mode of regulation by design. *Information, Communication & Society, 20*(1), 118–136. https://doi.org/10.1080/1369118X.2016.1186713

Algorithmic Heuristics

6

How People Evaluate the Ethics of Deepfakes

INTRODUCTION

Deepfakes are highly realistic synthetic creations generated using artificial intelligence (AI) (Ahmed, 2023). These intricate amalgamations, constructed by sophisticated algorithms and machine learning, can be used to seamlessly integrate the real-world visual and auditory characteristics of individuals into meticulously fabricated settings. This process leads to media content that looks strikingly authentic (Cover, 2022). While the development and utilization of deepfake technologies are still in their infancy (Wahl-Jorgensen & Carlson, 2021), continuous advances in machine learning have notably enhanced the authenticity of deepfakes. Scenarios portrayed can so closely resemble real-life situations (Hameleers, 2024; Shin, 2024) that it is becoming increasingly difficult to distinguish deepfakes from reality or authentic content (Goh, 2024).

The rapid development of deepfakes has highlighted a series of problems (Hancock & Bailenson, 2021). How do people perceive and to what extent do people trust artificially generated content? Due to their nearly indistinguishable resemblance to reality, deepfakes are seen as a dangerous viral threat (Chesney & Citron, 2019) and a potent form of disinformation (Ahmed, 2021) with the potential to deceive (Vassist & Krishnan, 2022). The widespread use of deepfakes presents significant challenges in discerning real information from artificial information (Cover, 2022; Weikmann et al., 2024), which can have serious societal implications. The inability of people to distinguish between real and fake content seriously undermines trust online and in democracy (Fallis, 2021). This raises the question of how we can enhance users' ability to detect deepfakes to reduce the negative impact of misinformation. Understanding how humans can identify deepfakes is crucial, given the technology's easy manipulation and detrimental impacts (Ahmed, 2023). Users' heuristics and sense-making models based on the roles of cognitive processes when encountering deepfakes can be important clues for countering AI misinformation (Di Domenico & Visentin, 2020; Li & Wan, 2023). Along these lines,

DOI: 10.1201/9781003530244-9

numerous approaches for combating misinformation have been researched, examining how individuals experience and consume deepfakes (e.g., Bryanov et al., 2020; Groth et al., 2022; Shin, 2024). Among all attempts to understand misinformation, it is worthwhile to focus on the processes that users engage with more critically or cognitively in responding to deepfakes (Molina & Sundar, 2022). Although users' cognitive processing mechanisms when it comes to deepfakes are critical in understanding how deepfakes are perceived, they have remained under-researched due to the complicated nature of user interaction with deepfakes. This underlines the need for further investigation into users' cognitive heuristics for diagnosing deepfakes, the related processes for discerning deepfakes, and the ensuing effects of deepfake–hallucination behavior.

Specifically, we examine how people perceive and process deepfake visuals in the context of news consumption. Understanding how users handle deepfaked information could contribute to developing both theoretical frameworks and practical solutions for the various issues stemming from the dissemination of AI-generated content (Jin et al., 2023). Our objective is to elucidate the role of cognitive traits and psychological ability in relation to the nature and significance of cognitive heuristics in deepfake processing. Building on concepts from heuristic systematic (HS) processing, this study puts forward a model that elucidates the cognitive processing and subsequent discernment of deepfakes and their sharing. The following research questions (RQs) drive this study:

RQ1: How do individuals cognitively reason about deepfakes? What are the cognitive processes underlying the reception of deepfake content and their impact on users' diagnosticity?

RQ2: What heuristic factors contribute to the judgment of deepfakes, and how are these factors related to users' processing and discernment?

By addressing these topics, this study offers insights into understanding cognitive heuristics in relation to deepfakes, specifically how users assess the credibility of deepfakes and how these affect deepfake discernability, to address the effects of deepfake misinformation. The results of this study contribute to the literature on AI by elucidating the deepfake effects of AI hallucination and the procedural uncertainty of AI. These findings further our comprehension of the relationship between users and deepfakes, specifically the cognitive mechanisms involved in users' processing, attitudes, and behaviors as consequences of deepfakes, equipping us with the knowledge to combat misinformation-related issues.

THEORETICAL HYPOTHESES: HOW DO INDIVIDUALS PERCEIVE DEEPFAKE ATTRIBUTES?

The rise of deepfake content has raised important questions: Can humans identify algorithmic visual manipulations, and how do they cognitively discern such manipulations? These questions can be approached through the cognitive HS theory.

UNDERLYING COGNITIVE PROCESSES OF DEEPFAKE EVALUATION

Although deepfakes have been an ongoing problem of the modern AI era (Ahmed, 2023), fairly little research has examined the cognitive processing of deepfakes, particularly from users' cognitive perspectives, with most extant studies exclusively focused on finding a means to combat deepfakes. The nature of human decision-making and its process and matrix have not been clarified, as prior research has primarily focused on the one-dimensional or monolithic properties of the mental impact of misinformation on individual behavior (e.g., Kwon et al., 2020). The limited research on the cognitive processing of deepfakes could constrain the knowledge of how individuals interact with deepfakes (Ahmed, 2023), particularly in contexts where deepfakes present sensitive political and health information (Vaccari & Chadwick, 2020). To fill this research gap, the proposed model is designed to explore the HS processing of deepfake content. Theoretically, this study builds on the principles of dual information theory by combining the cognitive and heuristic effect perspectives to examine the decision-making processes of users encountering deepfakes. The hypotheses are designed to examine the sense-making of users when they are presented with deepfakes and the effects of such sense-making on their decision-making on deepfake discernment.

HEURISTIC PROCESSING

The information processing model proposed by Chaiken et al. (1996) suggests that users engage in one or both modes of information processing when making decisions. The model distinguishes between heuristic and systematic processing mechanisms. Individuals tend to process information in a peripheral (heuristic) or central (systematic) mode. For instance, individuals may use the bandwagon heuristic as a mental shortcut when assessing content quality. This heuristic is triggered by specific cues, such as user popularity metrics, requiring minimal effort (Molina & Sundar, 2022). Online users often rely on cue-based information to systematically evaluate products and information (Shin et al., 2024).

In assessing the impact of deepfakes on user intentions and credibility evaluations, two forms of user-generated information are pertinent: user ratings and written reviews (Jin et al., 2023). Depending on whether quantitative or qualitative indicators are relied upon, distinct bandwagon effects may arise. According to the HS model, these two types of user feedback are likely to operate through different cognitive mechanisms, with user ratings serving as easier-to-process cues that prompt heuristic processing and qualitative reviews necessitating more intricate systematic processing.

Recent research has shown that heuristic cues are flexibly used by individuals depending on the situation. For instance, individuals may rely on the expertise heuristic, where experts are usually seen as credible, when encountering either an easy-to-process cue, such as the communicator being a professor, or when evaluating a more cognitively demanding argument for service quality (Karpinska-Krakowiak & Eisend, 2024). In this study on deepfake evaluation, we hypothesize that a bandwagon effect, based on the idea that following the behavior of others is good, may be triggered when individuals rely on either heuristic or systematic processing for determining credibility.

Bandwagon Heuristics

People tend to adopt certain behaviors, styles, or attitudes simply because others have exhibited them (Lammers et al., 2022). This bandwagon tendency is more obvious when users watch deepfake content, which normally does not feature relevant or useful information that users can use. Users' bandwagon cognitive heuristics, which implies social endorsement, affect veracity judgments when consuming misinformation and online content in general (Banas et al., 2022). Jin et al. (2023) reported that individuals accept the dominant view of the public when they judge the veracity of deepfakes. Similarly, Dogruel and Xiaoming (2016) found that when people saw signs or metrics that showed high popularity (e.g., the statistics of likes, visits, retweets, and shares), there were increased perceptions of injunctive and descriptive norms in terms of the number of shared tweets, which in turn led to higher perceived credibility. Ali et al. (2022) similarly reported that the number of likes increased the perceived believability of fake news. In light of this literature, the bandwagon effect in this study is hypothesized as follows:

> H1: Perceived bandwagoning will influence the perceived verisimilitude of the AI visuals.

Source Heuristics

Along with bandwagon heuristics, source information has traditionally been considered the primary basis for evaluating credibility in communication literature (Jin et al., 2023). For instance, Sundar (2008) reported that perceived source attribution plays a significant role in users' acceptance and experience of technologies. Similarly, Li et al. (2018) presented consumers with labels certified by a government source and found that the consumers saw the label as more trustworthy than the corporate source, leading to a positive attitude toward the labeled product. Source information serves as an important cue in understanding online content, as there is obviously extensive AI-generated content. Explanatory cues found in source attributions can be useful in informing users' attitudes toward AI media and content (Li et al., 2019; Norambuena et al., 2023), among which the summary of user reviews is a metric gauging the credibility of information. Source information is crucial for people to assess the credibility of the information presented (Li & Wan, 2023). People may perceive online content as more trustworthy if they have credible source information (Shen et al., 2019). The content then continues to propagate as more individuals discover popular and widely followed sources. Based on the ongoing research, source heuristics can be hypothesized to influence users' perceptions of realism in deepfake encounters:

> H2: Perceived source attributions influence the perceived verisimilitude of the AI visuals.

Perceived Verisimilitude

Deepfakes have grown in sophisticated realism (i.e., facticity) (Weikmann et al., 2024) and verisimilitude (i.e., truthfulness) (Kaate et al., 2023). While realism is the physical appearance of reality, verisimilitude is the quality of likeness to truth or being true. People may see deepfakes as real and further see them in terms of being true. In general, users perceive online content as realistic if they judge it to reflect real life in some meaningful way (LaMarre & Landreville, 2009). In the context of deepfakes manipulated by AI, perceived verisimilitude concerns how users understand the information presented by deepfake content or AI and its likeness to truth (Karpinska-Krakowiak & Eisend, 2024). The verisimilitude of deepfakes is related to the quality and relevance of the cues provided. The extent of verisimilitude in deepfakes has increased, as technology is enabling the replication of human cognition and likeness in ever more genuine ways (Campbell & Reiman, 2022). Users who view deepfake visuals as real are more likely to recognize presented claims to be correct than those who view deepfakes that have been proven to be false (Ahmed, 2021). An individual's perception of the verisimilitude of events, remarks, or actions depicted in deepfakes could influence their beliefs about the content, thereby influencing their perceptions of the credibility and accuracy of the content (Karpinska-Krakowiak & Eisend, 2024). The realistic verisimilitudes of deepfakes provoke and guide the perceiver's perceptions, thoughts, inferences, heuristics, recognition, and persuasion (Pennycook et al., 2021). Thus, the verisimilitude hypotheses are proposed:

> H3: Perceived verisimilitude positively influences the perception of the credibility of AI visuals.
> H4: Perceived verisimilitude positively influences the perception of the accuracy of AI visuals.

SYSTEMATIC PROCESSES FOR DIAGNOSTICITY

The concept of "diagnosticity" was recently introduced to enhance the HS model of information processing in the context of misinformation (Chen & Cheng, 2020). Diagnosticity refers to the extent to which individuals perceive information as valuable and relevant based on their judgment and decision-making (Chen et al., 2024). Extensive research has consistently established diagnosticity as a fundamental driving force behind users' attitudes and behavioral decisions (Shin, 2024). In the context of AI, information perceived as highly diagnostic carries more weight in users' understanding and experience

(Chen & Cheng, 2020). Therefore, diagnosticity can influence how users systematically or heuristically process messages when using AI. Specifically, in the context of AI, diagnosticity can impact the extent to which users believe that information is true when evaluating AI-generated content. Once users recognize the diagnosticity of a system, they begin to decide whether to trust the system and systematically assess misinformation by evaluating the credibility and accuracy of the information (Kwon et al., 2020). When dealing with misinformation from AI-powered machines, the indicators of diagnosticity are closely linked to users' understanding of the credibility and accuracy of information, that is, the reliability and correctness of the suggested information. Building on these insights from previous research, Shin (2024) proposed a conceptual model that emphasizes users' heuristic processes and how the perceived diagnosticity of misinformation may influence users' intentions. This highlights the significance of users' perception of diagnosticity in combating misinformation (e.g., Chen & Cheng, 2020).

Accuracy and Diagnosticity

Relevant studies have consistently shown the impact of perceived verisimilitude on the evaluation of online messages (Goh, 2024). The extent to which a narrative is perceived to depict a specific individual or event from the real world (plausibility) describes the emotional engagement with a narrative that, in turn, contributes to the perception of realism and the overall assessment of the message/narrative and its potential effect (Miller et al., 2023). The individual's perception and cognitive ability to correctly identify the proposed message plays a critical role in online interaction (Ahmed & Chua, 2023). The perceived accuracy of deepfakes is related to participants' discernment of sharing intention (Shin & Ahmad, 2023). In the absence of clear cues, users might unknowingly share deceptive deepfakes if they believe them to be authentic. The credibility assessment of misinformation mediates the relationship between online engagement and the sharing of misinformation (Shin & Ahmad, 2023). Message evaluation (Araujo, 2019; Shin 2023) impacts the propensity to share content on social media due to the perceived verisimilitude (Cho et al., 2021) and authenticity of the communicative act (Shin 2023). Based on this research, the following hypothesis can be established:

> H5: The perceived accuracy of deepfakes has a positive influence on users' perception of diagnosticity.

Credibility and Diagnosticity

Perceived credibility refers to how people perceive the authenticity of information in deepfakes. While perceived credibility has been extensively researched in the general media context (Ahmed, 2021; Cho et al., 2014; Shin, 2024), there is limited research on how people assess the credibility of deepfakes. Several studies have consistently shown that users' perceived credibility significantly influences their intention to share content online (Shin, 2024). This relationship can be applied to deepfakes, as users tend to share content when they believe it to be true. Ahmed (2021) found that credible cues impact people's perceptions of authenticity, which affects their intention to share deepfakes. The study also found that individuals with higher cognitive abilities were better at identifying deception and that the addition of labels about the fake nature of the video helped prevent inadvertent sharing. Iacobucci et al. (2021) found that providing perceived credible information increased the recognition of a video's fakeness and deterred the intention to share it. Based on these ongoing findings, it is worthwhile to test this relationship in the context of deepfakes. As such, we established the following hypothesis:

H6: The perceived credibility of deepfakes influences users' perception of diagnosticity.

Explanatory Cues as a Moderator

Individuals evaluate the message within a deepfake, considering factors such as its accuracy, and use this information as a cue to judge the overall quality and originality of the information (Metzger, 2007). The use of semantic words is crucial in people's cognitive processes, as such words provide relevant information. In addition to the information itself, the process of explaining helps in understanding and predicting user behaviors, as well as making sense of the quality of messages. Previous research has indicated that the act of explaining has a greater impact than the actual content of the explanation (Li et al., 2019). Providing clear labels and using content-proofing tools such as digital fact-checkers for any modified materials can give users a basis for evaluating the quality of a message. The proposed model includes the moderating effects of explanatory cues (fact-checking) on users' capability to distinguish deepfakes from genuine video footage (Figure 6.1).

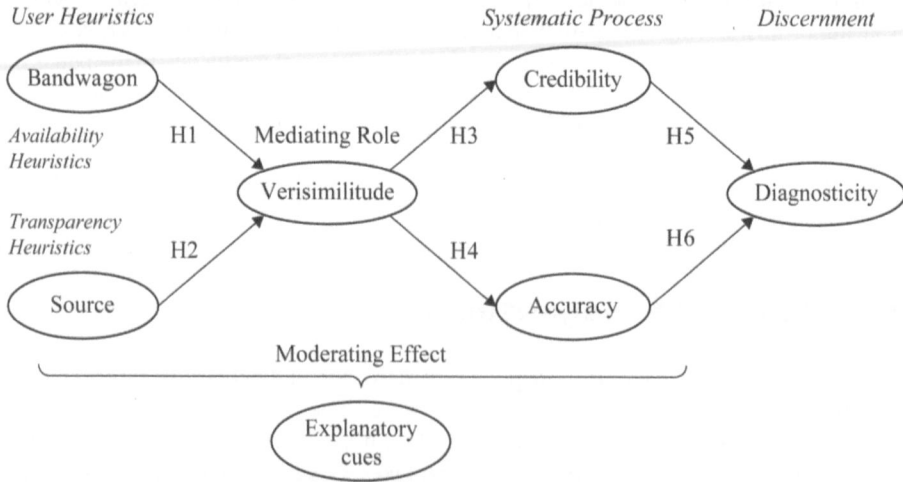

FIGURE 6.1   Users' cognitive processing of deepfakes.

METHODS

Materials and Manipulation

To investigate the cognitive processing of deepfakes and identify the factors influencing this process, we conducted an experiment that involved embedded authentic and deepfake visuals on political news. We acquired existing deepfakes of online news created by BuzzFeed Video (37 seconds). The two types of visuals (authentic vs. deepfake) were prepared for respondents. The original news in the edited videos was modified by adding heuristic cues for the experiment. These deepfakes were edited to have a high audiovisual quality, making the edited traces virtually undetectable. The augmented deepfakes featured explanatory cues, such as reference labeling, embedded metadata, digital fingerprints, and watermarked information, that helped users mitigate the concerning nature of AI production. The visuals in this experiment were framed in a Google visual framework to make them look like the search results, and users watched them in real contexts, such as in their everyday lives.

Within the framework, edited explanatory cues (e.g., the frequency of likes and the number of user views) were included. Two experiments were prepared. For Group 1, we made explanatory versions of CNN's deepfakes with transparency cues on the visuals, such as time history, creator information, source rating, and fact-checking results. The number of followers was designed to be single-digit (8) for the low bandwagon effect and 796,000 for the high bandwagon effect. The bandwagon effect was simulated by the number of likes and views (low = 19 likes and 392 views, high = 29,428 likes and 839,392 views). The source effect was simulated by the information on the number of likes and viewers' endorsements. Conversely, Experiment 2 was carried out with opposite cues (low followers and low likes) to test the effects of bandwagon heuristics and popularity heuristics.

Participants

A total of 597 respondents from the United States participated in the study, of whom 298 were women (49.1%), 301 were men (50.9%), and 11 did not identify or identify as a third gender (2.0%). Their mean age was 45.0 ($SD = 13.0$; $Range_{Age} =$ 19–59 years old). Half of the respondents (200) watched the experimental visual (high popularity, clear source attributions, and objective explanatory cues). The rest of the respondents (200) watched the controlled visual (low popularity, unclear source attributions, and without explanatory cues). All the respondents who were recruited completed the survey. Any surveys that were not fully complete were dropped.

Measures

Perceived Verisimilitude

We used an adapted version of the perceived verisimilitude scale from Campbell et al. (2022), taking one item from each dimension of verisimilitude: factuality, plausibility, perceptual quality, and narrative consistency. A four-factor correlated model was tested with adequate goodness-of-fit (GoF) (χ^2 [df] = 10420.88 [91], $p < .001$, $CFI = .96$, $TLI = .97$, $RMSEA$ [90%CI] = .06 [.06, .07]). Internal consistency reliability estimates were adequate for the four subscales ($\omega_{plausability} = .78$, $\omega_{factuality} = .85$, $\omega_{consistency} = .93$, $\omega_{quality} = .91$).

Perceived Accuracy

We used Ahmed and Chua's (2023) three-item scale of perceptual accuracy. The model in this sample had excellent GoF (χ^2 [df] = 4987.78 [10], $p < .001$, $TLI = 1.00$, $CFI = 1.00$, $RMSEA$ [90%CI] = .06 [.04, .08]), and we obtained good internal consistency and reliability ($\omega = .95$).

Perceived Credibility

We used three adapted items following Jin et al. (2023) to measure the users' perceptions of the credibility of the deepfake content. The credibility scales had adequate GoF (χ^2 [df] = 834.67 [6], $p < .001$, $TLI = .96$, $CFI = .98$, $RMSEA$ [90%CI] = .08 [.05, .12]), and internal consistency reliability was .74 ($\omega = .74$). Internal consistency reliability was under the desired threshold ($\omega = .53$).

Perceived Diagnosticity

We used Chen and Cheng's (2020) three-item scale of perceptual diagnosticity. The model in this sample had good GoF (χ^2 [df] = 4987.78 (10), $p < .001$, $CFI = 1.00$, $TLI = 1.00$, $RMSEA$ [90%CI] = .05 [.03, .08]), and we obtained good internal consistency and reliability ($\omega = .91$).

Procedure

Each respondent viewed one deepfake of each condition (299 for the experimental group and 298 for the control group). The videos were shown in a randomly assigned order. Immediately after viewing each video, the respondents completed the questionnaire on the study variables. Data were collected through Qualtrics. Participants were volunteers and were reimbursed $3.00 USD.

Data Analysis

Two-group analysis using structural equation modeling (SEM) was performed as a function of the cues used by users in the analysis of the deepfakes. Specifically, we compared the behaviors in an explanatory cue setting and those in other settings. For the SEM, we used the factor scores of variables and specified the single-item measure of intention to share as a latent variable. We assessed GoF following Hu and Bentler (1998). To evaluate measurement invariance between the experimental conditions, we first fixed the factor loadings between the two groups and then fixed the intercepts.

RESULTS

The HS Process of Deepfake Information Processing

The SEM results confirmed the structural validity of the hypotheses, which had a good fit with the hypothesized model (Figure 6.2). The path coefficients for each hypothesis were statistically significant ($p < .001$ or $p < .0001$; Table 6.1). The perceived verisimilitude was significantly influenced by heuristic factors ($\beta = .14, p < .05$) and subsequently influenced the systematic processing of deepfakes ($\beta = .17, p < .05$). Both perceived bandwagon and perceived source significantly influence the perceived verisimilitude of information. Together, these heuristic evaluations accounted for 49.2% of the variance in verisimilitude. The diagnosticity was significantly affected by the systematic processing of deepfakes, with systematic factors explaining 20.1% of the variance in diagnosticity. The model showed a significant portion of the variance in each factor. Furthermore, the significant paths indicated a causal relationship between the heuristic and systematic processes moderated by verisimilitude.

Multigroup Comparison

A multigroup analysis was performed to assess the invariance of latent constructs from the model to the control and experimental groups. The structural invariance test was

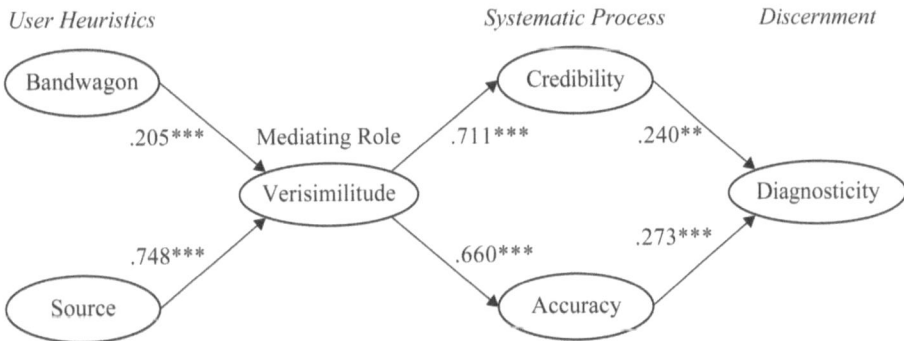

FIGURE 6.2   Users' cognitive processing of deepfakes.

TABLE 6.1   Testing results

PATHS	ESTIMATE	STANDARD ERROR	CRITICAL RATIO	P VALUE
H1: Bandwagon → Verisimilitude	.205	.032	5.745	***
H2: Source → Verisimilitude	.748	.051	15.35	***
H3: Verisimilitude → Credibility	.711	.050	8.913	***
H4: Verisimilitude → Accuracy	.660	.046	13.57	***
H5: Credibility → Diagnosticity	.249	.087	3.002	**
H6: Accuracy → Diagnosticity	.273	.054	4.017	***

**1.96: 95.9% (.05).
***3.29: 99.9% (.001).

performed for the control and experimental groups with explanatory cues. The model in which factor loading values were controlled and other parameters were analyzed across the two groups was estimated as the baseline model; it demonstrated a good fit ($\chi^2 = 785.71$, df $= 129$, $p < .001$, TLI $= .861$, GFI $= .890$, AGFI $= .842$, CFI $= .883$, RMSEA $= .067$). Next, a fully constrained model was tested in which all the structural path coefficients were controlled. The comparison results between the fully constrained model and the baseline model ($\Delta\chi^2 = 23.21$, Δdf $= 5$, $p < .001$) indicated significant differences in certain structural path coefficients across the groups. Then, the critical ratio test was conducted to assess the origin of the structural invariance, and the pairwise parameter values were compared. A critical ratio value smaller than -1.96 or greater than $+1.96$ reflected variances across groups at the .05 significance level. Five path coefficients (H1, H2, H3, H4, and H6) varied significantly between the control and experimental respondents (Figure 6.3). The experimental respondents who viewed the explanatory cues and had more positive realism showed higher levels of systematic processing ($\beta = .39$, $p < .001$) and diagnosticity ($\beta = .26$, $p < .001$), whereas the control respondents' heuristics and

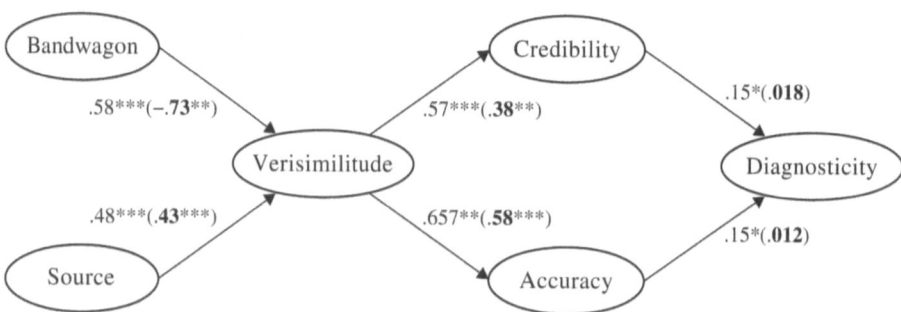

FIGURE 6.3   Results of the compared models. *p < .05, **p < .01, ***p < .001; _ for the control group is in bold; solid paths show that the structural coef_cients differ between the groups.

perceived verisimilitude showed insignificant effects on their level of diagnosticity they engaged in ($\beta = -.20$, $p = .029$).

Both groups had good fits with the data and also showed distinctive structures that implied different cognitive processes between the groups. The results revealed significant differences in item path formation and composition, shedding light on the effects of heuristic cues on deepfake judgment. The effects of verisimilitude on accuracy and credibility were more significant in the experimental group than in the control group. In comparing the two groups, the experimental group showed higher values for systematic processes, and the control group showed higher values for heuristic processes. Thus, it can be inferred that initial heuristic cues played a facilitating role in the systematic evaluations of decision-making processes and that their effects were greater in the systematic evaluations than in the heuristic evaluations. The results of the squared multiple correlations also support the underlying role of explainability. The R^2 values for credibility and accuracy in the control group were greater than those in the experimental group. Furthermore, the R^2 value of intention in the experimental group was noticeably higher than that in the control group.

The results of the two comparisons showed that heuristic cues had a positive influence on verisimilitude, credibility, and accuracy. Users' heuristics based on the cues had a significant positive role in systematic processes. The results imply that the users tended to exhibit more believability and confidence when they perceived higher realism, which triggered more effortful evaluations of credibility and accuracy when they held positive perceptions of the cues. This finding echoes prior findings (e.g., Ahmed, 2023; Ali et al., 2022; Jin et al., 2023; Kaate et al., 2023) that people showed a significant increase in heuristic and systematic processes through the interventions of transparency cues, which led to an improvement in their ability to discern AI. While prior findings have shown the significant effects of perception of available cues on users' heuristic cognition (Molina & Sundar, 2022), the present study advances knowledge on the effects of heuristic influence of explainable cues on the verisimilitude and discernability of deepfakes.

DISCUSSION

AI-Generated Deepfakes and Human-Generated Heuristics

As discussed by the cognitive heuristics literature (e.g., Sundar, 2008, 1998), using effective heuristics can help users engage in cognitive processes and lead to the correct diagnosis of deepfakes. This study aimed to understand how users cognitively appraise deepfakes and systematically evaluate their discernability. The results of the study revealed that the users' HS processing significantly influenced their perceptions and attitudes. Users' experiences with deepfakes were heuristically invoked and systematically driven: users appraised deepfake information with available heuristics and systematic information to assess diagnostic judgment. The findings from this study show the impact of heuristic cues and algorithmic features on users' diagnostic assessments, providing insight into how users process information in and about deepfake content. We found that the more users used heuristic cues in detecting and evaluating information, the more likely they were to determine the credibility and accuracy of information. Moreover, the more likely users perceived that the information was systematically reliable (credible or accurate), the more likely they were to accept it. Heuristic cues significantly influenced users' perceptions of credibility and the subsequent diagnosticity of that information. Moreover, the explanatory cues provided alongside the information affected how believable and trustworthy the information seemed. The high-level mental processing was influenced by how informative the information seemed, and this was also affected by how easy it was to understand the explanations provided by the AI system. Overall, how transparent and understandable the information was played a significant role in how users were influenced by misinformation and how they behaved as a result.

Theoretical Implications: AI Heuristic Effects on Deepfake Discernability

This study examined how heuristic cues affected deepfake discernability and associated decision-making. It extended HS theory by applying it to the context of deepfakes generated by AI and examining the cognitive process of judging deepfakes. The findings illustrate how HS theory can inform the understanding of deepfake acceptance and provide insights into ways to debias AI algorithms, thereby ensuring the equitable use of AI. The findings contribute relevant theoretical implications for understanding the effects of heuristics on the judgment of deepfakes (Goh, 2024).

First, although the HS theory has been extensively researched and applied, the present study elaborated on the duality of information processing when users view deepfake content. Specifically, we simulated a circumstance where users processed deepfakes heuristically, and such heuristics triggered an introductory notion of realistic verisimilitude, which then facilitated effortful systematic understanding. We found that users relied on popularity and source credibility as heuristics in viewing deepfakes. While this finding is consonant with previous studies (e.g., Ahmed, 2023), we further clarified the relationship between these heuristics and a cognitive mediator. Verisimilitude serves as a motivator or facilitator of heuristic processes and links them to systematic processes. Heuristic cues on popularity and source play a key role in bringing heuristics into the evaluation process, and verisimilitude serves as a catalyst for the further evaluation of deepfakes in terms of systematic evaluation.

Second, the findings show how HS theory can inform the evaluation of AI visuals and illustrate ways to debias AI algorithms, thereby promoting the discernable use of deepfakes. Specifically, we identified a set of heuristics that emerged during the consumption of deepfake visuals. The realism heuristic (e.g., Miller et al., 2023; Sundar, 2008) is linked to the idea that users are more likely to accept realistic videos since their visuals have a high similitude to the real world. This realism is triggered by audiovisual resemblance, but it is further enhanced by the user heuristics (bandwagon and source) and affects users' notion of verisimilitude. Popularity and bandwagon heuristics occur because users want to know the reliability and source attribution of AI, and realism heuristics occur as a motivation to further investigate AI systematically. How these heuristics are related is an important cue in understanding user cognition and decision-making. The elucidation of this relationship can be a theoretical advancement, as there remains a gap in understanding how these processes are related. By identifying the role of realism heuristics, this study linked heuristics to systematic processing in the deepfake context. The dual process of cognitive assessment, along with the mediating role of realism, can fill the gap in research on user behaviors related to deepfakes that previous research had attempted to address (e.g., Goh, 2024; Kim et al., 2021; Molina & Sundar, 2022).

Third, the findings clarified the role of diagnosticity in AI discernment. We applied the concept of perceived diagnosticity to the deepfake content and showed that diagnosticity is a critical construct in discerning the misinformation in deep-fakes (e.g., Chen et al., 2024) and further corroborated that HS processing of deep-fakes concurrently influences the intention of users to process misinformation via dual paths (e.g., Shin, 2024). Previous research has primarily focused on the unidi-rectional influence of deepfakes from a functional perspective, exploring such topics as deepfake traits, with little research holistically examining the cognitive process-ing of deepfakes. Our study advances ongoing research by illuminating how heuristic and functional dimensions can increase users' diagnostic appraisal and how users evaluate the accuracy and credibility of deepfakes. Our approach revealed relevant factors in the cognitive–psychological processes and enriches the understanding of the relationship between how deepfakes inform users' attitudes and how their attitudes toward the information and sources of AI-generated deepfakes influence the diagnosticity of misinformation; this coevolving relationship was mediated and facilitated by users' HS processing. While the literature has focused on conceptu-alizing the existence of realism in the context of AI (e.g., Goh, 2024; Kaate et al., 2023), we offer hypothetical and empirical evidence of the underlying relationship between realism, diagnosticity, and algorithmic attributes: when a visual is generated by algorithms in realistic, credible, and trustable ways, users perceive it with a high level of diagnosticity, which invokes their motivation to systematically appraise the message within.

Lastly, the model addressed the conceptual difference between realism and verisi-militude by clarifying the mediating roles of realism in the HS processing of AI. The verisimilitude in AI is the semblance of reality (relates truth) in information, while realism involves what is actually real. AI presents seemingly real information to users and users evaluate messages' verisimilitude through how other people see the mes-sages and these cues help users assess the truthfulness of messages. The mediating role of verisimilitude in influencing heuristic evaluations and the systematic cognitive pro-cess is noteworthy. The mediating effect clarifies and demonstrates why AI visuals are considered to be more authentic than real human visuals (Miller et al., 2023). People's perceptions of realism are enhanced by relevant heuristics, such as popularity cues and source metrics. Enhanced realism conveys high verisimilitude, which acts as a cognitive trigger for switching from heuristic to systematic processing, working as a conduit that channels evaluation efforts from heuristic factors into systematic processes. Previous discussions of HS theory have assumed discrete processes of separate mechanisms in which disconnected processes have little to do with each other or with interactional relations (e.g., Chaiken et al., 1996). In the context of AI-generated deepfakes, realism is associated with important functions that play a key role in the following two ways: (1) due to the uncertain source credibility of information, users evaluate the attributes of deepfakes intuitively and heuristically, and (2) given the harmful effects of deepfakes, users appraise the generated information holistically and systematically. The mediating role of verisimilitude revealed that the more assured users were about the systems being popular and verified by others, the more likely they were to technologically diagnose the information. These results are consistent with earlier research (e.g., Ali et al., 2022; Miller et al., 2023) suggesting that users' perceptions of realism are formed by user-generated cues, and this realism affects the conducting of systematic evaluations, which leads to materialized algorithmic attributes. The results further indicated that when AI users had a sufficient level of understanding of accuracy and credibility, they could react to the deepfakes consciously and with a higher, more effortful systematic process, becoming more confident and capable of diagnosing misinformation.

Overall, the findings from the model highlight the new role of heuristics in deepfake information processing: users seek available heuristic cues, and those who seek available cues are likely to further look for systematically generated cues for their heuristic understanding. This means that heuristics are not only an initial route of evaluation but also an antecedent for conscious efforts to reach a systematic understanding of AI content. Heuristics in deepfakes can result from cues and from their function as an activator in conducting systematic processing. This argument serves as a useful theoretical advancement because it elucidates the processing capacity of users through heuristics. The heuristic principle in deepfakes may refer to users' heuristics in probing the salience of algorithmic features using available cues and optimal inferences. Users' heuristics are context-oriented and can acquire significant diagnostic value if the diagnostic object is extended to include a systematic matrix.

Practical Implications: Design of Intervention Strategies for Deepfakes

The findings offer a practical understanding of deepfakes for stakeholders across the AI industry and the broader AI community, specifying how AI models can better address integrity issues across their platforms. The results offer useful, practical guidelines for AI to improve users' diagnostics, to counter deepfakes, and to reveal how information processing influences users' heuristic and procedural knowledge of deepfakes. Our findings regarding cognitive heuristics have practical implications for decision-making processes in the AI fields. Since cognitive heuristics are rooted in human nature, AI developers will need to consider them in their design and development. These heuristics can be used effectively to diagnose deepfakes. For example, cognitive heuristics can be used to nurture the digital efficacy and literacy of users. Realism may depend on the quality of realistic audiovisual elements, but user-perceived realism is affected by available heuristics and relevant cues that users use in their decision-making. Users' perceptions of verisimilitude are a processed form of user heuristics that influences users' notions of diagnosticity. Deepfake diagnosticity could rely on the AI system's technological features, as well as contextual and perceptual factors. Users' perceptions of diagnosticity may depend heavily on their interpretation of the AI's attributes. Therefore, attention should be given to improving the technical features and competence of systems for both diagnosticity and accuracy, and practitioners should present the credibility of AI to enhance the literacy of users encountering deepfakes.

LIMITATIONS AND FUTURE RESEARCH

Deepfakes have become a complicated issue due to the advancement of generative AI and the growth of the digital media landscape. We laid the groundwork for understanding human decision-making when it comes to deepfakes and presented a user-driven approach to user deepfake analysis and characterization. This study has shortcomings that should be considered.

First, to make our study more focused, we deliberately limited the scope of the HS model, leaving out important components such as processing characteristics, conditions of heuristic use, and motivational assumptions. The motivation to carefully process AI-generated information can be influenced by contextual factors and time-related considerations. For instance, users may need to balance their desire for quick information with the need for accuracy. Due to the exclusion of this factor from our study, the applicability of the HS model was constrained.

Second, the study was conducted during the inception of deepfakes. It is likely that the technology will develop and continue to change as it advances. Many generative AIs are in the early stages of development, and many more variations and possibilities will come. Although the affordances examined in this study included only those with which we are currently familiar, AI's potential growth will go beyond what is currently possible. Research on deepfakes must be advanced to keep up with the challenges and risks, including those related to both technological and user-related affordances, before they achieve widespread adoption.

Third, as this study primarily focused on a deepfake cognitive model within a single-user psychological schema, it neglected the algorithmic side of deepfake processing. Future research can consider the deepfake features of information processing when using the model to more comprehensively test it. Further comparisons and investigations can be worthwhile to consider. For example, researchers might determine how and to what extent the different dimensions in the deepfake processing model are shaped by the HS processing of users and how they affect the overall discernable efficacy of deepfakes and the subsequent behaviors of users in turn.

Our results indicate a connection between accuracy, usefulness, and trustworthiness, suggesting a link between false information, knowledge, and confidence. It would be valuable to explore how this connection relates to other cognitive and contextual factors. Future research could investigate the connections among realistic computer-generated content, trustworthiness, and usefulness to better understand what influences users' cognitive abilities when they encounter deepfakes. The limitations of this study highlight the need for a stronger theoretical and empirical approach to understanding the underlying processes of behaviors surrounding = deepfakes in different situations.

REFERENCES

Ahmed, S. (2021). Fooled by the fakes: Cognitive differences in perceived claim accuracy and sharing intention of non-political deepfakes. *Personality and Individual Differences, 182,* 111074. https://doi.org/10.1016/j.paid.2021.111074

Ahmed, S. (2023). Navigating the maze: Deepfakes, cognitive ability, and social media news skepticism. *New Media & Society, 25*(5), 1108–11129. https://doi.org/10.1177/14614448211019198

Ahmed, S., & Chua, H. (2023). Perception and deception: Exploring individual responses to deepfakes across different modalities. *Heliyon, 9,* 220383. https://doi.org/10.1016/j.heliyon.2023.e20383

Ali, K., Li, C., Zain-ul-abdin, K., & Zaffar, M. A. (2022). Fake news on Facebook: Examining the impact of heuristic cues on perceived credibility and sharing intention. *Internet Research, 32*(1), 379–397.

Araujo, T. (2019) The Impact of Sharing Brand Messages: How Message, Sender and Receiver Characteristics Influence Brand Attitudes and Information Diffusion on Social Networking Sites. *Communications, 44*(2), 162–184. https://doi.org/10.1515/commun-2018-2004

Banas, J., Palomares, N., Richards, A., Keating, D., Joyce, N., & Rains, S. (2022). When machine and bandwagon heuristics compete: Understanding users' response to conflicting AI and crowdsourced fact-checking. *Human Communication Research, 48*(3), 430–461. https://doi.org/10.1093/hcr/hqac010

Bryanov, K., Watson, B. K., Pingree, R. J., & Santia, M. (2020). Effects of partisan personalization in a news portal experiment. *Public Opinion Quarterly, 84*(S1), 216–235. https://doi.org/10.1093/poq/nfaa011

Campbell, C., Plangger, K., Sands, S., & Kietzmann, J. (2022). Preparing for an era of deepfakes and AI-generated ads: A framework for understanding responses to manipulated advertising. *Journal of Advertising, 51*(1), 22–38. https://doi.org/10.1080/00913367.2021.1909515

Campbell, D., & Reiman, A. (2022). Has social psychology lost touch with reality? *Journal of Experimental Social Psychology, 98,* 104255. https://doi.org/10.1016/j.jesp.2021.104255

Chaiken, S., Giner-Sorolla, R., & Chen, S. (1996). Beyond accuracy: Defense and impression motives in heuristic and systematic information processing. In P. M. Gollwitzer & J. A. Bargh (Eds.), *The psychology of action: Linking cognition and motivation to behavior* (pp. 553–578). Guilford Press.

Chen, K., Tsai, C., Hu, Y., & Hu, C. (2024). The effect of review visibility and diagnosticity on review helpfulness. *Decision Support Systems, 178,* 114145. https://doi.org/10.1016/j.dss.2023.114145

Chen, Z. F., & Cheng, Y. (2020). Consumer response to fake news about brands on social media. *Journal of Product & Brand Management, 29*(2), 188–198. https://doi.org/10.1108/JPBM-12-2018-2145

Chesney, R., & Citron, D. (2019). Deepfakes and the new disinformation war: The coming age of post-truth geopolitics. *Foreign Affairs, 98*(1), 147–155.

Cho, H., Shen, L., & Peng, L. (2021). Examining and extending the influence of presumed influence hypothesis in social media. *Media Psychology, 24*(3), 413–435. https://doi.org/10.1080/15213269.2020.1729812

Cho, H., Shen, L., & Wilson, K. (2014). Perceived realism: Dimensions and roles in narrative persuasion. *Communication Research, 41*(6), 828–851. https://doi.org/10.1177/0093650212450585

Cover, R. (2022). Deepfake culture: The emergence of audio-video deception as an object of social anxiety and regulation. *Continuum, 36*(4), 609–621. https://doi.org/10.1080/10304312.2022.2084039

Di Domenico, G., & Visentin, M. (2020). Fake news or true lies? Reflections about problematic contents in marketing. *International Journal of Market Research, 62*(4), 409–417. https://doi.org/10.1177/1470785320934719

Dogruel, L., & Xiaoming, H. (2016). Movie selection and E-WOM preference. *International Journal of Communication, 10*, 21. https://ijoc.org/index.php/ijoc/article/view/5221/1687

Fallis, D. (2021). The epistemic threat of deepfakes. *Philosophy & Technology, 34*(4), 623–643. https://doi.org/10.1007/s13347-020-00419-2

Goh, D. (2024). He looks very real: Media, knowledge, and search-based strategies for deepfake identification. *Journal of the Association of Information Science and Technology.* https://doi.org/10.1002/asi.24867

Groth, M., Epstein, Z., Firestone, C., & Picard, R. (2022). Deepfake detection by human crowds, machines, and machine-informed crowds. *Psychological and Cognitive Sciences, 119*(1), e2110013119. https://doi.org/10.1073/pnas.2110013119

Hameleers, M. (2024). Cheap versus deep manipulation: The effects of cheapfakes versus deepfakes in a political setting. *International Journal of Public Opinion Research, 36*(1), edae004. https://doi.org/10.1093/ijpor/edae004

Hancock, J. T., & Bailenson, J. N. (2021). The social impact of deepfakes. *Cyberpsychology, Behavior, & Social Networking, 24*(3), 149–152. https://doi.org/10.1089/cyber.2021.29208.jth

Iacobucci, S., De Cicco, R., Michetti, F., Palumbo, R., & Pagliaro, S. (2021). Deepfakes unmasked: The effects of information priming and bullshit receptivity on deepfake recognition and sharing intention. *Cyberpsychology, Behavior, & Social Networking, 24*(3), 194–202. https://doi.org/10.1089/cyber.2020.0149

Jin, X., Zhang, Z., Gao, B., Gao, S., Zhou, W., Yu, N., & Wang, G. (2023). Assessing the perceived credibility of deepfakes: The impact of system-generated cues and video characteristics. *New Media & Society.* https://doi.org/10.1177/14614448231199664

Kaate, I., Salminen, J., Santos, J., Jung, S., Olkkonen, R., & Jansen, B. (2023). The realness of fakes: Primary evidence of the effect of deepfake personas on user perceptions in a design task. *International Journal of Human-Computer Studies, 178*, 103096. https://doi.org/10.1016/j.ijhcs.2023.103096

Karpinska-Krakowiak, M., & Eisend, M. (2024). Realistic portrayals of untrue information: The effects of deepfaked ads and different types of disclosures. *Journal of Advertising.* https://doi.org/10.1080/00913367.2024.2306415

Kim, J., Merrill, K., & Collins, C. (2021). AI as a friend or assistant: The mediating role of perceived usefulness in social AI vs. functional AI. *Telematics and Informatics, 64*, 101694. https://doi.org/10.1016/j.tele.2021.101694

Kwon, Y., Park, J., & Son, J. (2020). Accurately or accidentally? Recommendation agent and search experience in over-the-top services. *Internet Research, 31*(2), 562–586. https://doi.org/10.1108/INTR-03-2020-0127

LaMarre, H. L., & Landreville, K. D. (2009). When is fiction as good as fact? Comparing the influence of documentary and historical reenactment films on engagement, affect, issue interest, and learning. *Mass Communication and Society, 12*(4), 537–555. https://doi.org/10.1080/15205430903237915

Lammers, J., Bukowski, M., Potoczek, A., Fleischmann, A., & Hofmann, W. (2022). Disentangling the factors behind shifting voting intentions: The bandwagon effect reflects heuristic processing, while the underdog effect reflects fairness concerns. *Journal of Social and Political Psychology, 10*(2), 676–692. https://doi.org/10.5964/jspp.9241

Li, H., Wang, C., Meng, F., & Zhang, Z. (2019). Making restaurant reviews useful and/or enjoyable? The impacts of temporal, explanatory, and sensory cues. *International Journal of Hospitality Management, 83*, 257–265. https://doi.org/10.1016/j.ijhm.2018.11.002

Li, M., & Wan, Y. (2023). Norms or fun? The influence of ethical concerns and perceived enjoyment on the regulation of deepfake information. *Internet Research*. https://doi.org/10.1108/INTR-07-2022-0561

Li, N., Brossard, D., Scheufele, D. A., Wilson, P. H., & Rose, K. M. (2018). Communicating data: Interactive infographics, scientific data and credibility. *Journal of Science Communication, 17*(2). https://doi.org/10.22323/2.17020206

Metzger, M. (2007). Making sense of credibility on the Web: Models for evaluating online information and recommendations for future research. *Journal of the American Society for Information Science and Technology, 58*(13), 2078–2091.

Miller, E., Steward, B., Witkower, Z., Sutherland, C., Krumhuber, E., & Dawel, A. (2023). AI hyperrealism: Why AI faces are perceived as more real than human ones. *Psychological Science, 34*(12), 1390–1403. https://doi.org/10.1177/09567976231207095

Molina, M., & Shyam, S. (2022). When AI moderates online content: Effects of human collaboration and interactive transparency on user trust. *Journal of Computer-Mediated Communication, 27*(4), zmac010. https://doi.org/10.1093/jcmc/zmac010

Norambuena, B., Farina, K., Horning, M., & Mitra, T. (2023). Watching the watchdogs: Using transparency cues to help news audiences assess information quality. *Media and Communication, 11*(4). https://doi.org/10.17645/mac.v11i4.7018

Pennycook, G., Epstein, Z., Mosleh, M., Arechar, A. A., Eckles, D., & Rand, D. G. (2021). Shifting attention to accuracy can reduce misinformation online. *Nature, 592*(7855), 590–595.

Shen, C., Kasra, M., Pan, W., Bassett, G. A., Malloch, Y., & O'Brien, J. F. (2019). Fake images: The effects of source, intermediary, and digital media literacy on contextual assessment of image credibility online. *New Media & Society, 21*(2), 438–463. https://doi.org/10.1177/1461444818799526

Shin, D. (2023). Embodying algorithms, enactive AI, and the extended cognition: You can see as much as you know about algorithm. *Journal of Information Science, 49*(1), 18–31. http://doi:10.1177/0165551520985495

Shin, D. (2024). *Artificial misinformation: Exploring human-algorithm interaction online.* Springer. https://doi.org/10.1007/978-3-031-52569-8

Shin, D., & Ahmad, N. (2023). Algorithmic nudge: An approach to designing human-centered generative artificial intelligence. *Computer, 56*(8), 95–99. http://doi:10.1109/MC.2023.3278156

Shin, D., Koerber, A., & Lim, J. (2024). Impact of misinformation from generative AI on user information processing: How people understand misinformation from generative AI. *New Media & Society*. https://doi.org/10.1177/14614448241234040

Sundar, S. S. (1998). Effect of source attribution on perception of online news stories. *Journalism & Mass Communication Quarterly, 75*(1), 55–68. https://doi.org/10.1177/107769909807500108

Sundar, S. S. (2008). The MAIN model: A heuristic approach to understanding technology effects on credibility. In M. J. Metzger & A. J. Flanagin (Eds.), *Digital media, youth, and credibility* (pp. 73–100). The John D. and Catherine T. MacArthur Foundation Series on Digital Media and Learning. The MIT Press. http://doi:10.1162/dmal.9780262562324.073

Vaccari, C., & Chadwick, A. (2020). Deepfakes and disinformation: Exploring the impact of synthetic political video on deception, uncertainty, and trust in news. *Social Media+ Society*, *6*(1), 2056305120903408. https://doi.org/10.1177/2056305120903408

Vasist, P. N., & Krishnan, S. (2022). Deepfakes: An integrative review of the literature and an agenda for future research. *Communications of the Association for Information Systems*, *51*(1), 14.

Wahl-Jorgensen, K., & Carlson, M. (2021). Conjecturing fearful futures: Journalistic discourses on deepfakes. *Journalism Practice*, *15*(6), 803–820. https://doi.org/10.1080/17512786.2021.1908838

Weikmann, T., Greber, H., & Nikolaou, A. (2024). After deception: How falling for a deepfake affects the way we see, hear, and experience media. *The International Journal of Press/Politics*. https://doi.org/10.1177/19401612241233539

PART THREE

Epistemology of
AI Ethics

*Mechanism of
Understanding AI Ethics*

PART THREE

Algorithmic Equity
How Humans Understand AI Morality

7

HOW PEOPLE MAKE SENSE OF ALGORITHMIC EQUITY

Generative artificial intelligence (AI) (GAI) is increasingly affecting the everyday lives of millions of people (Schlagwein & Willcocks, 2023). Algorithms are popular and influential in practice, but their popularity has been built on limited transparency, systematic discrimination, and ambiguous accountability (Wu et al., 2024). While GAI offers useful and pertinent content presented in innovative and interactive formats, ethical concerns about GAI have arisen as a result of the way the technology has been and is developed (Koerber et al., 2024). Challenges regarding how to safeguard the values, goals, and personalization processes of GAI; how and to what extent personal information about users is shared with algorithms; and how to balance ethics and innovation in AI remain unaddressed (Schoenherr, 2022). Underlying these issues are imperatives on how to address discrimination and mitigate bias in data, as well as how to ensure the responsible development of GAI technologies (Klenk, 2024). As ethical concerns have hit an all-time high and deeply embedded themselves in the public's consciousness recently with the breakthrough of generative techniques, the opacity of black-box algorithm operations has led to calls for research on algorithmic equity (AE) (Osoba et al., 2019; Yarger et al., 2020). Therefore, understanding the transformative effects of GAI and the awareness of its associated risks has become an urgent matter. These critical issues will become even more relevant as people become increasingly reliant on GAI and as its algorithms advance drastically. The key question, therefore, is how to manage these emerging algorithms ethically and legitimately while ensuring that they are ethically sound and socially desirable.

Despite the importance of GAI ethics, research have examined the ethical issues of algorithms in GAI contexts. The rapid innovation cycles in AI development and the abundance of related normative research in ethics, alignment, and safety make it difficult to keep track of their work. This imbalance highlights the need for a more

DOI: 10.1201/9781003530244-11

robust discussion on what it means for an algorithm to be equitable or ethical. Previous research has engaged in extensive assessments of AI ethics in general (e.g., Freiman, 2022), but we still do not know how people "make sense" of the equity related to AI activities impacting people's decisions. How people make sense of AI ethics in their use of machine learning, how users construe algorithmic fairness, and how they identify generative-based processes will be critical issues to consider as GAI becomes even more prominent and pervasive in people's everyday lives (Koerber et al., 2024). These normative concerns have given rise to calls for a better morality framework that squarely explains AI ethics (Coeckelbergh, 2020). Therefore, we examine these concerns from an ethical sensemaking process (Schoenherr, 2022). Specifically, we assess how people understand the ethical issues of GAI and how this understanding of ethics influences users' decision-making behaviors, with a focus on how people formulate decisions to trust GAI following ethical evaluations. As such, we combine the sensemaking model (Weick, 2001) with ethical decision-making models (Kumar, 2016) to explore the ethical sensemaking exercised by users when confronted with ethical choices in AI. We examine academic researchers' sensemaking of algorithms influencing their work in the empirical context of information search and scholarly research. Professional researchers' understanding may be based on industrial standards or ethical values, creating tension between uniform norms deemed to conform with normative requirements and those that potentially diverge from user expectations. Nevertheless, little is known about how users' ethical values have been conceptualized and how users perceive AI ethics. To address this gap, this study investigates the algorithmic factors and mechanisms that influence the sensemaking of AI equity in the higher education sector, specifically how GAI users (researchers) engage in the sensemaking of ethical values underpinning a GAI system. In leveraging the frame of sensemaking, we focus on how users' roles in algorithmic practices influence their judgments to adopt a GAI service in particular ways, with differing acceptance outcomes based on their own assessments. Our primary goal is to contribute to the development and implementation of GAI systems that are fair, transparent, and ethically responsible. Thus, we seek to understand algorithmic fairness in AI and to conceptualize specific and user-centered definitions of various aspects of platforms, with implications for both design and development as well as sociological and ethical frameworks. The proposed ethical framework could serve as a standard moral guideline for GAI and be broadly applicable to other AI contexts.

LITERATURE REVIEW: HOW PEOPLE MAKE SENSE OF AE

GAI has gained widespread popularity, but its adoption comes with a degree of ethical risk (Klenk, 2024). AE is a vital factor dictating GAI adoption, as algorithms are increasingly influencing various aspects of society, from personal decisions to large-scale policy implementation (Malmborg, 2023; Osoba et al., 2019).

Algorithmic Equity

Many people who drive cars may not have a deep understanding of the internal workings of their vehicles, but this does not hinder them from having a strong moral compass about the appropriate use of cars. The same principle applies to AI: people do not need to be AI experts to have a sense of ethical values. Moreover, most advanced AI models lack transparency in their decision-making processes, making it challenging to verify the ethical nature of their outputs. Therefore, it is crucial to carefully consider the ethical implications of AI systems, particularly when they are involved in decision-making tasks.

AE refers to the principle of designing, developing, and implementing algorithms in ways that ensure fairness, justice, and equal treatment for all individuals, particularly those from historically marginalized or underrepresented groups (Wu et al., 2024). The goal of AE is to avoid and mitigate biases that might arise in algorithmic decision-making processes, which can perpetuate or exacerbate existing inequalities (Yarger et al., 2020). Key aspects of AE have been researched. These include fairness, transparency, and accountability. In addition to the idea of equity proposed initially, new ideas regarding equity have recently been proposed, such as bias mitigation, inclusiveness, and explainability. The principles of AE are evolving; therefore, continuous efforts from stakeholders are required to redefine and create systems that support fair and equitable outcomes for all (Osoba et al., 2019).

AI equity significantly influences user decision-making by shaping how individuals decide whether to trust these systems and perceive the outcomes of AI-driven processes (Lim et al., 2024). There has been extensive research on algorithmic ethics, such as trust in AI systems (i.e., ethical transparency) (Crain, 2018), perceptions of fairness (i.e., bias and discrimination) (Hoffmann, 2019), informed decision-making (i.e., explainability and adoption) (Dolata & Crowston, 2024), and user empowerment and agency (i.e., respecting user privacy and preferences) (Heimann & Hübener, 2023). Overall, AI ethics profoundly impacts user decision-making by fostering trust, ensuring fairness, enhancing transparency, and empowering users to make informed choices. The ethical considerations embedded in AI systems can lead to greater acceptance, more responsible use of AI, and positive societal outcomes (Schlagwein & Willcocks, 2023).

With the emergence and proliferation of GAI, the need to define AE has become an urgent matter. In GAI, the question of transparency and fairness has taken on greater relevance and importance (Koerber et al., 2024). These issues are fundamental attributes working against the increasing adoption of machine learning algorithms for processing huge user data. Algorithms embedded in GAI can replicate human prejudices and biases encoded in data. As platforms dominate markets and reduce user agency, the social responsibility of enterprises should be required, as fairness and accountability in their conduct are imperative to protect against the prioritizing of the profitability of a single enterprise. While governments and practitioners have addressed the legal and ethical issues resulting from prevalent algorithm diffusion, there has been minimal effort to explicate how we can define AE in GAI and how equitable algorithms can be embedded and embodied in an operational GAI system (Koerber et al., 2024). We approach ethics-aware systems from a user perspective for enhancing these systems' transparency. Additionally, we aim to establish the AE equation to understand what constitutes AE in GAI.

Sensemaking of Ethical Judgment

Sensemaking refers to understanding, comprehending, and explaining complex or uncertain events (Schildt et al., 2020). It is the process by which people attribute meaning to their individual or collective experiences through priming (providing cues), editing (feedback), and triggering (careful evaluation) processes (Weber & Glynn, 2006). Sensemaking theories address cognitive processes, and their information-processing perspective has shown its usefulness in revealing the nuances of algorithmic sensemaking (Dervin, 2003). Previous research on AI adoption and users' construction of meaning (e.g., Möhlmann et al., 2023) showed the significance of clarifying users' sensemaking mechanisms, values, and needs in their particular contexts when working with algorithms (Engstrom et al., 2024).

Based on a sensemaking lens, dual process theory is a valuable complement aiding explorations of the ethical judgment of AI. Dual process theories of moral judgment propose that moral decisions involve two or more related but different processes (Moors, 2014). The processes are related in the sense that the conditions that affect whether they occur and which results they generate overlap. The processes are various in the sense that their results can conflict. The theories suggest that people engage in dual processing when making ethical judgments. Type 1 processing is rapid, emotional, and intuition-driven, and Type 2 is deliberative, slow, and calculated, requiring conscious deliberation of a high cognitive load. Some moral judgments arise as a flash of perception, while others follow mindful deliberation (Kumar, 2016, p. 791).

This dual process is consonant with the sensemaking process of priming, triggering, and editing. *Priming* acts as a cognitive constraint on sensemaking by providing social cues, *editing* is the action of internalizing particular understandings through social feedback processes, and *triggering* involves embodying particular institutional methods of evaluation by posing puzzles through ambivalence and contradiction. The dual process is helpful in understanding how people form ethical values and how they evaluate the ethics of something. The three mechanisms form a conceptual framework for the ethical heuristics of AI, such as the ethical information formation and moral processing model. While extensive research has been done on general information processing, ethical sensemaking in AI has remained unexplored. This study aims to fill this knowledge gap by applying the theory of the dual processing of ethical judgment to GAI.

Research Questions: Understanding Users' Sensemaking of AE

Understanding what constitutes AE and how algorithm ethics is formulated and applied is essential to the sustainable practice of ethical evaluation as an effective gadget for platforms and users (Schlagwein & Willcocks, 2023). Despite the significance of AE, little effort has been made to develop a robust operational definition of AE (Lim et al., 2024). We aim to address this literature gap by identifying the effects of algorithmic factors on the perceptions of ethics and uncovering underlying mechanisms that link heuristics to sensemaking. We define and conceptualize AE in connection with the use of algorithms, explaining the significance of such factors in the use of GAI and filling the current gap in our understanding of the relevant relationships between ethical heuristics and information processing. The research questions are as follows:

1. *How do users make sense of AE in GAI?*
2. *How is AE processed and used in the context of algorithmic generations from GAI?*
3. *How do users make sense of normative value assessments in algorithmic generation?*

These questions aim to clarify how equity can be integrated into GAI design and what forms of ethical evaluations underpinning platforms are effective for users. By ensuring that GAI operates based on normative values, we can help enhance users' trust in and engagement with GAI.

METHODS

Responding to the need to develop equitable and ethical AI, we present a qualitative method for examining sensemaking in the context of AE issues in GAI.

Data Collection

In leveraging sensemaking theory, we used an interpretative data collection approach to elicit responses revealing users' sensemaking in academic research contexts (perceptions and interpretations of AE in GAI). We focused on the human-led process of sensemaking that harnesses the capabilities of AI to decipher ethical evaluations. The qualitative method was designed to enable cognitive mapping as a way of eliciting views, feelings, opinions, and heuristics of how users think and make sense of AE. To reveal the principle of AI equity that is most compatible with a user's observation of ethics, we used semi-structured interviews and think-aloud methods as a framework to facilitate open and dynamic discussions. The interview guide is attached in the Appendix 1.

In a preliminary interview, we hired a sample of 21 graduate students from a large public university in the United States. All students had prior exposure to or ongoing experience with GAI systems. We also recruited a sample of 23 researchers from universities in the United States (Table 7.1). The interview was designed to reveal the dimensions of users' experiences with algorithms; categorize the subjective sensemaking of underlying ethics in relation to GAI algorithms; and analyze the awareness, perceptions, and evaluations of algorithms in relation to platforms, news comment prioritization, and online recommendations. The respondents were

TABLE 7.1 Demographics of samples

	ONLINE INTERVIEW (N = 39 FIRST ROUND)	THINK-ALOUD (N = 11 SECOND ROUND)
GENDER		
Male	17	5
Female	20	6
Other	2	0
EXPERIENCE WITH GAI		
Less than 1 year	10	6
More than 1 year	29	5
PROFESSION		
Student	14	3
Researcher with a master's degree	11	7
Researcher with a PhD	10	
Teacher/professor	4	1
FIELDS		
Humanities/social science	17	5
Computing/engineering	18	5
Other	4	1

selected from research groups conducting research on AI ethics, policy, and management. Screening interviews were conducted to gauge the degree of GAI experience. The pre-survey comprised four inquiries: (1) Which GAI platforms are you currently using? (2) How much time do you spend on these platforms per week? (3) What do you use the platforms for? (4) What content does GAI recommend to you? Unqualified respondents (non-users, light users, and insincere responses) were dropped.

Second, we designed field experiments that leveraged a think-aloud method where respondents were asked to express their thinking as they completed a task (N = 11). As a priming statement, we cited ethical requirements stipulated by the European Union Trustworthy Ethics Guidelines for Trustworthy AI (Malmborg, 2023) as our reference for baseline ethical requirements. The think-aloud method focused on three major topics: (1) relationships among platform participants; (2) participants' understanding of the GAI algorithm and their perceptions of transparency, fairness, and accountability; and (3) users' sensemaking of GAI algorithms and specific research responses. Specific questions were: What do you immediately think of when you hear the concept of AI ethics? What do you think AI should be? Should it perform based on normative values? In what ways can AI be utilized based on best ethics? What consequences could AI ethics have for your work? This open method gave some insight into participants' sensemaking processes of ethics and equity, interaction behavior, and content acceptance. We asked participants about their past experiences with GAI systems and their understanding of algorithms and bias. They were asked to describe their current knowledge about how these systems work and what AI ethics meant to them in this context. The interviews included questions on general perceptions of AI, AI as a research tool, and the dynamics of AI within interactions with other researchers. The think-aloud methods were done both face-to-face and online, depending on respondents' preferences.

Considering that GAI in academia is a multidisciplinary domain, most researchers found themselves at the intersection of two or more areas of scholarly research areas. For instance, 35% of the participants specialized in engineering and computer science with algorithmic programming expertise. Approximately 40% of the respondents were in the humanities and social sciences and had research experience using GAI. The interviews lasted approximately 30 minutes to 1 hour. If requested, participants could have more time. We completed an ethics clearance requirement with the ethics committee of the institution the authors are affiliated with.

Data Analysis

Our analysis strategy was informed by reflexive thematic analysis (Pratt et al., 2019). Transcribed interviews were entered into the ATLAS.ti tool for qualitative data analysis. The raw data were subject to reflexive thematic analysis to create rigor in the qualitative analysis. This procedure, which allowed open coding of the data, was adopted to facilitate the generation of new concepts and theories. This approach allowed us to identify complex patterns of meaning within the data. Through our analysis, we gained an understanding of the complexities involved in developing AI ethics for research. Additionally, we captured distinctive sensemaking patterns. After multiple rounds of analysis and reflection, we identified key themes that highlighted the practical concerns related to AI ethics in education and research. We reached theoretical saturation following 39 interviews, and we completed the coding after implementing 11 think-aloud protocols. Our ongoing research informed our interpretation of the data and led to the development of overarching ethical questions regarding GAI in education and research.

The first step followed open coding, which involved coding the raw data into first-order concepts based on what respondents expressed just like the grounded approach. We referred to the jargon expressed by the respondents when labeling the concepts as references. This step in the coding method produced 54 first-order concepts from the respondents' think-aloud protocols. The subsequent step involved coding the first-order concepts based on differences and similarities (second-order themes—a second level of abstraction of first-order concepts). This step was carried out by the researchers after discussing the central meaning of the first-order concepts and collaboratively deciding how the concepts related to each other. This produced eight recurrent thematic domains (second-order themes). In this study, these second-order themes are considered the results of our empirical analysis. We then combined the second-order themes into two dimensions. The third step was carried out by collaboratively discussing and conceptually analyzing how the aggregated dimensions

TABLE 7.2 Data analysis procedure

TRANSCRIBED RAW DATA	FIRST ROUND MAPPING SENSEMAKING PROCESSES	SECOND ROUND FACTORIZING DISTINCT CONCEPTS	THIRD ROUND CAPTURING SENSEMAKING PATTERNS
	Grounded in reflexivity	Thematic analysis	Patterning
Selected remarks	First-order concepts	Second-order themes	Aggregate patterns
"…*knowing the internal information about the processes and decisions made by GAI.*"	Exploratory shortcuts to abstract issues	Themes	Type 1 heuristic abstract priming
	Non-discrimination, impartiality, and due process	Fairness	
	Responsibility, auditability, and controllability	Accountability	
	Visibility, understandability, and observability	Transparency	
"…*wonder how accurate and to what extent AI gets my personal information.*"	Quality, correctness, and fact	Accuracy	Type 2 systematic concrete triggering
	Opportunity, benefits, and risks	Reliability	
	Security, data, and consent	Privacy	
	Interpretable, understandable, and awareness	Explainability	
	Engagement, faith, and stability	Trust	Mediation editing
	Risk, misinformation, and fake	Hallucination	
Frames	*AI ethics paradox*	*AI as a social actor*	*Dual process*

Source: Modified from Engstrom et al. (2024).

connect to theories of dual processing. This analysis procedure was iterative and co-influencing. First-order concepts and second-order themes were iteratively modified per the research process and identifications of central meanings in the collected material. Table 7.3 shows the number of references within the final second-order themes discovered during the coding method and the instances of focus groups in which they were included.

TABLE 7.3 Recurrent themes and topics discovered during the coding procedure

CODING TOPICS	THEMES	SENSEMAKING MECHANISM	NO. OF REFERENCES
Involves an equilibrium between treatment and outcomes; without bias/prejudice	Fairness	*Priming*: Acting as cognitive cues on ethics	31
Users can see whether algorithms have been thoroughly checked and make sense, and they can comprehend why certain decisions have been drawn	Transparency		29
Firms should be held legally liable for the results of their encoded generation.	Accountability		45
Trustworthiness, expertise, and reliability	Trust/credibility	*Editing*: Acting as internalization of primed messages	39
GAI generates a response that is inaccurate but statistically similar to factually correct data. While the response is false, it has a semantic or structural resemblance to what the model predicts as likely.	Hallucination		36
Relevant and correct responses	Accuracy	*Triggering*: Embodiment of particular ways of evaluating AI features	32
Users can recognize why certain predictions or recommendations have been made	Explainability		42
Concerns about the possibility for GAI to compromise an individual's privacy by revealing personal data to breaches or through other forms of unauthorized sharing	Privacy		38

RESULTS: HOW SCHOLARLY RESEARCHERS MAKE SENSE OF AE

Our analysis identified the process of sensemaking that users engaged in to make sense of AI ethics: priming through fairness, accountability, and transparency; editing for adjustment of trust and hallucination; and triggering for systematic concrete evaluations. We observed that ethical judgments occurred for each of the three patterns of sensemaking, leading us to develop the new construct of the dual process of ethical sensemaking, which is mediated by the editing process. In the priming process, users are engaged in distinctive sensemaking patterns: *AI as a fair tool* (AaaF), *AI as an open model* (AaaO), and *AI as a responsible agent* (AaaR). Users were triggered to systematically evaluate concrete features through the editing process, in which users engaged in the sensemaking of hallucination and trust (Table 7.2).

Type 1: Priming Process

In Type 1 processing, moral judgments arise as a flash of feeling, with fast, unconscious, spontaneous, and emotional processing. This process includes users' understanding of GAI's fairness, transparency, and accountability. These factors came up in association with Type 1 processing because people usually had a weak or abstract sense of these concepts and thus made fast heuristic judgments of AI. These were used to evaluate fast and frugal heuristics to capture the ethical quality of AI. These cognitive processes occurred in response to emotive cues based on previous experiences informed by human systems and ingrained heuristics.

AaaF

The evaluation of fairness is based on three sub-components: non-discrimination, impartiality, and due process. Fairness was by far the most discussed issue among the respondents, reflecting its status as a paramount concern. As more decisions and processes of great importance are being made by AI in various domains, people are becoming apprehensive about the fairness of algorithmic consequences. The concerns involve training data biases leaching into machine learning, causing adverse effects like racism, ideological leanings, stereotyping, and marginalization of certain groups. Concerns regarding GAI's tendency to perpetuate and reinforce existing biases when training new generative models with information from biased sources were raised. The monopolization or centralization of power by GAI firms that own and operate generative models, which are exorbitantly costly to develop, was also raised as a concern. Moreover, there are concerns regarding the imposition of values embedded in GAI systems on cultures distinct from those where the systems were developed. Many respondents claimed that fairness involves being neutral and impartial, without any bias or favoritism. Respondents discussed the ideas of treating everyone equally, being neutral, and ensuring unbiased results from algorithmic filtering and generations. They unanimously agreed that fairness is a crucial aspect of GAI platforms. When asked how to address issues of unfairness or bias, one respondent emphasized the importance of accurate results: "*I want the recommendations are free of bias. If ChatGPT is fair and transparent, I trust and take it.*" This highlights the need for precision in the field. In terms of due process, it was shown that an algorithmic system should adhere to an impartial due process without any bias. Based on the participants' responses, it is clear that fairness goes beyond mathematical equality and includes concepts such as impartiality, unbiased treatment, and accuracy.

AaaO

The concept of openness or transparency consists of three main ideas: visibility, understandability, and observability. Transparency has been recognized as a crucial aspect of platforms. However, since transparency is an abstract concept, respondents had differing opinions. The respondents emphasized the importance of logical interpretability and the need to explain internal mechanisms in GAI machine learning. Respondents stressed that given the complexity of GAI algorithms, the decisions or processes automated by AIs should be interpretable, itemizable, and understandable to the users who adopt, consume, and control the algorithms and AI services. Regarding understandability, one respondent mentioned, "AI systems are more and more complicated and are often difficult to figure out for laypeople and for those impacted by the decisions being generated." When it comes to visibility, another source stated, "The specifications of GAI are neither confirmable nor checkable. Many of these systems are designed by commercial firms, and their specifics are privately-owned." Another respondent emphasized, "It's impossible to explore how they work and who is responsible for the decisions they generate." Others emphasized the need for a clear explanation: "Any consequences from a GAI should be spelled out to the public affected by those results." The critical factors of transparency identified were explainability, observability, visibility, and verifiability.

AaaR

This theme was proposed based on 49 references from 23 interviews (Table 7.4). Overall, the references pointed to the emergence of three first-order concepts: responsibility,

TABLE 7.4   Data extracts reflecting Type 1 processing: heuristics for AI equity

DATA EXTRACTS	EXTRACTED CUES
Fairness: *"I believe that fairness is the most critical component of GAI. It's a topic that's gaining increasing attention, and transparency is key to understanding the fairness and impartiality of GAI. The critical role of fairness in AI is underscored by our heavy reliance on GAI. I expect the providers of GAI to act with fairness and integrity. Unfortunately, I've observed several instances of unfair responses and judgmental answers from GAI." (Respondent 3 [JA])*	GAI telling, prompting biased information at times
Transparency: *"I desired to have access to detailed information about the processes and decisions made by GAI, with the goal of making them visible, understandable, and transparent to both me and the individuals impacted by the algorithms utilized in these systems." (Respondent 7 [DS])*	People do not understand the process of generation and data collection.
Accountability: *"Every time I use AI, I wonder who's responsible for incorrect information or misinformation from AI. I hope that those designing, procuring, and using flawed AI are held accountable for their actions and the impacts of those algorithms. The more AI is held accountable, the higher I evaluate its ethical and trustworthy nature." (Respondent 12 [KF])*	Who is responsible for misinformation from GAI?

auditability, and controllability. Respondents viewed algorithmic responsibility in GAI as the idea that the AI providers must be held accountable for a system's design, implementation, and recommendation processes, and outcomes. Common concerns were expressed that algorithmic decisions are vulnerable to blunders that may lead to unintended results. Respondents stated that algorithms are likely to cause problems due to an incapacity to deal with prejudice or due to simple mistakes. One source said, "One of the critical challenges is of privacy protection and ensuring data. For GAI, it is difficult to main full confidentiality. What if AI leaks personal sensitive data? Who's responsible and what does it mean to the individuals who are already damaged." Another respondent used an example that AI is not a legal entity. How to assign accountability when GAI are involved in decision-making is the common issue raised. It was concluded that who should be held responsible if AI makes poor choices is unclear. One respondent noted, "Shared accountability across multiple stakeholders may be optimal but supported by testing, oversight committees, guidelines, and regulations." Another respondent seconded, "There seems to be a substantial divide between the principle of responsible AI and the practical ways of dealing with accountability in GAI." Based on this sensemaking process, three factors of responsibility were inferred—auditability, legality, and accountability.

Type 2: Triggering Process

This process involves conscious deliberation, as it is cognitively demanding. It is deliberate and controlled, requiring reasoned processing. During this process, users engage in elaborate and conscious sensemaking to assess accuracy, privacy, interpretability, and reliability. Type 2 processing involves the conscious evaluation of things based on some combination of utility, benefit, risk, and impact.

AI as an accuracy (AaaA)

The most common concern raised by the respondents was how accurate and truthful GAI is. Because GAI tools do not reveal their rules or the relationships within their underlying training data, they produce neither repeatable nor explainable results. One user's outputs might be different from another's, and the outputs are often inaccurate. If data are incomplete or biased, the results will also be incomplete or biased. Respondents commonly noted that GAI cannot reliably distinguish between biased information and unbiased facts when constructing its responses.

AI as a privacy (AaaP)

GAI systems have the potential to generate content that may inadvertently or intentionally defame individuals or organizations. Respondents noted that GAI can breach data privacy when models' training involves datasets that include personally identifiable information. Massive data foraging can expose sensitive information, resulting in significant privacy invasion through GAI. Data scraped from online may randomly reproduce and exaggerate personal information about people and related data about their associations. For example, a photo or resume that people posted or shared online can be repurposed for training AI systems, often without their consent or knowledge and sometimes with direct civil rights implications. Some respondents expressed a concern that people cannot simply erase information that has been recorded by GAI. Once a platform has been trained on something, there is almost no way to untrain it.

AI as an explainable agent (AaaE)

Respondents saw explainability as the most critical but least recognized attribute of algorithms. Respondents described explainability as how mechanisms and processes in machine learning should be understood by humans. Respondents expressed that algorithms can be rationalized in terms of how AI decisions are made in such a manner that people can comprehend them. Some AI systems' algorithms use black-box practices that lay users cannot understand. Another respondent seconded this point: "In most contemporary GAI applications, there is no clear clarification of how the AI produced certain results or decisions." It is noted that "offering interpretable explanations can be important in certain domains like health and medicine." Respondents raised a need for explainability beyond understandability to make algorithms logically acceptable to people. Respondents expressed that generated content should be accompanied by easy-to-understand descriptions.

Mediation by Editing

In the editing stage, users aim to modify or internalize standard values derived from Type 1 processing, which helps users make sense of Type 2 processing (Madan & Ashok, 2024).

AI as a trust (AaaT)

Trust is considered to be critical in GAI. Respondents agreed that trust is the most fundamental attribute of GAI. Many discussed trust in terms of transparency, arguing that these two factors should be embedded in GAI's design, not just as afterthoughts. Most respondents are wary about trusting AI systems and have moderate or low recognition of GAI. Therefore, they raised trustworthy AI as a need. One of the cornerstones of trustworthy AI is transparency built on explainable algorithms and data sources so that people can comprehend how decisions are made and ensure a lack of bias and sound ethics. Trust manifests when GAI prioritizes transparency and safety for users.

AI as a hallucination (AaaH)

Respondents raised critical concerns about GAI intentionally or unintentionally generating misleading or false information (Table 7.5). People are worried that inaccurate results generated by AI models could be a problem for systems that make critical decisions, such as health care and public services. Not only have various types of reasoning errors in AI been identified, but risks associated with specific types of misinformation,

TABLE 7.5   Data extracts reflecting Type 2 processing: systematic evaluation of AI equity

DATA EXTRACTS	EXTRACTED CUES
Accuracy: *"I found accuracy is important in constituting AI ethics. When I seek information from GAI, of course I expect the answers to be accurate and truthful. This is the most important feature as well as the highest standard of AI ethics."* (Respondent 21 [DP])	Is content generated by GAI correct?
Privacy and risk: *"I believe my acceptance of AI is tied to the type of data involved. I found it problematic for AI to be utilized to predict my preferences and information."* (Respondent 20 [DP])	How does GAI access/analyze my data?
Reliability: *"I consider a GAI service to be reliable if it is built in compliance with data protection requirements, makes unbiased and comprehensible decisions, and can be managed by humans. These should be the essential ethical attributes of GAI."* (Respondent 2 [KA])	To what extent is GAI reliable?
Trust: *"Trust in AI matters because individual adoption, societal diffusion, political support, knowledge development, and innovation all depend on it. I trust AI if I have a firm belief in the truth or ability of AI."* (Respondent 11 [GQ])	Credibility of GAI
Explainability: *"I hope GAI allows us to comprehend and trust the output and results generated by algorithms."* (Respondent 22 [OP])	Explainability of results

such as health misinformation or political misinformation, have also been examined (Koerber et al., 2024). Because AI has a tendency to produce flawed results as a result of flawed reasoning and manipulated citations, it has been raised the importance of individual fact-checking and the validation of AI models' outputs.

DISCUSSION

This study explored how AI users make sense of adopting GAI in their work. Our findings revealed how the perceived attributes of GAI systems initiate sensemaking processes and subsequently impact GAI's usage and adoption.

Algorithmic Sensemaking of Ethical AI

The methods employed in this study unveiled the process, components, and dimensions of AE in GAI. The interpretive methods revealed how perceptions, judgments, and the usage of GAI affect ethical decision-making. The findings provide insights into various themes that are crucial in ensuring fairness and equality within algorithms. Additionally, these dimensions shed light on the dynamics of algorithmic filtering and emphasize the importance of addressing equity issues in the development and implementation of algorithms across different domains.

First, people often consider AIs to be social actors, so they apply similar norms, social rules, and ethics to their interactions with AIs (Heimann & Hübener, 2023). AIs are considered social actors because they interact with the world. Humans unconsciously apply social heuristics used in human interactions in AI interactions, as they evoke similar social features as humans. This is similar to the Computers as Social Actors (CASA) paradigm (Nass & Moon, 2000) in which people mindlessly apply rules and expectations to computers. It seems that CASA has been extended to include AI, which is a significant extension of AI as social actors (AASA).

To understand this interdependence between AI and people, we must understand how AI mediates human ethics, opinions, and behaviors.

People apply ethical rules such as reliability, trust, truthfulness, and integrity to their interactions with others. They apply the same ethical standards to their interactions with AIs. These standards are unconscious mental patterns that humans have developed to interact effectively with each other. AIs bring up ethical questions because they are autonomous, self-learning agents. These features make humans view AIs as human-like ethical entities. Therefore, all human expectations and ethics are relevant and applicable in human–AI interactions. This is understandable because people are increasingly relying on GAI, and it is essential that GAI provides users with reliable and trustworthy answers. AIs are ethical agents in the sense that they can have ethical implications and impact (Foster & Wunsch, 2023). If AIs are ethical entities, then human ethics needs to be them into consideration.

Second, an emerging ethical paradigm can be seen from the heuristic–systematic process of AI (Sundar et al., 2020). Sensemaking triggered by the more abstract features of AI points to a heuristic cognition path. However, sensemaking prompted by the concrete features of an AI promotes systematic evaluation paths, integrating the social and technical systems in AI adoption. This dual process of the heuristic–systematic evaluation reveals two distinct modes of figuring out AI ethics. Heuristic processing involves focusing on salient and easily comprehended cues that activate well-learned judgmental shortcuts, whereas systematic processing engages attempts to thoroughly understand any available information through deliberate analysis, deep configuration, and intensive reasoning (Chaiken et al., 1996).

In reasoning about AI ethics, people employ a heuristic–systematic process. People process AI ethics heuristically and in ways that interweave perceptive, effective, and more systematic phases. This processing does not usually follow a simple progression but evidences trial-and-error processing that is consistent with the logic of heuristic processing more generally. While people have similar ethical expectations for both humans and AIs, they usually do not understand the technical operations or inner workings of algorithms. Concepts like transparency and fairness represent abstract ideologies to them, and they do not know how such concepts are concretely applied to real usages or everyday lives. For example, people know and agree regarding the importance of transparency and fairness but do not understand the specifics of such ethics, such as how to measure their presence and what should be done to ensure such ethics both from an organizational perspective and individual users' point of view. Thus, in many ways, users' sensemaking involves heuristic processes that rely on simple, readily available concepts or pre-existing knowledge (Gu et al., 2021). This may lead to bias or prejudice if their existing mindsets are biased or prejudiced. Heuristic processing can be successful if cues are correct and effective. In such cases, the process is relayed to a systematic process that looks at algorithmic features closely in an effortful manner. During the systematic process, people evaluate AI in terms of accuracy, responses, factuality, or quality of responses. These two processes are interrelated or co-occur, impacting each other.

Third, an ethical AI paradox reveals a disconnect between stated values and actual behaviors. Recent research on AI ethics has shown discrepancies between users' attitudes and their actual behaviors regarding what ethics should be in GAIs. While users claim to be very concerned about the ethics of AI, they nevertheless accept and continue to use GAI services without taking any precautious actions or doubts. Additionally, while people are concerned about the accuracy of GAI, they nevertheless continue to use, accept, and search for related information. Many participants expressed concerns over GAI hallucinations, but they use GAIs or even encourage others to adopt them. People are aware that these hallucination errors can be caused by a variety of reasons, including low quality of data/biases in the data used to train a model, incorrect assumptions made by a model, or insufficient training data. Such concerns, plus concerns over fairness and transparency, do not diminish user adoption. People prioritize efficiency, convenience, and service delivery over ethics. This phenomenon can be attributed to an algorithm ethics paradox.

IMPLICATIONS

This study focused on AE and explored how users make sense of ethical AI to examine their algorithm sensemaking processes when interacting with GAI. As GAI algorithms direct information curation, user design is progressively becoming an activity of sensemaking. That is, there is an increasing awareness of which aspects could be or should be managed. A dual-process framework provides a nuanced account of how AI ethics can arise in two different ways or as a result of two different reasoning processes. This theory shows that AI ethics is socially and cognitively constructed by users instead of stipulated by society or directed by AI.

Theoretical Implications

How do people configure and perceive algorithmic ethics? Our results contribute to the answering of this question by building upon literature on algorithms from a sensemaking perspective. The findings revealed dual sensemaking mechanisms, priming, and triggering, which are mediated by editing. These are connected to the ethical sensemaking process, providing heuristics as to whether an AI is ethical or moral.

Our results also contribute to theoretical refinement by highlighting how ethical values are created, sustained, and used in interactions with GAI. Specifically, we offer three theoretical contributions. First, the results enhance our understanding of what constitutes AE in GAI. While the characteristics of AI ethics in general have been studied, their empirical conceptualization within a specific context has been lacking.

Second, the study elucidated the roles and processes of sensemaking in an algorithmically mediated context, where sensemaking occurs through a mediated dual process. It defined sensemaking as a tool for understanding the processes leading to ethical manifestations. Third, the results revealed active users' role in the sensemaking process. The notion of active sensemaking challenges the previous assumptions of passive users and singular, deterministic meanings transmitted by AI. Our findings reveal the dynamics of sensemaking within different socially constructed realities.

1. **Understanding AE from Users' Sensemaking.** A majority of ethical concerns raised by the respondents echoed previous research, shedding light on a tacit disregard for the human perspective or user-centered views. Previous studies relied on statistical analyses that focused exclusively on algorithms or AI-centric perspectives (Dolata & Crowston, 2024), neglecting human perspectives or anthropomorphic focuses on ethical issues (Salge et al., 2022; Schildt et al., 2020). By focusing on how algorithms make sense of information, the literature failed to specify how users and researchers specifically make sense of the algorithms influencing them. This study uncovered ethical sensemaking in relation to algorithms by theorizing its sub-components and the relationships among the ethical components. Our results suggest that algorithmic ethical sensemaking consists of a dual process of priming and triggering evaluations, allowing them to heuristically and systematically keep up with algorithmic performance. This finding extends previous literature (e.g., Möhlmannn et al., 2023; Scarbrough et al., 2024) by showing that algorithmic sensemaking serves as a heuristic frame, linking users' concerns and their behavioral decisions. Sensemaking goes beyond being a simple way to give meaning to AI interactions (Engstrom et al., 2024); it helps clarify the ethical issues that allow for the full exploitation of AI interactions in maximizing the benefits and controlling the risks of GAI. Sensemaking in AI reveals what attributes are essential in GAI, how people sense them, and what ethical values are at play.

2. **How Do Humans Perceive AE?** Just as ethical standards have been deemed to be essential qualities of typical systems, so too have they been applied to algorithm-based GAI platforms (Koerber et al., 2024). The findings suggest that people have general normative values regarding ethics and expect GAI to have these values as well. People's understanding of normative values plays an essential role in their adoption of and interactions with GAI. Not only do normative values play a significant role in formulating perceived quality, but they also facilitate users' perceptions of the quality and performance of platforms. Users consider a system fair when understandable interpretations are available, and they perceive it to be more transparent when there is a higher level of perceived responsibility. Users' understanding of algorithm-driven platforms is nonlinear and not organized into structured ready-made automatic processes (Obreja, 2024). How users sense, perceive, cognize, and use algorithms hinges on how they process algorithmic attributes and the information through such attributes. Users actively process the algorithmic

TABLE 7.6   Comparison of AI perspectives and sensemade meanings

AE	AI PERSPECTIVE	USER SENSEMAKING
Fairness	Mechanical fairness Mathematical equalness	Beyond statistical fairness Qualitative equity
Transparency	Sharing algorithmic source code and model	Human reasoning efficacy
Explainability	Open source of algorithm specification	Who the explanation is intended for Interpretability
Accountability	Legal responsibility	Shared corporate responsibilities

decisions they receive from their cognitive processes and simulate them along with normative concepts of fairness, transparency, and accountability (Koerber et al., 2024). Thus, the meanings derived from their sensemaking are different from the concepts delivered by an AI (Table 7.6).

3. **Active Sensemaking.** The algorithmic ethics evaluation process implies the subsistence of active roles (committed and conscious) for users in assembling their perceptions of algorithms in GAI (Obreja, 2024). This role is consistent with the proposition of sensemaking that meaning is contextually constructed through interactions (Engstrom et al., 2024). The process of ethics construction is reciprocal with the help of GAI. With the rise of algorithm-driven technologies, the user's role has shifted from being a passive recipient of automated processes through GAI to a proactive creator of a preference profile who generates, modifies, and influences algorithms depending on the framing and contexts of their consumption. Users want to view their desires and preferences reflected on screens. As a result, their desires are reinforced through the algorithmic process. This new conceptualization of active sensemaking highlights that users actively harness and leverage the human ability to perceive and actively form patterns in an AI context, adding meaning to such patterns to generate insights and provide a foundation for the design and development of algorithmic systems. Active sensemaking highlights an interactionist view and is an essentially social process: users' interpretations and behaviors are significantly affected by interactions with algorithms that allow users to comprehend their contexts and take action collectively (Madan & Ashok, 2024).

Practical Implications: AI Ethics as a Process of Sensemaking

There is an urgent need for more solid AI ethics to be built into AI to support a human-led sensemaking process. Our results can serve as a reference point by helping practitioners of GAI platforms advance ethical design and improve user experiences with their products. For example, AI platforms may instrumentalize the black box of their algorithms to create acceptable ethical values, encouraging trust and acceptance. Since AE comprises users' sensemaking of algorithmic platforms, the industry may develop a strategy that applies a user-centric protocol to generative mechanisms. How to design de-biasing systems, how to ensure transparent interactions, and how to incorporate ethics in an interface are pressing questions.

Second, our findings regarding heuristic methods can be useful in designing heuristic algorithms in AI systems to produce approximate human-like solutions rather than automatic algorithmic solutions. Principles that revolve around how humans think can offer insightful design guidelines in ensuring an AI solution executes the optimum decision-making processes. Understanding how users sense and perceive their interactions with algorithms allows GAI practitioners and algorithm developers to perform more ethically and responsibly. Our results offer AI industry guidelines on how to address ethical issues in other features, such as how to collect user data and/or implicit feedback effectively while supporting users' trust in and adoption of AI. The algorithmic ethics processing model provides insights into integrating equity with usability factors and behavioral mechanisms. Our model serves as a bridge to develop human-centered and ethics-aware AI.

LIMITATIONS AND FUTURE DIRECTIONS

While there is abundant research on AI ethics for theoretical discussions, there is limited empirical evidence on the practical challenges perceived by experts when it comes to developing ethically aligned AI for the education sector. Therefore, our results are essential in providing evidence that may help bridge the gap between the theory and practice of AI ethics for education. Through our interpretive analysis methodology, we collected rich data and conducted an in-depth exploration of sensemaking and insights associated with ethical judgments.

First, our conclusions might have been biased by the limited sample size and convenience samples. Participant-level noise may have confounded the interpretations and analyses we performed. For the context of our interviews, "GAI" was used as a general term that could have led to users interpreting AI differently or focusing specifically on machine learning. During the think-aloud protocols, we emphasized supportive GAI as generative algorithms. However, some respondents had different understandings, mistaking more autonomous and advanced scenarios for AI. AI is a constantly evolving topic that is still under development, with many open questions yet to be determined by research and education. This highlights a broader challenge for research and ethics guidelines to define and research AI in specific applications, subjects, and contexts. While our study demonstrated the ethical reflection needed to address practical challenges in AI development, it is essential to note that our results are specific to the study population and may not be generalizable.

Further research is required to determine if similar insights can be obtained in other areas of domains. Future quantitative studies can explore whether participants from different educational backgrounds have different views or concerns about the use of AI in pedagogy. Further research in various algorithmic, socioeconomic, and international contexts is necessary.

CONCLUSION

The potential of GAI to bring transformative changes across various domains is undeniable, but it also presents unique ethical challenges. As new powerful technologies emerge, they bring with them enhanced capacities to act, necessitating new concepts of ethics to guide what constitutes just and fair actions. This study introduced the principles of AE as a moral requirement for GAI. Our results make a contribution by elucidating the interconnected concept of AE and proposing new algorithmic ethics. The development of AE draws from prior discussions in computer and information ethics, as well as broader philosophical traditions of ethics. As GAI becomes more advanced and autonomous, ethics can play a crucial role in constraining adverse effects and shaping the new technological landscape in a way that aligns with human values. Ethical values may pose challenges to user acceptance and the long-term sustainability of AI technology. The conceptual and methodological framework proposed in this study offers an approach to addressing these ethical concerns and provides guidelines for prototyping, developing, and deploying ethical GAI systems. Adhering to this framework can ensure the responsible use of GAI, maximizing its benefits while minimizing ethical risks.

REFERENCES

Chaiken, S., Giner-Sorolla, R., & Chen, S. (1996). Beyond accuracy: Defense and impression motives in heuristic and systematic information processing. In P. M. Gollwitzer; & J. A. Bargh (Eds.), *The psychology of action: Linking cognition and motivation to behavior* (pp. 553–578). Guilford Press.

Coeckelbergh, M. (2020). *AI ethics*. The MIT Press. https://doi.org/10.7551/mitpress/12549.001.0001

Crain, M. (2018). The limits of transparency. *New Media & Society, 20*(1), 88–104. https://doi:10.1177/1461444816657096

Dervin, B. (2003). Sense-making's journey from metatheory to methodology to methods. In B. Dervin (Ed.), *In sense-making methodology reader* (pp. 141–146). Hampton Press, Inc.

Dolata, M., & Crowston, K. (2024). Making sense of AI systems development. *IEEE Transactions on Software Engineering, 50*(1), 123–140. http://doi:10.1109/TSE.2023.3338857

Engstrom, A., Pittino, D., Mohlin, A., Johansson, A., & Mirzaei, E. (2024). Artificial intelligence and work transformations. *Information Technology & People.* https://doi.org/10.1108/ITP-01-2023-0048

Foster, J. A., & Wunsch, D. C. (2023). The ethical status of an AI. In X. Huang; J. H. Moore; & Y. Zhang (Eds.), *Integrative bioinformatics for biomedical big data: A no-boundary thinking approach* (pp. 135–146). Cambridge University Press.

Freiman, O. (2022). Making sense of the conceptual nonsense trustworthy AI. *AI and Ethics,*, *3*(2), 1351–1360. http://doi:10.1007/s43681-022-00241-w

Gu, J., Yan, N., & Rzeszotarski, J. (2021). Understanding user sensemaking in machine learning fairness assessment systems. *Proceedings of the Web Conference.* ACM, New York. https://doi.org/10.1145/3442381.3450092

Heimann, M., & Hübener, A.-F. (2023). AI as social actor. *Journal of Digital Social Research*, *5*(1), 48–69. https://doi.org/10.33621/jdsr.v5i1.159

Helberger, N., Karppinen, K., & D'Acunto, L. (2018). Exposure diversity as a design principle for recommender systems. *Information, Communication & Society*, *21*(2), 191–207. https://doi:10.1080/1369118X.2016.1271900

Hoffmann, A. (2019). Where fairness fails. *Information, Communication & Society*, *22*(7), 900–915. https://doi:10.1080/1369118X.2019.1573912

Klenk, M. (2024). Ethics of generative AI and manipulation. *Ethics Information Technology*, *26*, 9. https://doi.org/10.1007/s10676-024-09745-x

Koerber, A., Shin, D., & Lim, J. (2024). Impact of misinformation from generative AI on user information processing. *New Media and Society.* https://doi.org/10.1177/14614448241234040

Kumar, V. (2016). The empirical identity of moral judgment. *The Philosophical Quarterly*, *66*(265), 783–804. http://doi:10.1093/pq/pqw019

Lim, J., Ahmad, N., & Ibarahim, M. (2024). Understanding user sensemaking in fairness and transparency in algorithms. *AI & Society*, *39*, 447–490. https://doi.org/10.1007/s00146-022-01525-9

Madan, R., & Ashok, M. (2024). Making sense of AI benefits. *Information System Frontiers.* https://doi.org/10.1007/s10796-024-10475-0

Malmborg, F. (2023). Narrative dynamics in European Commission AI policy: Sensemaking, agency construction, and anchoring. *Review of Policy Research*, *40*(5), 757–780. https://doi.org/10.1111/ropr.12529

Möhlmannn, M., Salge, A., & Marco, M. (2023). Algorithm sensemaking: How platform workers make sense of algorithmic management. *Journal of the Association for Information Systems*, *24*(1), 35–64. http://doi:10.17705/1jais.00774

Moors, A. (2014). Examining the mapping problem in dual process models. In *Dual-process theories of the social mind* (pp. 20–34). Guilford.

Nass, C., & Moon, Y. (2000). Machines and mindlessness: Social responses to computers. *Journal of Social Issues*, *56*(1), 81–103. https://doi.org/10.1111/0022-4537.00153

Obreja, D. M. (2024). When stories turn institutional: How TikTok users legitimate the algorithmic sensemaking. *Social Media+Society*, *10*(1). https://doi.org/10.1177/20563051231224114

Osoba, O., Boudreaux, B., Saunders, J., Irwin, J., Mueller, P., & Cherney, S. (2019). *Algorithmic equity. A framework for social applications.* RAND Research report.

Pratt, M. G., Kaplan, S., & Whittington, R. (2019). Decoupling transparency from replication in establishing trustworthy qualitative research. *Administrative Science Quarterly*, *65*, 1–19. https://doi.org/10.1177/0001839219887663

Salge, C. A., Karahanna, E., & Thatcher, J. B. (2022). Algorithmic processes of social alertness and social transmission. *MIS Quarterly*, *46*, 229–260. https://doi.org/10.25300/misq/2021/15598

Scarbrough, H., Chen, Y., & Patriotta, G. (2024). The AI of the beholder: Intra-professional sensemaking of an epistemic technology. *Journal of Management Studies.* https://doi.org/10.1111/joms.13065

Schildt, H., Mantere, S., & Cornelissen, J. (2020). Power in sensemaking processes. *Organization Studies*, *41*(2), 241–265. https://doi.org/10.1177/0170840619847718

Schlagwein, D., & Willcocks, L. (2023). ChatGPT et al.: The ethics of using generative AI. *Journal of Information Technology*, *38*(3), 232–238. https://doi.org/10.1177/02683962231200411

Schoenherr, J. (2022). *Ethical artificial intelligence from popular to cognitive science trust in the age of entanglement.* Routledge.

Sundar, S., Kim, J., Beth-Oliver, M., & Molina, M. (2020). Online privacy heuristics that predict information disclosure. *CHI '20*, April 25-30, 2020. https://doi.org/10.1145/3313831.3376854

Weber, K., & Glynn, M. (2006). Making sense with institutions. *Organization Studies*, *27*, 1639–1660. https://doi.org/10.1177/0170840606068343

Weick, K. (2001). *Making sense of the organization*. Blackwell.

Wu, W., Huang, Y., & Qian, L. (2024). Social trust and algorithmic equity. *Decision Support Systems*, *178*, 114115. https://doi.org/10.1016/j.dss.2023.114115.

Yarger, L., Cobb, P., & Neupane, B. (2020). Algorithmic equity in the hiring of underrepresented IT job candidates. *Online Information Review*, *44*(2), 383–395. https://doi.org/10.1108/OIR-10-2018-0334

APPENDIX 1: QUESTIONNAIRE FOR SEMI-STRUCTURED INTERVIEWS WITH RESEARCHERS

Thank you for participating in this research. With the approval of the Institutional Review Board from our university, we are conducting a study on AI ethics for academic researchers. Any information you provide will be kept confidential and anonymized. Your identity will never be disclosed by law. Your responses will only be recorded for transcription purposes and will be destroyed afterward.

First, we are interested in learning about your experience with generative AI and how you use it in your research and work. What benefits do you find in using generative AI? Can you describe a typical interaction with AI and how you engage with it? What qualities and capabilities do you think generative AI should possess? Have you encountered any ethical dilemmas or problems while using generative AI? If so, how were these problems resolved? What aspects of the service do you appreciate and what do you find to be drawbacks?

Second, we are interested in your thoughts on the generative AI service. Have you received an explanation of the service? What information does it provide about the service? Have you experienced any instances of the service not working properly or providing misinformation? Has the service changed over time? Do you think the service operates transparently or is it a black box? The service algorithms aim to provide users with personalized content. Do you believe this personalization infringes on your privacy? Do you think the recommended content is fair? Do you believe the service is responsible for its actions and consequences?

Third, we would like to understand how you comprehend (make sense of) the AI system. How familiar are you with the ethical values of the system? Is it important for you to understand the underlying logic of how the system works or how it generates relevant information for you? If you receive incorrect information, what do you do? Do you speak to the provider about it?

The Ethics of AI Acceptance

How Ethical Heuristics Drive AI Adoption

8

INTRODUCTION

The role of ethics in artificial intelligence (AI) acceptance is crucial, as it significantly influences how people perceive and trust AI systems (Sallam, 2023). Ethical considerations in AI encompass a range of principles and practices aimed at ensuring that AI technologies align with human values, respect individual rights, and promote societal well-being (Afful-Dadzie et al., 2023; Schomakers et al., 2022). Understanding the factors that influence people's decision-making processes and continued usage intentions for generative artificial intelligence (GAI), services can aid in designing more human-centered GAI systems and foster the equitable development of AI technologies within the evolving GAI landscape (Ivanov & Webster, 2024). Users' cognitive heuristics exert a key influence on their behaviors and decisions when interacting with GAI systems (Sundar & Kim, 2019). Traditional approaches, such as the unified theory of acceptance and use of technology (UTAUT) and the technology acceptance model (TAM), have shown significant explanatory power in understanding technology adoption. These models, however, often focus on the adoption outcomes of using technology rather than the acceptance process, which involves various cognitive heuristics for evaluating both benefits and risks. To better understand AI acceptance, research should emphasize processes that enable users to critically engage with and assess the technology (Molina & Sundar, 2024). A handful of studies (Shi et al., 2020; Yada & Head, 2019) have applied dual-process information processing theories to technology adoption decisions. For instance, taking perceived risk into account, Shi et al. (2020) examined how heuristic and systematic cues influenced user adoption decisions of AI-based travel recommendation systems, particularly under varying levels of perceived risk.

Although users' cognitive processing mechanisms for GAI acceptance decisions are important, they are under-researched due to the technology's nascent stage and the complex GAI–human interaction. The exact responses of users to GAI and the impact

DOI: 10.1201/9781003530244-12

of benefit–risk assessments on behavior remain unclear. This research, grounded in the heuristic–systematic model (HSM), explores the psychological mechanisms behind GAI acceptance decisions, specifically focusing on the role of user empowerment heuristics. Users' perceived user empowerment (PUE) acts as a mental shortcut, facilitating systematic judgments in accepting GAI systems. We empirically illustrate the interplay between algorithmic attributes, empowerment heuristics, attitudes, and their influence on continued use and willingness to pay for premium GAI systems. Our findings will unravel the role of risk and benefit heuristics and their influence on users' behavioral decisions.

THEORETICAL BACKGROUND: MECHANISMS BEHIND COGNITIVE HEURISTICS IN GAI ACCEPTANCE

To examine the cognitive processes that underlie users' GAI heuristics for acceptance, two theoretical frames are integrated—the heuristic systematic (HS) processing framework and the construct of user empowerment—to investigate the antecedents and consequences of information processing by GAI users.

HS Processing in AI Adoption: Dual-Processing Theory

The HS processing model posits that users use one or both modes of information processing when evaluating information to arrive at a decision. Heuristic processing involves using cognitive heuristics to arrive at a judgment more easily, while systematic processing entails a deliberate and effortful examination and comparison of information (Chaiken, 2014). According to Chaiken (2014), both processes are influenced by contextual factors such as the user's motivation and ability to process information. For example, when a topic is personally relevant to a user and their motivation to process accurately is high, they tend to use systematic cues to process information. Someone with high prior knowledge about a topic and the motivation to process information will process in accordance with both systematic and heuristic cues. Often, heuristic and systematic processing occur simultaneously or in sequence in specific contexts (e.g., generative machine learning and AI), which can be highly probable (Chaiken & Maheswaran, 1994). Shi et al. (2020) found that while both cues are utilized by users, systematic cues have a stronger effect on adoption decisions, especially when perceived risk is high. Emotional trust, influenced more by heuristic cues, plays a critical role in adoption as a delegated agent.

This research uses the HS process model to understand how users make behavioral decisions regarding using and paying for premium features of a GAI system. The HSM is particularly relevant as the overarching theoretical framework because it explains how users manage cognitive overload by using various heuristics to make evaluative judgments during complex interactions. HSM clarifies how algorithmic features influence users' understanding and sensemaking processes when using GAI (Zrnec et al., 2022). Users often tend to apply heuristics to evaluate the attributes and quality of the information generated by GAI, which ultimately impacts their adoption decisions (Sundar & Kim, 2019). In this process, PUE and perceived ease of use (PEOU) serve as benefit heuristics, while privacy concerns and hallucinations function as risk heuristics. The interplay of these benefit–risk heuristics can influence user attitudes toward using GAI. These attitudes, in turn, act as heuristics, playing a crucial role in decisions regarding continued use and intention to pay for premium services where more systematic processing is involved.

Psychological Empowerment as a Heuristic in Decision-Making

Along these lines, the concept of psychological empowerment is proposed to complement the HS theory of information processing in the context of GAI. While the HS model focuses on user perceptions of technological cues, it overlooks how technologies empower users to plan, decide, and perform tasks effectively. Some studies have incorporated the concept of self-efficacy in examining technology acceptance (Cheung & Vogel, 2013), but they do not fully capture the critical role of the human agent in interacting with a system, as illustrated by Bandura's (1977) self-efficacy theory. The concept of user control is particularly critical in GAI as it empowers users to tailor their interactions, evaluate risks and benefits, and feel a strong sense of freedom over their AI experiences. Users are human agents who can be empowered by assistive technology such as GAI. As a result, the empowered human agent can employ more effective skills to complete a task and make a positive impact on their work while remaining autonomous. Empowerment has been shown to be a significant factor in information-seeking behavior and decision-making (Ivanov & Webster, 2024), and it is a key predictor of technology adoption (Shin, 2024).

User empowerment exerts a strong influence on the decision to adopt GAI technology. If users perceive greater empowerment through these technologies, they are more likely to adopt and continue using GAI services. The construct of cognitive empowerment emerged as "a motivational construct manifested in four cognitions: meaning, competence, self-determination, and impact" (Spreitzer, 1995, p. 1444).

- *Impact*: The impact dimension of user empowerment refers to the user's belief in their ability to make a difference in the outcome through their use of the technology (Thomas & Velthouse, 1990). It encompasses the user's sense of contributing meaningfully to broader goals through their engagement with technologies (Afful-Dadzie et al., 2023).
- *Competence*: The competence dimension reflects the user's confidence in their capacity to effectively and skillfully utilize a technology tool (Thomas &

Velthouse, 1990). User empowerment can be influenced by one's perceptions of themselves in relation to their experiences and sensemaking of technology in their work environments (Spreitzer, 1995; Thomas & Velthouse, 1990).

- *Self-determination*: It reflects the user's autonomy in using technology (Schweitzer & Simon, 2021) and the user's control over the initiation and regulation of their interaction with technologies, fostering a sense of independence and choice in their use (Schweitzer & Simon, 2021).
- *Meaning*: It concerns the perceived value of a task's aim according to the user's standards or ideals (Thomas & Velthouse, 1990). It considers how well an activity's goals fit with an individual's personal beliefs, values, and internalized norms (Schweitzer & Simon, 2021).

RESEARCH QUESTIONS: THE ROLE OF HEURISTICS IN AI DECISION-MAKING

Previous research in the TAM-related literature has mainly addressed the specific factors or conditions influencing technology acceptance (Davis et al., 1989). While these approaches have produced useful insights on adoption as a consequential dependent variable, they potentially failed to fully account for the cognitive, psychological, and contextual dimensions of heuristic understanding and systematic assessment (Shin, 2024). Cognitive processes are influenced by motivations and perceptions, which can be categorized as heuristic and systematic processing. Understanding the nexus between different processes is critical in grasping the context of AI decision-making. Although the existing research indicates that heuristics play a significant role in shaping the attitudes and decisions of users (Sundar, 2008), there is a need to understand how heuristics are developed, interpreted, connected, and applied by users in the context of general artificial intelligence (GAI). This study is guided by the following research questions (RQs):

RQ. What are the cognitive mechanisms underpinning users' decision-making surrounding GAI adoption?
1. How do heuristics evolve for acceptance of GAI systems?
2. How do users develop their attitudes toward GAI and what are the effects of AI heuristics on the HS process?

CONCEPTUAL MODEL AND HYPOTHESIS

The proposed model is designed to analyze the impact of AI heuristics on acceptance decisions (Figure 8.1). AI heuristics describe a rule of thumb that AI-like characteristics are reflected in the information transmitted by GAI (Sundar, 2008; Sundar & Kim, 2019).

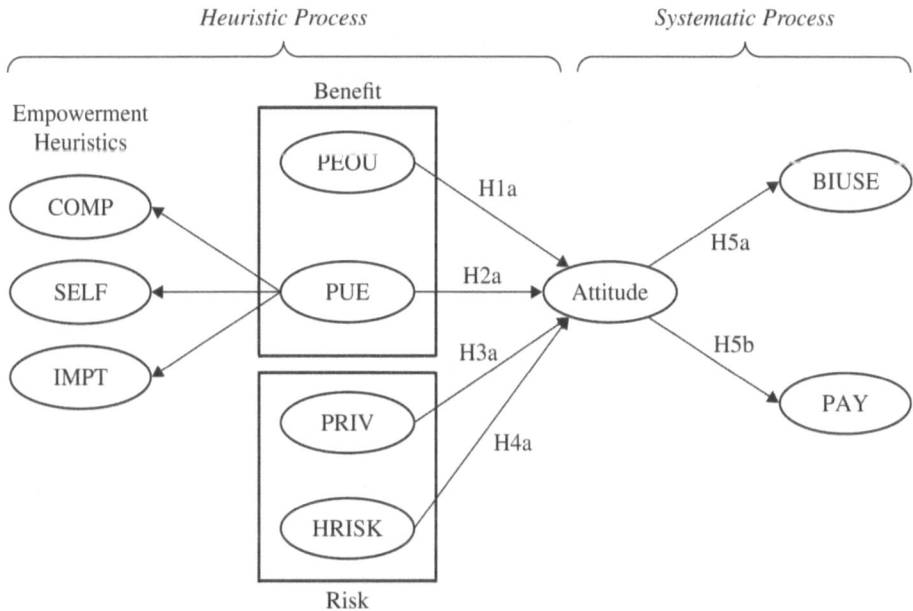

FIGURE 8.1   Heuristic systematic process of generative AI acceptance.

When people interact with GAI, any AI cues will cue users to apply the mental shortcut of assessing the benefits and risks of GAI, thereby shaping their judgments of the AI attributed to that source. Our hypotheses test and find the process of AI heuristics (how users invoke heuristics as they make judgments about adoption decisions) and the effects of AI heuristics on users' behavioral intentions. The goal of this study is to advance the HS model to provide a more comprehensive explanation of user attitudes and behavioral intentions, encompassing continued use and intention to pay for the premium GAI services after users have assessed both benefits and risks.

Benefit Heuristics

PEOU

To study benefit heuristics, we included PEOU, a robust predictor in TAM. PEOU is assumed to induce a positive attitude toward using technology (ATTAI). PEOU is the extent to which users think that using GAI requires minimal effort and is assumed to directly impact attitudes toward GAI. If people believe GAI tools are easy to navigate and utilize, they exhibit more positive attitudes toward using these tools, an increased intention to continue using them, and a greater willingness to pay for these tools. Therefore, the following hypothesis is proposed:

H1: PEOU positively influences (a) attitudes toward using GAI services, (b) continued usage intention, and (c) willingness to pay for premium services.

PUE

PUE is treated as a second-order latent factor comprising three properties: impact, competence, and self-determination. We posit that PUE influences attitudes toward using GAI. Additionally, we hypothesize that PUE has a positive correlation with users' intentions regarding the continued use of GAI or continued usage intentions (BIUSE) and willingness to pay (PAY) for premium services. Thus, the following hypothesis is proposed:

> H2: PUE positively influences (a) attitudes toward using GAI services, (b) continued usage intention, and (c) willingness to pay for premium services.

Risk Heuristics

Perceived privacy

Privacy concerns involve a user's worries about the extent to which their use of a system or the sharing of personal data through a system might lead to a loss of control over their personal information (Lutz et al., 2018; Shin, 2010). Such concerns have to do with users' perceptions of how effectively a GAI system manages and safeguards their personal and sensitive information (Gupta et al., 2023). Relevant studies have shown that concerns about privacy have an adverse effect on people's attitudes toward adopting technology services (Dhagarra et al., 2020). This relationship can be hypothesized to GAI, as such technologies involve numerous privacy dimensions. The usage of GAI systems introduces significant challenges regarding ensuring user privacy and data security. Users often question whether such technologies might inadvertently expose them to privacy risks (Albayati, 2024). Díaz-Rodríguez et al. (2023) have emphasized the lack of transparency in data management practices and the potential misuse of user information by GAI systems. They point out that inadequate privacy protection throughout the AI life cycle can result in misuse of personal information and a subsequent loss of trust in AI systems. Additionally, the phenomenon of hallucination, where GAI outputs nonsensical or misleading content (Ji et al., 2023), poses a risk that can negatively impact user trust and adoption. These user concerns regarding privacy and data security can act as barriers to the adoption of GAI. Based on the previous research, we hypothesize the following:

> H3: Privacy concern (PRIV) negatively impacts (a) attitudes toward using technology (ATTAI), (b) intention of continued usage (BIUSE), and (c) willingness to pay for the premium services (PAY).

Hallucination risk in GAI information

Hallucinations are a well-known limitation of GAI systems, involving unreliable outputs in the form of text, audio, visual, or other types (Nah et al., 2023). Hallucinations in GAI can be caused by various factors, including biased data, prejudiced training data, and incorrect assumptions. The hallucination issue in GAIs can be exploited by those who are aware of the hallucination as well as those who do not have an adequate understanding of them. Perceived hallucination risk (PHR) in the GAI context involves the user's understanding of the risk associated with a GAI system's generation of convincing yet inaccurate or fabricated content (Nah et al., 2023). Research highlights several concerns associated with the performance of GAI, emphasizing the propensity of deep learning-based generative models to produce hallucinated text. This appraisal of performance risk affects users' perceptions of both the likelihood and the potential impact of encountering such fake content while using GAI services. Using inaccurate information from GAI could harm a user's professional credibility if the erroneous information is applied in critical contexts. Moreover, hallucinations can pose a serious threat in critical fields such as medicine, where inaccurate information could have life-threatening consequences (Ji et al., 2023; Sallam, 2023). Thus, unintended outputs can degrade system performance and fail to meet users' expectations, particularly in the case of practical applications where accuracy is crucial (Ji et al., 2023). Based on previous studies, PHR is posited to exert a negative impact on attitudes and behavioral intentions toward using GAI services.

> H4: PHR has a negative impact on (a) attitudes toward using GAI services (ATTAI), (b) intention of continued usage (BIUSE), and (c) willingness to pay for the premium services (PAY).

Attitude Heuristics

Humans unconsciously and consciously use attitude heuristics to evaluate GAI for behavioral decisions. Attitude heuristics refer to the cognitive processes involving the use of positive or negative attitudes in establishing favorable or unfavorable communication and intentions (Pratkanis, 1989). Attitude toward technology use is a core variable assumed to influence behavioral intentions to utilize a technology system (Davis et al., 1989). Attitude has consistently been a solid heuristic of the intent to adopt technology across various contexts (Gopinath & Kasilingam, 2023). Given the favorable and unfavorable facts about GAI, a user's behavior toward it would be consistent with their attitude. Individual's adoption decisions are influenced by their attitude heuristics and knowledge of the GAI system.

Research has demonstrated GAI's predictive power in diverse settings, including mobile navigation (Yang et al., 2021), mobile health services (Rajak & Shaw, 2021), AI voice assistants (Choung et al., 2023), web course tools (Ngai et al., 2007), web-based learning platforms (Sánchez & Hueros, 2010), television commerce (Yu et al., 2005), non-fungible tokens (NFTs) for hotels (Liu et al., 2023), personalized AI news services (Lim & Zhang, 2022), and AI applications in workplaces (Park et al., 2024). A meta-analysis by Tao et al. (2020) identified attitude as the strongest predictor of BIUSE. In a meta-analytic structural equation modeling (SEM) model for the use of an AI-based chatbot, the attitude has been found to be the most influential predictor of BIUSE (Gopinath & Kasilingam, 2023). These results indicate an increasing importance of user attitudes in AI adoption research, suggesting that further investigation into how attitudes are formed and their effects on technology use is warranted to enhance the predictive capability of TAM. Given the increasing importance, this hypothesis examines how users' interactions with GAI and perceptions and evaluations of benefits and risks influence attitudes toward GAI adoption.

> H5: Attitudes toward using GAI services positively influence (a) continued usage intention and (b) willingness to pay for premium services.

METHODS

SEM was used to examine the HS process of acceptance and to evaluate whether the model is appropriate for determining acceptance decisions. A national survey was conducted in the United States to test the model. The survey was administered in mid-March 2024 using the Prolific Academia platform. Panelists were recruited under the condition that they had used a GAI service, including ChatGPT, Gemini, or Copilot, more than ten times in the past year. Respondents were given a monetary reward for their voluntary participation. The total sample for analysis was 783 respondents. Table 8.1 presents descriptive statistics on the sample's demographics. The sample included 45.8% females and 51.9% males, with their average age being 39.47 years (SD = 12.51). Approximately 64.4% of the sample were non-Hispanic White, 10.9% as African American, and 10.9% as Asian/Asian American. In terms of education level, 13.2% held a high school degree, while 37.8% had a college degree. About 39.1% of respondents had an annual household income of $75,000 or more. Only 9.2% of respondents were using a paid premium version of the AI service.

Measures

Multi-item scales, adapted from previous research, were used to measure all key constructs. All questions were presented with a 5-point Likert scale ranging from 1 (strongly disagree) to 5 (strongly agree). The questionnaire items for each item are listed in Table 8.2.

To measure PUE, we used three dimensions from the user empowerment theory: self-determination, competence, and impact. We excluded the meaning dimension as it was not directly relevant to the context of GAI services. Users understand that GAI empowers them to plan, decide, and perform tasks better, enhancing their confidence in completing tasks more efficiently and effectively while maintaining autonomy in their interactions with GAI. Each dimension was measured employing three constructs adapted from Afful-Dadzie et al. (2023) and Schweitzer and Simon (Schweitzer & Simon). An example item for each of these three dimensions is "My confidence in handling complex tasks has increased due to GAI," "I have significant control over how I engage with the service in my work," and "My work makes a substantial difference when I use it," respectively.

TABLE 8.1 Demographic information (*N* = 783)

DEMOGRAPHICS	BRACKETS	N	%
Gender	Male	406	51.9
	Female	359	45.8
	Other	18	2.3
Age	18–24	76	9.7
	25–34	236	30.1
	34–44	226	28.9
	45–54	133	17.0
	55+	112	14.3
Ethnicity	Non-Hispanic White	504	64.4
	Hispanic	72	9.2
	Black/African American	85	10.9
	Asian/Asian American	85	10.9
	Other	37	4.7
Education	Less than High school	11	1.4
	High school graduates	103	13.2
	Some college credit, no degree	148	18.9
	Trade/technical/vocational training	27	3.4
	Associate degree	82	10.5
	Bachelor's degree	296	37.8
	Graduate degree	116	14.8
Income	Less than $30,000 a year	158	20.2
	Between $30,000 and $74,999 a year	319	40.7
	$75,000 or more a year	306	39.1

PEOU reflects a user's perception of how effortlessly they can interact with and leverage the GAI service's functionalities to achieve their goals. We adapted four items from Rajak and Shaw (2021) to measure this dimension. Sample items include "I find it easy to use the GAI service to do what I want" and "It is easy for me to become skilled in using it."

Hallucination risk was assessed using four items that evaluated users' perceptions of content produced by GAI as accurate and credible. These constructs were taken from Hannigan et al. (2023) and Ji et al. (2023) and included "I doubt the accuracy of information provided by GAI" and "I question the believability of responses that seem plausible yet doubtful."

Regarding privacy concerns in using GAI, respondents were required to indicate the level of concern regarding the potential misuse or unauthorized use of personal data by GAI services. Four items adapted from Ioannou and Tussyadiah (2021) were

TABLE 8.2   Assessing measurement model for latent variables

FACTOR AND ITEMS	MEAN (SD)	ESTIMATE	S.E.	Z	CR	AVE
PERCEIVED EASE OF USE (PEOU)						
PEOU1: Learning how to use the generative AI service is easy for me.	4.35 (.713)	.856	.020	42.656***	.872	.634
PEOU2: It is easy for me to become skilled in using generative AI services.	4.17 (.765)	.809	.021	38.646***		
PEOU3: I can use the generative AI service with minimal technical support.	4.48 (.713)	.651	.032	20.127***		
PEOU4: I find it easy to get the generative AI service to do what I want.	4.12 (.784)	.667	.031	21.807***		
COMPETENCY (COMP)						
COMP1: I feel empowered in my ability to complete tasks using generative AI.	4.05 (.867)	.798	.020	39.595***	.816	.596
COMP2: My confidence in handling complex tasks has increased due to generative AI.	3.76 (1.00)	.795	.020	39.727***		
COMP3: I am confident in utilizing generative AI for effective task management.	4.07 (.867)	.721	.026	27.545***		
SELF-DETERMINATION (SELF)						
SELF1: I can customize generative AI to suit my unique work requirements	3.83 (.905)	.763	.025	30.549***	.758	.511
SELF2: I have significant control over how I engage with generative AI in my work	4.10 (.868)	.698	.026	26.371***		
SELF3: I feel a sense of autonomy when using generative AI.	3.85 (.944)	.682	.027	25.361***		
IMPACT (IMPT)						
IMPT1: My work makes a substantial difference when I use generative AI.	3.63 (1.06)	.888	.015	57.686***	.906	.762
IMPT2: The outcomes of my tasks are significantly better due to generative AI.	3.78 (1.03)	.885	.014	62.929***		

(Continued)

TABLE 8.2 *(Continued)*   Assessing measurement model for latent variables

FACTOR AND ITEMS	MEAN (SD)	ESTIMATE	S.E.	Z	CR	AVE
IMPT3: My use of generative AI is significantly influencing the outcomes of my projects.	3.56 (1.08)	.845	.016	53.032***		
ATTITUDE TOWARD USING GENERATIVE AI (ATTI)						
ATTI1: Using the generative AI system/tool is effective	4.37 (.695)	.844	.017	48.727***	.855	.664
ATTI2: Using the generative AI system/tool is helpful.	4.53 (.641)	.839	.020	42.965***		
ATTI3: Using the generative AI system/tool is practical.	4.36 (.733)	.758	.031	24.552***		
PRIVACY CONCERNS (PRIV)						
PRIV1: My input could be used for Gen AI model training without permission.	3.69 (1.15)	.663	.030	22.064***	.911	.722
PRIV2: I worry about the generative AI service sharing my information without my consent.	3.40 (1.27)	.935	.009	99.485***		
PRIV3: Unauthorized access to my data by Gen AI systems concerns me.	3.47 (1.27)	.894	.014	66.114***		
PRIV4: Generative AI systems might misuse my personal information.	3.45 (1.19)	.880	.014	64.176***		
HALLUCINATION-CAUSING RISK (HRISK)						
HRISK1: I am skeptical about whether generative AI outputs are based on real data or are made up.	3.16 (1.21)	.867	.014	60.245***	.904	.702
HRISK2: I doubt the accuracy of information provided by generative AI.	3.02 (1.15)	.871	.013	65.758***		
HRISK3: I question the believability of responses that seem plausible yet doubtful.	3.30 (1.14)	.855	.015	55.538***		
HRISK4: I come across generative AI content that appears real but could be fabricated.	3.58 (1.15)	.751	.023	32.121***		

(Continued)

TABLE 8.2 *(Continued)* Assessing measurement model for latent variables

FACTOR AND ITEMS	MEAN (SD)	ESTIMATE	S.E.	Z	CR	AVE
CONTINUE TO USE (BIUSE)						
BIUSE1: I intend to continue using this generative AI service for various tasks.	4.48 (.708)	.895	.017	51.706***	.839	.643
BIUSE2: I want to use this generative AI service's other products.	3.79 (.955)	.568	.031	18.468***		
BIUSE3: I will continue using this generative AI service as long as I can access them.	4.50 (.711)	.897	.017	54.072***		
PAY FOR PREMIUM (PAY)						
PAY1: I am willing to pay a higher price for this service than similar services offered by competitors.	2.50 (1.31)	.923	.008	115.307***	.932	.775
PAY2: I will continue to use services from this generative AI provider even if the price increases somewhat.	2.69 (1.29)	.923	.010	94.052***		
PAY3: Even with significant price increases, I would continue using this generative AI service.	2.40 (1.25)	.911	.008	109.612***		
PAY4: The values and advantages offered by this generative AI service are worth paying more for.	2.92 (1.26)	.855	.014	61.065***		

[a] Standardized estimates
[b] Composite reliability = (Σ std. loadings)^2/ (Σ std. loading)^2 + Σ measurement error
Note: Model Fit indices: χ^2 = 1273.909, df = 410, χ^2/df = 3.11, RMSEA = .052 [90% CI =.049–.055], CFI = .949, TLI = .942, SRMR = .052. ***$p < .001$.

included, such as "Unauthorized access to my data by the GAI service concerns me" and "My input could be used for GAI service training without permission."

Attitude toward using GAI services was measured based on users' evaluations and feelings regarding the use of such technologies. Three items, based on Ma and Huo (2023), were used, including "The GAI system/tool is effective." and "Using the GAI system/tool is helpful."

To gauge users' intentions to continue using the GAI service, three items were adapted from Liu and Huang (2024). Examples include "I intend to continue using it for various tasks" and "I will continue using the service as long as I can access it."

Willingness to pay for the premium GAI service (PAY) was assessed using four items adapted from Chatterjee and Kumar (2017), including "The values and advantages offered by this service are worth paying more for" and "I am willing to pay a higher price for the premium version of it."

Measurement Model, Discriminant Validity, and Convergent Validity

Prior to running the structural path model, we performed confirmatory factor analysis (CFA) by following the theoretical measurement model for each construct. The model fit indices ($\chi^2 = 1273.909$, $df = 410$, $\chi^2/df = 3.11$, RMSEA = .052 (90% CI = .049–.055), CFI = .949, TLI = .942, SRMR = .052) were higher than the criteria suggested by Hu and Bentler (1999). It suggests that the measurement model fits the data adequately. The average variance extracted (AVE) and construct reliability (CR) for each construct (Table 8.2) passed the recommended cutoff levels, .70 and .50, respectively (Fornell & Larcker, 1981). Thus, it suggests that all items effectively converged on their respective constructs and indicates the high internal consistency and reliability of the items within each construct. To test the discriminant validity, the square root of the AVE for each construct was analyzed against other correlation values among the latent variables. The correlations of the latent variables are presented in Table 8.3, with the square root of AVEs placed along the diagonal. Table 8.3 shows that most of the endogenous variables' square root values were greater than correlations with other exogenous variables, confirming the discriminant validity of the constructs (Fornell & Larcker, 1981).

TABLE 8.3 Estimated correlation matrix for the latent variables

	PEOU	COMP	SELF	IMPT	AIII	PRIV	HRISK	BIUSE	PAY
PEOU	**.796**	–	–	–	–	–	–	–	–
COMP	.513	**.772**	–	–	–	–	–	–	–
SELF	.439	.716	**.715**	–					
IMPT	.466	.760	.651	**.873**	–	–	–	–	–
ATTI	.526	.694	.594	.630	**.815**	–	–	–	–
PRIV	−.184	−.188	−.161	−.170	−.218	**.850**	–	–	–
HRISK	−.112	−.309	−.265	−.281	−.356	.492	**.838**	–	–
BIUSE	.390	.595	.510	.541	.748	−.222	−.259	**.802**	–
PAY	.174	.489	.419	.444	.350	−.160	−.223	.354	**.880**

Note. PEOU: perceived ease of use; COMP: competence; SELF: self-determination; IMPT: impact; ATTI: attitude toward using generative AI; PRIV: privacy concerns; HRISK: hallucination-causing risk; BIUSE: continue to use; PAY: willingness to pay for premium.
The diagonal values (shown in bold) represent the square root of AVE.

Structural Model

To check the proposed hypotheses, we employed covariance-based SEM (Dash & Paul, 2021; Hair et al., 2017) with mediation analysis using Mplus 8. The hypothesized structural model demonstrated a good fit to the data: $\chi^2 = 1273.909$, df = 410, χ^2/df = 3.11, RMSEA = .052 (90% CI = .049–.055), CFI = .949, TLI = .942, and SRMR = .052. Indirect effects were checked using 95% bootstrapped confidence intervals (CIs) with 10,000 resamples. The estimated standardized coefficients of the direct and indirect paths are summarized in Table 8.4.

TABLE 8.4 Estimated standardized coefficients for direct and indirect paths

STRUCTURAL EQUATION MODEL (DIRECT EFFECTS)				95% CI	
PATHS	ESTIMATE	S.E.	Z	LOWER	UPPER
PEOU → ATTI	.162	.050	3.241**	.064	.259
PUE → ATTI	.625	.049	12.655***	.528	.722
PRIV → ATTI	.003	.038	.078	−.071	.077
HRISK → ATTI	−.127	.039	−3.241**	−.205	−.050
PEOU → BIUSE	−.073	.047	−1.53	−.166	.020
PUE → BIUSE	.227	.082	2.787**	.067	.387
PRIV → BIUSE	−.09	.033	−2.750**	−.154	−.026
HRISK → BIUSE	.075	.036	2.066*	.004	.147
ATTI → BISUE	.621	.073	8.467***	.477	.765
PEOU → PAY	−.173	.048	−3.644***	−.267	−.080
PUE → PAY	.693	.075	9.290***	.546	.839
PRIV → PAY	−.066	.042	−1.571	−.149	.016
HRISK → PAY	−.012	.047	−.261	−.105	.081
ATTI → PAY	−.103	.077	−1.340	−.255	.048
MEDIATION ANALYSIS					
	ESTIMATE	S.E.	Z	LOWER	UPPER
PEOU → BIUSE					
Total Effect	.028	.059	.469	−.088	.144
Total Indirect Effect	.100	.034	2.961**	.034	.167
Specific Indirect: PEOU → ATTI → BIUSE	.100	.034	2.961**	.034	.167
PUE → BIUSE					
Total Effect	.616	.054	11.352***	.509	.722
Total Indirect Effect	.389	.055	7.022***	.280	.497

(Continued)

TABLE 8.4 *(Continued)*   Estimated standardized coefficients for direct and indirect paths

MEDIATION ANALYSIS					
	ESTIMATE	*S.E.*	*Z*	*LOWER*	*UPPER*
Specific Indirect: PUE → ATTI → BIUSE	.389	.055	7.022***	.280	.497
HRISK → BIUSE					
Total Effect	−.004	.044	−.089	−.090	.082
Total Indirect Effect	−.079	.027	−2.910**	−.133	−.026
Specific Indirect: HRISK → ATTI → BIUSE	−.079	.027	−2.91**	−.133	−.026
PRIV → BIUSE					
Total Effect	−.088	.038	−2.303*	−.164	−.013
Total Indirect Effect	.002	.024	0.078	−.045	.048
Specific Indirect: PRIV → ATTI → BIUSE	.002	.024	0.078	−.045	.048
PEOU → PAY					
Total Effect	−.190	.046	−4.171***	−.279	−.101
Total Indirect Effect	−.017	.013	−1.250	−.043	.009
Specific Indirect: PEOU → ATTI → PAY	−.017	.013	−1.250	−.043	.009
PUE → PAY					
Total Effect	.628	.044	14.178***	.541	.715
Total Indirect Effect	−.065	.051	−1.263	−.165	.036
Specific Indirect: PUE → ATTI → PAY	−.065	.051	−1.263	−.165	.036
HRISK → PAY					
Total Effect	.001	.047	.018	−.091	.092
Total Indirect Effect	.013	.010	1.297	−.007	.033
Specific Indirect: HRISK → ATTI → PAY	.013	.010	1.297	−.007	.033
PRIV → PAY					
Total Effect	−.067	.041	−1.609	−.148	.015
Total Indirect Effect	.000	.005	−0.063	−.010	.009
Specific Indirect: PRIV → ATTI → PAY	.000	.005	−0.063	−.010	.009

Note: PEOU: perceived ease of use; COMP: competence; SELF: self-determination; IMPT: impact; ATTI: attitude toward using generative AI; PRIV: privacy concerns; HRISK: hallucination-causing risk; BIUSE: continue to use; PAY: willingness to pay for premium. Model Fit indices: $\chi^2 = 1273.909$, df $= 410$, χ^2/df $= 3.11$, RMSEA $= .052$ [90% CI $= 049$-$.055$], CFI $= .949$, TLI $= .942$, SRMR $= .052$. **$p < .01$, ***$p < .001$.

RESULTS

The findings suggest that both the heuristic and systematic processes influence users' adoption decisions. Empowerment heuristics are used as a benefit–risk assessing method. Users' benefit–risk assessments had direct effects on heuristic and systematic processes, and these influences were mediated by users' attitudes. Users utilized the benefit and risk assessment as a heuristic to form their attitude based on their judgment of GAI. The effects of heuristic processes on decision-making were stronger compared to systematic processes (willingness to pay for premium services was not supported). Attitude was found to mediate the relationships between heuristic and systematic processes.

Direct Effect of Benefit and Risk Heuristics on Attitudes

This study predicted that the benefit heuristics—PEOU and PUE—have positive effects on attitudes toward using GAI services. First, PEOU was shown to positively influence attitude ($\beta = .162$, $p < .001$). PUE also had a strong positive effect on attitude ($\beta = .625$, $p < .001$). Thus, the benefit perception factors hypotheses, H1a and H2a, were supported.

The study identified two risk heuristics that are inherent in GAI services—hallucination risk (HRISK) and privacy concerns (PRIV). We posited the more concerns users had about hallucination and privacy, the more significant their negative attitude toward using GAIs. HRISK was identified to negatively influence ATTAI ($\beta = -.127$, $p < .001$), while PRIV did not show any significant effect on ATTAI ($\beta = .003$, $p = .998$). The hallucination risk hypothesis, H4a, was supported, but the privacy hypothesis, H3a, was not supported.

Direct Effect on Systematic Processes

PEOU did not show a significant impact on BIUSE ($\beta = -.073$, $p = .126$), while PUE exerted a significant impact on BIUSE ($\beta = .227$, $p = .005$). Thus, H1b was rejected, while H2b was supported. As for the risk factors, hallucination risk was shown to exert a positive influence on BIUSE ($\beta = .075$, $p = .039$), while privacy concern had a negative direct effect on BIUSE ($\beta = -.090$, $p = .006$). Thus, H3b was supported, but H4b was not. Regarding the intention to pay for the premium version (PAY), PUE was found to have a strong direct effect on PAY ($\beta = .693$, $p < .001$). Unexpectedly, PEOU had a significant negative impact on PAY ($\beta = -.173$, $p < .001$). As for the risk factors, both HRISK ($\beta = -.012$, $p = .794$) and PRIV ($\beta = -.066$, $p = .116$) did not have a direct influence on PAY. Thus, H1c, H3c, and H4c were not supported, whereas H2c was supported.

Relationship Between Attitude and Behavioral Intentions

As TAM studies consistently find, ATTAI   had a strong positive effect on BIUSE (β = .621, p < .001). However, ATTAI did not have a significant impact on PAY (β = −.103, p = .180). Thus, H5a was supported while H5b was rejected.

Indirect Effect Routes

The mediation analysis identified three significant indirect effect routes. The PUE route (PUE → ATTAI → BIUSE) exhibited a strong effect size (effect = .389, p < .001), which indicated partial mediation. Thus, PUE has two routes through which it positively contributes to BIUSE. It boosts the positive ATTAI, thereby increasing BIUSE. The PEOU route (PEOU → ATTAI → BIUSE) was also significant (effect = .100, p = .003). The hallucination risk route (HRISK → ATTAI → BIUSE) indicates how the perceived risk of hallucination eventually led to lower intention for continued use by lowering ATTAI (effect = −.079, p = .003). However, this indirect effect was canceled out by the direct effect of HRISK on BIUSE. Thus, the total effect of HRISK was insignificant. As for PAY, none of the indirect routes were significant.

DISCUSSION

Drawing on HSM and the theory of user empowerment, we examined how perceptions of GAI use, attitude heuristics, and their impact on behavioral decisions. The findings show that HSM is a useful theoretical framework for evaluating and predicting user acceptance. Attitudes toward using GAI, stemming from PEOU and PUE, enable users to make positive choices, taking action to advance systematic evaluation and execute adoption decisions. Systematic processing could be predicted by a greater positive attitude, while heuristic processing was predicted by benefit–risk assessment. These findings have implications for applying HSM in technology acceptance research, especially in emerging GAI fields, by expanding our understanding of heuristic factors in GAI acceptance decisions.

The Benefit Heuristics and Attitude

This study introduces the concept of attitude heuristics in GAI acceptance, exploring how users form these heuristics in response to benefit heuristics assessments. The significant path from PEOU to ATTAI indicates that PEOU contributes to positive attitudes toward using GAI, which in turn boosts behavioral intentions for continued use. However, PEOU showed no significant direct effect on BIUSE, as its total effect on BIUSE became insignificant due to the canceling out of its direct effect.

In the classic TAM, PEOU lowers adoption costs by reducing the learning curve. Our results confirm that PEOU generates favorable attitudes toward using GAI, thereby increasing the intention for continued use. PEOU is a unique feature of GAI because it lowers the barrier to entry. For example, ChatGPT's user interface allows interaction with AI using natural language, likely contributing to its rapid adoption. However, in our model, PEOU did not directly affect BIUSE, suggesting that after using GAI services, users may find other factors more critical for continued use.

Notably, contrary to expectations, PEOU had a negative direct effect on willingness to pay for premium services (PAY). The simple bivariate correlation between PEOU and PAY was weakly positive (Table 8.3). However, the path from PEOU to PAY turned negative when other factors, such as PUE, ATTAI, hallucination risk, and privacy concerns, were taken into account. One possible explanation for this negative effect is the influence of PUE. PUE shows a strong positive correlation with PAY (.69) and a very strong influence on ATTI (.63), suggesting that users who feel empowered by the GAI system are more willing to pay for premium features. This strong influence of PUE may overshadow the effect of PEOU when both are considered simultaneously, leading to a negative path coefficient for PEOU to PAY. Furthermore, the negative impact of PRIV and HRISK on ATTI and BIUSE can also contribute to this effect. Although these factors have direct negative effects, their presence in the model may cause users to scrutinize the necessity of premium features more critically, especially if they already find the system easy to use. This critical scrutiny might reduce the perceived need for upgrading to premium features. Another statistical insight is that users with high PEOU might be more confident in using the free version of the GAI system efficiently. When users find the system easy to use, they may not see significant additional value in the premium features, especially when they also feel empowered (high PUE) and have a positive ATTI. This dynamic can reduce their willingness to pay for premium features despite finding the system easy to use.

The User Empowerment Heuristics

The model tested in this study shows that PUE enhances heuristics for evaluating GAI risks and benefits. The underlying factors of PUE—competence, impact, and autonomy—were found to be the most powerful predictors of BIUSE through two significant routes: a direct effect on BIUSE and an indirect effect on BIUSE via ATTAI. The results indicate that positive ATTAI, bolstered by PUE, significantly affects BIUSE but not PAY. Furthermore, PUE demonstrated a strong direct effect on PAY.

The *competence factor* shows that users are sure about their capacity to use GAI to complete tasks. It confirms the role of technology self-efficacy (Compeau & Higgins, 1995) in predicting attitudes toward technology use (Kulviwat et al., 2014). Furthermore, PUE encompasses the ability to instrumentally use GAI services to successfully perform the necessary tasks. This requires more than just knowing how to use GAIs. A certain level of technical proficiency and domain knowledge is required to be able to use technology successfully for specific tasks.

The impact factor reflects users' experience that using GAI helps produce better output compared to what could have been generated without GAI. The findings of the

PUE to ATTAI pathway align with the role of positive result expectations in social cognitive theory (Bandura, 1986). People form a positive attitude toward technology when they expect it to lead to positive outcomes. Evaluating GAI technology involves assessing the quality of outcomes produced and perceived competence. User empowerment is initiated by users and embodied by their perceptions and actions. This empowerment serves as a heuristic, guiding users to form positive attitudes, which influence their subsequent systematic processes.

PUE empowers users to overcome identified risks and form positive attitudes, which then influence their behavioral intentions. PUE has both an indirect and direct influence on behavioral intentions. Users' confidence in AI invokes positive feelings about AI adoption, leading to systematic and effortful assessments of further use or engagement in services. Once users feel confident and know how to assess GAI, they feel assured and reliable, resulting in positive attitudes. If users find GAI tools easy to navigate and understand, their attitude toward using these tools is likely to be more positive. Additionally, PUE, which encompasses users' interactions with GAI in terms of competence, autonomy, and impact factors, directly predicts attitudes toward using GAI.

The Role of the Privacy Heuristic

Privacy concerns directly impacted systematic processing but had no effect on heuristic processing. This suggests that BIUSE might be decreased by privacy concerns about user data being out of the user's control once submitted to GAI services. This significant negative effect aligns with previous findings. Research has indicated that worries about privacy can have a negative impact on people's willingness to use technology, especially in privacy-sensitive domains like healthcare and smart home technology (Sundar et al., 2020). Ratten (2015) found that concerns about privacy are inversely related to the likelihood of using cloud computing services. Similarly, Guhr et al. (2020) examined the extent to which users' privacy concerns influence their intention to adopt smart home technology, which requires sharing a lot of private information with the tech cloud. They found significant direct and indirect negative effects on smart home use intention. Higher privacy concerns led to a decreased intention to use smart home technology. If users are more worried about not being able to control their personal information, they will seek to minimize the risk of privacy violations, which can discourage their intention to continue using the technology.

Practically, privacy issues can be a significant risk factor that may discourage the use of GAIs. Initially, privacy concerns were not considered an imminent threat until users realized that data—including prompts, conversation histories, and sensitive personal information submitted to GAI services—are used for training and improving the model unless users opt out. When used in training, user data can be exposed to human reviewers. Carlini et al. (2023) showed that large language models can be manipulated to recover and produce sensitive personal information from the training data, including email addresses, phone numbers, and postal addresses. Their study highlights that diffusion models, similar to language models, can memorize individual images from their training data and emit them during generation. Despite ChatGPT's privacy protection tools, such as blocking access to personal data about individuals and removing personally identifiable information during training, complete prevention of training data leakage is not guaranteed (Wu et al., 2024). Thus, it is important for GAI services to provide clear warning messages about opt-out options to enhance privacy protection and minimize user concerns.

The Role of Hallucination Heuristics

Regarding risk factors, the results showed that the perceived HRISK had a direct adverse influence on ATTAI while having a slightly positive direct effect on BIUSE. Although users were aware of the hallucination risk, they intended to keep using GAI. The hallucination concern had an indirectly discouraging effect on BIUSE via negative ATTAI. However, when combining the direct and indirect effects, the hallucination concern did not have any significant effect on BIUSE. The perceived risk of hallucination also did not have any effect on PAY.

GAI services tend to produce hallucinations due to mismatches between their training data and the real-world information they generate, known as source-reference divergence, as well as the choices made in their training and modeling processes (Ji et al., 2023). AI companies acknowledge this fundamental limitation of current large language models but cannot yet completely resolve the issue. Instead, they provide warning messages on their GAI user interfaces to remind users of the potential risks. For instance, Gemini says, "Gemini may display inaccurate info, including about people, so double-check its responses," while ChatGPT says, "ChatGPT can make mistakes. Consider checking important information." Our results suggest that the hallucination factor does not deter or slow down the adoption of GAI services. While being aware of and tolerating the hallucination risks, users may be careful while continuing to use GAI services by validating AI-generated outputs and sparingly using them for unfamiliar domains.

Attitude and Behavioral Intentions

The path from attitude to behavioral intention was significant, confirming that attitude toward technology precedes the intention to use it. Users leveraging attitude heuristics showed a higher acceptance of algorithmic services since they were able to understand the system better and enhance their algorithmic attributes. Users' attitudes serve as cues to assess and evaluate the qualities of an algorithm. People rely on attitude heuristics to observe the credibility of algorithms; these heuristics provide a mechanism for evaluating algorithmic attributes and functions. In other words, attitudes guide users in understanding algorithmic qualities and help them change their behaviors. Attitude heuristics are antecedents to perceived value and simultaneously affect intention. Users do not simply accept GAI; they evaluate algorithmic attributes to determine if they are beneficial, useful, and competent. Through heuristic processes, users estimate the value of an algorithmic system. When these attributes are confirmed through cognitive processes, people begin to believe and accept the technology.

IMPLICATIONS

There is an increasing need to understand users' cognitive heuristics at both the practical and theoretical levels. The cognitive heuristic has received increasing research attention in recent days, especially given users' growing reliance on GAI for information search. This study contributes to the understanding of cognitive heuristics in AI adoption by focusing on the effects of AI heuristics on users' adoption behaviors. In line with ongoing literature (e.g., Shin, 2023, 2024), the current study found that higher use of cognitive heuristics was significantly associated with formulating attitudes and triggering behavioral intention, in which a statistically significant relation was discovered between the two variables, thereby supporting the idea of AI heuristics. These implications can be explained in theory and practice.

Theoretical Implications: Linking Heuristic– Systematic Processing to AI Adoption

This study contributes to the research on HSM and TAM in GAI acceptance by proposing and testing theoretical linkages between these models. The findings reveal the relative roles of different perceptual heuristics and how they relate to decision-making in GAI acceptance. The results confirm that GAI acceptance stems from an interconnected cognitive process closely tied to the development of perceptual heuristics through user empowerment. These findings offer a dynamic view of the determinants of user attitudes, highlighting the combined influence of benefit and risk heuristics within the HSM framework.

Specifically, this study advances the TAM literature by (1) incorporating the user empowerment factors that strengthen the role of GAI as a human assistant tool, (2) identifying factors contributing to continued use intentions and the intention to use premium GAIs beyond initial adoption, and (3) examining the role of the risk factors that are inherent in GAIs. The findings revealed that the two benefit heuristics positively contribute to improving attitudes toward using GAI services, which in turn increases intentions. However, the risk heuristics of hallucination and privacy concerns had an insignificant influence on BIUSE and PAY. In other words, the risk heuristics did not deter continued use intention or willingness to pay for premium services.

Among the benefit heuristics, user empowerment factors were significant determinants of attitude heuristics and behavioral intentions. The opaque, black-box nature of GAI may cause concern and fear, prompting users to find ways to evaluate GAI features. Users' perceived empowerment serves as a heuristic that helps them make decisions using available risk-benefit information, leading to the formulation of attitudes and intentions.

Empowerment heuristics enhance users' cognition, facilitating the assessment and judgment of GAI. This concept aligns with self-efficacy and perceived control in the extended TAM. When users are confident and possess strong self-efficacy, they tend to evaluate technology quality and system performance more effectively. The use of empowerment heuristics underscores the importance of users' self-efficacy in interactions with GAI. Users' sense of empowerment plays a vital role in GAI acceptance and in managing data, privacy, and risk. Our results highlight the existence and significance of the empowering heuristic, which positively influences perceived values, attitudes, and intentions.

Second, this study significantly contributes to the AI acceptance literature by identifying the heuristic factors that influence attitudes toward GAI. Besides the technological attributes of AI, it's crucial to understand how users develop attitudes and perceptions about the technology's performance. This study builds on existing research (e.g., Molina & Sundar, 2024) that highlights the cognitive effects of AI as a communication tool. We found that users' AI heuristics, which include both benefits and risks, are vital in shaping their evaluations of GAI. This study is one of the first to explore how evaluating the risks and benefits of AI predicts users' attitudes and to examine how these attitudes mediate behavioral intentions. As motivational and intentional factors become more important in AI adoption, our findings provide valuable insights.

Additionally, this study advances theoretical understanding by clarifying how attitudes are formed and how these attitudes mediate systematic processes leading to different aspects of behavioral intentions. Previous research on technology acceptance mainly focused on factors affecting technology adoption but rarely examined the mechanisms of attitude formation and its impact on subsequent behavior. Our findings show that while a positive attitude toward using GAI contributes to the intention to continue using it, it does not lead to the willingness to pay for premium services. One possible explanation is that most users use GAI for simple tasks that can be completed with the free version. As a result, they might not see the need to upgrade to premium services. This is supported by Hsu and Lin (2015), who found that satisfaction did not significantly influence the intention to purchase a premium app when free alternatives were available.

By clarifying the relationships between perceived features, attitudes, and intentions, this study illuminates the interconnections between algorithmic properties, AI experiences, and user interactions with GAI. These links reveal the cognitive properties of cues: how algorithmic properties provide users with perceptual cues that shape their attitudes and how these attitudes enable users to interact with algorithms feeling both empowered and cautious. The findings contribute to the emerging sub-domain of human–AI interaction by demonstrating a feedback loop: how users' attitudes and behaviors influence algorithms' outputs through empowerment mechanisms. These findings provide a potential path for further development of GAI and overall AI systems.

Practical Implications: Identifying and Operationalizing AI Heuristics

The immediate practical contributions are the relevant guidelines for new GAI service developments. The implications of this study can advance system performance and user acceptance of their products for the developers of algorithm-based systems or other related services associated with machine learning. Given the roles of the benefit and risk heuristics in algorithms, the AI industry may develop a new framework that applies a user HS approach to algorithmic and machine learning systems.

The first practical recommendation for the AI industry is to strategically prioritize user heuristics in GAI design and development. By applying user heuristics, the industry can design GAI services that provide user control, ensuring a positive user experience. User heuristics and cognitive processes are key to understanding how users experience algorithm-based services. The results will be constructive for the GAI industry to analyze and understand the importance of user heuristics and how they affect their decision-making. Understanding users' tendency to use cognitive heuristics can help develop effective marketing and promotional strategies for AI. The findings from this study can be instrumental in helping GAI systems to solve problems by providing user-centered ways of evaluating benefit–risks of AI.

Second, users' perceptions and heuristics related to algorithmic systems are a major factor in GAI. The perceptions and heuristics of users toward algorithmic systems greatly influence their perceived value and behavior, ultimately impacting their decision to use an AI system. Users may be open to using GAI services, but they still have concerns about associated risks. Building user trust in the reliability, credibility, and accuracy of algorithmic systems can promote their acceptance. Understanding user heuristics will be crucial in predicting their future behaviors, but this can be challenging due to users' ever-changing interests and the rapidly evolving nature of the industry. The insights provided by the algorithm model in this work will help in addressing risks and privacy issues. Overall, the aim of algorithmic and automated process systems is to move toward user-centered and human-based GAI services, which necessitates a better understanding of algorithms and their implications for governance.

LIMITATIONS AND SUGGESTIONS FOR FUTURE RESEARCH

This study combined the TAM with the HSM of dual processes, which provides a nuanced perspective on user adoption decision processing. Our results, however, have some limitations that need to be further addressed through future work. First, for the sake of a theoretical parsimonious model, this study intentionally narrowed the applicability of the HS model, leaving out some of its critical components, such as the characteristics of processing, conditions of heuristic use, and motivational assumptions. The motivation to process AI-generated information carefully can also be related to contextual factors and factors related to time. Because this study overlooked such factors, the applicability of the HS model was limited.

Second, this study was conducted during the inception of GAI. Thus, it is likely that the technology will develop and continue to expand as it advances. Many GAIs, including ChatGPT, are in the initial stages of development, and many more variations and possibilities will come. Although the heuristics examined in this study included only those with which we are currently familiar, AI's potential growth will go beyond what is now possible. Research on GAI can be furthered to keep up with challenges and risks, including both technological and user-related heuristics before it achieves widespread adoption. The limitations of this study call for a more robust theoretical and empirical approach to theorize and operationalize AI heuristics for future GAI.

REFERENCES

Afful-Dadzie, E., Clottey, D. N. K., Kolog, E. A., & Lartey, S. O. (2023). Information technology consumerization in primary healthcare delivery: Antecedents, fit-viability, and perceived empowerment. *Health and Technology, 13*(3), 413–425. https://doi.org/10.1007/s12553-023-00749-z

Albayati, H. (2024). Investigating undergraduate students' perceptions and awareness of using ChatGPT as a regular assistance tool: A user acceptance perspective study. *Computers and Education: Artificial Intelligence, 6*, 100203. https://doi.org/10.1016/j.caeai.2024.100203

Bandura, A. (1977). Self-efficacy: Toward a unifying theory of behavioral change. *Psychological Review, 84*(2), 191–215. https://doi.org/10.1037/0033-295X.84.2.191

Bandura, A. (1986). *Social foundations of thought and action: A social cognitive theory.* Prentice-Hall.

Carlini, N., Hayes, J., Nasr, M., Jagielski, M., Sehwag, V., Tramer, F., Balle, B., Ippolito, D., & Wallace, E. (2023). Extracting training data from diffusion models. 32nd USENIX Security Symposium (USENIX Security 23).

Chaiken, S. (2014). The heuristic model of persuasion. In M. P. Zanna, J. M. Olson, & C. P. Herman (Eds.), *Social influence* (pp. 3–39). Psychology Press.

Chaiken, S., & Maheswaran, D. (1994). Heuristic processing can bias systematic processing: Effects of source credibility, argument ambiguity, and task importance on attitude judgment. *Journal of Personality & Social Psychology, 66*(3), 460–473. https://doi.org/10.1037/0022-3514.66.3.460

Chatterjee, P., & Kumar, A. (2017). Consumer willingness to pay across retail channels. *Journal of Retailing and Consumer Services, 34*, 264–270. https://doi.org/10.1016/j.jretconser.2016.01.008

Cheung, R., & Vogel, D. (2013). Predicting user acceptance of collaborative technologies: An extension of the technology acceptance model for e-learning. *Computers & Education, 63*, 160–175. https://doi.org/10.1016/j.compedu.2012.12.003

Choung, H., David, P., & Ross, A. (2023). Trust in AI and its role in the acceptance of AI technologies. *International Journal of Human-Computer Interaction, 39*(9), 1727–1739. https://doi.org/10.1080/10447318.2022.2050543

Compeau, D. R., & Higgins, C. A. (1995). Computer self-efficacy: Development of a measure and initial test. *MIS Quarterly, 19*(2), 189–211. https://doi.org/10.2307/249688

Dash, G., & Paul, J. (2021). CB-SEM vs PLS-SEM methods for research in social sciences and technology forecasting. *Technological Forecasting and Social Change, 173*, 121092. https://doi.org/10.1016/j.techfore.2021.121092

Davis, F. D., Bagozzi, R. P., & Warshaw, P. R. (1989). User acceptance of computer technology: A comparison of two theoretical models. *Management Science, 35*(8), 982–1003. https://doi.org/10.1287/mnsc.35.8.982

Dhagarra, D., Goswami, M., & Kumar, G. (2020). Impact of trust and privacy concerns on technology acceptance in healthcare: An Indian perspective. *International Journal of Medical Informatics, 141*, 104164. https://doi.org/10.1016/j.ijmedinf.2020.104164

Díaz-Rodríguez, N., Del Ser, J., Coeckelbergh, M., López de Prado, M., Herrera-Viedma, E., & Herrera, F. (2023). Connecting the dots in trustworthy artificial intelligence: From AI principles, ethics, and key requirements to responsible AI systems and regulation. *Information Fusion*, *99*, 101896. https://doi.org/10.1016/j.inffus.2023.101896

Fornell, C., & Larcker, D. F. (1981). Evaluating structural equation models with unobservable variables and measurement error. *Journal of Marketing Research*, *18*(1), 39–50. https://doi.org/10.2307/3151312

Gopinath, K., & Kasilingam, D. (2023). Antecedents of intention to use chatbots in service encounters: A meta-analytic review. *International Journal of Consumer Studies*, *47*(6), 2367–2395. https://doi.org/10.1111/ijcs.12933

Guhr, N., Werth, O., Blacha, P. P. H., & Breitner, M. H. (2020). Privacy concerns in the smart home context. *SN Applied Sciences*, *2*(2), 247. https://doi.org/10.1007/s42452-020-2025-8

Gupta, M., Akiri, C., Aryal, K., Parker, E., & Praharaj, L. (2023). From ChatGPT to ThreatGPT: Impact of generative AI in cybersecurity and privacy. *IEEE Access*, *11*, 80218–80245. https://doi.org/10.1109/ACCESS.2023.3300381

Hair, J. F., Matthews, L. M., Matthews, R. L., & Sarstedt, M. (2017). PLS-SEM or CB-SEM: Updated guidelines on which method to use. *International Journal of Multivariate Data Analysis*, *1*(2), 107–123. https://doi.org/10.1504/ijmda.2017.087624

Hannigan, T., McCarthy, I. P., & Spicer, A. (2023). Beware of botshit: How to manage the epistemic risks of generative chatbots. *Business Horizons*, *67*(5), 471–486. DOI: 10.2139/ssrn.4678265

Hsu, C.-L., & Lin, J. C.-C. (2015). What drives purchase intention for paid mobile apps? – An expectation confirmation model with perceived value. *Electronic Commerce Research and Applications*, *14*(1), 46–57. https://doi.org/10.1016/j.elerap.2014.11.003

Hu, L.-T., & Bentler, P. M. (1999). Cutoff criteria for fit indexes in covariance structure analysis: Conventional criteria versus new alternatives. *Structural Equation Modeling*, *6*(1), 1–55. https://doi.org/10.1080/10705519909540118

Ioannou, A., & Tussyadiah, I. (2021). Privacy and surveillance attitudes during health crises: Acceptance of surveillance and privacy protection behaviors. *Technology in Society*, *67*, 101774. https://doi.org/10.1016/j.techsoc.2021.101774

Ivanov, S., & Webster, C. (2024). Automated decision-making: Hoteliers' perceptions. *Technology in Society*, *76*, 102430. https://doi.org/10.1016/j.techsoc.2023.102430

Ji, Z., Lee, N., Frieske, R., Yu, T., Su, D., Xu, Y., Ishii, E., Bang, Y. J., Madotto, A., & Fung, P. (2023). Survey of hallucination in natural language generation. *ACM Computing Surveys*, *55*(12), Article 248. https://doi.org/10.1145/3571730

Kulviwat, S., C. Bruner Ii, G., & P. Neelankavil, J. (2014). Self-efficacy as an antecedent of cognition and affect in technology acceptance. *Journal of Consumer Marketing*, *31*(3), 190–199. https://doi.org/10.1108/JCM-10-2013-0727

Lim, J. S., & Zhang, J. (2022). Adoption of AI-driven personalization in digital news platforms: An integrative model of technology acceptance and perceived contingency. *Technology in Society*, *69*, 101965. https://doi.org/10.1016/j.techsoc.2022.101965

Liu, C.-H., Dong, T.-P., & Vu, H. T. (2023). Transformed virtual concepts into reality: Linkage the viewpoint of entrepreneurial passion, technology adoption propensity and advantage to usage intention. *Journal of Retailing and Consumer Services*, *75*, 103452. https://doi.org/10.1016/j.jretconser.2023.103452

Liu, Y.-L. E., & Huang, Y.-M. (2024). Exploring the perceptions and continuance intention of AI-based text-to-image technology in supporting design ideation. *International Journal of Human-Computer Interaction*. https://doi.org/10.1080/10447318.2024.2311975

Lutz, C., Hoffmann, C. P., Bucher, E., & Fieseler, C. (2018). The role of privacy concerns in the sharing economy. *Information, Communication & Society*, *21*(10), 1472–1492. https://doi.org/10.1080/1369118X.2017.1339726

Ma, X., & Huo, Y. (2023). Are users willing to embrace ChatGPT? Exploring the factors on the acceptance of chatbots from the perspective of AIDUA framework. *Technology in Society*, *75*, 102362. https://doi.org/10.1016/j.techsoc.2023.102362

Molina, M. D., & Sundar, S. S. (2024). Does distrust in humans predict greater trust in AI? Role of individual differences in user responses to content moderation. *New Media & Society*, *26*(6), 3638–3656. https://doi.org/10.1177/14614448221103534

Nah, F. F.-H., Zheng, R., Cai, J., Siau, K., & Chen, L. (2023). Generative AI and ChatGPT: Applications, challenges, and AI-human collaboration. *Journal of Information Technology Case and Application Research*, *25*(3), 277–304. https://doi.org/10.1080/15228053.2023.2233814

Ngai, E. W. T., Poon, J. K. L., & Chan, Y. H. C. (2007). Empirical examination of the adoption of WebCT using TAM. *Computers & Education*, *48*(2), 250–267. https://doi.org/10.1016/j.compedu.2004.11.007

Park, J., Woo, S. E., & Kim, J. (2024). Attitudes towards artificial intelligence at work: Scale development and validation. *Journal of Occupational and Organizational Psychology*. Advance Online Publication. https://doi.org/10.1111/joop.12502

Pratkanis, A. R. (1989). The cognitive representation of attitudes. In A. G. Greenwald; A. R. Pratkanis; & S. J. Breckler (Eds.), *Attitude structure and function* (pp. 71–98). Lawrence Erlbaum Associates, Inc.

Rajak, M., & Shaw, K. (2021). An extension of technology acceptance model for mHealth user adoption. *Technology in Society*, *67*, 101800. https://doi.org/10.1016/j.techsoc.2021.101800

Ratten, V. (2015). Social cognitive theory and the technology acceptance model in the cloud computing context: The role of social networks, privacy concerns and behavioural advertising. In A. Brem & É. Viardot (Eds.), *Adoption of innovation: Balancing internal and external stakeholders in the marketing of innovation* (pp. 43–56). Springer International Publishing. https://doi.org/10.1007/978-3-319-14523-5_4

Sallam, M. (2023). ChatGPT utility in healthcare education, research, and practice: Systematic review on the promising perspectives and valid concerns. *Healthcare*, *11*(6), 887. https://doi.org/10.3390/healthcare11060887

Sánchez, R. A., & Hueros, A. D. (2010). Motivational factors that influence the acceptance of Moodle using TAM. *Computers in Human Behavior*, *26*(6), 1632–1640. https://doi.org/10.1016/j.chb.2010.06.011

Schomakers, E.-M., Lidynia, C., & Ziefle, M. (2022). The role of privacy in the acceptance of smart technologies: Applying the privacy calculus to technology acceptance. *International Journal of Human-Computer Interaction*, *38*(13), 1276–1289. https://doi.org/10.1080/10447318.2021.1994211

Schweitzer, V., & Simon, F. (2021). Self-construals as the locus of paradoxical consumer empowerment in self-service retail technology environments. *Journal of Business Research*, *126*, 291–306. https://doi.org/10.1016/j.jbusres.2020.11.027

Shi, S., Gong, Y., & Gursoy, D. (2020). Antecedents of trust and adoption intention toward artificially intelligent recommendation systems in travel planning: A heuristic–systematic model. *Journal of Travel Research*, *60*(8), 1714–1734. https://doi.org/10.1177/0047287520966395

Shin, D. (2010). The effects of trust, security and privacy in social networking: A security-based approach to understand the pattern of adoption. *Interacting with Computers*, *22*(5), 428–438. https://doi.org/10.1016/j.intcom.2010.05.001

Shin, D. (2023). Embodying algorithms, enactive artificial intelligence and the extended cognition: You can see as much as you know about algorithm. *Journal of Information Science*, *49*(1), 18–31. https://doi.org/10.1177/0165551520985495

Shin, D. (2024). *Artificial misinformation: Exploring human-algorithm interaction online*. Palgrave Macmillan.

Spreitzer, G. M. (1995). Psychological empowerment in the workplace: Dimensions, measurement, and validation. *Academy of Management Journal, 38*(5), 1442–1465. https://doi.org/10.5465/256865

Sundar, S. S. (2008). The MAIN model: A heuristic approach to understanding technology effects on credibility. In M. J. Metzger; & A. J. Flanagin (Eds.), *Digital media, youth, and credibility* (pp. 73–100). The MIT Press.

Sundar, S. S., & Kim, J. (2019). *Machine heuristic: When we trust computers more than humans with our personal information* Proceedings of the 2019 CHI Conference on Human Factors in Computing Systems, Glasgow, Scotland UK. https://doi.org/10.1145/3290605.3300768

Sundar, S. S., Kim, J., Rosson, M. B., & Molina, M. D. (2020). *Online Privacy Heuristics that Predict Information Disclosure* Proceedings of the 2020 CHI Conference on Human Factors in Computing Systems, Honolulu, HI. https://doi.org/10.1145/3313831.3376854

Tao, D., Wang, T., Wang, T., Zhang, T., Zhang, X., & Qu, X. (2020). A systematic review and meta-analysis of user acceptance of consumer-oriented health information technologies. *Computers in Human Behavior, 104*, 106147. https://doi.org/10.1016/j.chb.2019.09.023

Thomas, K. W., & Velthouse, B. A. (1990). Cognitive elements of empowerment: An "interpretive" model of intrinsic task motivation. *Academy of Management Review, 15*(4), 666–681. https://doi.org/10.5465/amr.1990.4310926

Wu, X., Duan, R., & Ni, J. (2024). Unveiling security, privacy, and ethical concerns of ChatGPT. *Journal of Information and Intelligence, 2*(2), 102–115. https://doi.org/10.1016/j.jiixd.2023.10.007

Yada, N., & Head, M. (2019). Attitudes toward health care virtual communities of practice: Survey among health care workers. *Journal of Medical Internet Research, 21*(12), e15176. https://doi.org/10.2196/15176

Yang, L., Bian, Y., Zhao, X., Liu, X., & Yao, X. (2021). Drivers' acceptance of mobile navigation applications: An extended technology acceptance model considering drivers' sense of direction, navigation application affinity and distraction perception. *International Journal of Human-Computer Studies, 145*, 102507. https://doi.org/10.1016/j.ijhcs.2020.102507

Yu, J., Ha, I., Choi, M., & Rho, J. (2005). Extending the TAM for a t-commerce. *Information & Management, 42*(7), 965–976. https://doi.org/10.1016/j.im.2004.11.001

Zrnec, A., Poženel, M., & Lavbič, D. (2022). Users' ability to perceive misinformation: An information quality assessment approach. *Information Processing & Management, 59*(1), 102739. https://doi.org/10.1016/j.ipm.2021.102739

Responsible AI and the Newsroom

9

How Does AI Journalism Make Sense of AI Ethics?

INTRODUCTION

Artificial intelligence (AI) and automation have become pervasive in news media, influencing all aspects of journalism, from news gathering to news distribution (Simon, 2024). Additionally, the use of machine learning continues to grow in the world of journalism. As algorithms are increasingly making editorial decisions, specific concerns have been raised with regard to the responsible, accountable, and fair use of AI-driven tools by news media, contributing to new regulatory and ethical questions (Diakopoulos et al., 2024).

As society desires the provision and consumption of high-quality journalistic content, scholars and industry experts are arguing for the responsible use of AI (Simon, 2024). Responsible AI principles can help adopters harness the full potential of these tools while minimizing unwanted outcomes. The AI adopted and used by media organizations should be trustworthy, and for stakeholders to trust AI, it must be transparent (Wilczek & Eder, 2024). Technology companies must be clear about who trains their AI systems, what data were used in that training, and, most importantly, what went into their algorithm's recommendations. If we are to use AI to help make important decisions, the decisions must be explainable.

For reasons of social responsibility, AI applications in journalism should not only increase editorial efficiency but also contribute to local media's democratic role in society by adhering to professional values and ethical standards (Paik, 2024). They should also ensure news exposure diversity in ways that fit the editorial missions and business models of media organizations (Wilczek & Eder, 2024). There is a growing consensus that AI journalism should adhere to the principles of responsible AI (Paik, 2024). These

DOI: 10.1201/9781003530244-13

principles help guide the design, development, deployment, and use of AI—building trust in AI solutions that have the potential to empower organizations and their stakeholders (Trattner et al., 2022). Responsible AI involves the consideration of the broader societal impact of AI systems and the measures required to align these technologies with stakeholder values, legal standards, and ethical principles (European Council, 2024). Responsible AI aims to embed such ethical principles into AI applications and workflows to mitigate risks and adverse outcomes associated with the use of AI while maximizing positive outcomes (Porlezza, 2023). As AI is influencing a range of social domains from law and medicine to journalism, government, and education, it must be accountable for a host of societal, ethical, legal, and other human-centered concerns in these domains.

Against this background and the limited practice of responsible AI by the media industry, this study analyzes whether and to what extent the use of AI in news media and journalism focuses on journalists' sensemaking of AI ethics. To analyze the complex interplay between journalists and algorithms, a sensemaking approach to ethical judgment is applied to examine the epistemologies of AI ethics, how journalists develop an understanding of AI and ethics-related practices, and how they utilize these conceptions in their sensemaking of AI use in their practice. The sensemaking frame is useful for investigating how journalists derive the meaning of AI in their journalistic contexts and for identifying the emerging ethical relationship between journalists and algorithmic systems.

By leveraging sensemaking, this study proposes AI ethical principles for journalism as a path toward responsible AI journalism. Specifically, the study aims to establish a comprehensive understanding of AI journalism by defining the principles and practices of responsible AI in journalism. Ultimately, the study aims to offer insights into new methods for researching and promoting the development of responsible AI in the journalism and media sectors. We illustrate ethical and responsible AI journalism in the context of applying AI technologies in the journalism domain. Juxtaposing the nature of journalism ethics against the values embedded in algorithmic platforms, we derive insights on how expansive the value gap is between the two interconnected ecosystems and whether this gap is continuing to widen.

The results of the study reveal the ethical challenges of using AI technologies in journalism, the editorial difficulty of integrating AI into professional practices, the decision to adopt journalistic AI systems, and the process of this adoption. Critical analysis positions journalistic sensemaking within a broader organizational, societal, political, and cultural context and highlights the ethical issues related to algorithmic biases, the perceptual discrepancy between journalistic values and AI ethics, problems related to using algorithms, and the knowledge gaps in utilizing AI platforms. Newsrooms approach AI cautiously, estimating whether it can deliver on its promises while upholding conventional journalistic values. These findings help us to understand journalists' responsibilities toward the public, the optimization of journalistic values and AI ethics, and the future model of algorithmic journalism. Theoretical implications can be drawn for promoting responsible AI journalism as a normative ethical framework to be adopted. Practical discussions are made around the responsible AI journalism model and how AI journalism can be practiced while maintaining the integrity of democratic values embedded in journalism ethics. The findings of this study will assist media organizations in developing policies and guidelines to integrate AI responsibly into journalism.

LITERATURE REVIEW

Algorithmic Journalism

Journalistic AI systems can be used to execute many different tasks. AI is being used in all processes of news production, from discovery and production to dissemination (Simon, 2024). Newsrooms utilize machine learning to analyze massive quantities of data and discover patterns that humans would normally never be able to pick up. Journalists turn to algorithms for story angles and rough proxies of public response. AI has been used in journalism for several years, but the advent of generative AI tools has ignited a thorny public debate (Shi & Sun, 2024). Although there is great potential for machine learning and algorithms in journalism, it is also an emerging technology creating new ethical challenges for newsrooms. These technologies appear to surpass human capabilities in structuring information and producing publishable content. However, concerns persist regarding widening global asymmetries, the effectiveness of these technologies in combating or exacerbating disinformation, and even how journalism reports on these technologies while being increasingly dependent on them, and therefore, on the big tech companies profiting from them (Opdahl et al., 2023).

Algorithmic journalism or journalistic AI systems can be used for news production, for example, in data analysis for investigative journalism and fact-checking (Paik, 2024). They can be used to create automated text, video, and audio as well as to complete routine support tasks like translation and transcription (Shin, 2024). In terms of dissemination, AI systems can be used to match content with audiences through personalization and news recommender algorithms or to organize or customize content. Algorithmic journalism can also be a means of engaging with audiences, for example, through virtual assistants and chatbots or new pricing models.

Diakoupolus et al. (2022) argued that AI intersects with core journalism principles like accuracy, context, trust, and transparency. The content produced by AI may contain misinformation or lack a factual basis. Additionally, there may be ethical issues with a journalism organization's transparency, which can damage the credibility of an outlet. How newsrooms use AI and interact with algorithms can offer valuable insights for understanding the principles and practices of responsible AI for journalism (Trattner et al., 2022).

Responsible AI for Media

The integration of AI into journalism and media necessitates responsible implementation, prioritizing not only technical features but also ethical considerations (Trattner et al., 2022). Responsible AI in journalism involves ethical configuration, development, and implementation, ensuring privacy, ethics, and bias mitigation (Zerfass et al., 2020). AI systems used in journalism are obligated to observe journalistic ethics, such as protecting the sensitive personal data they collect or process and following data protection guidelines. In short, responsible AI for journalism should ensure AI tools are incorporated into journalism in a fair, secure, understandable, and robust way (Shin, 2024). The European Council (2023) developed a framework for AI integration into journalism featuring the following components: trust, fairness, privacy and security, explainability, transparency, governance, explainability, accuracy, transparency and traceability, robustness, and privacy. The general principles of responsible AI closely resemble established journalism ethics, but they must be applied to journalism due to the different situations and contexts between responsible AI and journalism. Recently, the need for responsible AI has surged with the use of generative AI in newsrooms. Thus, every single newsroom has been urged to implement an ethics policy to govern the use of generative AI (Arguedas & Simon, 2023).

Responsible AI in journalism involves addressing ethical and social considerations related to AI, such as bias, disinformation, and privacy concerns. To achieve this, designers should first identify fundamental domain values and incorporate them as requirements during the design process. This involves generating configurations for technical and organizational features that support those values.

Ethics by design methods, which incorporate ethical principles into the design and development of products, services, and systems, can be used to help translate journalistic ethics into the design features of AI journalism (Gutierrez et al., 2023). After identifying the value requirements during the design phase, AI designers must then build their systems to reflect these values. For example, an editorial algorithm that filters news feeds can be trained by news editors. They evaluate content based on ethical guidelines, such as whether it meets journalistic values or an organization's public service goals. Aligning data and metrics to values is a non-trivial challenge, as principles can be vague and multivalent, potentially hiding ethical conflicts (e.g., around notations of algorithmic ethics). Success in the build stage requires clear definitions of values so that training data can be appropriately operationalized (Porlezza, 2023). Responsible AI assists newsrooms in establishing the trust, fairness, and governance necessary for journalism to thrive in the AI era (World Economic Forum, 2024).

Heuristic–Systematic Model of Ethics Processing: Making Sense of AI in Journalism

Sensemaking refers to understanding, comprehending, and explaining complex or uncertain events (Edgerly, 2021). It is the process by which people attribute meaning to their individual or collective experiences through priming (providing cues), editing (feedback), and triggering (careful evaluation) processes (Weber & Glynn, 2006). Addressing cognitive processes, sensemaking perspectives have been used in analyzing AI and have shown their usefulness in revealing the nuances of algorithmic sensemaking (Lim et al., 2024). Previous research on AI adoption and users' construction of meaning (e.g., Möhlmannn et al., 2023) showed the significance of clarifying users' sensemaking mechanisms, values, and needs in their particular contexts when working with algorithms (Engstrom et al., 2024).

Based on a sensemaking lens, dual-process theory is a valuable complement aiding explorations of the ethical judgment of AI journalism. Dual-process theories of moral judgment propose that moral decisions involve two or more related but different processes (Powell et al., 2018). Much of human cognition involves two types of reasoning: Type 1 processing is rapid, emotional, and intuition-driven, and Type 2 is deliberative, slow, and calculated, requiring conscious deliberation of a high cognitive load (Kumar, 2016, p. 791). This dual process makes sense in reasoning about AI ethics because journalists may rely on heuristics and their existing values, such as ongoing journalistic values, when dealing with AI at first. Upon further evaluation, journalists may closely assess the features of AI and determine the benefits and risks it can bring to their work. The dual process can clarify how journalists form ethical values regarding AI and how they use AI ethics in their practices.

From Journalistic Heuristics to Responsible AI for Media

Journalism ethics and professional standards have been significant aspects of modern journalism since its inception (Shi & Sun, 2024). Several organizations have developed codes of ethics to outline the expected conduct for journalists and news organizations in relation to their societal role. Today, most professional journalists and media organizations have committed to upholding ethical principles by developing their own codes of ethics or adhering to established declarations, such as those proposed by the *Society of Professional Journalists* (SPJ), *International Federation of Journalists*, and *Global Charter of Ethics for Journalists* (2019). These ethics have become important values and have been used as journalistic heuristics in journalistic practice. While each code of ethics has its own specific focus, widely accepted ethical heuristics and professional standards can be identified:

- Truthfulness and accuracy: Journalists should strive for truth and accuracy, give all the relevant facts in their possession, and verify them. Journalists should not act on behalf of any kind of special interest.
- Impartiality and fairness: Journalists must try to be as objective as possible by reporting different viewpoints fairly.
- Minimize harm: Journalists are sometimes asked to act in the public interest when they face the choice of whether to publish content.
- Privacy: Journalists must respect the right to privacy unless the disclosure of information is essential for the purpose of the published content.
- Accountability and liability: Journalists should improve the services of the media for the public and restore the prestige of the media in the eyes of the general population.

These journalism principles work as heuristics that have long been a cornerstone guiding journalistic practices (Shin, 2024), but there is a growing need to advance ethical standards toward responsibility-aware AI ethics for AI journalism (Diakopoulos et al., 2024). The responsible implementation of AI in journalism is essential to ensure that AI is used in ways that benefit journalism and democracy as a whole (Paik, 2024). This involves a commitment to ethical practices, transparency, accountability, and continuous optimization and adjustment. AI applications in journalism should increase the efficiency of newsrooms and adhere to specific quality standards. Accordingly, there is a need to bring about a paradigm shift in journalism ethics to promote responsible AI for media (Wilczek & Eder, 2024). It is important to explore the similarities and differences between journalism ethics and the broader principles of responsible AI. It is therefore meaningful to examine how the ethical framework of AI journalists differs from traditional journalistic guidelines in AI newsrooms, as well as how public perceptions of responsible AI ethics diverge from traditional journalism principles.

Research Questions

This study assesses how journalists utilize and perceive AI and discusses the implications of AI ethics to develop a responsible AI journalism model. The study focuses on the sensemaking process through which journalists interpret AI journalism and aims to understand how AI ethics are incorporated into their work. The following research questions guide this study:

> RQ1: How do journalists frame AI journalism to make sense of their experience using AI in their journalistic work?
> RQ2: How are newsrooms responsibly utilizing AI in their work? What are the ethical dilemmas engendered by the adoption of AI within the journalistic domain?
> RQ3: How is AI ethics processed and practiced in the context of responsible AI journalism?

These questions delve into the interactions between journalists and AI and propose new paradigms for ethical standards in journalism.

METHODS

We present a qualitative empirical study based on an online survey to examine journalists' sensemaking of ethical AI in their use of AI in journalistic practice. Drawing on 39 interviews with news professionals in 37 news organizations in the United States and 25 international experts working in academia, technology, and policy, this study examines journalists' ethical understanding when using AI across the editorial, production, and dissemination domains with an eye to the ethical implications of AI for news organizations.

Data Collection

In leveraging the sensemaking theory of qualitative methods, we used an interpretative approach to data collection to elicit users' sensemaking responses in media contexts (perceptions and interpretations of ethical AI in journalism). In-depth interviews were conducted with 39 newsroom journalists across the United States. We focused on the journalist-led process of sensemaking that harnesses the capabilities of AI to decipher ethics. The *SPJ* of the United States, the *Paris Charter on AI and Journalism* (Reporters Without Borders, 2023), and the European Council's *Guidelines on the Responsible Implementation of AI in Journalism* were used to guide interview questions to determine how AI platforms impact media professionals' ethics and their sensemaking of AI.

To determine the notion of AI ethics in journalism that is most compatible with journalists' perceptions of ethics, we used semi-structured interviews as a framework to facilitate open and dynamic discussions. This method was designed to produce cognitive mapping as a way of eliciting thoughts, feelings, views, and heuristics, elucidating how users outline and make sense of ethical AI in journalism. The interview guidelines are attached in the Appendix.

As part of an initial exploratory study, we gathered a sample of 25 researchers specializing in journalism and media from universities. These preliminary interviews helped to shape the formal interviews with journalists. The respondents were selected for their research on AI ethics, policy, and management, and they were found through their publications featured on Google Scholar. For data collection, we recruited a sample of 39 editors, journalists, and media professionals in the United States, all of whom had prior exposure to or ongoing experience with algorithmic journalism (Table 9.1). Invitations to participate in a semi-structured, in-depth interview were sent via email to interviewees found through newsroom websites and journalist association listservs, as well as via direct messaging on various social media platforms. The interviews were conducted from December 2023 to May 2024.

The interviews were designed to reveal the dimensions of journalists' experiences with algorithms, identify the subjective sensemaking of underlying ethics in relation to algorithmic journalism, and analyze challenges, perceptions, and evaluations of algorithms in journalistic practices, such as news comment prioritization, data analytics, and online recommendation. Screening interviews were conducted to measure the degree of algorithmic understanding and its usage in journalism. The preliminary survey featured four questions: (1) which algorithms are you currently using in your work? (2) In what dimensions are you using AI in your newsroom practice? (3) What and why do you use algorithms? (4) How can newsrooms integrate news values into their AI practice and how do labor issues intersect with AI?

Online interviews were conducted via Zoom or Microsoft Teams and recorded with the interviewees' consent. The audio files were uploaded to Rev, an online transcription service. The data were processed concurrently as interviews were scheduled. Participants were asked about their daily workflow, social media use for audience building and new distribution channels, challenges and opportunities using web analytics tools, and the various areas of tension they experience in upholding ethical practices in AI journalism. Participants are referred to by their identification codes, and the region in which their newsroom is located is presented (Table 9.1). On average, the interviews lasted 1 hour each. We completed an ethics clearance procedure with the ethics committee of the university with which the authors are affiliated.

TABLE 9.1 Demographics of samples

	NEWSROOM JOURNALIST (N = 39)
GENDER	
Male	18
Female	20
Other	1
AI USE IN NEWSROOM	
Less than 1 year	10
1–2 years	11
More than 2 years	18
COMPANY SIZE	
Small local newsroom	2
Medium-sized media	14
<1000 employees	9
National news	5
AI USE IN NEWSROOMS (ALL THAT APPLIED)	
Researching topics and story discovery	8
Content production	9
Information gathering	7
Audience and trend analytics (AI-assisted interpretation of audience feedback)	4
Reporting/editing	9
Customization/dissemination	10
Fact-checking/fake news detection	11

Data Analysis

Our analytical strategy was informed by reflexive thematic analysis (Pratt et al., 2019). Data obtained from interviews were analyzed thematically. Transcribed interview scripts were entered into the ATLAS.ti tool for qualitative data analysis. The raw data in ATLAS.ti were analyzed according to reflexive thematic analysis to create rigor in the qualitative analysis (Dworznik-Hoak, 2020; Paik, 2024). This procedure, which allows open coding of the data, was adopted to facilitate the generation of new concepts and theories. This approach allowed us to identify complex patterns of meaning within the data. Through our analysis, we gained a relevant understanding of the complexities involved in developing AI ethics for journalism. We captured distinctive sensemaking patterns stemming from the interpretive data. After multiple rounds of analysis and reflection, we identified key themes that highlighted the practical ethical concerns related to AI ethics in journalism and media. Theoretical saturation was reached at 39 interviews, and coding was completed at the identification of nine second-order themes. Our ongoing research informed our interpretation of the data and led to the development of overarching ethical questions regarding AI in journalism and media.

The first step involved coding the raw data into first-order concepts based on what respondents shared in the interviews without any particular themes or theories in mind (open coding). We refer to the terminology used by the respondents when describing the concepts as references (Table 9.2). This first step in the coding procedure resulted

TABLE 9.2 Data analysis procedure

FIRST ROUND	SECOND ROUND	THIRD ROUND	DUAL PROCESS OF ETHICAL REASONING	
Mapping sensemaking process	Factorizing distinctive concepts	Capturing sensemaking patterns		
Reflexive grounded	Thematic analysis	Patterning		
First-order concepts	Second-order themes	Aggregate patterns	Common applications of AI in newsrooms	
Exploratory shortcuts to abstract issues	Themes		Production process	AI use in newsrooms
Non-discrimination, impartiality, due process	Fairness	Type I: Heuristic priming using FAT	Access and observation	Story discovery Trend detection Searching for stories
Responsibility, auditability, controllability	Accountability	Anchoring process between heuristic/ algorithmic	Selection and filtering	Automated collection and analysis
Visibility, understandability, observability	Transparency			Content categorization Analysis of datasets
Quality, correctness, fact	Accuracy		Processing and editing	Verification, fact-checking
Opportunity, benefits, risk	Reliability Robustness	Type II: Computational triggering using REAP		Formatting of content Copyediting, adaptation Tagging of content
Security, data, consent	Privacy		Publishing and distribution	Personalization and recommendation
Interpretable, understandable, awareness	Explainability			Audience analytics Content moderation

Source: Modified from Engstrom et al. (2024).

in 54 first-order concepts reflecting interpreted meaning from the respondents' think-aloud. The second step involved coding the first-order concepts based on differences and similarities (second-order themes—a second level of abstraction of the first-order concepts). This step was conducted by researchers discussing the central meaning of the first-order concepts and collaboratively deciding how the concepts related to each other. This produced eight recurrent thematic domains (second-order themes). In our study, these second-order themes are considered the results of our empirical analysis. We then aggregated the second-order themes into two dimensions. The third step was conducted by collaboratively discussing and theoretically analyzing how the aggregated dimensions relate to theories of workplace learning. This analysis procedure was iterative and co-influencing. First-order concepts and second-order themes were constantly renegotiated according to the research process and discoveries of central meaning based on the collected material.

RESULTS: HOW JOURNALISTS MAKE SENSE OF AI ETHICS

The results of the analysis bring attention to the tension between ethical considerations and the innovative use of AI in journalism. It also revealed the process of journalistic sensemaking of algorithms to make sense of AI ethics. This process entailed heuristic priming through fairness, accountability, and transparency (FAT) and triggering for computational/algorithmic evaluations. Ethical judgment was involved in each of the dual sensemaking patterns, leading us to propose a new model of responsible AI journalism. In the priming heuristic process, journalists are engaged in distinctive sensemaking patterns: fairness, transparency, and accountability.

Type 1: Journalistic Heuristics

In Type 1 processing, moral judgments arise as a flash of feeling, with fast, unconscious, spontaneous, and emotional processing. Journalists use rules of thumb, short-cuts, and experience-based techniques to find cognitive dimensions of AI quickly and efficiently; this is referred to as journalistic heuristics (Lim et al., 2024). Journalists rely on their own existing perceptions of AI as there is no established set of ethical guidelines ("There are no set best practices yet, and we don't know how to see AI") and a lack of expertise regarding the technical aspects of algorithms ("I have no clue about how algorithms work, and I'm not really interested in understanding AI for my job"). Thus, journalists use existing heuristics or conventional journalism ethics or their cognitive schemas to evaluate the ethical values of AI journalism. Journalists use existing journalism ethics (e.g., impartiality, objectivism, accuracy, and accountability) in evaluating AI and its ethics. This process includes users' understanding of AI's FAT.

These factors came up in association with Type 1 processing because people usually had a weak or abstract sense of these concepts and thus made fast heuristic judgments of AI. These were used to evaluate fast and frugal heuristics to capture the ethical quality of AI (Hong & Tewksbury, 2024). Additionally, these cognitive processes occurred in response to journalistic cues based on previous journalism experiences informed by human systems and ingrained heuristics.

Fairness: Extension of the impartiality concept in journalism

The critical meaning of the first dimension, fairness, was the most touted topic, implying a paramount concern. This notion of fairness is transferred or translated from the impartiality and objectivism of journalistic ethics. Just like in conventional journalism, the importance of fairness in ethical AI is widely recognized by journalists. They viewed that fairness is the most complex and multifaceted issue surrounding fairness and bias in AI, encompassing sources of bias, their impacts, and proposed mitigation strategies.

Respondents saw fairness as exploring all sides of an issue and reporting the findings accurately. They believed that fairness principles should be applied in algorithmic journalism:

> Fairness is important in algorithmic journalism. We should not exaggerate the importance of a story. As a journalist, you have a responsibility to examine your own motives and ensure that your personal feelings and emotions do not influence what you report, who you talk to, or which elements of a story you highlight.

Many respondents often claimed that fairness involves being objective and impartial, without any discrimination or favoritism ("News consumers fear that the use of AI in journalism will worsen societal isolation among people and will hurt marginalized groups"). Respondents discussed the ideas of treating everyone equally, being neutral, and ensuring unbiased results from algorithmic filtering and recommendations. They unanimously agreed that fairness is a crucial aspect of algorithmic platforms. When asked how to address issues of unfairness or bias, one respondent emphasized the importance of accurate results, saying, "I hope the results are free of bias. When I believe the algorithm is fair and transparent, I trust and accept it." This highlights the need for precision in the field. In terms of due process, it was noted that an algorithmic system should adhere to an impartial due process without any prejudice. Based on participant responses, it is clear that fairness goes beyond mathematical equality and includes concepts such as impartiality, unbiased treatment, and accuracy ("AI generates debate over newsroom fairness").

Overall, the journalists' perceptions of the meaning of algorithmic fairness were often unclear. However, the majority of journalists agreed that newsrooms should understand concepts of fairness and bias. Many saw AIs as having inherent bias. People considered bias to be a computational error in decision-making processes that results in unfair outcomes. One respondent cited the example of the COMPAS system used in the US criminal justice system, which is used to predict the likelihood of a defendant reoffending.

Many viewed fairness as being about how to detect and minimize bias from AI. Respondents listed kinds of bias (sampling bias, algorithmic bias, representation bias, confirmation bias, measurement bias, and generative bias). It seems that newsrooms interpret fairness in terms of bias. Many understood the benefits of using AI in journalism, but they also experienced risks and challenges. One of the key concerns cited was the negative impacts of bias from AI on news and reporting. It was understood that bias in AI can perpetuate and often amplify existing inequalities, leading to discrimination against marginalized groups and distorted images. One respondent noted,

> In addition to perpetuating gender stereotypes and discrimination, AI can also lead to new forms of discrimination based on skin color, ethnicity, or physical appearance. To ensure that AI systems for journalism are fair, equitable, and serve the needs of the public, it is crucial to identify and mitigate bias in AI….

Others seconded by stating,

> Objectivity is not to use biased data and AI…using biased AI can cause a bunch of ethical issues like discrimination and put a lot of responsibility on developers and policymakers. It can also make people lose trust in technology and limit human freedom. We all need to team up to fix these problems. As journalists, we can help out by creating ethical guidelines and rules that make sure AI systems are fair, open, and answerable.

In general, the interviews showed that journalists still prioritize traditional notions of objectivity. They believe that objectivity and impartiality are the key components of fairness in algorithmic journalism. According to many respondents, algorithmic journalism should not take sides in disputed issues. Impartiality also involves presenting all sides of an argument fairly, which is often referred to as objectivity.

Transparency: Concept derived from the ideas of journalistic truth and accuracy

Transparency was raised and advocated as a critical principle in algorithmic journalism. This notion is derived from media transparency, the audience's right to know, and the accuracy of journalistic values. Transparency is viewed, based on the concept of media transparency (transparent media or media opacity), as how and why news is being produced, distributed, and handled by media professionals. Journalists argued that their news should be produced in a way that allows the audience to evaluate the credibility of their work.

Respondents viewed transparency as an established ethical principle for traditional journalism and argued that it should apply to algorithmic journalism. Transparency is viewed as a core journalistic ethic and value fueled primarily by the drastic development of AI. Algorithmic advances in journalism have gradually increased the availability of and demand for more data and information on the news and its editorial process. The advancement of AI instilled in the public an expectation of the right to know. Respondents argued that the introduction of AI has provided more means of disclosing information, interacting with journalists, and examining news production. One respondent said, "News consumers want disclosure from journalists about how they are using AI—but there is less consensus on what that disclosure should be, when it should be used, and whether it can sometimes be too much."

Respondents agreed that news organizations must ensure transparency in their usage of AI, disclose any automated content creation, and uphold journalistic values such as accuracy, objectivity, fairness, and responsibility. One editor viewed transparency as a two-sided principle, pairing the disclosure elements of transparency with explainability. Additionally, there is a need for diversity and inclusivity in AI development to prevent algorithmic biases and promote balanced reporting. Many respondents expressed concerns that news media is not being transparent about their intentions regarding the use and adoption of AI. Furthermore, there are worries about the lack of transparency in AI systems.

However, because transparency is a complex concept, respondents had differing opinions on how, where, and why their newsrooms should disclose the use of AI tools in their reporting, editing, and production processes. For example, some people had not fully grasped the importance of logical interpretability and the need to explain the internal mechanisms of machine learning. One respondent with technical knowledge of AI emphasized the importance of logically interpreting the algorithmic model in journalism: "The decisions or processes automated by AIs should be interpretable, explainable, and observable to the users who adopt, consume, and control the algorithms and algorithmic services." Another respondent noted,

> Maintaining transparency in the use of AI is critical for preserving public trust. It is important for news organizations to clearly disclose when and how AI systems are used in the creation of data analyses and content. This explanation includes clarifying the algorithms used and the data sources so that the public can assess the credibility of an article.

While the importance of transparency was observed, the respondents did not notice the concept of algorithmic transparency except for its importance as a normative principle. Challenges such as technical limitations and adversarial behaviors that can lead to deviations from expected operations were not observed in our analysis of the data. The lack of understanding of the application of a transparency model in journalism was a recurring trend in the interviews ("The risks for newsrooms relying on AI are that first, media professionals do not fully understand ChatGPT and second, a financial risk that the adoption of these technologies may further complicate journalistic practices"). They had no opinion on the evaluation of disclosures around computational news products in ensuring transparency in algorithmic journalism. For example, while people understood the importance of transparency for maintaining an accountable media industry, they did not think to extract design criteria and identify intentional biases in algorithms.

In short, respondents' understanding of media transparency reflected the relationship between journalists and news sources. This perspective further reflects the journalism-oriented view that contrasts with an audience's view of the right-to-know principle.

Accountability: A concept derived from media accountability

The theme of accountability is derived from media accountability or the social responsibility of the media in journalism ethics. This theme was generated from 49 references found across 23 of the interviews. The concept of accountability in journalism is often seen from a journalistic perspective. It involves the responsibility of journalists and news organizations to maintain ethical standards, ensure accuracy and credibility in their reporting, and uphold the public's trust. One respondent noted, "To serve the public, journalism must be accurate, independent, impartial, and accountable, as well as show humanity." Another noted, "Accountability in journalism encompasses traditional investigative reporting, but much more. It includes fact-checking political speech, digging into digital data, and aggressive beat coverage to reveal as much as possible about what is really going on."

When it comes to accountability, people tend to focus on media accountability. However, when asked about algorithmic accountability, the majority of respondents either had no awareness of the concept or were unable to provide specific responses. Some respondents argued that platform providers should be held liable for considerations surrounding platform design, development, recommendation processes, and outcomes. Respondents expressed concerns that algorithmic decisions are vulnerable to errors that may lead to unwanted consequences. Respondents further stated that algorithms are likely to create problems due to an inability to deal with bias or simple oversight.

Respondents agreed that newsrooms using algorithms should somehow be held liable for the consequences of their programmed machine learning results. In cases where algorithms deliver discriminatory outputs due to biases embedded in training data, systems should be responsible for the harm done as a consequence of this discrimination. One respondent noted, "I wish I could examine and review the behavior of [the] algorithm system." Another respondent expressed, "Algorithms can be equipped to change a system using only certain manipulations."

In summary, the survey respondents demonstrated a tendency to view accountability through the perspective of traditional media. While most recognized the importance of accountability in algorithmic journalism, many did not fully understand how it should be put into practice and supervised. In general, the references indicated three main concepts: media accountability, social responsibility, and watchdog or investigative journalism.

Type 2: Computational Algorithmic Evaluation

After evaluating the abstractive values in AI through the heuristic process, journalists then judged the specifics of algorithmic attributes. This process involves conscious deliberation, as it is cognitively demanding. It is also deliberate and controlled, requiring reasoned processing. During this process, journalists engage in elaborate and conscious sensemaking to assess reliability, explainability, accuracy, and privacy (REAP). This algorithmic evaluation (Type 2) involves conscious sensemaking, evaluating things based on some combination of utility, benefit, risk, and effectiveness. This is a conscious sensemaking of REAP.

AI reliability through source reliability

Reliability is essential in both AI and journalism ethics. Respondents argued that reliability has become imperative in journalism and algorithmic journalism. The issue is how news organizations can leverage AI to enhance their reporting while maintaining trust and credibility. Furthermore, they need to determine the implications of AI-generated content on the public's perception of news. In particular, the rise of generative AI in journalism has provided a powerful tool for creating news content, but it has also raised complex ethical questions around trust, credibility, and the role of human journalists.

The journalists interviewed tended to view reliability from a source reliability (credibility) perspective. Source credibility in media refers to a communicator's positive characteristics that affect a receiver's acceptance of a message. This frame was used in evaluating AI. Many talked about reliability in terms of source credibility ("How can I validate generated news content from generative AI?"), and some argued that reliability and transparency should be embedded in design, not just as an afterthought. How to verify and cross-reference sources, evaluate content track records, and assess bias while using generative AI were the main concerns as to reliability.

Most journalists were wary about trusting AI systems as a credible source and generally had low recognition of AI. The need for trustworthy AI was raised as a concern. One respondent working in data journalism observed, "News consumer trust is strikingly low on AI journalism. Issues with consumer trust that exist in journalism are about how we use AI tools in news making. We have to do rigorous fact-checking when using AI tools."

Another respondent noted,

> There are three categories of risk that AI poses to journalism. First, generative AI in particular can be used to supercharge disinformation campaigns, making them faster, more targeted, and possibly more persuasive using "deepfake" video and audio. Second, AI tools can introduce errors and biases in journalists' own work. Third, journalists could lose their jobs if they are replaced by AI systems, some of which were trained on content created by journalists. All of these developments could undermine public trust in journalism.

One of the cornerstones of trustworthy AI is transparency, meaning explainable algorithms and data sources must be understood so people can comprehend how decisions are made and ensure decision-making is performed in an unbiased and ethical manner. Trust comes when AI prioritizes transparency and safety for users. One editor concluded, "We're continuing to pursue AI ethically and responsibly." One journalist working in a digital newsroom said,

> I don't think generative AI should be used for journalistic reporting. There is too much ethical debt these systems are creating upstream before the tools even reach journalists. You may have editors review the generated text for accuracy and facts, but it will be harder to catch regressive biases in categorization and characterizations.

In short, reliability is framed within the traditional media perspective. The respondents believed that reliability is a fundamental component of a functioning democracy because it directly affects how the public perceives news and the credibility of the media. They viewed reliability as a tool to establish trust in AI journalism ("Trust in AI journalism is super important for the newsroom to do its job well in algorithmic journalism. It gives us the information we need to make good decisions about the news we read"). Having trust in algorithms ensures that people have confidence in the fairness, accuracy, and reliability of these systems. While the importance of reliability is well-understood, there is a limited understanding of the practical aspects of validating and evaluating the reliability of AI.

Explainability: From explanatory journalism

Explainability is derived from the journalistic values of the right to know, accuracy, and truth (factuality). Respondents considered explainability or interpretability as essential in AI, but it seems that the concept was a new or noble concept to them. They viewed transparency as a coupling concept. One respondent used the example of explanatory journalism as a way "to present news stories in an understandable and accessible manner by providing greater context than would be presented in traditional news sources." Another noted the example of *The New York Times* lawsuit and emphasized the urgency for clarity in AI's decision-making processes:

> The lawsuit filed against *The NYT* is a pivotal moment that emphasizes the importance of transparency in the data usage of AI systems and the need for clear explanations of their content-generation processes. It serves as a call to action for developers and policymakers to align AI innovations with ethical standards.

Respondents explained explainability as how the mechanisms and processes used by algorithms should be perceived by audiences. Respondents expressed that algorithms can be rationalized in terms of how specific recommendations are produced in such a manner that humans can understand them. It was raised that some AI systems use algorithms based on black-box practices that layman users cannot comprehend. Another respondent seconded this view: "In most current AI systems, there is no clear explanation of how the AI produced certain results or values." They noted that "providing interpretable explanations can be critical in certain fields." Respondents raised a need for explainability beyond explainability to make news algorithms understandable to people. Respondents stated that recommendations for content should be accompanied by more straightforward descriptions than algorithmic decisions.

Understandability was proposed as a coupling concept of explainability ("understandable by the audience and explainable by the journalist"). Regarding understandability, one respondent mentioned, "AI systems are [becoming] increasingly complicated and are often hard to understand for laypeople and for those impacted by the decisions being generated." This point was seconded by another reporter, saying, "I get why understandability and visibility are important, but I'm not really familiar with AI." As for visibility, another newscaster stated, "The design of news algorithms is neither confirmable nor checkable. Many of these systems are designed by outsourced contractors, and their details are proprietary." Another respondent emphasized, "It's impossible to know what AI is doing and who is responsible for the decisions it makes." Others also emphasized the need for explanation, stating, "Any news produced by an algorithmic system should be spelled out to the people affected by those outputs."

In short, the principle of explainability is crucial in algorithmic journalism, representing a norm with both conceptual and ethical implications. However, there is still uncertainty surrounding the specific application of, practice of, and approach to explainability in the context of algorithmic journalism. Often, explainability was viewed from the journalistic visibility point of view (journalists' ability to understand) instead of audiences' ability to understand news production (the right to know). Journalists currently lack an algorithmic and operational understanding of how explainability should function within algorithmic journalism.

Accuracy in AI vs. accuracy in reporting

Journalists consider accuracy in journalism to be accurate reporting of quality journalism or precision journalism ("The overriding ethical consideration is accuracy in journalism"). Accuracy is often juxtaposed to dis- and misinformation and fake news. Journalists consider accuracy to be a key part of fact-based journalistic discourse and one of the features of quality journalism ("I think quality journalism presents accurate, factual, and truthful portraits of reality"). Accuracy in journalism is an essential ethical guideline. Accuracy has been discussed along with other journalistic values like factuality, credibility, and truthfulness. Accuracy in AI raises epistemological questions of whether and how AI journalism is capable of portraying reality accurately and objectively without bias. Accuracy means that a journalist is responsible for checking whether the information generated by AI is true. In algorithmic journalism, accuracy is viewed as the correct data used to train AI models.

A majority of respondents viewed accuracy as entailing internal consistency between and within news stories, whereas there was a minor view that accuracy is a metric that measures how often algorithmic tools correctly predict news outcomes. Respondents expressed operational difficulties in evaluating accuracy in algorithmic journalism:

> We used an algorithmic tool to retrieve data and classify police misconduct records in our city, helping to identify 54 allegations related to missing persons in just four years. But crucially, the training data for the tool were created by 200 volunteer workers from the community, who manually labeled the records wrongly and by mistake.

The most touted concern in sensemaking responses was how accurate and truthful AI is. Because news algorithms do not express their rules or the relationships within their underlying training data, they produce neither repeatable nor explainable results. Many people mentioned that AI is not always able to accurately differentiate between biased information and unbiased facts when it uses data to form its responses. They believe that journalists' assessments may be more reliable because algorithms might not recognize certain inconsistencies, the (lack of) credibility of information sources, or misinterpretations of new factual developments. While accuracy is ideal, it is viewed that perfect accuracy is rarely achieved in algorithmic journalism. This relates to a statistical limitation: extremely high accuracy can be a sign of overfitting, whereby a model fits its training data too closely and so performs poorly when tested on other data. Knowing this difficulty, newsrooms seem to approach accuracy in terms of practical accuracy based on best efforts.

In short, accuracy is considered the cornerstone of traditional journalism. However, there is a lack of understanding of how accuracy is defined and implemented within the evolving field of algorithmic journalism.

Data privacy vs. source confidentiality

When asked about privacy, journalists tended to see privacy as a person's right to privacy (source privacy) if a journalist unreasonably intrudes (physically, electronically, or otherwise) upon an area in which that person has a reasonable expectation of privacy. Journalists mentioned they have a limited First Amendment right not to be forced to reveal source information and news sources. Some journalists view privacy as a reporter's privilege, as journalism is not required to reveal source information.

Commonly, privacy is viewed as a critical issue in journalism that involves balancing the public's right to know with individuals' rights to privacy. Journalists safeguard sources' rights, maintain ethical integrity, and ensure responsible reporting ("We have to comply with regulations like the General Data Protection Regulation and California Consumer Privacy Act"). Journalists discussed facing ethical and legal challenges when reporting on sensitive matters that may invade personal privacy. AI systems have the potential to generate content that may inadvertently or intentionally defame individuals or organizations. Respondents noted that using AI in their journalism can breach data privacy when an algorithm's training involves datasets that include personally identifiable information.

In writing news stories, journalists are often required to protect the identities of their sources. Many of the most impactful works of journalism have relied upon such an arrangement, yet the balancing act between publishing information that is vital to a story and protecting the person behind that information can present untold challenges, especially when the personal safety of the source is at risk:

> When using a dataset as a source in a story, we are put in the new position of having to evaluate the sensitivity of the information at hand. These challenges are particularly heightened in this age of omnipresent data collection. AI tools have enabled large volumes of data processing, which in turn promotes efforts to monetize data or use them for surveillance.

One editor attributed data privacy concerns to the role of AI instead of journalists. They pointed to recent examples of privacy violations, such as Cambridge Analytica's use of personal data for ad targeting and invasive data tracking by smart devices. They believe that AI is responsible for data leaks and breaches.

Some journalists talked about privacy in terms of data privacy or privacy in AI. For example, using anonymization techniques can shield individual identities or ensure the ethical management of personal data. A massive data forage can expose sensitive information, resulting in significant privacy invasion through AI. Data scraped from online randomly may reproduce and exaggerate personal information about people and their relational data about their associations. Yet, this viewpoint is less common, as the majority of the present-day focus is on privacy in journalism.

One respondent's view serves as a concluding remark on privacy: "Journalists need to deeply understand AI data policy because it is only then that you can apply it." Another editor echoed this importance by saying,

> Similar to handling confidential sources, it's important to assess the information and decide what to publish without disclosing unnecessary personal details. While certain personal information may be necessary, most stories can be published without identifying every individual in a dataset.

It is clear from the interviews that AI journalists use various methods to protect individuals' privacy. Respondents agreed that establishing robust data and AI governance practices and safeguards to protect end user privacy and sensitive data is critical. They wish to communicate data usage policies, obtain informed consent, and comply with AI data protection regulations.

Summary

From the data, it is clear that media organizations are struggling with the question of how to handle AI applications responsibly. The interviews brought to light various issues concerning AI ethics, including (1) the absence of ethical guidelines for AI use and implementation, (2) the importance of human oversight of AI-generated content, (3) the need for transparency in disclosing whether content was created by AI or humans, (4) setting limits on the use of generative AI by journalists, (5) avoiding the disclosure of private information to AI platforms and ensuring human responsibility for published content, and (6) addressing the risk of bias in AI tools.

It is also highlighted that newsrooms have not established general rules or recommendations for the use of other AI technologies like generative AI, recommender systems, data mining tools, or predictive models. Overall, the interviews conducted suggested that traditional journalistic ethics continue to play a significant role in newsrooms. It is evident that journalists acknowledge the significance of ethical values in algorithmic journalism; however, there appears to be a lack of specific understanding regarding the appropriate or effective use of AI in this context. While AI has rapidly replaced traditional forms of news media, journalists' ethical principles remain rooted in the old paradigm. This underscores the critical need to develop a comprehensive and detailed ethical framework and guidelines for the responsible integration of AI into journalism.

Discussion: Shifting Journalistic Values to AI Journalistic Values

As AI assumes a more prominent role in journalism, newsrooms need to adapt to a changing landscape where AI plays a significant role in news production. This shift will challenge traditional conceptions of journalistic practice, necessitating the development of new ethical standards. One significant risk is that the fundamental principles of journalistic ethics may face challenges in this evolving paradigm (Paik, 2024). The ethical issues confronting AI in journalism are often similar to those that journalists already encounter, albeit in varied degrees and contexts. For instance, ensuring the availability of accurate and trustworthy data is crucial for both journalism and AI-generated content. There is a parallel need for transparent and disclosure policies for generated content, a requirement that media organizations already stick to in investigative journalism. Accuracy has been a critical criterion in precision journalism, which is also a pivotal factor in algorithmic journalism. These similarities are the reasons why journalists' views on AI ethics remain within the frame of conventional journalism ethics. While there are ethical codes both for journalism and AI, there are no widely adopted ethical codes for AI journalism. Journalists stressed the need for ethical codes guiding the use of AI in newsrooms to uphold their responsibility to the public while balancing freedom and societal interests.

In the absence of ethical guidelines, responsible AI can be a relevant solution to the current problems in AI journalism. In responsible AI journalism, it is essential that traditional journalistic values such as autonomy, accuracy, diversity, lack of bias, truthfulness, and objectivity remain relevant. However, these values might need to be reconsidered or redefined in light of the new opportunities and risks associated with the use of AI in journalism.

The guidelines of the SPJ can serve as fundamental principles for establishing new ethical values in journalism (Paik, 2024). The first principle of journalism is seeking truth, which involves ensuring the accuracy of published information, providing interpretive context to avoid distortion, citing sources, and labeling commentary. This principle aligns with the accuracy and reliability of responsible AI principles, where accuracy is crucial and refers to aligning predictions with a given set of data or expected outcomes. AI journalists should strive for truth and accuracy, declaring all relevant facts and verifying them.

The second principle of journalism is minimizing harm. This principle can be related to accountability and bias in AI journalism. Accountability is becoming a very important concept in AI journalism. Algorithmic journalism should strengthen high-quality journalism and serve the public interest by maximizing the benefits that AI could bring to data analytics, personalization, and prediction. AI journalism can reduce bias by effectively using fact-checking, data mining, strengthening and scaling investigative journalistic projects, and enabling automatization.

The third principle of journalism is impartiality and fairness. Traditional journalists were required to conduct themselves as objectively as possible by reporting different viewpoints fairly. This notion of fairness can be precisely transferred to algorithmic journalism, where fairness is a core principle of responsible AI. The respondents advocated for the practice of developing AI systems in a fair way that is ethical, reliable, and transparent. Algorithmic journalism should be designed to treat people fairly and consider how they impact different groups of people, such as by gender or ethnicity.

The last principle of journalism is accountability (Table 9.3). Traditional journalists had a responsibility to provide accurate, balanced, and ethical reporting. This principle

TABLE 9.3 Juxtaposing journalistic ethics and AI ethics

	CONVENTIONAL JOURNALISM ETHICS	RESPONSIBLE AI JOURNALISM
Fairness	Journalistic objectivity—impartiality of views and opinion	The quality or state of being fair, especially fair or impartial treatment
Accountability	Social responsibility of media: Watchdog or investigative journalism; plurality	Being held liable in data, bias, and process of reporting
Accuracy	Truth and accuracy	Accuracy without bias
Privacy	Privacy of informants or information sources (confidentiality)	Privacy and security of data (privacy-preserving algorithms)
Transparency	Truth and accountability	Providing a window into the inner workings of AI, helping people understand and trust how these systems work
Harm	Public value	Accountability of news algorithms

can be extended to responsible AI. Developers and organizations are responsible for the behavior and impact of their AI systems. Algorithmic journalism should give audiences ways to hold them accountable. No technology, regardless of how sophisticated it is, can replace the trust journalists build with their audiences. To be accountable, relevant actors must be able to assure others that the AI systems they are developing or deploying are worthy of trust and face consequences when they are not. There are several ways to ensure accountability in algorithmic journalism: establishing clear guidelines and ethical standards for AI use; addressing fairness concerns if a model does not perform well for a small minority of cases; and predicting and controlling what AI generates to reduce bias and ethical risk.

ALGORITHMIC JOURNALISM ETHICS

A Model of Artificially Responsible and Socially Desirable AI Journalism

This study examined AI ethics and explored how journalists make sense of ethical AI when using AI in their practices. A dual-process framework provides a nuanced account of how AI ethics can arise in two different ways or as a result of two discrete reasoning processes. The theoretical model suggests the necessity of shifting journalism values toward AI ethics and implementing a responsible AI journalism framework.

Theoretical Implications: Sensemaking of Balancing Journalism Heuristics and AI Ethics

How do newsroom journalists configure and perceive AI ethics? Our results contribute to the answering of this question by building upon literature on algorithms from a sensemaking perspective. The findings revealed dual sensemaking mechanisms: a heuristic process of priming and an algorithmic evaluation of triggering. These are connected to the ethical sensemaking process, providing heuristics as to whether an AI is ethical or moral. Our results also contribute to theoretical refinement by highlighting how ethical values are created, adjusted, and used in interactions with AI in a specific professional domain. Specifically, we offer three theoretical contributions.

First, the sensemaking framework proved to be a valuable tool for elucidating which values are encountered by journalists using AI and how they choose to make sense of AI use. This is a heuristic part of understanding how and why journalists develop AI ethics in their work and can be used to create guidelines that may help them to practice responsible AI journalism. This study contributes to the sensemaking framework by expanding it into the journalism field and applying it to the specific context of AI as experienced by journalists. The results explicate the constituency of AI ethics in journalism. While the characteristics of AI ethics in general have been debated and studied, their empirical conceptualization within the specific journalism context has been lacking. This study uncovered journalistic sensemaking in relation to algorithms by theorizing its subcomponents and the relationships among the responsible AI ethical components.

Second, the study elucidated the roles and processes of sensemaking in an algorithmically mediated context, where sensemaking occurs through a mediated dual process. It defined sensemaking as a tool for understanding the processes leading to ethical manifestations in AI journalism. Our results suggest that algorithmic ethical sensemaking consists of a dual process of priming and triggering, allowing journalists to heuristically and computationally (algorithmically) keep up with algorithmic performance. This finding extends previous findings (e.g., Edgerly, 2021; Scarbrough et al., 2024) by showing that algorithmic sensemaking serves as a heuristic framework linking journalistic concerns and editorial decisions. Journalists have existing journalism ethics and expect AI to share these values. Journalists often view AI systems as an extension of traditional media outlets, which indicates that they use a conventional paradigm of sensemaking to interpret new innovations.

Journalists' understanding of ethical values plays an essential role in their utilization and integration of AI into journalism (Dworznik-Hoak, 2020). Not only do ethical values play a significant role in informing perceived quality, but they also facilitate journalists' perceptions of the quality and the performance of AI. Journalists consider a system fair when understandable interpretations are available, and they perceive it to be more transparent when there is a higher level of perceived responsibility. Journalists' understanding of algorithm-driven technologies is nonlinear and not organized into structured ready-made automatic processes. How journalists sense, perceive, cognize, and use algorithms in their work hinges on how they process algorithmic attributes and the information through such attributes. Sensemaking goes beyond being a simple way to give meaning to AI interactions (Engstrom et al., 2024);

it helps clarify the ethical issues that allow for the full exploitation of AI interactions in maximizing the benefits and controlling the risks of AI. Sensemaking in AI reveals what attributes are essential in AI, how people sense them, and what ethical values are at play (Kiesow et al., 2021).

Practical Implications: Why Journalists Should Pay Attention to Responsible AI

Practical implications include the effective use of sensemaking in AI ethics and guidelines for responsible AI practice in journalism. First, utilizing sensemaking pathways can help newsroom editors better support their journalists in the use of AI. AI technologies in journalism pose numerous unresolved challenges and societal risks, such as biased algorithms, the spread of misinformation, and the amplification of echo chambers. While AI innovation and progress are positive, it is crucial for newsrooms to adopt and use AI ethically and responsibly. An ethical policy for AI, rooted in the core principles of journalism, is essential for the sustainability and competitiveness of journalism in the AI era. In addition to using AI ethically and professionally, journalists must collaborate to prevent AI from generating biased content and misinformation.

Second, this study highlighted the need for a new ethical model of AI in journalism. The findings clarified how journalistic values can be established in the AI era, balancing the potential benefits of algorithms—such as increased accuracy, efficiency, analytics, and predictions—with the need to uphold the core principles of journalistic integrity, including fairness, accuracy, transparency, and accountability. In the era of AI, journalists should act as sense-makers rather than just messengers or dispensers of news. AI journalists should be responsible for seeking, parsing, sorting, and analyzing information to ethically and effectively transform data into news. Using AI responsibly in this way will enhance transparency, minimize biases and prejudices, and ensure the fairness and credibility of AI applications (Ouchchy & Dubljević, 2020). It is essential to bridge the knowledge gap and provide journalism and the public with a clear understanding of AI journalism with responsible principles of AI. The ability to innovate and use journalistic AI systems in accordance with professional ethics and human rights can contribute to the resilience of journalism in the digital age. The findings provide the fundamentals for carving out principles for responsible AI journalism and media organizations that implement journalistic AI systems.

Recommendation: FAT–REAP Framework for Responsible AI Journalism

The study findings indicate that both heuristic (FAT) and computational/algorithmic factors (REAP) play fundamental roles in journalists' sensemaking. As a result, we suggest implementing the FAT–REAP framework in journalism to promote a responsible AI model in newsrooms.

FAT as heuristics for journalistic values

FAT is essential in journalism, and the same principle applies to algorithmic journalism (Shin, 2024). It is vital for AI-powered journalism to be impartial and free of unintentional bias. In responsible AI journalism, fairness means that AI systems should not prioritize any group, individual, or value. This concept extends the idea of impartiality in traditional journalism, where impartiality signifies unbiased, balanced, objective, and open-minded reporting that avoids favoring one side over another. Fairness in responsible AI is a key goal for AI ethics, as it can foster fairness, justice, and accountability. Some functions, like using generative AI for automatic political news writing, may inherently carry biases based on the editors' political stances, which is generally accepted in newsrooms. However, it is important to disclose these biases when creating algorithms in responsible AI journalism. Additionally, conducting tests to ensure that there is no social bias present in news algorithms is essential.

In the context of journalism, accountability mainly refers to the media's social responsibility toward the public. It aims to improve media services for the public and restore public trust in the media. It also aims to protect freedom of speech and the press and ensure that the media can operate independently to support democracy and the betterment of society. Journalists and news outlets are accountable to the public, and they can address professional, public, and political criticisms through press councils, ombudsmen, media criticism, and digital forms of media accountability. However, AI and algorithm accountability refer to the idea of making algorithms legally responsible for their actions. This means that AI journalists whose algorithms significantly impact the public and society should be held accountable for any mistakes. To achieve this, there should be standards for versioning and commenting, along with best practices for logging, to create a clear audit trail.

REAP as functional and utilitarian requirements

The importance of explainability in journalism has traditionally been underestimated (Trattner et al., 2022). In the past, there was no perceived need for news outlets to provide explanations about their news, stories, or editorial opinions to the public. However, in today's AI age, and particularly in responsible AI practice, understanding the technical aspects of transparency in algorithmic journalism is crucial. Explainability is a fundamental element of responsible AI journalism because it makes AI systems transparent and helps the audience and public comprehend their functioning (Wilczek & Eder, 2024). It plays a significant role in fostering trust in AI systems and the outcomes they generate. The goal is not only to make AI journalism transparent but also to make their operations understandable and reliable in data analysis to the public.

In addition to explainability, trust in journalism is highly valued, and reliable news is seen as an essential standard that shapes people's views on news credibility. In algorithmic journalism, trust is even more crucial than in traditional journalism. Trust in AI is closely linked to the transparency of data, sources, and the process of data analysis. Developers and approvers of algorithms should transparently disclose the purpose, principles, and values guiding an algorithm's development. This self-disclosure ensures that those involved are purposeful in their actions and mindful of the impact and consequences of algorithms. As AI becomes increasingly integrated into journalism, ensuring that these systems are both sturdy and transparent will be essential for their ethical integration into society. Algorithmic journalism should be evaluated based on its societal risks, and any algorithm that has a human impact must be explainable.

The key assumption of the FAT–REAP model is that journalists need to undergo a fundamental shift in their role. They need to go beyond just producing information and become proactive fact-checkers. It is their journalistic responsibility to meticulously verify the credibility of news generated by AI across various topics and domains. Journalists must also actively inform the public of the truth and critique any content that does not meet the ethical standards of journalism. They should focus on enhancing their cross-disciplinary integration skills, not just discovering news but also effectively integrating and organizing content from various sources and perspectives. Moreover, journalists must develop vital planning, organizing, and coordinating abilities by leveraging and enhancing their practical experience. By leveraging their innate human cognition, such as intuition, empathy, creativity, critical thinking, and sense of humanity, journalists can maintain their agency and integrity in collaboration with AI.

CONCLUSION

Newsrooms today are grappling with the challenges and opportunities that come with using AI systems. Most of the interviewed journalists were aware of the changes and dynamics driven by AI in newsrooms. However, journalists have doubts about algorithmic issues, which suggests the difficulty associated with understanding and using the innovation. The significant ethical challenges arising from AI in journalism cannot be overlooked. In adopting AI in journalism, it is essential to recognize the dangers and limitations of AI. As the importance of AI ethics continues to grow, there is a need for a consensus on the responsible configuration and use of AI algorithms in journalism. This study introduced the principles of algorithmic ethics as a moral requirement for responsible AI journalism. Our results make a relevant contribution to AI journalism by elucidating the interconnected concept of algorithmic ethics and journalistic values and proposing new framework based on an optimum model combining the two arenas.

The integration of responsible AI in journalism requires careful consideration to ensure that AI serves as a tool to support human journalists rather than replace them. Human control, moral judgment, and ethical responsibility remain essential components of responsible AI journalism. In line with ongoing research, our results resonate with the need to create a set of codes of conduct for responsible AI journalism. This code would be voluntarily adopted and practiced in each local newsroom, providing a set of ethical guidelines for the development and use of AI algorithms. It would be a reference for decision-making when creating and using such algorithms in newsrooms. Additionally, it could be used during audits or to clarify the limitations of an algorithm's role in journalism.

REFERENCES

Arguedas, A., & Simon, F. (2023). *Automating democracy: Generative AI, journalism, and the future of democracy* (p. 21). Balliol Interdisciplinary Institute, University of Oxford.

Diakopoulos, N., Trattner, C., Jannach, D., Meijer, I., & Motta, E. (2024). Leveraging professional ethics for responsible AI. *Communications of the ACM, 67*(2), 19–21. http://doi:10.1145/3625252

Dworznik-Hoak, G. (2020). Making sense of Harvey: An exploration of how journalists find meaning in disaster. *Newspaper Research Journal, 41*(2), 160–178. https://doi.org/10.1177/0739532920919822

Edgerly, S. (2021). Audience sensemaking: A mapping approach. *Digital Journalism, 10*(1), 165–187. https://doi.org/10.1080/21670811.2021.1931388

Engstrom, A., Pittino, D., Mohlin, A., Johansson, A., & Mirzaei, E. (2024). Artificial intelligence and work transformations. *Information Technology & People.* https://doi.org/10.1108/ITP-01-2023-0048

European Council (2023). *Guidelines on the responsible implementation of artificial intelligence systems in journalism.* Council of Europe. Adopted by the Steering Committee on Media and Information Society in November 2023.

European Council. (2024). Responsible AI guideline. EU Research Report.

Gutierrez, M., Porlezza, C., Cooper, G., Makri, S., MacFarlane, A., & Missaoui, S. (2023). A question of design: Strategies for embedding AI-driven tools into journalistic work routines. *Digital Journalism, 11*(3), 484–503. https://doi.org/10.1080/21670811.2022.2043759

Hong, C., & Tewksbury, D. (2024). Can AI become Walter Cronkite? Testing the machine heuristic, the hostile media effect, and political news written by artificial intelligence. *Digital Journalism, 12*, 1–24.

Kiesow, D., Zhou, S., & Guo, L. (2021). Affordances for sense-making: Exploring their availability for users of online news sites. *Digital Journalism, 11*(6), 962–981. https://doi.org/10.1080/21670811.2021.1989316

Kumar, V. (2016). The empirical identity of moral judgment. *The Philosophical Quarterly, 66*(265), 783–804. http://doi:10.1093/pq/pqw019

Lim, J., Ahmad, N., & Ibarahim, M. (2024). Understanding user sensemaking in fairness and transparency in algorithms: Algorithmic sensemaking in over-the-top platform. *AI & Society, 39*, 447–490. https://doi.org/10.1007/s00146-022-01525-9

Möhlmannn, M., Salge, A., & Marco, M. (2023). Algorithm sensemaking: How platform workers make sense of algorithmic management. *Journal of the Association for Information Systems, 24*(1), 35–64. http://doi:10.17705/1jais.00774

Opdahl, A., Tessem, B., Dang-Nguyen, D., Motta, E., Setty, V., & Throndsen, E. (2023). Trustworthy journalism through AI. *Data & Knowledge Engineering, 146*, 102182. https://doi.org/10.1016/j.datak.2023.102182.

Ouchchy, C., & Dubljević, V. (2020). AI in the headlines: The portrayal of the ethical issues of artificial intelligence in the media. *AI & Society, 35*, 927–936.

Paik, S. (2024). Journalism ethics for the algorithmic era. *Digital Journalism.* https://doi.org/10.1080/21670811.2023.2200195

Porlezza, C. (2023). Promoting responsible AI: A European perspective on the governance of artificial intelligence in media and journalism. *Communications: The European Journal of Communication Research, 48*(3), 370–394. https://doi.org/10.1515/commun-2022-0091

Powell, T. E., Boomgaarden, H. G., De Swert, K., & de Vreese, C. H. (2018). Framing fast and slow: A dual processing account of multimodal framing effects. *Media Psychology*, 22(4), 572–600. https://doi.org/10.1080/15213269.2018.1476891

Pratt, M. G., Kaplan, S., & Whittington, R. (2019). Editorial essay: The tumult over transparency: Decoupling transparency from replication in establishing trustworthy qualitative research. *Administrative Science Quarterly*, 65, 1–19.

Reporters Without Borders (2023). The *Paris Charter on AI and Journalism*. Paris, France.

Scarbrough, H., Chen, Y. & Patriotta, G. (2024). The AI of the beholder: Intraprofessional sensemaking of an epistemic technology. *Journal of Management Studies*. https://doi.org/10.1111/joms.13065

Shi, Y., & Sun, L. (2024). How generative AI is transforming journalism: Development, application and ethics. *Journalism and Media*, 5(2), 582–594. https://doi.org/10.3390/journalmedia5020039

Shin, D. (2024). *Artificial misinformation: Exploring human-algorithm interaction online*. Switzerland: Springer Nature. https://doi.org/10.1007/978-3-031-52569-8

Simon, F. (2024). Artificial intelligence in the news how AI retools, rationalizes, and reshapes journalism and the public arena. Tow Center for Digital Journalism. Columbia Journalism School.

Society of Professional Journalists. (n.d.). Code of Ethics. https://www.spj.org/pdf/spj-code-of-ethics.pdf

Trattner, C., Jannach, D., Motta, E., Costera, I., & Diakopoulos, N. (2022). *Responsible media technology and AI: Challenges and research directions. AI and Ethics*, 2, 585–594. https://doi.org/10.1007/s43681-021-00126-4

Weber, K., & Glynn, M. (2006). Making sense with institutions. *Organization Studies*, 27, 1639–1660. https://doi.org/10.1177/017084060606834

Wilczek, B., & Eder, M. (2024). Developing responsible AI in local journalism with design thinking. In G. Hooffacker, W. Kenntemich, & U. Kulisch (Eds.), Neue Plattformen – *neue Öffentlichkeiten*. Springer VS. https://doi.org/10.1007/978-3-658-44659-8_3

World Economic Forum (2024). *The principles for future responsible AI for media in the era of AI*. White Paper, January 2024. World Economic Forum Report.

Zerfass, A., Hagelstein, J. and Tench, R. (2020). Artificial intelligence in communication management: a cross-national study on adoption and knowledge, impact, challenges and risks. *Journal of Communication Management*, 24(4), 377–389. https://doi.org/10.1108/JCOM-10-2019-0137

APPENDIX: QUESTIONNAIRE FOR SEMI-STRUCTURED INTERVIEWS FOR JOURNALISTS

Thank you for participating in this research. With the approval of the Institutional Review Board from our university, we are conducting a study on AI ethics for journalists in the media industry. Any information you provide will be kept confidential and anonymized. Your identity will never be disclosed by law. Your responses will only be recorded for transcription purposes and will be destroyed afterward.

First, we are interested in learning about your experience with AI (e.g., generative AI) and how you use it in your work in your professional settings. What benefits do you find in using AI in newsrooms? Can you describe a typical interaction with AI and how you engage with it? What qualities and capabilities do you think AI should possess? Have you encountered any ethical dilemmas or problems while using AI? If so, how were these problems resolved? What aspects of the service do you appreciate and what do you find to be drawbacks?

Second, we are interested in your thoughts on the AI service in journalism. Have you received an explanation of the service? What information does it provide about the service? Have you experienced any instances of the service not working properly or providing misinformation? Has the service changed over time? Do you think the service operates transparently or is it a black box? The service algorithms aim to provide users with personalized content. Do you believe this personalization infringes on your privacy? Do you think the recommended content is fair? Do you believe the service is responsible for its actions and consequences? What do you think about the implications of AI in journalism?

Third, we would like to understand how you comprehend (make sense of) the AI system in journalism. How familiar are you with the ethical values of the system? Is it important for you to understand the underlying logic of how the system works or how it generates relevant information for your news production and dissemination? If you receive incorrect information, what do you do? Do you speak to the provider about it? What are your thoughts on the potential impact and development of AI journalism?

Fourth, we would like to know about generative AI and journalism. What is the impact of generative AI on newsrooms and journalism, and how are these technologies being implemented? What issues arise regarding algorithmic biases (misinformation from ChatGPT), and the potential vulnerabilities created by the reliance on and increasing use of generative AI in journalism? Can generative AI be used to address some of journalism's current challenges while preserving the role of human involvement and the credibility of news? What roles do newsroom policies and structures play in shaping the use of generative AI news, and what tensions may arise between journalism and generative AI performance? What are the skill gaps and challenges faced by newsrooms in implementing generative AI effectively? What issues arise around copyright, accountability, accuracy, and privacy?

PART FOUR

Governance of AI Ethics

Striking the Right Balance Ethics and Regulation

The Moral Code
The Intersection of Ethics and Regulation in AI

10

THE EMERGENCE OF ALGOCRACY

"Algocracy," or algorithmic governance, refers to a system in which algorithms and machine learning play a central role in decision-making across various spheres of life (Danaher, 2020). This approach is increasingly seen in areas such as law enforcement, regulatory practices, transportation management, land registration, and within both public and private sector operations (Lorenz et al., 2021). By leveraging data-driven insights, these systems can streamline processes, improve efficiency, and make decisions based on predictive patterns and statistical analyses. However, as algorithms become more embedded in these areas, questions arise about transparency, accountability, and potential bias. Algorithmic governance has the potential to make decision-making more consistent and objective, yet it can also lead to opaque, "black-box" processes, where the rationale behind decisions is not easily understood or accessible (Floridi & Taddeo, 2023). This lack of clarity can be particularly concerning when algorithms are applied in critical sectors, such as policing or credit scoring, where biased or erroneous data may perpetuate social inequalities (Shin, 2024). When artificial intelligence (AI) is applied to these domains, the governance rational has moved from technical rationality and technological feasibility to a higher ethical and moral quest.

Currently, AI governance and ethics are areas fraught with complexity and redundancy as each society is creating its own AI governance and ethical frameworks to advance its own jurisdiction needs. One reason for the complexity may be that determining when and where to regulate automated decision-making systems and how they affect society is complex. In a nutshell, AI governance poses a dual dilemma. The first challenge lies in the epistemological question, which raises doubts about the effectiveness of regulating a fast-changing technology with fixed rules. Since AI is drastically

DOI: 10.1201/9781003530244-15

evolving, existing regulatory frameworks can quickly become outdated or restrictive, leading to concerns about the necessity for governance that can adapt and remain flexible. The second challenge is the weighting dilemma, which should take precedence in regulatory efforts. Should the focus be on specific applications of AI, particular industries, or the risks involved? This challenge also considers which values should be prioritized. Notably, these trade-offs are not strictly oppositional; achieving a balance among various and frequently conflicting interests is intricate and depends on the context.

Despite the dilemmas, sustainable governance frameworks are necessary to ensure AI operates in ways that are fair, transparent, and accountable, thus maintaining public trust in AI-driven systems (James et al., 2023). AI governance seeks to strike a balance between the innovative potential of AI and its societal implications, emphasizing ethics while addressing risks such as bias, privacy concerns, and human rights (Binns, 2023). Effective governance works not only to prevent harmful outcomes but also to establish standards that align AI's influence with societal values and priorities, thereby promoting equitable benefits and avoiding disproportionate impacts on marginalized groups (Shin, 2025). A key aspect of AI governance is establishing transparent structures that distribute both risks and rewards fairly, ensuring that AI technologies do not unfairly advantage or disadvantage particular groups within society (Waldman & Martin, 2022). This is particularly important as AI systems increasingly impact individual lives in ways that can be opaque or even harmful if not properly managed. To address this, a governance framework for algorithms must weigh the benefits of these technologies against potential risks, striving for accountability similar to that found in other areas of public interest. A well-structured governance model provides the necessary oversight through regulatory bodies and compliance mechanisms that help balance these considerations and foster public confidence in the ethical use of AI (Binns & van Zoonen, 2023).

The relationship between AI ethics and AI governance is intimate and crucial, especially when it comes to managing AI risks and enacting benefits (Cave & Dignum, 2023). Without ethics, our understanding of AI risks and benefits would be completely detached from the human experience, causing a slew of cascading problems across domains such as responsible AI development, risk management, and, most importantly, governance. Thus, this chapter argues in favor of the principle that AI governance frameworks and approaches should be grounded in, guided by, and driven by AI ethics. Ethics-based AI governance is more than moral guidance; it necessitates enforceable standards to ensure that values such as fairness and transparency are upheld in practice (Floridi & Taddeo, 2023). Ethical guidelines serve as the moral compass guiding AI governance. Regulations establish clear expectations for accountability, data privacy, and fairness in AI systems, turning ethical ideals into concrete standards that organizations must adhere to. For instance, assessments of algorithmic fairness, data protection laws, and accountability protocols are regulatory tools designed to ensure that AI systems align with these ethical principles (Finocchiaro, 2024). While ethics provide aspirational goals, regulation enforces them, establishing legal frameworks that hold developers accountable for upholding these values (Chesterman et al., 2024).

ETHIC-CENTRIC AI GOVERNANCE: CORE PRINCIPLES

Ethic-centric AI governance emphasizes the importance of ethical values in embedding policies, frameworks, and practices for developing and deploying AI (Table 10.1). This approach prioritizes values such as fairness, transparency, accountability, and respect for human rights, ensuring that technological advancements align with societal needs and moral considerations. The following principles can be summarized with actionable ideas paired with mechanisms through which they can be implemented and upheld.

TABLE 10.1   Key principles of ethic-centric AI

PRINCIPLES	JUSTIFICATIONS	MECHANISMS
Trustworthiness	AI systems should operate reliably and consistently, be developed sustainably, respect human rights and democratic values, and promote inclusive growth along with broad benefits. The role and intended purpose of an AI system, particularly in high-impact situations, should be clearly defined and communicated. Furthermore, individuals involved in the operation of AI systems should be held to high standards of accountability and expertise. Organizations that utilize or develop AI should also collaborate openly with policymakers, AI safety researchers, responsible AI practitioners, and consumers or users when applicable.	Authentication of AI-generated content, Human oversight and involvement, and continuous maintenance of AI inventories.
Transparency and explainability	The design, functionality, intended purpose, outputs, use cases, risks, and impacts of an AI system should be transparently communicated and easily understood by all relevant stakeholders, including policymakers, senior management, end users, and the general workforce. Within an organization, it is equally important to share critical information with key personnel regarding AI initiatives, integration strategies, objectives, potential challenges, bottlenecks, and organizational silos, along with compliance and business requirements. Particular attention must be given to high-risk and high-impact AI systems, especially during deployment and integration phases, to ensure effective oversight and responsible implementation.	Publicly accessible communication and feedback channels, AI lifecycle documentation and reporting, and AI system registration.

(Continued)

TABLE 10.1 *(Continued)*   Key principles of ethic-centric AI

PRINCIPLES	JUSTIFICATIONS	MECHANISMS
Reliability and validity	The outputs produced by AI systems should be both valid and reliable over time. If these systems undergo significant modifications or changes, such processes need to be documented, and the systems should undergo additional assessments for performance, risk, and impact. AI outputs must be fact-based and truthful. In cases where the systems perform unreliably, procedures for recalling or withdrawing them should be established and implemented to prevent adverse impacts from further use. Additionally, it is essential to communicate the capabilities and limitations of AI systems to all those involved in their operation.	Expert-in-the-loop, continuous testing, remediation, and improvement, risk assessments, and input validation.
Resilience and robustness	AI systems must operate reliably in new and changing environments, be resistant to adversarial threats and cyberattacks, maintain their operational integrity during infrastructural failures, and quickly recover to a functional state after such failures. To enhance robustness and resilience, AI systems should undergo regular updates and continuous monitoring. They need to be tested in diverse environments and subjected to various testing procedures. Additionally, they should be designed with redundancy in mind to prevent potential vulnerabilities from leading to catastrophic failures. Organizations should also consider the potential dual-use cases that may arise from the AI systems they implement or develop.	Adversarial training and testing, failure mode discovery and fail-safe implementation, and performance evaluation across novel and/or changing environments.
Privacy and security	AI systems, their training data, and the data they process must be managed with the highest standards of security and responsibility. They should never be deployed in ways that infringe on individuals' fundamental rights to privacy, such as in workplace surveillance or biometric categorization. Any sensitive data used to train or processed by an AI system must be obtained with explicit, informed consent from the data subjects. Robust security measures must be implemented to mitigate risks such as model inversion attacks, where adversaries attempt to reverse-engineer model outputs to uncover sensitive information. These measures should include state-of-the-art encryption protocols, secure model architectures, and regular audits to detect vulnerabilities.	Data governance, cybersecurity protocols, predictive threat intelligence, and identification and protection of AI assets.

(Continued)

TABLE 10.1 *(Continued)*   Key principles of ethic-centric AI

PRINCIPLES	JUSTIFICATIONS	MECHANISMS
Autonomy and human dignity	AI systems should never be used to manipulate, coerce, or undermine individuals, and their outputs must not compromise a person's fundamental human rights and autonomy—the ability to govern oneself. Organizations should invest significant time and resources in promoting AI awareness and skills development on a large scale. Additionally, their AI initiatives should focus on human augmentation rather than human replacement. In situations where AI-driven automation inevitably replaces human jobs, organizations should implement mechanisms to help affected individuals upskill and reskill, thereby preserving human value and dignity.	AI skills development, awareness, and upskilling/reskilling initiatives.
Fairness	AI systems should perform non-discriminately, and training data should possess a high degree of integrity, such that it accurately represents real-world contexts—data lineage should also be scrutinized appropriately. State-of-the-art techniques to identify and mitigate bias in AI models and datasets should be implemented and administered regularly, and the results of these assessments should be openly reported and documented. AI systems should also be leveraged in line with their intended use cases, as specified by AI providers and developers.	Bias audits and real-time impact assessments.

CAN AI ETHICS BE ENFORCED OR REGULATED?

The question of whether AI ethics can be regulated is both challenging and essential in today's AI landscape (Peters, 2023). With AI systems increasingly influencing key domains, establishing and enforcing ethical standards has become urgent. Although theoretically possible, regulating AI ethics involves turning abstract principles into actionable laws and guidelines, which is complex. The most fundamental difficulty is that AI ethical principles are often too broad or abstract, making it difficult to apply them effectively in practice. Ethical values vary by culture and application, demanding flexible approaches. AI's rapid evolution and global disparities in governance priorities add to the complexity. Traditional governance structures only worked for slower AI and can't keep pace with innovation. This mismatch creates gaps in oversight, leaving room for ethical breaches or unintended consequences. Without clear, actionable guidelines or specific frameworks, organizations struggle to implement these principles meaningfully in real-world AI systems. For example, ethics such as fairness, transparency, and accountability are crucial but tend to be vague, leaving room for wide interpretation. This is why regulation is needed in AI ethics to ensure that developers and companies adhere to core principles such as fairness, accountability, transparency, and privacy (Binns, 2023). This could include requiring regular checks for bias, enhancing AI explainability, and setting up accountability structures to minimize harm. Such measures would foster a culture of ethical awareness in AI development, encouraging more socially responsible practices.

Nevertheless, various practical hurdles persist in translating ethical values into practical regulation. One of the main difficulties in regulating AI ethics lies in the inherent subjectivity of ethical principles. Ideas like fairness and transparency can vary significantly, both in interpretation and application. For instance, one group's definition of fairness may be seen as biased by another, making it challenging to create universally accepted regulatory standards (Hacker et al., 2024). Furthermore, as AI evolves, ethical questions may shift, demanding that regulations be flexible enough to adapt to new technological and ethical landscapes. This raises a fundamental question: how can regulators establish guidelines that remain relevant in a rapidly advancing field?

Balancing regulation and innovation is also a key task. On the one hand, strong regulatory frameworks are essential to ensure ethical practices, protect users from potential harm, and uphold societal values. Without adequate oversight, there is a significant risk of AI systems perpetuating bias, violating privacy, or being used in unethical ways. On the other hand, imposing overly stringent regulations can have unintended consequences, such as discouraging developers from exploring bold and creative solutions. This risk aversion may hinder technological advancements that could bring substantial societal benefits. Thus, the key lies in crafting regulations that are both effective and adaptive—rigorous enough to safeguard public interests, yet flexible enough to foster innovation and encourage progress (Koene & Gennaro, 2023).

The global nature of AI technology further complicates regulation. Because AI often crosses borders, a fragmented regulatory approach can create confusion and make accountability difficult for multinational organizations. Each country might adopt different ethical standards and regulatory practices, making consistent enforcement challenging. To address this, international cooperation is needed to create cohesive ethical guidelines that can be applied globally, fostering a more harmonized and responsible AI ecosystem.

A robust regulatory framework for AI ethics also requires input from a diverse range of stakeholders. Involving ethicists, technologists, policymakers, and the public in regulatory discussions can provide valuable perspectives and foster a comprehensive approach (Leprince & Kreiss, 2020). Such inclusivity helps align regulation with societal values, increasing public trust in AI by showing a clear commitment to ethical standards. Public trust is vital for the widespread adoption of AI, and transparent regulatory processes are essential to maintaining that trust.

Although governing AI ethics is possible and necessary, in reality, it is a complex endeavor that requires strategic management (Jobin et al., 2019). An effective regulatory framework must define clear ethical principles, balance regulation with innovation, encourage international collaboration, and engage diverse voices. As AI continues to evolve, these frameworks will need to adapt to keep ethical considerations at the forefront of technological progress (Weissinger, 2024). Ultimately, a robust model of AI ethics will help ensure that AI advances responsibly, serving the public good and minimizing potential risks.

SHOULD AI BE REGULATED, ETHICIZED, OR BOTH

The debate surrounding the regulation and ethical guidelines of AI is both complex and multifaceted, reflecting the diverse challenges and perspectives involved in governing this transformative technology (Binns & van Zoonen, 2023). While ethics provides a foundational framework to guide the moral considerations behind AI development, regulation is essential for enforcing these principles and holding organizations accountable. Ideally, AI should be ethicized and regulated, as each approach addresses distinct aspects of responsible AI development and deployment aspects. Ethicizing AI takes a proactive stance, encouraging developers and organizations to consider social implications early in the design process, before deploying AI systems. For instance, in the healthcare sector, AI systems are increasingly used for diagnosing diseases and recommending treatments. Ethicizing AI in this context would necessitate developers prioritizing patient autonomy and informed consent, ensuring that algorithms are trained on diverse datasets to mitigate biases that could lead to unequal treatment outcomes. By promoting fairness and transparency, ethicizing AI aims to create systems that serve all individuals equitably.

Incorporating ethical considerations into the development process of AI can foster a culture of accountability and responsibility. Principles such as fairness, transparency, and respect for human rights can guide developers in creating AI solutions that benefit society. However, relying solely on ethical guidelines is problematic, as they depend on voluntary compliance and the goodwill of organizations. While ethical frameworks urge developers to consider the societal implications of their work, regulation offers a means of enforcement, holding parties accountable when ethics are neglected (Hacker et al., 2024). By integrating both ethical and regulatory approaches, we can establish a balanced framework where ethical values shape the design and direction of AI, while regulations ensure that these values are practiced in reality. This combination could lead to a responsible environment for AI innovation, ultimately serving society while minimizing risks.

However, while ethics can create a strong internal culture of responsibility, ethical principles alone lack enforceability. Organizations may interpret or prioritize these principles differently, leading to inconsistent applications and potential harms. Conversely, regulation establishes legally enforceable standards to ensure ethical AI principles are consistently upheld. Regulatory frameworks impose requirements for accountability, transparency, and safety, providing mechanisms for redress if AI systems cause harm or infringe on users' rights. For example, regulations such as the California Consumer

Privacy Act enforce data privacy, which is an ethical concern but with legally binding consequences. The regulation also addresses the limitations of voluntary ethical compliance by creating standardized requirements and consequences for non-compliance, which can help prevent harmful outcomes.

The optimal approach is to combine both ethics and regulation in AI governance. Ethicizing AI fosters a culture of responsibility and awareness of societal impacts, while regulation guarantees consistent enforcement and accountability. Together, they create a comprehensive framework that encourages developers to act responsibly and provides society with mechanisms to enforce these principles, resulting in AI systems that are both ethically sound and legally compliant. This integrated approach can optimize AI's benefits while mitigating risks, fostering technology that serves the public good in a manner that is transparent, fair, and secure.

DILEMMA BETWEEN ETHICS AND REGULATION: BINARY ETHICS AND THE LAW

Regulation and ethics in AI are not exclusive but rather complementary (Lorenz et al., 2021). While they each have distinct roles, they often intersect and support one another to guide the responsible development and deployment of AI technologies (Binns, 2023).

Ideally, self-regulation in AI ethics offers a valuable opportunity to complement external regulation by allowing developers and organizations the flexibility to adapt ethical practices to align with technological advancements and specific contexts. This approach encourages innovation and fosters a sense of accountability, as companies take responsibility for the societal impact of their AI systems. Moreover, self-regulation can lead to the establishment of industry-wide standards through voluntary codes of conduct and ethical guidelines, creating a proactive framework to effectively address emerging challenges in the evolving landscape of AI. By embracing self-regulation, we can cultivate a more responsible and responsive AI ecosystem.

Self-regulation in AI ethics allows developers and organizations to adapt ethical practices flexibly in line with technological advancements and specific contexts. It encourages innovation by avoiding overly rigid external rules and fosters accountability as companies take ownership of their AI's impact. Self-regulation promotes industry standards through voluntary codes of conduct and ethical guidelines, enabling flexibility to address emerging challenges. However, self-regulation alone is often insufficient in enforcing responsible behavior. Since ethics relies on voluntary adherence without formal consequences, it may not be universally followed, especially if ethical guidelines conflict with profit motives or competitive pressures. Regulatory frameworks translate ethical principles into concrete rules, offering mechanisms for compliance and penalties for non-compliance. For example, privacy regulations such as the General Data Protection Regulation uphold ethical principles related to data protection by setting clear guidelines for data handling and imposing fines for violations. In this way, regulation serves as a safeguard, especially in high-risk applications with significant social impact, ensuring that ethical principles are effectively implemented. Rather than viewing ethics and regulation as mutually exclusive, they work best in tandem. Ethics can inform the creation of regulations, helping lawmakers understand what principles need protection, while regulation can give teeth to ethical guidelines and ensure consistent application. Both are necessary: ethics inspires responsible innovation, while regulation enforces it. In this way, a balanced approach that combines ethical guidance with regulatory oversight can promote the development of AI that is not only innovative but also fair, safe, and trustworthy (Grieman, 2024).

Regulating AI presents significant challenges due to its complexity, scale, and ever-evolving nature. Values such as transparency and fairness are difficult to define and categorize, with their interpretations varying depending on the context (Weissinger, 2024). Additionally, the rapid progress of AI across sectors like healthcare, finance, and law enforcement adds complexity to the task of keeping regulatory frameworks current and effective. Traditional regulatory methods are often ill-suited for the dynamic, adaptable, and opaque nature of AI systems. These challenges highlight the need for flexible, adaptive regulations to address AI's unique risks while fostering innovation. However, the inherent nature of AI complicates regulatory oversight (Möhlmann & Vohs, 2021).

One of the main difficulties in regulating AI lies in its inherent complexity and opacity (Peters, 2023). Many AI systems, particularly those powered by machine learning and deep learning, operate as "black boxes," where the processes leading to a particular decision are not easily interpretable, even to the experts who developed them (Wright & Schultz, 2021). This opacity poses significant challenges to transparency and accountability, both crucial for effective regulation. When regulators cannot understand how an AI system reaches its conclusions, it becomes challenging to determine whether the system's decisions are fair or unbiased, or to hold developers accountable when errors or biases arise.

This lack of interpretability limits the capacity of existing regulatory frameworks to monitor and control AI effectively, underscoring the need for new methods and tools to understand and oversee algorithmic processes (Shadbolt & Wilks, 2023). Moreover, the vast scope and adaptability of AI applications complicate regulation. Unlike many traditional technologies, AI systems are capable of learning from new data and adapting their behavior over time, which means their outputs can change unpredictably based on new information (Zeng & Li, 2023). This adaptability challenges traditional regulatory models, which often rely on static assessments or periodic reviews that may not capture the ongoing evolution of AI systems. Regulatory frameworks must therefore be designed to monitor AI in real-time or adopt mechanisms for continuous oversight, which requires significant resources and new, advanced tools. Such adaptability also means that regulations cannot be overly rigid, as they need to accommodate new AI capabilities and applications as they emerge.

Privacy and ethical concerns introduce further regulatory challenges, as AI often relies on large volumes of personal data to function effectively (Shin, 2024). The more data an AI system has, the more accurate it can be, yet this also heightens the risks associated with data misuse or breaches of privacy. Regulators face a dilemma in balancing the need for data-driven innovation with the public's right to privacy and data protection. Different countries have varying standards for privacy, as exemplified by the European Union's General Data Protection Regulation, which sets stringent requirements for data handling and algorithmic transparency. The diversity of privacy standards worldwide complicates regulation, as multinational AI developers must navigate a complex web of requirements that may conflict with each other, hindering their ability to create universally compliant AI solutions (Zaidan & Ibrahim, 2024).

Finally, the fast-evolving nature of AI technologies further challenges regulation, which often outpaces existing regulatory frameworks. This rapid advancement presents a significant challenge for policymakers, who struggle to keep pace with the innovations being developed in the field. As AI systems advance, incorporating capabilities like deep learning, natural language processing, and autonomous decision-making, their implications become increasingly complex. Traditional regulatory frameworks, typically designed for more stable industries, may lack the agility required to address the dynamic and often unpredictable nature of AI technology. For example, when new AI applications are introduced—such as predictive policing—regulatory bodies may find themselves reacting to issues after they have arisen, rather than proactively addressing potential risks. This reactive approach can lead to gaps in regulation, allowing harmful practices to proliferate unchecked, as stakeholders exploit the lag between innovation and regulation. Moreover, the technical intricacies of AI systems can make it difficult for policymakers to understand the specific risks associated with their deployment, leading to oversights and misinformed regulations (Binns, 2023). Regulating AI is challenging because of its complexity, adaptability, dependence on personal data, and global implications. To tackle these challenges, we need innovative regulatory frameworks that emphasize transparency, ongoing oversight, and international collaboration. By developing adaptable and cooperative regulations, society can maximize the benefits of AI while minimizing its potential risks.

HOW TO OPTIMIZE ETHICS AND REGULATION

Balancing ethics and regulation in AI development is key, as each approach tackles different parts of responsible AI use. Ethics provides a values-based foundation, encouraging developers, companies, and users to reflect on the broader impact of their work. On the other hand, regulation offers enforceable standards, holding entities accountable and ensuring compliance, particularly in sensitive areas like healthcare, finance, and criminal justice. When it comes to choosing one approach as the primary method, regulation often proves to be more effective. Since regulations are legally binding, they ensure that everyone meets required standards and can face consequences for violations. For instance, laws like the EU's AI Act and the Colorado AI Act enforce ethical standards of fairness and transparency by demanding clarity in AI algorithms and imposing fines for non-compliance. While ethics is essential for guiding responsible design, it often relies on voluntary adherence, which can falter in competitive markets where profit and innovation are paramount. Ethical guidelines can lack the clarity and enforcement that regulations provide, making them hard to follow without legal support. However, ethics is crucial in shaping regulations, as many laws are built on principles like fairness and respect for human rights, ensuring that regulations adapt to changing societal values.

One way to optimize a balance between ethics and regulation is by integrating ethical considerations into the design and development phases of AI technologies (Waldman & Martin, 2022). This method is called "Ethics by design," embedding ethical principles directly into the development, deployment, and lifecycle management of AI systems (Brey & Dainow, 2024). Google and Microsoft have implemented ethical principles that guide their AI projects. These guidelines address crucial concerns such as fairness, safety, privacy, and bias prevention, ensuring that ethical risks are identified early in the process. By embedding these principles directly into the development lifecycle, developers can proactively address potential issues and ensure their technologies align with societal values before they are deployed in the real world (Binns, 2023). To be effective, this ethical embedding approach should be accompanied with a context-specific approach. That is, tailoring ethical frameworks to different applications or industries should be done. For instance, prioritize transparency in healthcare AI, while focusing on safety in autonomous vehicles.

Another effective strategy for optimizing AI ethics and regulation is the use of regulatory sandboxes (Chesterman et al., 2024). These controlled environments allow AI technologies to be tested in real-world conditions with regulatory oversight, minimizing the risk of harm. Countries such as Singapore and South Korea have pioneered regulatory sandboxes, allowing AI systems to be tested in industries like healthcare and finance. This approach gives regulators the chance to observe the technology's impacts and adjust regulations as needed, ensuring innovation continues while reducing potential risks to public safety and well-being. Additionally, integrating human-in-the-loop systems can be useful for maintaining oversight in critical applications such as criminal justice. This approach not only ensures that complex ethical issues, such as transparency and accountability, are considered, but it also reinforces public trust by showing that AI systems are designed to prioritize ethical considerations. Human oversight in AI applications helps balance efficiency with fairness and transparency, thereby promoting better outcomes while safeguarding societal values (Binns & van Zoonen, 2023; Schuilenburg & Peeters, 2021).

Achieving the equilibrium requires the establishment of frameworks that can adapt to technological progress while also reflecting a wide array of societal values. Involving a diverse group of stakeholders—such as technologists, ethicists, policymakers, and those affected by AI—is essential. These varied perspectives help ensure that ethical guidelines resonate across different cultural, social, and economic contexts, promoting equity and inclusivity in AI. When contributors from diverse backgrounds participate in shaping the ethical framework, AI regulations are better equipped to consider the diverse potential consequences of these technologies on society. It should be noted that optimizing ethics and regulation in AI is an ongoing process of balancing innovation with oversight, adapting to technological changes, and fostering a shared commitment to societal values (James et al., 2023). Effective AI governance requires flexible yet robust policies that allow AI systems to evolve responsibly while safeguarding the rights, privacy, and well-being of individuals and communities.

AI REGULATION AND ETHICS IN THE WORLD: GLOBAL PERSPECTIVES

The landscape of AI regulation is rapidly evolving, with various countries implementing their frameworks to address the ethical and societal implications of AI technologies. The regulatory approaches in the United States, the EU, the United Kingdom, and South Korea highlight their unique strategies and challenges in governing AI.

United States

In the United States, the approach to AI regulation is characterized by a decentralized and sector-specific framework (Donoghue et al., 2024). There is no comprehensive federal AI regulation; instead, oversight is largely left to individual states and industry sectors. Various federal agencies, such as the Federal Trade Commission (FTC) and the National Institute of Standards and Technology (NIST), are actively engaged in developing guidelines and recommendations for AI governance. For instance, NIST has initiated efforts to create a framework for managing AI risks, focusing on reliability, privacy, and bias mitigation. Moreover, there has been growing interest in legislative proposals aimed at regulating AI technologies. The Algorithmic Accountability Act, introduced in 2022, aims to require companies to assess the impact of their automated systems on accuracy, fairness, and privacy. Despite these efforts, challenges remain, including the fragmented nature of the regulatory landscape, which can create confusion and hinder accountability across states and sectors.

European Union

The regulatory approaches to AI in the EU and the United States differ significantly in structure, philosophy, and implementation, reflecting each region's unique priorities and values. In the EU, the regulatory landscape is characterized by a comprehensive and centralized approach. The proposed EU AI Act is a prime example, establishing a risk-based classification system that categorizes AI applications into four tiers: unacceptable, high-risk, limited-risk, and minimal risk (European Commission, 2021). This framework mandates varying degrees of regulatory scrutiny, with unacceptable AI practices, such as social scoring by governments, being outright banned. High-risk AI systems, which have substantial implications in critical areas like healthcare and law enforcement, are subject to stringent requirements, including rigorous assessments and transparency mandates. This structured approach is grounded in the EU's commitment to aligning AI technologies with fundamental rights, emphasizing ethical standards and accountability in their deployment. Conversely, the United States adopts a more decentralized and sector-specific approach to AI regulation.

Ethics and rights are central to the EU's regulatory framework, which strongly emphasizes safeguarding individual rights and promoting ethical AI development. The EU AI Act protects fundamental rights such as privacy and non-discrimination, aiming to ensure that AI systems operate transparently and responsibly. This commitment to ethical governance reflects the EU's broader values and societal priorities. Moreover, the EU's strategy aims to establish common standards that may influence global AI governance, positioning the EU as a leader in ethical AI regulation. The intent is to create a cohesive framework that other regions might adopt, thereby reinforcing its commitment to ethical standards on an international scale.

The EU AI Act emphasizes the importance of transparency and user awareness. For limited-risk and minimal-risk AI applications, developers are required to inform users about the nature of the AI systems they interact with. This transparency not only fosters public trust but also empowers users to make informed decisions about their engagement with AI technologies. By prioritizing user awareness, the EU aims to create an environment where individuals feel confident in the AI systems they encounter. Moreover, the EU's approach to AI regulation is grounded in its commitment to fundamental rights and ethical principles. The regulatory framework aims to ensure that AI development is in line with the EU's core values, such as respect for human dignity, privacy, and non-discrimination. By embedding ethical considerations into the regulatory process, the EU aims to ensure that AI technologies are developed and deployed in a manner that upholds societal values and protects individuals' rights.

The EU AI Act is a groundbreaking initiative to establish a comprehensive regulatory framework for AI technologies. By adopting a risk-based approach, emphasizing transparency, and protecting fundamental rights, the EU aims to effectively tackle the complexities of AI regulation. As the landscape of AI continues to evolve, the EU's proactive stance will likely serve as a model for other regions seeking to address AI technologies' ethical and societal implications.

United Kingdom

The United Kingdom is taking a more centralized approach to AI regulation, with a focus on creating a framework that fosters innovation while ensuring ethical standards are met (Roberts et al., 2023). The UK government published the "National AI Strategy" in 2021, which outlines its vision for AI development, emphasizing the importance of trust and transparency in AI systems. The strategy encourages collaboration between government, industry, and academia to establish best practices for responsible AI deployment. In addition, the United Kingdom is exploring the establishment of an AI regulatory framework that balances innovation and ethical considerations. The Centre for Data Ethics and Innovation plays a vital role in advising the government on the ethical use of data and AI. Recent discussions have centered around the need for principles rather than prescriptive rules, enabling flexibility as AI technologies evolve. However, the United Kingdom faces challenges in addressing potential biases in AI systems and ensuring public trust in AI applications.

South Korea

South Korea has adopted a proactive approach to AI regulation, recognizing its strategic importance in its economic development. The government has implemented various initiatives to support AI innovation while ensuring ethical practices. The "Artificial Intelligence National Strategy," launched in 2020, aims to position South Korea as a global leader in AI by promoting research and development, education, and infrastructure. South Korea established the "Guidelines for Ethical AI" to address ethical concerns in 2021. These guidelines outline principles for responsible AI development and deployment. They emphasize transparency, fairness, and accountability and aim to build public trust in AI technologies. Additionally, South Korea is actively engaging in international discussions on AI governance, participating in forums like the OECD's AI Policy Observatory to share insights and collaborate on best practices.

The regulatory approaches to AI in each country reflect its unique context and priorities. The United States leans toward a decentralized, sector-specific framework, while the United Kingdom aims for a more centralized and principles-based approach. South Korea stands out with its proactive national strategy and commitment to ethical AI development. As AI technologies continue to evolve, these countries will need to adapt their regulatory frameworks to address emerging challenges and ensure that AI serves the public good. Collaborative efforts at both national and international levels will be essential in establishing effective and cohesive AI governance that fosters innovation while protecting individuals and society.

In sum, the United States emphasizes self-regulation and industry-led initiatives but lacks a comprehensive federal framework, which has raised concerns about inconsistent protection of rights. In contrast, the European Union has taken a more proactive approach, proposing the AI Act, which aims to establish clear, broad regulations addressing AI risk, ensuring compliance with strict ethical standards like transparency and accountability (Novelli et al., 2024). The United Kingdom, while similar to the EU in its emphasis on ethical considerations, has taken a slightly more flexible approach, focusing on fostering innovation while mitigating risks, through frameworks like the AI Strategy. South Korea has adopted a practical approach with its own regulatory sandbox model, focusing on creating environments for testing AI in sectors such as healthcare and finance, while promoting innovation alongside strong ethical and regulatory oversight. Across these regions, the balance between encouraging innovation and ensuring ethical safeguards varies, but they all share a common focus on ensuring that AI advances responsibly while minimizing risks to privacy and society.

WHAT AI ETHICAL VALUES EMERGE IN THE NEAR FUTURE?

The principles of AI ethics are continually progressing in response to rapid advancements, leading to the anticipation of new principles arising in the future (Mäntymäki et al., 2022).

The following principles will guide the design and development of AI governance in ways that enhance human dignity, autonomy, and purpose.

- *Access equity.* In the future, equity in access to AI will be critical, ensuring equal access to the benefits of AI. While AI has the potential to improve various aspects of life significantly, these benefits may not be evenly distributed. Certain populations, particularly those in low-income or rural areas, may lack access to the technology and infrastructure necessary to harness the benefits of AI. For example, AI-driven medical technologies may be available in well-funded hospitals but not in under-resourced healthcare systems, leaving marginalized communities without access to cutting-edge treatments. Similarly, AI-powered educational tools may be available to richer students but not those in underserved areas. As AI continues to evolve, it will be crucial to ensure that the technology does not widen the gap between the privileged and the disadvantaged but instead promotes inclusivity and equal opportunity for all.

- *Legitimacy of authority* will be a cornerstone concept in the future development of AI governance frameworks. In organizations, the rules and policies governing AI systems derive their legitimacy from the consent of those affected by them. This legitimacy hinges on actively engaging stakeholders in the creation and refinement of these frameworks. Such participation ensures that governance strategies address the multifaceted challenges and opportunities presented by AI rather than imposing one-size-fits-all solutions. Here, consent transcends mere acquiescence and represents an active endorsement of the governance system by stakeholders. This endorsement signifies that the system aligns with their values, needs, and objectives. A governance framework that earns broad support is more likely to navigate the inherent complexities of AI responsibly and effectively. Conversely, frameworks that fail to engage stakeholders risk alienating those they aim to serve, leading to resistance or non-compliance and diminishing their overall efficacy.

- *Individualistic moral fidelity.* In the evolving landscape of AI, adherence to individual moral principles becomes increasingly significant. Staying true to our moral compass is not only an ethical obligation but also a necessary component of responsible AI governance. Moral fidelity requires that we critically assess and refine our beliefs when confronted with new challenges or insights. Humans possess an inherent moral intuition, shaped by universal emotions such as guilt, shame, and empathy. While these instincts guide our reactions to ethical dilemmas, they are not infallible. Engaging with AI—an entity capable of amplifying societal issues such as bias and discrimination—necessitates heightened moral vigilance. The harm caused by AI often mirrors preexisting societal inequities, exposing systemic flaws. By confronting these issues, we can use AI as a tool for introspection and societal improvement. Furthermore, the uncertain and unpredictable nature of AI's impact demands that individuals and organizations rely on their moral instincts to navigate ethical dilemmas. These instincts serve as a compass during moments of ambiguity, guiding actions that prioritize fairness, accountability, and the collective good.

- *The role of temperance.* Temperance, or the practice of self-restraint and moderation, will be vital in managing the opportunities and risks associated with future AI. While AI has the potential to enhance many aspects of life, it is critical to deliberate on the boundaries between human effort and technological intervention. Work and personal endeavors are fundamental to a sense of purpose and self-worth. Delegating excessive responsibilities to AI risks diminishing these experiences, replacing them with convenience at the expense of meaning. For instance, an overreliance on AI in professional settings could erode creativity and critical thinking, while in personal contexts, it might undermine the value of effort and perseverance. Temperance requires striking a balance between leveraging AI to optimize processes and preserving spaces for human ingenuity and effort. By thoughtfully determining which tasks to delegate to AI and which to retain, individuals and organizations can maintain control, purpose, and a deeper connection to their activities and goals.
- *Enrichment through human agency.* The principle of enrichment through human agency will be important in designing AI systems that empower individuals, enhance their capacities, and respect their autonomy. This principle extends beyond simply avoiding harm; it involves fostering environments where people can actively engage in meaningful behaviors and decision-making processes without undue manipulation or coercion. By supporting human agency, AI can contribute to personal growth, societal advancement, and the preservation of human dignity. Human agency will be even more important to decision-making, personal growth, and the ability to influence one's environment. AI should complement these capacities by offering tools that support informed choices and purposeful actions.

WHO GOVERNS THE MACHINES? SHAPING THE FUTURE OF AI GOVERNANCE

Governing AI effectively demands a collaborative framework that combines regulatory oversight, technological standards, and cross-sector engagement. Policymakers should establish adaptive regulations that prioritize safety, fairness, and transparency, enabling AI systems to be robustly monitored and held accountable. Industry and research organizations play a key role by developing technical standards for ethical AI design, data privacy, and algorithmic fairness. Additionally, governance should involve regular assessments, allowing AI systems to be adjusted as societal needs and technological capacities evolve. International cooperation is essential to address cross-border implications, and involving diverse voices from academia, industry, and civil society ensures a balanced approach that reflects broad societal values. This governance model fosters innovation while mitigating risks, ensuring AI develops in ways that are aligned with public interest and trust.

The future of AI regulation is likely to involve a multifaceted approach that balances innovation with ethical considerations, ensuring that AI technologies benefit society while minimizing risks (Birkstedt et al., 2023). This evolution will require adaptive frameworks, international collaboration, and a focus on transparency, accountability, and fairness in AI systems. A critical factor in the future of AI regulation is the need for adaptive frameworks. Traditional regulatory models often fail to keep up with the fast-paced evolution of technology, creating gaps in oversight that can lead to negative outcomes (Hoffman & Kairouz, 2021). To tackle this challenge, regulators must create adaptable guidelines that can keep pace with the evolving nature of AI. This involves setting up ongoing monitoring and evaluation mechanisms, enabling real-time adjustments to regulations as new risks and ethical issues emerge. By fostering a proactive regulatory environment, governments can ensure that AI systems are developed and deployed responsibly, aligning with societal values and expectations.

For future guidelines, ethics-driven AI regulation is preferred (Shin, 2024). Ethics-driven AI regulation is a governance approach that roots AI policies and legal standards in ethical principles to ensure responsible, transparent, and fair use of technology. This approach recognizes that AI technologies impact fundamental human values, such as fairness, privacy, accountability, and transparency, and seeks to translate these ethical imperatives into enforceable standards that shape AI development and deployment. By embedding ethical values directly into regulatory frameworks, ethics-driven regulation aims to align AI innovation with societal values and protect public welfare, especially in high-stakes or sensitive applications. The foundation of ethics-driven AI regulation lies in addressing specific ethical concerns raised by AI applications. For instance, algorithmic bias is a significant concern, as AI systems can inadvertently perpetuate or amplify societal biases when trained on unbalanced data. An ethics-driven regulatory framework mandates practices such as data diversity, transparency in algorithmic decisions, and regular audits to identify and reduce bias. Moreover, ethics-driven AI regulation emphasizes accountability and transparency, particularly where AI systems have a significant social impact. This involves establishing clear protocols for human oversight, especially in high-risk applications such as healthcare, finance, and criminal justice, where AI decisions can greatly affect individuals' lives. Ethics-driven regulation may require companies to disclose how AI decisions are made, provide interpretability for complex algorithms, and assign responsibility for AI-related decisions, which fosters trust and minimizes the risk of harm. While ethics-driven regulation sets minimum standards, it also encourages a culture of ongoing ethical commitment, urging companies and developers to consider the broader implications of their technologies. For instance, in promoting transparency and fairness, ethics-driven regulation can inspire companies to go beyond compliance, encouraging responsible innovation aligned with evolving social values. This focus on continuous ethical engagement is particularly important in the fast-paced field of AI, where new challenges arise as technology advances.

Governing AI will remain challenging due to the inherent intricacy of its deployment and use in practice (Cave & Dignum, 2023). The future of AI governance will likely be in a middle ground between strict regulation and no regulation, relying on ethical issues (Finocchiaro, 2024). As developments unfold, the landscape of AI will hinge on how we approach this dichotomy. In the middle ground, adaptability will be a key component. As AI technologies advance, governance structures must remain flexible and able to respond to unforeseen developments without stifling innovation (Reynolds & Hallinan, 2024). This flexibility can be achieved through dynamic regulatory approaches, stakeholder engagement, and ongoing research into AI's ethical, social, and technical implications. Professionals in various fields may face conflicts between their ethical principles and the necessity for AI governance. Striking a balance between fostering innovation and addressing ethical considerations is a pressing issue that is expected to become even more critical in the near future (Floridi & Taddeo, 2023).

In conclusion, AI governance is critical for ensuring that AI aligns with ethical values and societal principles while promoting innovation and minimizing risks. By fostering transparency, accountability, and ethical considerations, governance frameworks help align AI development with societal values and goals. As AI evolves, effective governance will be essential to ensure that AI technologies enhance human well-being, uphold democratic principles, and support sustainable development. Through flexible and inclusive governance, society can leverage the potential of AI to shape a future that benefits everyone. The integration of AI ethics and regulatory frameworks is crucial for fostering AI development that resonates with societal ideals and safeguards individual rights. AI ethics lays down a moral groundwork by emphasizing key concepts such as fairness, transparency, and accountability. In contrast, regulation translates these principles into actionable standards and oversight practices. This combination establishes a comprehensive approach that facilitates responsible AI innovation, reduces potential risks, and builds public confidence.

REFERENCES

Binns, R. (2023). Legal taxonomies of machine bias: Revisiting direct discrimination. FAccT '23: Proceedings of the 2023 ACM Conference on Fairness, Accountability, and Transparency. Pages 1850–1858. https://doi.org/10.1145/3593013.3594121

Binns, R. (2024). If the difference principle won't make a real difference in algorithmic fairness, what will? Philosophy & Technology, 37, 119. https://doi.org/10.1007/s13347-024-00805-0

Birkstedt, T., Minkkinen, M., Tandon, A., & Mäntymäki, M. (2023). AI governance: Themes, knowledge gaps and future agendas. *Internet Research*, *33*(7), 133–167. https://doi.org/10.1108/INTR-01-2022-0042

Brey, P., & Dainow, B. (2024). Ethics by design for artificial intelligence. *AI Ethics*, *4*, 1265–1277. https://doi.org/10.1007/s43681-023-00330-4

Cave, S., Dihal, K., Drage, E., & McInerney, K. (2023). Who makes AI? Gender and portrayals of AI scientists in popular film, 1920–2020. Public Understanding of Science, 32(6), 745–760. https://doi.org/10.1177/09636625231153985

Chesterman, S., Gao, Y., Hahn, J., & Sticher, V. (2024). The evolution of AI governance. *Computer, 57*(9), 80–92. http://doi:10.1109/MC.2024.3381215.

Cobbe, J., & Singh, J. (2021). Artificial intelligence as a service: Legal responsibilities, liabilities, and policy challenges. *Computer Law & Security Review*, *42*, Article 105723. http://dx.doi.org/10.2139/ssrn.3824736

Danaher, J. (2020). Freedom in an age of algocracy. In Shannon Vallor (ed.), The Oxford handbook of philosophy of technology. https://doi.org/10.1093/oxfordhb/9780190851187.013.16

Donoghue, R., Huanxin, L., & Ernst, E. (2024). AI, regulation, and the world of work: The competing approaches of the US and China. *Political Science and Public Policy*, 353–365. https://doi.org/10.4337/9781803922171.00035

European Commission. (2021). Proposal for a regulation on a European approach for artificial intelligence.

Finocchiaro, G. (2024). The regulation of artificial intelligence. *AI & Society*, *39*, 1961–1968. https://doi.org/10.1007/s00146-023-01650-z

Floridi, L. (2024). The ethics of artificial intelligence: exacerbated problems, renewed problems, unprecedented problems. American Philosophical Quarterly, 61 (4), 301–307. https://doi.org/10.5406/21521123.61.4.01

Grieman, K. (2024). *Law, death, and robots: The regulation of artificial intelligence in high-risk civil applications.* Bloomsbury Publishing.

Hacker, P., Cordes, J., & Rochon, J. (2024). Regulating gatekeeper AI and data: Transparency, access and fairness under the Digital Markets Act, the General Data Protection Regulation and beyond. *European Journal of Risk Regulation*, *15*(1), 49–86. https://doi.org/10.1017/err.2023.81

Hoffmann, M., Boysel, S., Nagle, F., Peng, S., & Xu, K. (2024). Generative AI and the nature of work (Working Paper No. 25-021). Harvard Business School.

James, A., Hynes, D., Whelan, A., Dreher, T., & Humphry, J. (2023). From access and transparency to refusal: Three responses to algorithmic governance. *Internet Policy Review*, *12*(2). https://doi.org/10.14763/2023.2.1691

Jobin, A., Ienca, M., & Andorno, R. (2019). Artificial intelligence: The global landscape of AI ethics guidelines. *Nature Machine Intelligence*, *1*(4), 389–399. DOI: 10.1038/s42256-019-0088-2

Koene, A. (2024). A call to action: Designing a more transparent online world for children and young people. Journal of Responsible Technology, 19. 100093. https://doi.org/10.1016/j.jrt.2024.100093

Finocchiaro, G. (2023). The regulation of artificial intelligence. AI & Society, 39(4), 1–8. https://doi.org/10.1007/s00146-023-01650-z

Lorenz, L., Meijer, A., & Schuppan, T. (2021). The algocracy as a new ideal type for government organizations: Predictive policing in Berlin as an empirical case. *Information Polity, 26*(1), 71–86. https://doi.org/10.3233/IP-200279

Mäntymäki, M., Minkkinen, M., Birkstedt, T., & Viljanen, M. (2022). Defining organizational AI governance. *AI and Ethics*, 2, 603–609. http://doi:10.1007/s43681-022-00143-x

Möhlmann, M., & Vohs, K. D. (2021). The ethics of artificial intelligence: Implications for the regulation of AI. *Journal of Business Ethics*, *175*(4), 837–857. https://doi.org/10.1007/s10551-020-04534-3

Novelli, C., Taddeo, M., & Floridi, L. (2024). Accountability in artificial intelligence: What it is and how it works. *AI & Society, 39*, 1871–1882. https://doi.org/10.1007/s00146-023-01635-y

Peters, A. (2023). The challenges of AI governance: Ethics, law, and public policy. *Artificial Intelligence Review*, *56*(2), 1235–1252. https://doi.org/10.1007/s10462-022-10024-7

Reynolds, C., & Hallinan, B. (2024). User-generated accountability: Public participation in algorithmic governance on YouTube. *New Media & Society*, *26*(9), 5107–5129. https://doi.org/10.1177/14614448241251791

Roberts, H., Babuta, A., Morley, J., Thomas, C., Taddeo, M., & Floridi, L. (2023). Artificial intelligence regulation in the United Kingdom. *Internet Policy Review*, *12*(2). https://doi.org/10.14763/2023.2.1709

Schuilenburg, M., & Peeters, R. (2021). *The algorithmic society. Technology, power, and knowledge*. Routledge.

Shadbolt, N., & Wilks, Y. (2023). AI governance and the role of international cooperation: Lessons from global standards. *Journal of International Affairs*, *76*(1), 25–45. https://www.jstor.org/stable/10.5325/jinteaffai.76.1.0025

Shin, D. (2024). *Artificial misinformation: Exploring human-algorithm interaction online*. Springer Nature. https://doi.org/10.1007/978-3-031-52569-8

Shin, D. (2025). *Minds, machines, and misinformation*. Elsevier.

Singhal, A, Neveditsin, N., Tanveer, H., & Mago, V. (2024). Toward fairness, accountability, transparency, and ethics in ai for social media and health care. JMIR Med Inform, 12. e50048. doi: 10.2196/50048

Waldman, A., & Martin, K. (2022). Governing algorithmic decisions: The role of decision importance and governance on perceived legitimacy of algorithmic decisions. *Big Data & Society*, *9*(1). https://doi.org/10.1177/20539517221100449

Weissinger, L. B. (2024). AI, complexity, and regulation. In J. B. Bullock et al. (Eds.), *The Oxford handbook of AI governance*. https://doi.org/10.1093/oxfordhb/9780197579329.013.66

Wright, A. M., & Schultz, J. (2021). Regulating artificial intelligence: The role of states, markets, and civil society. Journal of Law, Technology & Policy, *2021*(2), 1–36. https://doi.org/10.2139/ssrn.3752440

Zaidan, E., & Ibrahim, I. A. (2024). AI governance in a complex and rapidly changing regulatory landscape: A global perspective. *Humanity Social Science Communication*, *11*, 1121. https://doi.org/10.1057/s41599-024-03560-x

Diversity-Aware AI

11

Designing AI Systems That Reflect Humanity

DIVERSITY-AWARE AI: NAVIGATING THE FUTURE WITH INCLUSIVITY AND FAIRNESS

In an increasingly digitized world, artificial intelligence (AI) shapes countless aspects of daily life—from the algorithms guiding medical diagnoses to the recommendation engines powering social media. However, as AI's influence expands, so does the recognition that these systems can perpetuate and even exacerbate societal biases if not carefully designed. Diversity-aware AI, a paradigm that advocates for the integration of diverse perspectives, values, and lived experiences, has emerged as a solution to these challenges (Shin & Zhou, 2024). It is a system that can adapt to different users/items and provide indiscriminate recommendation services to people. At first glance, this seems to be an oxymoron. AI is designed to provide personalized and customized services to people yet it still requires diversity. The key lies in the importance of diverse data and varied perspectives in developing effective AI systems (Shams et al., 2023). Diversity in data sources and the programming teams behind AI technologies ensures that the systems can understand and serve a wide range of users. This richness of input leads to more accurate recommendations, a better understanding of different cultures, and ultimately more effective solutions that resonate with a broader audience (Lin et al., 2024).

The concept of diversity in AI is not merely an ethical ideal but a practical imperative to develop systems that are genuinely capable of adaptation (Achon et al., 2024). Human intelligence is characterized by its ability to adjust to new information, unfamiliar situations, and different viewpoints. Traditional AI models, by contrast, often rely on static representations of problems and data, constraining their ability to adapt to new scenarios. As such, diversity-awareness becomes essential, as it facilitates a "model change" paradigm (Du et al., 2021). This means that rather than AI being bound by one set model, it must continually revise its own understanding in light of different perspectives and data inputs that may alter its perception of the problem space (Baumer, 2017).

DOI: 10.1201/9781003530244-16

Diversity-aware AI includes concepts similar to fairness-aware AI. While diversity-aware AI ensures that AI systems reflect a broad range of perspectives and representations, fairness-aware AI prioritizes the prevention of bias and discrimination within AI systems to ensure equitable treatment across all demographic groups (Jui & Rivas, 2024). The focus of fairness-aware AI is to create systems that do not systematically disadvantage any group based on protected attributes like gender, race, or socioeconomic background. While diversity-aware AI seeks to enhance variety and representation, fairness-aware AI addresses issues of justice and equal opportunity, working to prevent algorithms from unfairly benefiting or harming specific groups. In this sense, diversity-aware AI is a higher concept encompassing other value-aware AI such as fairness, transparency, trust, and ethics (Zhao et al., 2024). Designing diversity-aware AI actively promotes and showcases variety across different demographic and identity groups. The aim is not simply to prevent discrimination but to actively enhance the representation of traditionally underrepresented or marginalized groups in various AI-driven applications.

In a diversity-aware approach, AI systems are calibrated to promote a heterogeneous mix in their recommendations or outputs. For instance, in a recommendation system for music or movies, diversity-aware AI would not only prioritize items based on users' past preferences but would also introduce a range of content from artists of different backgrounds, genres, or cultures. In hiring algorithms, diversity-awareness might involve creating a candidate pool that reflects a variety of backgrounds, experiences, and skills, rather than disproportionately selecting candidates from a narrow, homogeneous group. The underlying assumption is that exposure to diverse perspectives enriches the user to experience and counteracts the reinforcement of echo chambers or "filter bubbles," which can arise when algorithms exclusively focus on optimizing for similarity and user engagement.

Diversity enables AI to expand beyond the "static model" approach, providing the groundwork for a system that can evolve alongside its changing environment (Currin et al., 2022). Without a diversity-aware foundation, AI systems run the risk of perpetuating biases, reinforcing stereotypes, and missing nuances that would otherwise be apparent to human decision-makers. These pitfalls not only hinder the utility of AI but can also result in harmful, exclusionary impacts on the very users AI is meant to serve. Thus, diversity-awareness is a requirement that underlies any model change, encouraging systems to explore the boundaries of current understanding and pushing AI toward more human-like adaptability (Evans et al., 2022).

DIVERSITY AS A CATALYST FOR ADAPTIVE, OPEN-ENDED INTELLIGENCE

Developing diversity-aware AI involves rethinking intelligence itself (Chen & Sundar, 2024). Human intelligence is characterized by its ability to synthesize and adjust to new perspectives, which often arise incrementally through exposure to varied experiences and viewpoints (Hermann, 2022). Similarly, diversity-aware AI must adopt an "open-ended" model of intelligence, where the system's understanding of tasks, values, and even its operational goals evolves over time through exposure to diverse data. This approach not only enhances the adaptability of AI systems but also fosters a type of intelligence that is more responsive to complex, evolving environments (Jesse & Jannach, 2021). For instance, an open-ended AI in a healthcare setting could adapt its treatment recommendations by learning from data reflecting a wide array of patient backgrounds, medical histories, and treatment outcomes. Such an AI would recognize that a single, universal model is insufficient for addressing the nuances of individual cases. Instead, it would incrementally incorporate insights from different populations, medical practices, and treatment modalities to refine its recommendations. This incremental synthesis of diverse perspectives represents a fundamental shift from traditional models, allowing AI to develop a richer, more context-sensitive understanding that approximates human adaptability (Crawford & Paglen, 2021).

The goal of diversity-aware AI is to ensure that AI systems are not only effective and efficient but also fair, inclusive, and reflective of the pluralistic societies in which they operate (Jin et al., 2023). At its core, diversity-aware AI is concerned with recognizing and respecting the diversity of human experiences, identities, and social contexts (Li & Liu, 2021). This includes, but is not limited to, aspects such as race, gender, socioeconomic status, culture, and language. Traditional AI models, primarily trained on data that reflects a limited subset of these dimensions, often fail to generalize well to diverse populations, leading to skewed results and reinforcing existing inequalities. For instance, facial recognition technologies have been shown to perform significantly better for certain demographic groups than others, often struggling with accuracy in identifying individuals from minority backgrounds. Such disparities underscore the urgency of designing AI that consciously accounts for diversity to avoid reproducing structural biases. The path to diversity-aware AI involves a multi-layered approach.

First, there is the need for inclusive datasets. In many cases, biases in AI arise because the data used for training and validation do not represent the full spectrum of human experiences (Holstein et al., 2019). When AI models are trained predominantly on data from specific demographics, such as North American or European populations, their accuracy for people outside these demographics suffers. Expanding data collection to incorporate broader and more representative samples helps to mitigate this issue. However, it is essential to approach this task ethically, ensuring that data collection respects privacy rights and does not exploit marginalized communities (Aguirre et al., 2016).

Moreover, the algorithms themselves must be designed to detect and adjust for biases rather than reinforce them. This requires transparency in model development, as well as the implementation of fairness measures that can identify and mitigate unfair patterns. Techniques such as adversarial debiasing and fairness-aware regularization are increasingly used to counteract inherent biases in data, but these technical solutions are just one part of a larger equation. Designing diversity-aware AI also requires ongoing human oversight and accountability. Interdisciplinary teams, including experts in social sciences, ethics, and law, should be involved in the development process to ensure that these models are not just technically sound but also socially responsible (Hanna et al., 2020).

Additionally, the importance of stakeholder engagement in building diversity-aware AI cannot be overstated. Engaging with communities that AI will impact is essential to understanding the nuances of how it might affect different groups. This participatory approach enables AI designers to gain insights into the specific needs, concerns, and values of these communities (Bastian et al., 2021). For example, when designing AI tools for healthcare, input from diverse patients and medical professionals can help developers anticipate how algorithms may impact various populations differently and guide them to design solutions that improve outcomes for all. The result is not only more equitable AI but also technology that enjoys greater public trust and legitimacy (Currin et al., 2022).

Diversity-aware AI also has a broader, societal value. By embedding diversity considerations into AI systems, organizations can create products that resonate with a global audience, fostering greater inclusion and understanding across cultural and geographical divides (Werder et al., 2024). For example, language processing models that accommodate linguistic diversity—such as dialects, nonstandard grammar, or multilingual inputs—can help break down barriers in communication, allowing more people to access technology in ways that are meaningful to them. In an age where AI mediates so many facets of human interaction, diversity-aware AI represents a powerful means of promoting cultural inclusivity and empowering underserved communities (Cachat-Rosset & Klarsfeld, 2023). However, pursuing diversity-aware AI presents significant challenges. There are technical limitations, as current methodologies for fairness and debiasing are still in nascent stages. Additionally, the need for vast, representative datasets clashes with privacy concerns and the logistical difficulties of collecting data from diverse populations. The field is also constrained by broader societal challenges, such as systemic biases that AI alone cannot address. For example, achieving truly equitable healthcare outcomes through AI is complicated by underlying disparities in access to medical resources. While AI can play a role in addressing these issues, it must operate within a broader framework of social reform (Zowghi & Mahmud, 2024).

Diversity-aware AI is both a technical endeavor and a societal commitment. It calls for innovative solutions, interdisciplinary collaboration, and continuous reflection on the ethical implications of AI in diverse contexts (Evans et al., 2022). As the technology becomes more ubiquitous, ensuring that AI systems are aware of and responsive to the diversity of human experience is not just a desirable goal but an essential one. In embracing diversity-aware AI, we take a step toward a future where technology enhances human potential without sacrificing fairness or inclusivity—a future where AI serves, respects, and uplifts all of humanity.

THE IMPORTANCE OF DIVERSITY-AWARE AI: A PATH TO EQUITABLE ALGORITHMS

In the modern digital landscape, AI is a powerful force shaping how we live, work, and communicate (Araujo et al., 2020). From predictive healthcare to personalized education, AI has the potential to drive remarkable advancements across sectors. However, as this technology pervades nearly every aspect of life, concerns around its fairness, inclusivity, and ethical use have come into sharper focus. Diversity-aware AI–AI that is explicitly designed to acknowledge and incorporate the range of human experiences, identities, and backgrounds—is a response to these concerns, aiming to create equitable and trustworthy technology for all. Diversity in AI is not merely a checkbox or an ethical ideal, but a practical necessity for creating systems capable of learning, adaptation, and realistic human interaction (Loecherbach et al., 2020). Traditional AI models often work within a "static model" paradigm, which relies on a predefined dataset and follows fixed protocols for interpreting and responding to new inputs. While effective within limited contexts, this static approach restricts an AI's ability to adapt to new circumstances, perspectives, or users. Such models can perpetuate biases, reinforce stereotypes, and struggle to interpret situations outside of narrowly defined norms (Roche et al., 2023). The importance of diversity-aware AI cannot be overstated, as it stands to prevent harm, enhance innovation, and ultimately contribute to a more just and inclusive society. The central reason for prioritizing diversity-aware AI is to prevent harmful biases from perpetuating or amplifying inequalities. AI systems are only as fair as the data and assumptions on which they are built (Mattis et al., 2022). When training data is skewed toward certain demographics, such as majority racial or socioeconomic groups, the resulting AI models may perform poorly for others, leading to adverse outcomes. For example, AI algorithms in healthcare have been shown to misdiagnose or inaccurately assess risk for certain populations due to underrepresentation in the training data. These biases are not merely technical flaws; they have real-world consequences that disproportionately affect already marginalized communities. Diversity-aware AI, by incorporating representative data and using bias-detection techniques, can work to prevent these discriminatory outcomes, ensuring that AI systems serve all people equitably (Chauhan & Kshetri, 2024).

Beyond preventing harm, diversity-aware AI is essential for fostering innovation and expanding the scope of AI applications (Møller, 2023). When AI is designed with diversity in mind, it is more adaptable to various contexts and environments, enabling it to address a wider range of challenges. For instance, natural language processing (NLP) systems that consider linguistic diversity are better equipped to understand and serve multilingual populations, improving accessibility for non-native speakers or people from diverse dialect backgrounds. This broader applicability not only enhances user experience but also stimulates innovation, as developers uncover new use cases and solutions for previously overlooked communities. The inclusive design of AI systems thus drives the field forward, broadening the reach and potential of AI technology (Drabiak, 2024).

Diversity-aware AI also plays a crucial role in building trust between technology providers and the communities they serve. Public trust in AI has been shaken by high-profile instances of bias, from facial recognition systems with higher error rates for minority groups to recruitment algorithms that inadvertently favor certain demographics over others. These incidents undermine confidence in AI's fairness and raise concerns about its influence on decision-making processes that directly impact people's lives (Zaid et al., 2022). By developing diversity-aware AI, organizations can demonstrate a commitment to ethical and inclusive practices, which can help rebuild trust. Transparent, diversity-focused design and evaluation practices signal to the public that

AI systems are developed responsibly, with an emphasis on respecting individual rights and reducing bias (Roche et al., 2023).

Moreover, diversity-aware AI has the potential to address broader social inequalities (Yin et al., 2023). In fields like employment, education, and criminal justice, AI is increasingly used to make or inform decisions with profound impacts on individuals' lives. Without attention to diversity, these systems can unintentionally reinforce existing biases within these sectors, exacerbating disparities rather than alleviating them. However, with a diversity-aware approach, AI can become a tool for promoting equity (Yeung, 2017). For instance, fairer algorithms in hiring can open opportunities for historically underrepresented groups, while diversity-aware AI in education can provide tailored resources that cater to diverse learning needs. As AI becomes intertwined with society, it has the potential not only to reflect but also to shape social structures, making its role in equity vital.

Another significant aspect of diversity-aware AI is its alignment with ethical principles. The ethical use of AI is increasingly becoming a priority for stakeholders worldwide, including policymakers, tech companies, and consumers. A diversity-aware approach to AI aligns with principles of fairness, respect for human dignity, and social responsibility. It recognizes the importance of designing technology that honors diverse perspectives and experiences, acknowledging that inclusivity is an ethical imperative in any society that values equity (Heitz et al., 2022). As AI ethics guidelines proliferate, diversity-awareness is emerging as a cornerstone for responsible AI, making it integral to the future regulatory landscape and guiding companies in sustainable AI practices (Zowghi & Mahmud, 2024).

Diversity-aware AI is important because it represents a more inclusive vision of technological progress. The digital revolution should be for everyone, and ensuring that AI systems consider diversity embodies this principle. Technology shapes societies in powerful ways, and diversity-aware AI ensures that all groups have a voice and presence in the digital future. It enables individuals from various backgrounds to participate fully and equitably in an AI-driven world, reducing digital divides and fostering a more inclusive global community (Jang et al., 2022).

In summary, diversity-aware AI is not just a technical aspiration but a fundamental necessity for a fair and inclusive society. It prevents the amplification of biases, fosters broader innovation, builds trust, and aligns with ethical principles that promote respect for all people. As AI continues to shape the future, integrating diversity into its design is essential to ensuring that this powerful technology serves everyone, not just a select few (Jesse & Jannach, 2021). By embracing diversity-aware AI, we take a step toward a world where technology advances without sacrificing fairness or equity, paving the way for a digital landscape that uplifts and empowers all of humanity (Møller, 2023).

ETHICAL DILEMMA IN DIVERSITY-AWARE AI

The development of diversity-aware AI systems seeks to make algorithms more inclusive by recognizing and supporting the needs of diverse user groups. These AI systems are designed to respect cultural, social, and demographic differences, ideally creating a more equitable user experience across communities. Yet, achieving true inclusivity in AI is complicated by a series of ethical challenges that raise questions about fairness, transparency, and the safeguarding of individual rights.

One of the central ethical issues in diversity-aware AI lies in the potential for biases within the data used to train these systems. AI systems depend on large datasets to learn patterns and make predictions, yet these datasets often contain historical biases that reflect societal prejudices or institutional inequalities. While the purpose of diversity-aware AI is to address and counteract such biases, there is a significant risk that it may inadvertently reinforce or even amplify them if not carefully managed. For instance, a diversity-aware hiring algorithm that aims to improve gender balance might still rely on biased historical data that favors certain genders or job profiles, leading to unintended discriminatory outcomes. Thus, the challenge of dealing with data bias is an ethical issue that requires careful scrutiny and ongoing efforts to audit and refine the training datasets.

Another ethical dilemma in diversity-aware AI is the question of how to define and measure diversity itself. Defining diversity within AI frameworks is not straightforward, as diversity spans a wide range of attributes, including gender, race, socioeconomic status, language, and ability, among others. Attempting to encapsulate these dimensions in a set of predefined categories can lead to oversimplification, risking the creation of AI models that treat identities as rigid rather than nuanced and fluid. For example, an AI system might classify users into fixed demographic categories that fail to account for intersectional identities or personal experiences, leading to outcomes that may feel exclusionary rather than inclusive. In this way, diversity-aware AI systems run the risk of fostering tokenism or reinforcing stereotypes rather than embracing the richness of human diversity.

Transparency and accountability are also major ethical concerns when designing and implementing diversity-aware AI. AI algorithms are often described as "black boxes," where the decision-making process is not fully transparent or understandable even to the engineers who develop them. This opacity becomes particularly concerning when these systems make choices that impact individuals based on diversity factors. For instance, if an AI-driven hiring platform filters applicants based on demographic traits in ways that are not transparent, users cannot hold the system accountable for potentially discriminatory decisions. The ethical imperative here is to ensure that diversity-aware AI systems are not only fair but also transparent, allowing users and stakeholders to understand how decisions are made and enabling them to contest or correct discriminatory outcomes.

Another key ethical issue associated with diversity-aware AI is related to informed consent and privacy. To tailor services to diverse groups effectively, diversity-aware AI systems often need to collect sensitive demographic information. While this data can help make the AI more responsive to different user needs, it also raises privacy concerns. Users may not be comfortable sharing personal information related to their race, gender, or sexual orientation, especially if they are unsure how this data will be used or protected. The lack of adequate privacy safeguards can erode user trust, as people may feel that their personal identities are being commodified or manipulated for algorithmic purposes. Therefore, ensuring robust privacy protections and obtaining informed consent from users is essential for maintaining ethical integrity in diversity-aware AI applications.

Diversity-aware AI holds the potential to make technology more inclusive and representative of various communities, but it also presents ethical challenges that must be carefully addressed. Bias in data, the complexity of defining diversity, lack of transparency, and concerns around privacy all pose significant hurdles that require ongoing ethical reflection and action. To fulfill the promise of diversity-aware AI, developers and organizations must adopt rigorous standards that prioritize fairness, accountability, and the protection of individual rights, ensuring that these systems genuinely serve all users rather than entrenching existing inequalities (Yu et al., 2024).

CASE STUDY: DIVERSITY-AWARE RECOMMENDATION SYSTEM

Recommender systems (RS) subtly nudge users to search for relevant online content and have the potential to play a critical role in shaping public opinion (Shin, 2024). As algorithms play as gatekeepers in RS (Scheffauer et al., 2023), concerns about misinformation and constrained perspectives have emerged, shedding light on the disruptive powers of news gatekeeping and recommendations by algorithms (Knudsen, 2023). Access to diverse sources of news and perspectives is more critical than ever in the AI-driven RS, as people often can find themselves diving into "rabbit holes" of news and opinions fed by news algorithms (Møller, 2023). Various attempts have been made to counter diverse problems, including using AI to nudge users to expose diverse news (Heitz et al., 2022) and auditing algorithms to recommend diverse content (Shin, 2024). Algorithmic nudges are one of these efforts using algorithm design components to lead users' behavior in algorithmically mediated contexts (Yeung, 2017).

News platforms use algorithmic nudges as a news gatekeeping tool at different dimensions, such as news recommending services, content purchasing suggestions, and prescriptive decision-making tools (Vermeulen, 2022). Although the consequences are still under debate and elusive, researchers have argued that algorithmically personalized news can work as a new form of gatekeeping (Napoli, 2015), which often leads to unintended consequences (i.e., self-reinforcing echo chamber; Cardenal et al., 2019), partisan personalization (Bryanov et al., 2020), and unwanted habits (i.e., selective exposure, addictive confirmation; Knudsen, 2023; Wu-Ouyang, 2023). The relationship between RS and AI in numerous studies illustrates how personalized and tailored algorithms can use persuasion and psychometrics to affect individual behavior in unintended ways (Jesse & Jannach, 2021). Concerns about hyper-personalized news—via behavioral and contextual data—in the algorithm environment (Yeung, 2017) have raised questions on how a news recommender system (NRS) can be more aligned with journalistic values with socially responsible and less algorithm-driven with technical personalization (Hermann, 2022) to facilitate rather than constrain the normative goals of journalism

(Joris et al., 2020). A number of obstacles stand in the way of RS and the legitimate use of algorithmic nudges in news platforms (Møller, 2023). The prevalence of RS has caused concerns about providing constrained perspectives, often called information cocoons, echo chambers, filter bubbles, self-reinforcement, and information enclaves (Knudsen, 2023). To keep users on a provided platform, users are fed content they like based on their interests in the name of personalization, without considering inclusive content or diverse viewpoints (Mitova et al., 2022). Despite its importance, the effects and mechanisms of algorithmic gatekeeping on user behaviors, particularly in RS, have been under-researched. The exact nature of how algorithmic nudges work under what conditions, how users respond to the nudges, and what impact nudges have on news personalization and the diversity of viewpoints regarding issues of public interest via RS remain inconclusive. There is a practical need to design contemporary RS to allow users to have options to access the diverse spectrum of news beyond algorithmically personalized news (Sax, 2022). The principle of diversity-aware news recommenders has emerged as a safeguard (Mattis et al., 2022). It is becoming increasingly imperative for journalistically sustainable, algorithmically efficient, and societally acceptable personalized RS (Heitz et al., 2022).

Side Effects of Algorithmic Personalization

With its prevalence and broad applicability, there are hot debates and controversies about RS and algorithmic personalization (Helberger, 2019). While effective in maneuvering user behaviors through the analytics of user data, concerns rise as algorithmic personalization has underlined the assumption of manipulative news recommendation (Møller, 2023). Personalized articles are based on the previously consumed news, and this creates a self-reinforcing cycle of filter bubbles around people. Issues about selective exposure and echo chambers through self-reinforcement in the algorithmic news environment trigger concerns regarding how RS can become more human-centered and promote normative principles of journalism (Bastian et al., 2021). As the level and sophistication of personalization increase, personalization and diversity become two essential principles of RS that keep journalistic principles while providing personalized news stories (Sax, 2022). Personalization and diversity can have trade-offs and conflicts, as too much personalization can lead to over-specialization and filter bubbles, while excessive diversity can lead to irrelevance and noise. This relation of personalization-diversity is different from traditional media nudge. In journalism, for example, algorithmic nudging has been used to increase news diversity in RS (Jürgens & Stark, 2022) by re-ranking news items in the interface (Araujo et al., 2020). News networks, such as *CNN,* the *BBC, USA Today,* and *The New York Times,* provide ubiquitous access to users, allowing them to surf through prioritized news using algorithm machine learning. To draw a higher volume of clicks to their sites, online platforms increasingly utilize algorithms in their RS to improve user engagement in their services. Yet, algorithms are intertwined with broader economic rationales and user preferences and are not always designed to prioritize news content as they should do. Loecherbach et al. (2020) illustrated that less preferred news items are likelier to be chosen if displayed at higher ranks or placed favorably on the page which readers easily catch. Algorithmic nudges can increase news diversity considerably (Sonoda et al., 2022), especially when readers face news overload or when AI systems recommend their news selections. Algorithmic nudges can support people who pursue but do not find diverse articles by making such articles more accessible and available or by providing diverse recommendations. These recommendations lead users to develop new interests, enabling recommendation algorithms to advance (Sax, 2022) and contributing to greater societal and journalism values. Readers' desire to seek diverse news aligns with the right to diverse information, as specified by the European Court of Human Rights (Article 10), which requires the media to adopt measures that guarantee citizens access to diverse information. These trends imply the imperative task of how to embed explainable, human-centered, diverse, and inclusive algorithms in RS (Hameleers et al., 2021; Shin, 2024).

Overly personalization in RS is the result of recommendation approaches that place an over-emphasis on prediction and accuracy. These typical accuracy-focused approaches may fail to consider other aspects of subjective user experiences, such as diversity (exposure to a different spectrum of news), inclusion (representing and respecting the variety of human perspectives), and equity (appreciating the balanced views of news) when assessing the recommendation quality. When developing a socially responsible RS, the industry can consider the beyond-accuracy aspects to evaluate the effectiveness of news recommendations. The findings of this study contribute to the design of contemporary RS in terms of equitable and ethical content recommendations, such as diversity-aware RS by clarifying the structural relations of journalistic values with news recommendations. How to build RS that is aware of ethical values, how to design RS that enables users to audit, and how to reflect transparency in the design of RS become key ethical issues as well as essential design criteria. There is an opportunity for future work on algorithmic nudges serving as an intermediary between readers and news organizations, pushing for more transparency to fully understand the intricacy of algorithmic gatekeeping and where the balance may lie between personalized news and diversified perspectives while protecting journalistic values of fairness and transparency.

Nudging toward Media Pluralism and News Diversity

As RS is widely used and accepted, diversity in recommendation systems has become a key issue (Evans et al., 2022) and the principle by which to consider avoiding the overfitting problem as well as a polarization of opinion (Currin et al., 2022), which poses a significant threat to a democratic discussion (Helberger, 2019). This importance comes from the fact that news diversity in the media has been a fundamental principle for safeguarding the satisfaction of the communicative rights of individuals and society at large (Baden & Springer, 2017). Numerous scholars warn of the potential threats of algorithmic gatekeeping (e.g., Cardenal et al., 2019). Among the concerns raised, scholars and practitioners have equally asked questions about how RS can be designed in a more user-centered way that preserves the normative goals of news journalism (Heitz et al., 2022). Optimizing the role of public values in news recommendations is an urgent task that should be followed by defining and operationalizing the diversity principle in NRS. Algorithmic nudges are proposed as a possible solution to this question. This study underlines the theoretical nexus between algorithmic nudges in NRS awareness of news diversity and inclusion as key drivers for personalized NRS. Such theoretical frames can provide practical implications for the technological feasibility of diverse news recommendations in NRS. Relevant research has examined nudging toward inclusion and news diversity, which can inform the conceptualization of diversity-aware news recommendations (e.g., Evans et al., 2022). Helberger (2019), for example, proposed normative ideals and measurable metrics of diversity and pluralism in NRS. Despite recent research, realizing and reflecting news diversity in the recommendation nudging process still needs to be researched. Despite its importance, research on how NRS can facilitate news diversity and pluralism has remained under-researched. How to design nudges in AI that guide users toward better decisions ethically and responsibly remains an open question for NRS and journalism.

Nudging toward Inclusion and News Diversity

Algorithmic journalism is increasingly seeking implicit and explicit algorithmic news personalization (Cardenal et al., 2019). This trend creates tension with news diversity, which has been an essential basis for media and journalism (Bernstein, 2022). As RS engineers technological architecture that helps shape public discourse, it has reduced news diversity and social diversity (Shin, 2024). As algorithmic personalization depends primarily on automated recommendation systems, these systems are often neither fair nor transparent because they are mainly driven by commercial interest and technological efficiency. This nonpublic value contrasts with the normative principles of news as a marketplace of ideas in which readers are entitled to a wide spectrum of news and viewpoints. As RS is widely used and accepted, diversity in recommendation systems has become an important issue (Shin, 2024) and the principle by which to consider avoiding the overfitting problem as well as a polarization of opinion (Currin et al., 2022), which poses a major threat to a democratic discussion (Helberger, 2019). This importance comes from the fact that news diversity in the media has been a key principle for safeguarding the satisfaction of the communicative rights of individuals and society at large (Baden & Springer, 2017).

Numerous scholars warn of the potential threats of RS, such as echo chambers and filter bubbles (Cardenal et al., 2019). Among the concerns raised, scholars and practitioners have commonly asked questions about how RS can be designed in a more user-centered way that preserves the normative goals of news journalism (Shin, 2024). Optimizing the role of public values in news recommendations is an important task, which should be followed by defining and operationalizing the diversity principle in RS. Algorithmic nudges are proposed as a possible solution to this question. This study underlines the theoretical development of algorithmic nudges in RS that are aware of news diversity and inclusion as key drivers for personalized RS. Such theoretical frames can provide practical implications for the technological feasibility of diverse news recommendations in RS. Relevant research has examined nudging toward inclusion and news diversity, which can inform the conceptualization of diversity-aware news recommendations (e.g., Vrijenhoek et al., 2021). Helberger (2019), for example, proposed normative ideals and measurable metrics of diversity and inclusion in RS. Despite recent research, realizing and reflecting news diversity in the recommendation process remains under-researched. To fully benefit from news recommendations, users should engage with diverse news and opinions in ways that lead to the marketplace of ideas and pro-social media effects.

A Two-Step Flow of Gatekeeping: Why RS Need More Than Personalization

Personalization is a key feature in RS, as it generates tailored news based on user pref-erences and popularity metrics. However, excessively personalized news stories limit users' exposure to different types and views of the news (Shin, 2024). At the user level, users may become dissatisfied with being exposed to similar kinds of news or stereo-typed articles (Monzer et al., 2020). Over-personalization may also influence a user's perspective and behavior (Monzer et al., 2020), leading them to seek counter-attitudinal (an attitude that reverses one's own beliefs) perspectives and opinions (Helberger, 2019). Our findings suggest a two-step flow of gatekeeping and personalization: readers per-sonalize their news through algorithms with the help of algorithmic gatekeeping, and in turn, the readers seek diverse news to view nonpersonalized news and other perspec-tives to compare and contrast a variety of different viewpoints (Figure 11.1).

Personalized messages are transmitted through RS to readers. Those messages are interpreted and moderated by algorithmic nudges which in turn suggest to read-ers diverse news different from the personalized news. This two-step flow is related to users' actions and the algorithm's reaction to make news more personalized and relevant. In contrast to the one-step flow of gatekeeping (or traditional gatekeeping), which holds that gatekeepers decide what news should move past them (through the

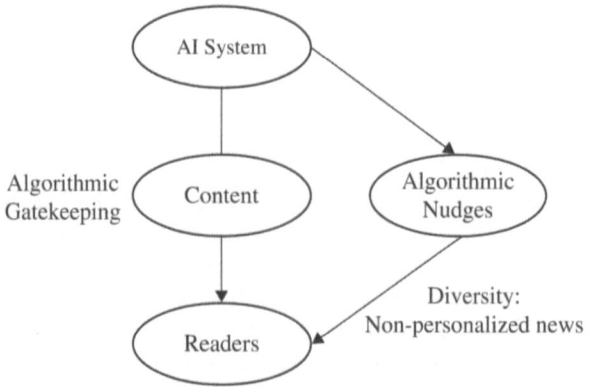

FIGURE 11.1   A two-step flow of personalization.

information "gate") to readers, the two-step flow model of personalization proposes an interactive and dependent relation between AI and readers that they co-construct personalized news with a mediation of algorithmic nudges. Opinion leaders in the one-step flow of gatekeeping can be algorithmic nudges acting as intermediary roles in the two-step flow. Gatekeepers in the one-step flow are equivalent to algorithms. Passive readers in the one-step flow can be active users with AI in the two-step flow. The process of selecting, filtering, and then customizing items of media is an iterative, interactive, and multi-tier dynamic process. These interactive gatekeeping decisions are made by AI every day to sort out the relevant items that audiences will view.

This two-step flow of personalization advances from the traditional model by proposing two heuristic implications. First, this two-step flow explains why diversity should be embedded into RS. While readers expect personalized news through RS, they also seek diverse news in RS. Greater personalization usually improves news relevance and user engagement, but it may also increase users' desire to seek diverse news and pursue different viewpoints. Personalized news serves as an anchoring effect, whereby users' decisions are influenced by a particular personalized referenced point, and from there, users explore other news (Currin et al., 2022) to make a comparison as a way of self-enhancement of the personalization (Buunk & Gibbons, 2000).

Second, the two-step flow of gatekeeping explains the personalization paradox (Aguirre et al., 2016) in RS contexts. While users desire personalized news, they seek diverse news to compare and contrast their personalization to other views. As much as users are satisfied with personalized news, they also seek diversified news. Personalization by algorithms can be a fundamentally flawed metaphor because personalization is a relative, situational concept (Kim & Pasek, 2020), and thus, an absolute state of personalization is technically impossible. Just as algorithmic personalization is not a permanent fixture of news and content, neither is users' personalization. Users' personalized interests are contextual (and thus a moving target) and comparative concerning the nonpersonalized marketplace of ideas. For example, when users show an interest in political elections, AI can personalize their web banners, political stories, suggested columns, etc., but what if their interests change? Due to its self-reinforcing loops (Noble, 2018), RS continue to recommend the users very narrowly defined news, and it will likely limit the potential of future personalization because of the self-favoring or self-reinforcing nature of personalization (Heitz et al., 2022), which becomes a downward spiral unless interventions are provided. RS should be varied and diversified, adapt quickly to new trends, and have the ability to modify quickly to process more user data. From this perspective, users are naturally curious about nonpersonalized views and opinions to (1) confirm that curated news is personalized, (2) compare their personalized view with other alternative views, and (3) evaluate the extent of personalization of the curated news. As user preferences and behavior are contextual, so is algorithmic personalization. Thus, personalization in RS contexts is a coupling concept with diversity and pluralism, which should be considered equally in its design (Evans et al., 2022).

This relation is theoretically relevant and constructive in developing diversity-aware RS. Theoretically, algorithmic personalization has yet to be well established and only a few studies have discussed algorithmic personalization as a positive effect of personalization on user adoption. The personalization paradox reveals interdependence and tensions between personalization and diverse news, which advocates the need for diversity and pluralism in RS. For example, Facebook's news feed recommendation system may incorrectly suggest a specific user's preference for political news tailored to conservative views based on their click/viewing history. Thus, it only recommends specific news from conservative political standpoints. Because users can only specify their preferences through the algorithmic mechanism run by the personalization codes, the algorithms are likely to recommend further the already curated preference due to the lack of other alternatives. In this way, personalization algorithms reinforce their user preferences without the possibility of adjusting user preferences. Thus, users and personalization algorithms will look for diverse sources and news for further personalization, as they are contextually and continuously changed.

Practically, the personalization paradox provides design guidelines for designing diversity-aware RS. RS can pursue personalization as well as diversity and inclusion in news recommendations. Personalization can be fulfilled through algorithms, and this, in turn, gives room for diversity-aware design. In RS, a series of parameters of specific personalization can be established as parameters for diverse news. For example, when conservative viewpoints of news (right-wing perspectives) are personalized, then as a piece of subsequent news or supplement suggesting news, liberal viewpoints of news (left-wing voices) are recommended to users. When a series of opposing and contradictory views of immigration is personalized to readers, favoring perspectives of immigration is recommended. Diversity-aware RS can be achieved by striking an optimum balance between personalization and diversity. Platforms can practice personalization and can, at the same time, achieve diversity and pluralism through personalization. RS can refine personalization through diversity, as it can reflect the opposite view of news selection. Diversity-optimizing RS can enhance tolerance for opposing views by promoting exposure to both pro-attitudinal and counter-social issues (Heitz et al., 2022). Such RS utilizes a collaborative filtering method, which shows users' similarity to other users and their preferences. This collaborative filtering can be reversely applied in RS; the so-called converse filtering or random dynamical nudge (Currin et al., 2022, p. 3) can identify the users' news spectrum from preferred news to diverse news. As a result of converse filtering, RS users can benefit from personalized news as well as diverse and inclusive news. The primary function of converse filtering is to promote discourse across different perspectives based on content that can be ideologically skewed. Personalization and diversity are two sides of the same coin in NRS, and one helps the other to recommend the quality of news to users.

OPERATIONAL ISSUES IN DIVERSITY-AWARE AI

Designing diversity-aware AI presents unique challenges that reflect both the technical intricacies of machine learning and the ethical imperatives of building inclusive systems. As AI increasingly shapes decisions in areas like healthcare, education, and criminal justice, the need for diversity-awareness has become urgent. However, building

AI capable of understanding and respecting diverse perspectives is no simple task. From data limitations to algorithmic bias, and from ethical concerns to practical implementation hurdles, several significant challenges make developing diversity-aware AI complex and multifaceted.

One of the primary challenges lies in data diversity and representation. AI systems rely on vast amounts of data to learn and make predictions, yet this data often lacks the diversity necessary to capture the full range of human experiences. Many datasets have historical biases or demographic imbalances, leading to AI models that may unintentionally reinforce stereotypes or underperform when used in contexts involving marginalized groups. For instance, an algorithm trained on predominantly Western datasets may struggle with language processing in non-Western dialects, creating accessibility barriers for users from different linguistic backgrounds. Even when datasets do contain diverse samples, they may reflect unequal distributions of certain groups, leading to the overrepresentation of some and the underrepresentation of others. Ensuring balanced representation within training datasets, while also respecting the nuances of each community, is a foundational yet complex step in building diversity-aware AI.

In addition to data representation, developing AI models that are sensitive to cultural, social, and individual differences presents a challenge in algorithmic design. AI often operates on generalizable patterns and probabilistic models, which can limit its ability to account for context-specific variations or nuanced differences. For instance, recommendation algorithms on social media platforms may group users with similar profiles into clusters, but these clusters may inadvertently overlook differences in cultural preferences, personal values, or life experiences. Addressing these challenges requires the development of algorithms that can identify and adapt to varied contexts, recognizing that certain choices and preferences are deeply personal or culturally specific. However, this context-aware approach can add significant complexity to model design, as it demands sophisticated methods for defining and dynamically adapting to diverse variables.

Bias in algorithmic decision-making is another significant challenge, as AI systems often inadvertently mirror the prejudices present in the data they are trained on. When biases are embedded in the datasets or the models themselves, AI can end up reproducing inequitable outcomes that disproportionately impact certain communities. For example, in the criminal justice system, predictive policing algorithms trained on historical crime data can reinforce racial disparities by targeting communities that were historically over-policed. Bias can emerge not only from the data but also from the assumptions and design choices of developers, who may unconsciously introduce their own perspectives into the model. Identifying, measuring, and mitigating these biases is a complex task that requires comprehensive evaluation techniques and a commitment to ethical standards in AI design. Bias-mitigation techniques, such as fairness-aware learning and adversarial debiasing, are being explored, but they often involve trade-offs that can affect model accuracy or introduce new complexities into the system.

Another challenge lies in creating transparent and explainable AI (XAI) systems that users can understand and trust. Diversity-aware AI is especially susceptible to issues of opacity, as models that adapt to diverse contexts may operate with sophisticated, often opaque decision rules that are difficult to interpret. For AI to be genuinely inclusive, users need to understand how decisions are made, particularly in high-stakes fields like healthcare, finance, and employment. However, creating transparency within complex, adaptive models remains a difficult problem. XAI seeks to address these issues by providing insights into the decision-making process, but achieving a balance between transparency and model complexity can be technically challenging. Users need sufficient information to trust that the system respects diversity, yet overly simplified explanations may fail to capture the true breadth of the AI's considerations, particularly when those considerations involve complex sociocultural factors.

The ethical and legal considerations surrounding diversity-aware AI add further layers of complexity. Diversity-aware AI often operates at the intersection of personal privacy, data protection, and inclusivity, raising concerns about how data is collected, stored, and utilized. To ensure diversity, developers may need access to personal data reflecting various demographic attributes, but this practice must be balanced against individuals' right to privacy and the need for data minimization. Compliance with legal frameworks, such as the General Data Protection Regulation (GDPR) in Europe, poses additional constraints, as these regulations place strict limits on how personal data can be used. Furthermore, ethical concerns arise regarding the potential for "positive" discrimination, where overly prescriptive diversity goals could lead to stereotyping or tokenism rather than genuine inclusivity. This ethical tension requires careful consideration of both the benefits and risks of using demographic data to guide model adjustments and must involve transparent, ethically informed decision-making.

Finally, the practical challenges of implementing diversity-aware AI extend to organizational structures and the allocation of resources. Building AI systems that genuinely reflect diversity is resource-intensive, requiring not only financial investment but also interdisciplinary collaboration. Effective diversity-aware AI development often requires insights from sociologists, ethicists, psychologists, and other experts who can help developers navigate complex cultural and ethical questions. However, securing this level of expertise and creating cross-functional teams can be challenging in technology-focused companies, where diversity considerations may be deprioritized in favor of rapid innovation and cost-efficiency. Additionally, diversity-aware AI requires continuous monitoring and refinement to adapt to changing social norms and values, which calls for ongoing investment that some organizations may be reluctant to commit. Without sufficient institutional support and resource allocation, the goal of creating truly diversity-aware AI may be compromised by practical limitations.

In conclusion, while diversity-aware AI holds the potential to make technology more inclusive, adaptive, and representative, it also presents a range of formidable challenges. Addressing issues of data diversity, algorithmic bias, transparency, ethical considerations, and resource allocation demands a thoughtful, multidisciplinary approach that extends beyond technical expertise alone. To build AI systems that reflect the diversity of human society, developers must remain vigilant in addressing biases, committed to transparency, and willing to engage with complex ethical questions. As AI continues to shape modern life, prioritizing diversity-awareness will be essential not only for the ethical development of AI but also for building systems that can genuinely understand and reflect the rich, multifaceted experiences of all users.

CONCLUSION

Diversity in AI remains a challenge as algorithms personalize our news feeds, make news recommendations, and target algorithmic curations (Heitz et al., 2022). Scholars and experts echo the need for diversity and transparency in NRS and algorithmic technologies in general (Jürgens & Stark, 2022). This study highlights how diversity nudges affect users and steer algorithms to enact choice architectures and nudges that influence user behavior relating to diverse news. While the various principles of algorithmic nudges account for recent developments in AI media, an essential proposition in algorithmic nudges is that users should understand the logic of algorithms (transparency), engage in the personalization process (two-tier processes), and remain in control of such nudges (Zaid et al., 2022). Although algorithmic gatekeeping is increasingly pervasive and embedded in many media services, it also creates unintended consequences where journalistic value and moral responsibility for their nudges cannot be suitably attributed to any particular editorial or contextual factors. Algorithmic nudging should enable users to make better news selection and consumption decisions by facilitating informed cognitive processes, extending engagement to construct data, and augmenting users' literacy to utilize insights from the data. It is critical to pay close attention to the complicated societal context within which algorithmic nudges are used and deployed to prevent algorithmic nudges from progressing past the limited perspective of traditional nudging as a simple user interface in AI environments. Equally important is to design algorithmic nudges in NRS as a platform for marketplace ideas and transparent user-centered mechanisms that contribute to overcoming users' emotional, cognitive, and psychological limits when they make decisions and perform actions that can promote discourse and ultimately strengthen democratic reflection in algorithmic media. To benefit from AI systems, users must engage with various views and diverse opinions in ways that translate into pro-social media effects. Thus, our study has valuable implications for how we can redefine personalization conceptually and design diversity-aware NRS practically to promote diverse news consumption.

WHERE DO WE GO FROM DIVERSITY-AWARE AI?

The future of diversity-aware AI holds promise for creating systems that not only perform tasks effectively but also respond sensitively to the complexities of human identity, culture, and values. As AI becomes more integrated into everyday decision-making processes—from healthcare to education to entertainment—its ability to understand and reflect diverse perspectives will be essential for ensuring fair and inclusive outcomes. Advances in data representation and algorithmic flexibility are enabling AI models to capture a broader range of human experiences, allowing these systems to adapt dynamically to varied user needs. Through increasingly sophisticated machine learning techniques, future diversity-aware AI could transcend rigid demographic categories to recognize more nuanced aspects of identity, such as cultural context and personal values, making it possible to tailor interactions more closely to each individual's unique background.

However, developing AI that meaningfully reflects diversity will require ongoing efforts in bias mitigation and transparency. Future models will likely incorporate fairness-aware learning processes that help mitigate biases at each stage of the development pipeline, from data collection to algorithmic training. Transparency will also play a critical role in enabling users to understand how diversity-aware AI makes decisions, fostering trust and allowing for public scrutiny of AI behavior. As new tools for XAI emerge, future systems could become more accessible and understandable, even as they grow more complex. In particular, innovations in "context-aware" systems, which tailor their responses based on specific user histories and social environments, could represent a major leap forward in the ethical and inclusive deployment of AI.

Looking ahead, interdisciplinary collaboration will be crucial for building truly diversity-aware AI. As technology intersects more deeply with social sciences and ethics, the future of AI development will depend on insights from fields like psychology, sociology, and cultural studies, ensuring that these systems are informed by a wide range of human perspectives. Additionally, as AI regulations evolve globally, frameworks for diversity-aware AI will need to adapt, embracing legal and ethical standards that uphold inclusivity and privacy. Governments, organizations, and AI developers will need to work together to ensure that these systems are both compliant and ethically aligned, supporting an inclusive digital future. If developed responsibly, diversity-aware AI could help foster greater equality, adapt to the diverse needs of global populations, and contribute meaningfully to a fairer and more understanding technological landscape.

REFERENCES

Achon, L., Souza, A., Hume, A., & Cernuzzi, L. (2024). A diversity-aware recommendation system for tutoring. *AI Communications, 37*(1), 1–23. http://doi.org/10.3233/AIC-230434

Aguirre, E., Roggeveen, A., Grewal, D., & Wetzels, M. (2016). The personalization-privacy paradox. *Journal of Consumer Marketing, 33*(2), 98–110. https://doi.org/10.1108/JCM-06-2015-1458

Araujo, T., Helberger, N., Kruikemeier, S., & Vreese, C. (2020). In AI we trust? *AI & Society, 35*(6), 611–623. https://doi.org/10.1007/s00146-019-00931-w

Baden, C., & Springer, N. (2017). Conceptualizing viewpoint diversity in news discourse. *Journalism, 18*(2), 176–194. https://doi.org/10.1177/1464884915605028

Bastian, M., Helberger, N., & Wijermars, M. (2021). Safeguarding the journalistic DNA: Attitudes towards the role of professional values in algorithmic news recommender designs. *Digital Journalism, 9*(6), 835–863. https://doi.org/10.1080/21670811.2021.1912622

Baumer, E. (2017). Toward human-centered algorithm design. *Big Data & Society, 4*(2). https://doi.org/10.1177/2053951717718854

Bryanov, K., Watson, B., Pingree, R., & Santia, M. (2020). Effects of partisan personalization in a news portal experiment. *Public Opinion Quarterly, 84*(S1), 216–235.

Buunk, P., & Gibbons, X. (2000). Toward an enlightenment in social comparison theory. In J. Suls & L. Wheeler (Eds.), *Handbook of social comparison. The springer series in social clinical psychology*. Springer. https://doi.org/10.1007/978-1-4615-4237-7_22

Cachat-Rosset, G., & Klarsfeld, A. (2023). Diversity, equity, and inclusion in artificial intelligence: An evaluation of guidelines. *Applied Artificial Intelligence*, *37*(1), 2176618.https://doi.org/10.1080/08839514.2023.2176618

Cardenal, S., Aguilar-Paredes, C., Cristancho, C., & Majó-Vázquez, S. (2019). Echo-chambers in online news consumption. *European Journal of Communication*, *34*(4), 360–376. https://doi.org/10.1177/0267323119844409

Chauhan, P. S., & Kshetri, N. (2024). The role of data and artificial intelligence in driving diversity, equity, and inclusion. *IEEE Access*, *12*, 37829–37843.

Chen, C., & Sundar, S. S. (2024). Communicating and combating algorithmic bias: Effects of data diversity, labeler diversity, performance bias, and user feedback on AI trust. *Human–Computer Interaction*. https://doi.org/10.1080/07370024.2024.2392494

Crawford, K., & Paglen, T. (2021). *Excavating AI: The politics of images in machine learning training sets. AI & Society*, *36*(4), 1159–1171.

Currin, C., Vera, S., & Khaledi-Nasab, A. (2022). Depolarization of echo chambers by random dynamical nudge. *Scientific Reports*, *12*, 9234. https://doi.org/10.1038/s41598-022-12494-w

Drabiak, K. (2024). AI and machine learning ethics, law, diversity, and global impact. *Bioethical Inquiry*, *16*(1), 1–17.

Du, Y., Ranwez, S., Sutton-Charani, N., & Ranwez, V. (2021). Is diversity optimization always suitable? Toward a better understanding of diversity within recommendation approaches. *Information Processing & Management*, *58*(6), 102721. https://doi.org/10.1016/j.ipm.2021.102721

Evans, R., Jackson, D., & Murphy, J. (2022). Google News and machine gatekeepers. *Digital Journalism*, *11*(9), 1682–1700. https://doi.org/10.1080/21670811.2022.2055596

Hameleers M., van der Meer T., & Vliegenthart R. (2021). Civilised truths, hateful lies? Incivility and hate speech in false information–evidence from fact-checked statements in the US. *Information, Communication and Society*, 25(11), 1596–1613. https://doi.org/10.1080/1369118X.2021.1874038

Hanna, A., Denton, E., Smart, A., & Smith-Loud, J. (2020). Towards a critical race methodology in algorithmic fairness. In *Proceedings of the 2020 conference on fairness, accountability, and transparency (FAT* 2020)*, 501–512.

Heitz, L., Lischka, J., Birrer, A., Paudel, B., Tolmeijer, S., Laugwitz, L., & Bernstein, A. (2022). Benefits of diverse news recommendations for democracy. *Digital Journalism*, *10*(10), 1710–1730. https://doi.org/10.1080/21670811.2021.2021804

Helberger, N. (2019). On the democratic role of news recommenders. *Digital Journalism*, *7*(8), 993–1012. https://doi.org/10.1080/21670811.2019.1623700

Hermann, E. (2022). Artificial intelligence and mass personalization of communication content. *New Media & Society*, *24*(5), 1258–1277. https://doi.org/10.1177/14614448211022702

Holstein, K., Wortman Vaughan, J., Daumé, I. I. I., Dudik, H., & Wallach, M., H. (2019). Improving fairness in machine learning systems: What do industry practitioners need? In *Proceedings of the 2019 CHI conference on human factors in computing systems*, 1–16.

Jang, W., Chun, J., Kim, S., & Kang, Y. (2022). The effects of anthropomorphism on how people evaluate algorithm-written news. *Digital Journalism*.https://doi.org/10.1080/21670811.2021.1976064

Jesse, M., & Jannach, D. (2021). Digital nudging with recommender systems. *Computers in Human Behavior Reports*, *3*, 100052. https://doi.org/10.1016/j.chbr.2020.100052

Jin, D., Wang, H., Zhang, Y., Ding, W., Xia, F., & Pan, S. (2023). A survey on fairness-aware recommender systems. *Information Fusion*, *100*, 101906. https://doi.org/10.1016/j.inffus.2023.101906

Joris, G., Grove, F., Damme, K., & Marez, L. (2020). News diversity reconsidered. *Journalism Studies*, *21*(13), 1893–1912. https://doi.org/10.1080/1461670X.2020.1797527

Jui, T. D., & Rivas, P. (2024). Fairness issues, current approaches, and challenges in machine learning models. *International Journal of Machine Learning and Cybernetics*, *15*, 3095–3125. https://doi.org/10.1007/s13042-023-02083-2

Jürgens, P., & Stark, B. (2022). Mapping exposure diversity. *Journal of Communication*, *72*(3), 322–344. https://doi.org/10.1093/joc/jqac009

Kim, D., & Pasek, J. (2020). Explaining the diversity deficit. *Communication Research*, *47*(1), 29–54. https://doi.org/10.1177/0093650216644647

Knudsen, E. (2023). Modeling news recommender systems' conditional effects on selective exposure. *Journal of Communication*. https://doi.org/10.1093/joc/jqac047

Li, B., & Liu, L. (2021). *Counteracting bias amplification through fairness-aware deep learning*. *IEEE Transactions on Neural Networks and Learning Systems*, *32*(8), 3441–3455.

Lin, Z., Guan, S., Zhang, W. , Lin, Z., Guan, S., Zhang, W., Zhang, H., Li, Y., & Zhang, H. (2024). Towards trustworthy LLMs: A review on debiasing and dehallucinating in large language models. *Artificial Intelligence Research*, *57*, 243. https://doi.org/10.1007/s10462-024-10896-y

Loecherbach, F., Moeller, J., Trilling, D., & van Atteveldt, W. (2020). The unified framework of media diversity. *Digital Journalism*, *8*(5), 605–642. https://doi.org/10.1080/21670811.2020.1764374

Mattis, N., Masur, P., Möller, J., & van Atteveldt, W. (2022). Nudging towards news diversity. *New Media & Society*. https://doi.org/10.1177/14614448221104413

Mitova, E., Blassnig, S., Strikovic, E., Urman, A., Hannak, A., de Vreese, C. H., & Esser, F. (2022). News recommender systems. *Annals of the International Communication Association*, 1–30. https://doi.org/10.1080/23808985.2022.2142149

Møller, L. (2023). Designing algorithmic editors. *Digital Journalism*. https://doi.org/10.1080/21670811.2023.2215832

Monzer, C., Moeller, J., Helberger, N., & Eskens, S. (2020). User perspectives on the news personalization process. *Digital Journalism*, *8*(9), 1142–1162. https://doi.org/10.1080/21670811.2020.1773291

Napoli, P. (2015). Social media and the public interest. *Telecommunications Policy*, *39*(9), 751–760. https://doi.org/10.1016/j.telpol.2014.12.003

Noble, S. (2018). *Algorithms of oppression: How search engines reinforce racism*. NYU Press.

Roche, C., Wall, P. J., & Lewis, D. (2023). Ethics and diversity in artificial intelligence policies, strategies and initiatives. *AI Ethics*, *3*, 1095–1115. https://doi.org/10.1007/s43681-022-00218-9

Sax, M. (2022). Algorithmic news diversity and democratic theory. *Digital Journalism*, *10*(10), 1650–1670. https://doi.org/10.1080/21670811.2022.2114919

Scheffauer, R., Goyanes, M., & Gil de Zúñiga, H. (2023). Social media algorithmic versus professional journalists' news selection. *Journalism*. https://doi.org/10.1177/14648849231179804

Shams, R. A., Zowghi, D., & Bano, M. (2023). AI and the quest for diversity and inclusion: A systematic literature review. *AI Ethics*. https://doi.org/10.1007/s43681-023-00362-w

Shin, D. (2024). *Artificial misinformation: Exploring human-algorithm interaction online*. Switzerland: Springer Nature. https://doi.org/10.1007/978-3-031-52569-8

Shin, D., & Zhou, S. (2024). A value and diversity-aware news recommendation systems: Can algorithmic gatekeeping nudge readers to view diverse news? *Journalism & Mass Communication Quarterly*. https://doi.org/10.1177/10776990241246680

Sonoda, A., Seki, Y., & Toriumi, F. (2022). Analyzing user engagement in news application considering popularity diversity and content diversity. *Journal of Computational Social Science*, *5*, 1595–1614. https://doi.org/10.1007/s42001-022-00179-3

Vermeulen, J. (2022). To nudge or not to nudge: News recommendation as a tool to achieve online media pluralism. *Digital Journalism*. https://doi.org/10.1080/21670811.2022.2026796

Werder, K., Cao, L., Ramesh, B., & Park, E. H. (2024). Empower diversity in AI development: Diversity practices that mitigate social biases from creeping into your AI. *Communications of the ACM*. https://doi.org/10.1145/3676885

Wu-Ouyang, B. (2023). Comparing media systems in Western democracies. *Journalism & Mass Communication Quarterly*. https://doi.org/10.1177/10776990231217482

Yeung, K. (2017). Hyper nudge: Big data as a mode of regulation by design. *Information, Communication & Society*, *20*(1), 118–136.

Yin, K., Fang, X., Chen, B., & Sheng, L. (2023). Diversity preference-aware link recommendation for online social networks. *Information System Research*, *34*(4). https://doi.org/10.1287/isre.2022.1174

Yu, X., Gao, Z., Zhao, C., Qiao, Y., Chai, Z., Mo, Z., & Yang, Y. (2024). Diversity-aware unbiased device selection for federated learning on non-IID and unbalanced data. *Journal of Systems Architecture*, *156*, 103280. https://doi.org/10.1016/j.sysarc.2024.103280

Zaid, B., Biocca, F., & Rasul, A. (2022). In platforms we trust? *Journal of Broadcasting and Electronic Media*, *66*(2), 235–256. https://doi.org/10.1080/08838151.2022.2057984

Zhao, Y., Wang, Y., Liu, Y., Cheng, X., Aggarwal, C., & Derr, T. (2024). Fairness and diversity in recommender systems. *ACM Transactions on Intelligent Systems and Technology*. https://doi.org/10.1145/3664928

Zowghi, D., Bano, M. AI for all: Diversity and Inclusion in AI. *AI and Ethics 4*, 873–876 (2024). https://doi.org/10.1007/s43681-024-00485-8

Algorithmic Inoculation

12

Immunizing Minds Against Bias

CAN HUMANS BE INOCULATED AGAINST BIAS?

In human beings, intelligence offers no immunity against prejudice and bias, and the same holds true for artificial intelligence (AI). Machine learning systems understand the world through the lens of human language and historical data, absorbing not only our best qualities but also our biases and prejudices (Basol et al., 2021). Consequently, these systems can internalize and perpetuate human bigotry just as readily as they can our ideals. There have been initiatives and efforts to address algorithmic bias. The inoculation approach has gained support in various contexts and shows promise in reducing susceptibility to both specific instances of misinformation and the broader techniques and strategies commonly used to mislead or misinform people (Compton, 2021).

The inculcation approach in AI involves systematically embedding specific values, beliefs, or cognitive skills into AI-driven systems to influence users' thinking and behavior in a beneficial way (Compton et al., 2021). Unlike traditional training or education, which relies on passive knowledge acquisition, algorithmic inoculation seeks to instill certain values or critical thinking skills by repeatedly exposing users to structured messages, guidance, or corrective information. The aim is to subtly shape user perceptions and decision-making in a way that promotes long-term understanding and resilience against harmful content, biases, or misinformation (Ecker et al., 2022).

AI-driven inculcation can involve algorithms that actively monitor user interactions and deliver timely, context-specific prompts that reinforce critical thinking or debiasing techniques (Batista et al., 2024). For instance, an AI system might interject with reminders about credible sources when users encounter questionable information or highlight

DOI: 10.1201/9781003530244-17

logical fallacies in contentious content. The goal of inculcation in AI is not merely to present information but to internalize these cognitive strategies in users, creating a more reflexive, adaptive, and skepticism-oriented approach to information (Kunst et al., 2024). This can be particularly valuable in fields like AI literacy, digital health, and online safety, where consistent reinforcement of values or attitudes is essential for long-term impact.

INOCULATION THEORY AND AI

Inoculation theory suggests that preemptively exposing users to a refuted or weakened version of a message can help build resistance to future persuasion attempts (Compton et al., 2021). Since its introduction in 1961, the theory has been widely applied to explain how beliefs and values are modified and how individuals maintain consistency in their cognition and perception in the face of attempts to influence them. Drawing an analogy to medical inoculation (which applies to beliefs rather than infections), the theory serves as a cognitive strategy to protect attitudes from persuasion by providing resistance to counter-attitudinal attacks. These attacks may come in the form of sustained pressures, direct or indirect influences, or psychological threats from various sources (Basol et al., 2021).

The theory provides a conceptual framework for a cognitive defense against the spread of falsehoods by strengthening mental resistance to future misinformation and manipulation, much like how medical vaccines build resistance to specific diseases (Traberg et al., 2022). Inoculation messages typically involve refutational preemption and motivational coercion. The coercion component alerts users that they may encounter both refutational preemption and psychological manipulation. This can either involve passively providing counterarguments to misinformation (passive inoculation) or actively engaging users in creating their own counterarguments (active inoculation) (Weiler et al., 2022). Active inoculation tends to be more effective, as it encourages users to generate their own resistance (antibodies) and counterarguments (Borukhson et al., 2022). By taking an active role in the inoculation process, users are nudged to initiate internal refutations (van der Linden, 2023), which can result in lasting effects due to increased psychological resistance (Pennycook, 2023).

Inoculation messages typically include both forewarning and refutational preemption (Compton et al., 2021). One approach involves alerting users to an impending misinformation threat (forewarning), while another involves exposing them to a weakened form of false information to preemptively counteract it (refutational preemption). Cognitive inoculation can be triggered through a motivational response to a perceived threat, where users defend themselves against attacks based on false information. For example, a message could inform users that "false and harmful information about immigration is being spread online and in ChatGPT." Alternatively, the inoculation can be a weakened dose of false propaganda, similar to debunking messages. For instance, "Immigrants eat dogs and cats and harm our culture and value" could be refuted with accurate information. In the context of the COVID-19 pandemic and debates over political correctness, inoculation theory has proven effective in developing interventions that help build psychological resistance to fake news and disinformation, including in areas like conspiracy theories, risky health behaviors, science denialism, political propaganda, and emotionally manipulative campaigns (Kunst et al., 2024; van der Linden, 2023; Vivion et al., 2022). Applied to AI, Inoculation Theory provides a valuable framework for designing interventions to enhance user resilience against misinformation and cognitive biases (Shin, 2024). AI algorithms can identify patterns in misinformation, recognize manipulative tactics (such as cherry-picking data or using emotional language), and generate "inoculation messages" tailored to counteract these strategies (Musi et al., 2023). For example, AI systems could expose users to examples of misinformation and demonstrate how biases or persuasive techniques were incorporated. This AI-driven method can be personalized to users' browsing habits and cognitive styles, making it both scalable and adaptive. By continuously refreshing the inoculation process to address emerging misinformation and persuasion tactics, AI systems can promote lasting resilience against digital manipulation, promoting a more discerning, critically minded audience (Pennycook & Rand, 2022).

COGNITIVE PROCESS OF INOCULATION

The inoculation approach draws on a series of cognitive processes—threat awareness, counterargument generation, schema adjustment, and the use of both slow and intuitive reasoning—to create a lasting mental defense against misinformation (Lu et al., 2023). This process works by engaging mental mechanisms that boost a person's ability to recognize, question, and reject misleading information in future scenarios. By activating certain cognitive pathways, inoculation strategies help to build a "mental immunity" that empowers people to maintain accurate beliefs and make informed decisions (Kuru, 2024).

Threat Awareness

The inoculation process begins with creating awareness of a potential "threat" to one's beliefs. By making people aware that misinformation exists and can manipulate them, this approach introduces a low level of cognitive dissonance—a mental state where people recognize a potential inconsistency between new information and their preexisting beliefs. This awareness acts as a cognitive alert, signaling to the brain that it should be cautious when encountering similar information in the future. Research shows that simply knowing about the risk of manipulation heightens people's vigilance, making them more discerning and critical when exposed to persuasive or misleading claims.

Counterargument Generation

Once people recognize that their beliefs may be challenged, they receive counterarguments or refutations of common misinformation tactics, equipping them with tools to defend their beliefs. This process involves *cognitive rehearsal*, where individuals mentally practice recognizing and rejecting false information. When they're given counterarguments or explanations about how misinformation operates, they essentially "rehearse" what they would do if confronted with misleading information. This rehearsal strengthens neural pathways that reinforce skepticism and critical evaluation, enhancing their ability to quickly recognize and reject similar claims in real situations.

Cognitive Dissonance Reduction

Inoculation also activates cognitive dissonance reduction, a psychological process in which people strive to resolve mental discomfort when they encounter contradictions to their beliefs. By exposing individuals to a "weakened" version of misinformation along with counterarguments, inoculation helps them reconcile the conflict before it escalates. Since they've already encountered, questioned, and resolved this information in a safe context, they experience less cognitive dissonance when they come across it again. This reduces the likelihood of belief change and reinforces their initial, correct beliefs.

Mental Schema Activation and Adjustment

Schemas are mental frameworks that help individuals organize and interpret information. Inoculation works by activating and adjusting these schemas so that misinformation can be quickly identified as irrelevant or misleading. For instance, if people learn that certain tactics, such as emotionally charged language, are used to spread misinformation, their schema for evaluating information adjusts to recognize these tactics as red flags. In this way, inoculation modifies their mental frameworks, allowing them to process future information with heightened scrutiny and skepticism, filtering out unreliable content.

Dual-Process Reasoning (System 1 and System 2 Thinking)

Inoculation taps into dual-process reasoning, where people use both automatic, intuitive thinking (System 1) and slower, reflective thinking (System 2). When individuals are exposed to inoculation messages, they initially engage in System 2 thinking, processing the information carefully and reflecting on the counterarguments (Shin, 2024). Over time, this critical response to misinformation tactics can be "internalized" and integrated into System 1 thinking, making individuals more instinctively skeptical. For example, after inoculation training, people may automatically notice emotional manipulation in headlines or social media posts without conscious effort, engaging System 1 as a faster, intuitive defense.

Strengthened Cognitive Bias Awareness

Cognitive biases, such as framing bias, can make individuals susceptible to misinformation. Inoculation addresses this by emphasizing these biases and making people aware of their own tendency to seek out agreeable information. When people understand these biases, they become more vigilant about questioning information, especially if it aligns too perfectly with their beliefs. This self-awareness fosters a mental habit of cross-checking and verifying information, counteracting the influence of biases that make them more susceptible to misleading claims (Roozenbeek et al., 2022).

Elaboration Likelihood Model Engagement

The Elaboration Likelihood Model posits that people process persuasive messages through either a central (thoughtful, focused) or peripheral (quick, superficial) route. Inoculation leverages the central route by encouraging people to actively think about and engage with the counterarguments presented. By elaborating on these arguments, individuals strengthen their cognitive defenses, making them less susceptible to superficial persuasion attempts later. When people are encouraged to engage deeply with information through central processing, they are better able to resist attempts to manipulate their beliefs through shallow or manipulative messaging (Schuetz et al., 2021).

Memory Encoding and Retrieval

Finally, inoculation assists with the encoding and retrieval of misinformation-resistance strategies. By actively engaging with inoculation messages and practicing counterarguments, people encode these lessons in their memory. When they encounter similar situations, these memory traces are more likely to be activated, helping them apply the inoculation lessons automatically. For example, if they remember a counterargument they previously learned, they are more likely to retrieve and apply it, allowing them to navigate new misinformation with confidence.

In the AI era, algorithms can enhance cognitive inoculation by flexibly scaling this process and providing tailored interventions (Shin & Akhtar, 2024). For instance, AI can identify trending misinformation and deliver personalized refutational messages, fostering cognitive resilience in users against evolving digital threats. Through this structured, repeated exposure, cognitive inoculation empowers users to navigate information with increased skepticism and confidence.

By preemptively strengthening these cognitive pathways, inoculation allows people to apply critical thinking instinctively, resist biases, and quickly identify manipulative tactics. This approach doesn't just offer information but builds a cognitive infrastructure that equips individuals to maintain accurate beliefs and make informed judgments when they face misleading information in everyday life (van der Linden, 2023).

PREBUNKING AND DEBUNKING

Prebunking and debunking are two distinct approaches used to counter algorithmic bias, each operating at different stages in the spread of false information (Tay et al., 2021). Prebunking is a proactive strategy aiming to "inoculate" people against misinformation by exposing them to a weakened version of misleading content before they encounter it in full form (Basol et al., 2021). This approach is based on the idea that forewarning individuals and providing them with cognitive mechanisms, like critical thinking cues and fact-checking techniques, can help them resist the impact of future falsehoods. For example, prebunking may involve campaigns that teach people about common misinformation tactics, such as sensationalist headlines or emotional manipulation. Research suggests that when people are exposed to misinformation in a controlled way and taught how to recognize it, they develop a kind of "cognitive immunity" and are less likely to fall for similar content later on (Lewandowsky & van der Linden, 2021). Tools like fairness checklists, simulation models, and bias detection software are often used to identify and address issues during development, minimizing the likelihood of biased outcomes when the algorithm is put into real-world applications (Mehrabi et al., 2021).

In contrast, debunking is a reactive approach that addresses misinformation after it has already circulated (Ecker et al., 2022). Debunking efforts often engage fact-checking and correcting false claims once they are publicly identified. This process typically involves providing accurate information and evidence-based corrections that clarify why a piece of information is incorrect or misleading. This approach may also include public awareness campaigns that explain how the bias emerged and what steps are being taken to address it. Debunking can be effective, but it faces challenges like the "continued influence effect," where people may still retain parts of the misinformation despite receiving a correction (Epstein et al., 2021). Once an algorithm is deployed, biased outcomes may have already affected individuals or groups, which can have lasting consequences—especially in high-stakes applications like healthcare, hiring, or criminal justice. Additionally, debunking may require complex fixes, such as retraining algorithms or overhauling them, which can be resource-intensive and may not fully remove the effects of prior biases.

In practice, both approaches have their pros and cons. Prebunking offers a preventive advantage, making it potentially more effective over time as people become less susceptible to misinformation. However, it requires public awareness campaigns and can be resource-intensive, as it involves anticipating misinformation trends. Debunking, while immediately useful in addressing specific false claims, often struggles against the "stickiness" of misinformation, as people sometimes hold onto their initial beliefs. Both strategies are used in misinformation management, with some experts suggesting that a combination of prebunking and debunking offers the most comprehensive defense against false information (van der Linden et al., 2021).

Together, prebunking and debunking form a complementary approach to reducing the impact of misinformation, addressing both preventive and corrective aspects of misinformation resilience.

HEURISTIC SYSTEMATIC INOCULATION PROCESSING

The influence of inoculation information processing on misinformed decision-making can be dual (Shin & Akhtar, 2024): heuristic (System 1 thinking) and systematic (System 2 thinking). Heuristic processing, the first line of defense, is a quick and intuitive response that relies on simple cues. When individuals encounter potentially deceptive information, they can rely on these cues—such as recognizing unreliable sources or identifying overly dramatic or misleading headlines—as initial red flags. This fast, surface-level judgment is designed to help people dismiss misinformation quickly without requiring much cognitive effort. This process is similar to System 1 thinking, which is fast, automatic, and relies on intuition and shortcuts. In inoculation messages, System 1 thinking is harnessed through simple cues or "heuristics" designed to help individuals make quick judgments. For instance, a person might learn to recognize certain patterns that often indicate misinformation, such as sensational language, emotionally charged headlines, or unreliable sources. When individuals receive an inoculation message, System 1 might be triggered to develop a "gut feeling" against misleading content. This instinctive, snap-judgment response doesn't involve much cognitive effort, yet it provides an immediate first line of defense by allowing individuals to recognize misinformation almost instantly. By cultivating specific, easily remembered rules or signals within the inoculation message, System 1 thinking becomes a tool for helping people reject misinformation without the need for deep analysis. This approach can be especially effective in contexts where people are exposed to a high volume of information and need a quick filter to distinguish credible from non-credible sources.

Systematic processing, on the other hand, is a more deliberate and analytical way of thinking. In the inoculation model, systematic processing takes individuals a step further by encouraging them to critically evaluate the content of the message itself. This is equivalent to System 2 thinking, which is deliberate and effortful reasoning. Rather than simply relying on cues, systematic processing involves analyzing the logic of the argument, checking for consistency, and assessing the evidence presented. This deeper level of engagement enables individuals to form more robust defenses against misinformation, making them better equipped to handle more subtle or complex cases of deception. This type of process is engaged when individuals go beyond surface cues to thoroughly evaluate the content of an inoculation message. In the context of inoculation, a systematic process is essential for developing a deeper, more robust mechanism against misinformation. By encouraging recipients to systematically analyze misleading information, System 2 thinking helps people consider the logical structure of the argument, check the evidence, and evaluate the overall coherence and validity of the claims.

For example, an inoculation message might present a common piece of misinformation along with detailed counterarguments that demonstrate why the information is misleading. The process of evaluating these counterarguments activates systematic thinking, as individuals are required to engage in critical reasoning, cross-referencing facts, and understanding the flaws in the deceptive content. This deeper cognitive processing not only reinforces immediate resistance to misinformation but also helps people build a more enduring defense that applies to new, related instances of misinformation.

In designing an inoculation message, these two processes are integrated and combined (Roozenbeek et al., 2022). People are introduced to a mild version of the misinformation along with simple rebuttals or corrections. The initial exposure to misinformation, even in a weakened form, helps to prepare individuals for real-life encounters with similar deceptive content. Then, as users delve further into the message, systematic thinking promotes a comprehensive understanding of why the information is misleading, reinforcing their initial instinct with careful analysis. This combined approach enhances both the speed and depth of individuals' responses to misinformation. The rebuttals are presented both as heuristics—simple rules or cues to help them identify misinformation at a glance—and as systematic arguments, providing a deeper analysis that helps them understand why the information is misleading.

Over time, individuals who engage with this dual-process inoculation method develop stronger mental resilience. The combination of quick heuristics and in-depth analysis becomes an internalized habit, allowing them to quickly identify and critically assess false claims, even when faced with new or complicated deceptive tactics. This layered approach not only enhances immediate identification of misinformation but also strengthens long-term cognitive immunity, creating a more informed and discerning audience (Pilditch et al., 2022).

THE PROCESS OF ALGORITHMIC INOCULATION

The inoculation approach to algorithmic bias seeks to empower individuals to recognize and resist deceptive information generated by AI. This strategy is enhanced by the principles of cognitive immunity, which can be likened to how vaccines work to strengthen biological immunity. By exposing individuals to weaker or less harmful forms of misinformation, this approach builds resilience, equipping people to detect and deflect similar forms of misinformation when encountered in real-life situations.

The first stage of algorithmic inoculation involves helping people understand what misinformation is and how it spreads (identifying and understanding misinformation). This foundation is crucial because it allows individuals to recognize when they are encountering false or misleading information, especially when it is tailored and amplified by algorithms. Once individuals are aware of the problem, the inoculation process begins with the introduction of controlled exposure to mild forms of misinformation (preemptive exposure). This could involve showing them exaggerated or misleading claims, but in a way that also provides them with the tools to critically evaluate such content. Just as a vaccine functions by exposing the body to a harmless dose of a virus to build immunity, this approach aims to "train" the mind to resist future encounters with similar falsehoods. By exposing individuals to misinformation in a structured manner, they are encouraged to analyze and debunk it, which helps them develop a kind of cognitive immunity (cognitive immunity). This immunity doesn't make them impervious to misinformation, but rather less susceptible to being swayed by it when they encounter it again. They become better equipped to identify the tactics used to spread false narratives and more adept at questioning the sources of the information they come across.

A key element of the inoculation process is debiasing, where individuals are not only shown misinformation but also provided with counterarguments or factual corrections. This helps individuals adjust their cognitive framework, incorporating new knowledge that strengthens their ability to resist manipulation. For example, showing someone a misleading headline alongside factual corrections allows them to learn how to spot inaccuracies or distortions.

Finally, similar to how vaccinations require boosters to maintain effectiveness, algorithmic inoculation requires reinforcement (reinforcement and practice). Continued exposure to information about how algorithms work and how to critically engage with content ensures that individuals don't lose their resistance to misinformation over time. This ongoing process of education and critical engagement helps to reinforce the skills needed to navigate an increasingly complex digital information environment, ultimately strengthening individuals' resilience against algorithmically driven misinformation. This phase of cognitive immunity building is critical, as it allows individuals to internalize lessons from controlled exposures and cultivate a natural resistance to similar forms of deception in the future. In essence, their brains become trained to recognize the structure and tactics of misinformation without falling for it. When they subsequently encounter AI-generated misinformation outside the controlled setting, they are more likely to recognize it as deceptive and respond skeptically. The inoculation approach, therefore, turns passive consumers of information into active, informed participants who are better equipped to navigate the complicated landscape of digital and AI-generated information (Martel et al., 2020).

ALGORITHMIC INOCULATION METHODS

As misinformation has proliferated in digital media, affecting everything from public health to politics, these inoculation methods have gained attention as a proactive approach to safeguard public understanding and discourse (Traberg et al., 2022). One primary method of misinformation inoculation is known as *prebunking*, a proactive strategy that involves exposing individuals to a "weakened" version of misinformation or educating them on common tactics used to spread it (Lazer et al., 2018). The concept is based on the idea that by experiencing a less intense or obvious form of misinformation, individuals will recognize these patterns when exposed to similar information in the future. For example, a prebunking session might involve showing participants a video that explains typical misinformation strategies, such as using emotionally charged language or presenting false authority figures, helping them develop an intuitive awareness of these tactics. In pre-exposure, participants in inoculation studies might be shown examples of how information can be distorted to mislead people—through methods like using false authority, emotional manipulation, or selective presentation of facts. This helps them build an awareness of these deceptive strategies. Once people understand these tactics, they become more alert to them in practice, making it easier to question and reject misleading information. This approach also involves *counter-arguing* exercises. By presenting a small dose of misinformation and guiding individuals through arguments that debunk it, inoculation exercises help people practice spotting logical flaws and building counterarguments. This not only induces skepticism but also equips people with the tools to actively counter misinformation when they see it again. Research shows that this process improves critical thinking and makes people less likely to passively accept or spread false information.

Another essential factor of misinformation inoculation is *critical thinking training*, which emphasizes developing skills for analyzing and evaluating the information people consume. Critical thinking training does not focus on specific facts but rather on equipping individuals with a mindset and skillset to assess information sources and content critically. By focusing on skills such as assessing evidence, identifying logical fallacies, and considering alternative perspectives, critical thinking training empowers individuals to doubt and scrutinize information, making them less likely to accept false claims at face value. Critical thinking is particularly valuable in addressing misinformation that aligns with people's preexisting beliefs or emotions, as it encourages a more reflective and less reactionary approach to information consumption.

Fact-checking and media literacy are also crucial components of misinformation inoculation (Ali et al., 2022). Media literacy programs train people on the principles of responsible information production and consumption, focusing on identifying reliable sources, recognizing bias, and understanding the motivations behind various media messages. Fact-checking, meanwhile, teaches individuals to verify information before accepting or sharing it, promoting habits of skepticism and verification. This approach has proven effective, particularly for younger audiences who frequently navigate a blend of facts and opinions in online environments. Developing a habit of fact-checking encourages a more cautious approach to information, fostering a form of "cognitive immunity" that helps guard against misinformation. Some educational initiatives have even incorporated fact-checking games that simulate real-world misinformation challenges, making the learning process interactive and memorable (Hu et al., 2023).

Simulated fact-checking and games are also used in inoculation approaches, particularly with younger audiences. These simulations engage individuals in activities where they practice identifying and debunking misinformation in controlled environments, often through interactive games or training modules. For instance, a simulation might present players with various social media posts and ask them to verify the content using provided fact-checking tools. By practicing fact-checking in a safe environment, individuals become more familiar with the techniques needed to verify information and are more likely to apply these skills when they encounter questionable information in real life. This approach combines learning and engagement, making the skills taught memorable and easier to adopt as part of daily media habits.

IS ALGORITHMIC INOCULATION REALLY EFFECTIVE?

As promising as this approach seems, the question remains: Is algorithmic inoculation truly working? Pilditch et al. (2022) argue that algorithmic inoculation does hold promise in building resilience against misinformation. By teaching individuals to recognize and critically analyze misleading content, it empowers them to question the validity of what they encounter online. Studies (Pennycook, 2023; Pennycook & Rand, 2022) have shown that individuals exposed to inoculation interventions are better equipped to detect misinformation and are less likely to be swayed by false narratives in the future. This critical engagement cultivates a form of "cognitive immunity," enabling individuals to more effectively distinguish between credible and misleading information (Martel et al., 2020). Additionally, inoculation proves especially effective in countering the subtle and widespread influence of algorithmically amplified misinformation (Lu et al., 2023). Algorithms curate content based on users' preferences and behaviors, often reinforcing existing beliefs and creating echo chambers. Inoculation helps users understand how these algorithms work and, in turn, enables them to navigate information more discerningly. By promoting awareness of algorithmic biases, inoculation can reduce the impact of misinformation that spreads through these personalized, algorithm-driven filters.

However, despite these positive outcomes, the effectiveness of algorithmic inoculation is not guaranteed across all contexts or for all individuals (Bessarabova et al., 2024; van der Linden, 2024). One of the main challenges is motivating users. Inoculation is most effective when individuals are already inclined to think critically about information. However, for those with strongly held beliefs or significant ideological polarization, inoculation may not produce the desired outcomes. In fact, there is the risk of the backfire effect, where exposure to counterarguments or misinformation can actually strengthen existing false beliefs rather than weaken them (Shin, 2024). The nature of the misinformation being targeted is also crucial in determining the effectiveness of inoculation. For example, easily debunked misinformation—such as false claims about factual events—may be more readily resisted through inoculation. However, more complex or emotionally charged misinformation, like conspiracy theories or ideological narratives, can be much harder to combat. These types of misinformation often tap into people's emotions or deeply held beliefs, making it difficult for inoculation to have the same impact.

Another key consideration is the context in which inoculation is applied (Ecker et al., 2022). In formal settings like classrooms or workplaces, where there is structured learning and a receptive audience, inoculation may be more effective. Conversely, the casual and often passive way people consume content on social media complicates efforts to engage them in inoculation interventions. Additionally, the relentless flow of new content on these platforms makes it difficult to sustain the long-term benefits of inoculation, which relies on periodic reinforcement to stay effective.

Additionally, the effectiveness of inoculation may be influenced by the type of misinformation involved (Chen & Cheng, 2020). Some forms of misinformation are easier to debunk than others. For instance, easily verifiable claims about concrete facts can be corrected more easily than more complex, nuanced misinformation that plays on emotions or biases. The inoculation approach is likely to be more successful in situations where the misinformation is relatively straightforward and can be addressed with clear facts and reasoning. More complex misinformation, such as conspiracy theories or ideological narratives, may require more sophisticated and nuanced interventions.

Despite these challenges, algorithmic inoculation remains a promising tool in the fight against misinformation (Compton et al., 2021). When used alongside other strategies, such as media literacy education and fact-checking, it can help individuals become more resilient to the persuasive power of false information (Kuru, 2024). Inoculation is not a silver bullet. While it is not a panacea, algorithmic inoculation can be a powerful constituency of a broader strategy to combat misinformation in an increasingly algorithmic world. By fostering critical thinking, increasing awareness of algorithmic influence, and promoting ongoing engagement with information, inoculation can contribute to a more informed and skeptical digital public.

THE PROS AND CONS OF ALGORITHMIC INOCULATION

As AI plays an increasingly influential role in the creation and dissemination of information, algorithmic inoculation seeks to build resilience against AI-generated falsehoods, empowering individuals to navigate digital spaces with greater critical awareness. While this approach has notable strengths, it also faces challenges that complicate its widespread implementation and effectiveness.

One of the key strengths of algorithmic inoculation is its preemptive defense against misinformation (Musi et al., 2023). Instead of attempting to correct false beliefs after they have taken hold, inoculation equips people with the cognitive tools to identify and resist misinformation before it impacts their views. This proactive approach is particularly valuable because research shows that once misinformation is accepted, it can be difficult to dislodge, even when corrected. By introducing individuals to controlled, weakened examples of misinformation, algorithmic inoculation trains them to spot deceptive elements, fostering a skepticism that prepares them for real-world encounters with misinformation. This strategy not only strengthens critical thinking but also reduces the risk of people being misled by the next wave of AI-generated content.

Another strength of algorithmic inoculation lies in its ability to foster long-lasting cognitive resilience (Spampatti et al., 2024). The process exposes individuals to patterns of manipulation commonly used in misinformation, such as selective editing, sensationalism, or emotional appeals. By repeatedly encountering these tactics in a safe, controlled environment, people develop a kind of "mental toolkit" that helps them recognize and reject these patterns when they appear in real-world content. This resilience-building extends beyond short-term effects, fostering lasting shifts in how individuals interpret and engage with information, cultivating a more critical and discerning public. Ideally, this learned skepticism can contribute to healthier information ecosystems, as inoculated individuals become less vulnerable to manipulative content (Shin, 2023).

Despite these advantages, algorithmic inoculation also faces significant weaknesses that can limit its effectiveness. One major challenge is the difficulty of scaling inoculation techniques to reach a broad audience. While small groups may benefit from inoculation training, it requires substantial resources to implement these strategies at the societal level. Educational initiatives, content moderation, and public campaigns are necessary to introduce inoculation on a wide scale, but they demand consistent funding, coordination, and policy support. In a landscape where misinformation keeps evolving, inoculation programs have to keep up, regularly refreshing their tactics and examples to outpace new forms of AI-generated manipulation. This ongoing adaptation, however, can be both time-intensive and expensive, making it hard to maintain these efforts in the long run.

Another limitation of algorithmic inoculation is its reliance on engagement and motivation. Not all individuals may be equally receptive to inoculation efforts; some may be uninterested in or resistant to participating in programs that promote critical thinking about information sources. This is especially true in polarized or highly ideological environments, where people may selectively reject inoculation content that challenges their existing beliefs. Moreover, inoculation can sometimes backfire if individuals perceive it as an attempt to control their beliefs, leading them to reject even legitimate information. This psychological reactance can create additional barriers to inoculation's success, as people who feel they are being "taught" not to believe certain things may be more resistant to future attempts at cognitive training.

Finally, algorithmic inoculation is limited by the inherent complexity of digital misinformation, especially as AI becomes more sophisticated in creating realistic and tailored content. While inoculation can prepare individuals to recognize specific tactics, the constant evolution of AI-generated misinformation means that new tactics will emerge that may circumvent existing defenses. For example, if inoculation programs focus on spotting emotionally charged language, AI systems may start generating misinformation that relies on factual distortions rather than emotional appeals, rendering the inoculation less effective. In this way, the dynamic nature of AI-generated content poses an ongoing challenge to maintaining effective inoculation techniques, as defenses can quickly become outdated.

In sum, algorithmic inoculation offers a valuable but imperfect solution to the problem of AI-generated misinformation. Its strengths lie in its proactive and resilience-building approach, preparing individuals to detect manipulation before it can influence their beliefs. However, its limitations—scalability, engagement challenges, and the adaptive nature of AI misinformation—highlight the need for a multi-faceted strategy that includes ongoing education, adaptive policies, and technological interventions. While algorithmic inoculation alone may not be sufficient to fully protect society from the harms of misinformation, it can serve as a foundational element in a broader, more comprehensive approach to maintaining the integrity of our information environments in the digital age.

ETHICAL CONSIDERATIONS OF ALGORITHMIC INOCULATION

Ethical considerations of inoculation approaches in addressing bias focus on issues of transparency, informed consent, potential psychological impacts, and unintended effects (Bessarabova et al., 2024). In inoculation methods, transparency and informed consent are crucial ethical pillars in this context. Inoculation techniques, especially when used in public information campaigns or educational settings, should ideally be accompanied by clear communication about their purpose and methodology. Without transparency, these interventions may be seen as covert persuasion, where individuals might feel manipulated rather than empowered to critically evaluate information (Lewandowsky et al., 2021). Ensuring that participants are aware of the inoculation process, particularly in sensitive contexts like public health or political messaging, aligns with ethical standards by promoting informed choice and reducing potential distrust.

The second ethical issue is autonomy (Molina & Sundar, 2023). Algorithmic inoculation relies on curated misinformation and corrective information that is often tailored based on user data. While the goal is to enhance users' resilience to misinformation, there is an ethical risk that users may feel manipulated if they are unaware of the system's purpose or if the process seems overly intrusive. Without clear communication, users may perceive these interventions as subtle forms of control rather than empowerment, raising questions about the ethical balance between protective interventions and personal freedom (Lewandowsky et al., 2020).

Privacy is also a concern in algorithmic inoculation approaches (Musi et al., 2023). These algorithms typically require user data to personalize and target misinformation inoculations effectively. While personalized inoculations may enhance the intervention's effectiveness, they also raise ethical concerns about data collection, consent, and potential misuse. Users must trust that their data is handled responsibly and solely for the intended purpose of combating misinformation, without being exploited for unrelated goals like targeted advertising or behavior profiling (Pennycook, 2023).

Another ethical consideration involves the long-term effects of inoculation (Roozenbeek et al., 2022; Tully et al., 2020). While inoculation has shown promise in enhancing misinformation resilience, it requires careful monitoring and follow-up to ensure that it does not lead to overconfidence or indiscriminate skepticism. Excessive skepticism could lead people to doubt even well-substantiated information, ultimately contributing to "epistemic mistrust," where individuals question the validity of all information sources (Lewandowsky & van der Linden, 2021). In this sense, inoculation methods need to be carefully balanced to promote critical thinking without encouraging a blanket distrust of information, especially from reputable sources.

The ethical deployment of inoculation methods requires transparency, respect for participants' autonomy, compliance with privacy, and vigilance regarding potential unintended consequences. Researchers and practitioners must weigh the benefits of inoculation against its risks, aiming to enhance public resilience to misinformation without compromising ethical standards or eroding trust in information systems. Through thoughtful application, inoculation methods can support an informed public, but they require continuous refinement and ethical consideration to avoid unintended negative impacts on individuals and society at large.

THE FUTURE DIRECTION OF ALGORITHMIC INOCULATIONS

The future of algorithmic inoculation holds significant potential as society grapples with the challenges of misinformation and manipulation in an increasingly AI-driven world. This approach, which builds cognitive resilience against misinformation through preemptive exposure to controlled, "weakened" versions of deceptive content, may evolve to become more adaptive, personalized, and integrated with other digital literacy tools. However, its continued development will depend on advancements in technology, policy support, and public receptiveness.

One of the most promising directions for the future of algorithmic inoculation is its potential to become more adaptive. As misinformation techniques evolve, AI-based inoculation systems will need to stay one step ahead, updating the misinformation examples and tactics they present to users in response to emerging trends. Advances in machine learning may enable inoculation algorithms to continuously scan and analyze current misinformation, rapidly identifying new patterns and developing corresponding "inoculation" techniques. For instance, if AI-driven misinformation increasingly uses deepfake videos or hyper-realistic images, inoculation programs could incorporate these elements into their training, helping users become resilient to these specific forms of manipulation. This dynamic approach would help inoculation remain effective even as misinformation techniques become more sophisticated.

Personalization is another area where algorithmic inoculation may advance. In the future, inoculation systems could tailor misinformation examples and resilience-building exercises to individual users, taking into account their personal vulnerabilities, information habits, and cognitive biases. Research has shown that people are often more susceptible to certain types of misinformation based on their beliefs, values, and social influences. With personalized inoculation, users would receive training that is specifically targeted at the types of misinformation they are most likely to encounter and believe. This approach could be more engaging and relevant for users, enhancing its effectiveness by tackling misinformation in a way that aligns with each individual's unique perspective and needs.

Additionally, algorithmic inoculation is likely to be increasingly incorporated into digital and media literacy programs, creating a well-rounded educational framework. As misinformation becomes an increasingly complex issue involving social, psychological, and technological dimensions, a multi-disciplinary approach will be essential. Future inoculation programs could be embedded within school curricula, workplace training, and even social media platforms. For example, platforms might offer interactive inoculation experiences, simulating misinformation scenarios in real time to give users hands-on practice in identifying manipulation tactics. Additionally, public health campaigns or government-led initiatives could include inoculation as part of broader media literacy efforts, ensuring that more people have access to cognitive defenses against misinformation.

Despite its promise, the future of algorithmic inoculation will also face challenges. Privacy concerns may arise as personalized inoculation systems gather and analyze user data to tailor misinformation defenses. Finding ways to safeguard users' privacy while delivering targeted inoculation will be a priority, and new privacy-preserving AI techniques may play a critical role in addressing this issue. Moreover, public trust and receptiveness will be essential. Algorithmic inoculation could face resistance from those who view it as an attempt to influence or control their beliefs, especially in polarized environments. Effective inoculation programs will need to be transparent and neutral to ensure broad acceptance, focusing on building critical thinking skills without promoting specific viewpoints.

The adaptability and accessibility of algorithmic inoculation will also depend on policy support. Governments, educational institutions, and tech companies will need to invest in developing and disseminating inoculation programs and ensure they reach diverse populations. Policymakers will play a crucial role in supporting digital literacy initiatives that incorporate inoculation, establishing guidelines and funding for the development of open-source inoculation tools, and encouraging platforms to integrate inoculation efforts without compromising user autonomy. In the long run, algorithmic inoculation could become a foundational skill in the digital age, empowering individuals to navigate the information landscape more independently and critically. As misinformation continues to pose risks to societies, economies, and democracies, algorithmic inoculation offers a pathway to a more resilient public, one that is less vulnerable to deception and more capable of informed decision-making. However, for algorithmic inoculation to reach its full potential, it will require continual technological innovation, thoughtful policy, and a commitment to fostering public trust and engagement.

REFERENCES

Ali, K., Li, C., Zain-ul-abdin, K., & Zaffar, M. (2022). Fake news on Facebook: Examining the impact of heuristic cues on perceived credibility. *Internet Research*, *32*(1), 379–397. https://doi.org/10.1108/INTR-10-2019-0442

Basol, M., Roozenbeek, J., Berriche, M., Uenal, F., McClanahan, W., & van der Linden, S. (2021). Toward psychological herd immunity: Cross-cultural evidence for two prebunking interventions against COVID-19 misinformation. *Big Data & Society*, *8*. https://doi.org/10.1177/20539517211013868

Batista, F., Bueno, S., Nunes, F., & Pavão, N. (2024). Inoculation reduces misinformation: Experimental evidence from multidimensional interventions in Brazil. *Journal of Experimental Political Science, 11*(3), 239–250. https://doi.org/10.1017/XPS.2023.11

Bessarabova, E., Banas, J., Reinikainen, H., Talbert, N., Luoma-aho, V., & Tsetsura, T. (2024). Assessing inoculation's effectiveness in motivating resistance to conspiracy propaganda in Finnish and United States samples. *Frontiers in Psychology, 15.* https://doi.org/10.3389/fpsyg.2024.1416722

Borukhson, D., Lorenz-Spreen, P., & Ragni, M. (2022). When does an individual accept misinformation? *Computational Brain & Behavior, 5,* 244–260. https://doi.org/10.1007/s42113-022-00136-3

Chen, Z. F., & Cheng, Y. (2020). Consumer response to fake news about brands on social media. *Journal of Product & Brand Management, 29*(2), 188–198. https://doi.org/10.1108/JPBM-12-2018-2145

Compton, J. (2021). Threat and/in inoculation theory. *International Journal of Communication, 15,* 4294–4306. https://ijoc.org/index.php/ijoc/article/view/17634

Compton, J., Linden, S., Cook, J., & Basol, M. (2021). Inoculation theory in the posttruth era: Extant findings and new frontiers for contested science, misinformation, and conspiracy theories. *Social and Personality Psychology Compas, 15,* e12602. https://doi.org/10.1111/spc3.12602

Ecker, U. K. H., Lewandowsky, S., Cook, J., Schmid, P., Fazio, L. K., Brashier, N., Kendeou, P., Vraga, E. K., Amazeen, M. A. (2022). The psychological drivers of misinformation belief and its resistance to correction. *Nature Review Psychology, 1,* 13–29. https://doi.org/10.1038/s44159-021-00006-y

Epstein, Z., Berinsky, A., Cole, R., Gully, A., Pennycook, G., & Rand, D. (2021). Developing an accuracy-prompt toolkit to reduce COVID-19 misinformation online. *Harvard Kennedy School Misinformation Review, 2*(3), 1–12. https://doi.org/10.37016/mr-2020-71

Hu, X., Yuan, Y., & Luo, J. (2023). Understanding the shifting nature of fake news research. Journal of the *Association for Information Science and Technology, 74*(10), 1123–1137. https://doi.org/10.1002/asi.24980

Kunst, J. R., Gundersen, A. B., Krysińska, I., Piasecki, J., Wójtowicz, T., Rygula, R., van der Linden, S., & Morzy, M. (2024). Leveraging artificial intelligence to identify the psychological factors associated with conspiracy theory beliefs online. *Nature Communications, 15,* 7497. https://doi.org/10.1038/s41467-024-51740-9

Kuru, O. (2024). Literacy training vs. psychological inoculation? Explicating and comparing the effects of predominantly informational and predominantly motivational interventions on the processing of health statistics. *Journal of Communication,* jqae032. https://doi.org/10.1093/joc/jqae032

Lazer, D. M. J., Baum, M. A., Benkler, Y., Berinsky, A. J., Greenhill, K. M., Menczer, F., Metzger, M. J., Nyhan, B., Pennycook, G., Rothschild, D., Schudson, M., Sloman, S. A., Sunstein, C. R., Thorson, E. A., Watts, D. J., & Zittrain, J. L. (2018). The science of fake news. *Science, 359*(6380), 1094–1096. https://doi.org/10.1126/science.aao2998

Lewandowsky, S., Ecker, U. K. H., & Cook, J. (2020). Beyond misinformation: Understanding and coping with the "Post-Truth" Era. *Journal of Applied Research in Memory and Cognition, 6*(4), 353–369. https://doi.org/10.1016/j.jarmac.2020.06.004

Lewandowsky, S., & van der Linden, S. (2021). Countering misinformation and fake news through inoculation and prebunking. *European Review of Social Psychology, 32*(2), 348–384. https://doi.org/10.1080/10463283.2021.1876983

Lu, C., Hu, B., Li, Q., Bi, C., & Ju, X. (2023). Psychological inoculation for credibility assessment, sharing intention, and discernment of misinformation: Systematic review and meta-analysis. *Journal of Medical Internet Research, 25,* e49255. https://doi.org/10.2196/49255

Martel, C., Pennycook, G., & Rand, D. G. (2020). Reliance on emotion promotes belief in fake news. *Cognitive Research, 47*(5). https://doi.org/10.1186/s41235-020-00252-3

Mehrabi, N., Morstatter, M., Saxena, F., Lerman, A., & Aram, C. (2021). A survey on bias and fairness in machine learning. *Association for Computing Machinery, 54*(6). https://doi.org/10.1145/3457607

Molina, M. D., & Sundar, S. S. (2024). Does distrust in humans predict greater trust in AI? Role of individual differences in user responses to content moderation. New Media & Society, 26(6), 3638–3656. https://doi.org/10.1177/14614448221103534

Musi, E., Carmi, E., Reed, C., Yates, S., & O'Halloran, K. (2023). Developing misinformation immunity: How to reason-check fallacious news in a human–computer interaction environment. *Social Media + Society.* https://doi.org/10.1177/20563051221150407

Pennycook, G. (2023). A framework for understanding reasoning errors. *Advances in Experimental Social Psychology, 67,* 131–208. https://doi.org/10.1016/bs.aesp.2022.11.003

Pennycook, G., & Rand, D. G. (2022). Accuracy prompts are a replicable and generalizable approach for reducing the spread of misinformation. *Nature Communications, 13,* 2333. https://doi.org/10.1038/s41467-022-30073-5

Pilditch, T. D., Roozenbeek, J., Madsen, J. K., & van der Linden, S. (2022). Psychological inoculation can reduce susceptibility to misinformation in large rational agent networks. *Research Society Open Science, 9*(8), 211953. https://doi.org/10.1098/rsos.211953

Roozenbeek, J., van der Linden, S., Goldberg, B., Rathje, S., Lewandowsky, S. (2022). Psychological inoculation improves resilience against misinformation on social media. *Science Advances, 8,* eabo6254. https://doi.org/10.1126/sciadv.abo6254

Schuetz, S., Sykes, T., & Venkatesh, V. (2021). Combating COVID-19 fake news on social media through fact-checking. *European Journal of Information Systems, 30*(4), 376–388. https://doi.org/10.1080/0960085X.2021.1895682

Shin, D. (2023). *Algorithms, humans, and interactions.* Routledge. https://doi.org/10.1201/b23083

Shin, D. (2024). *Artificial misinformation: Exploring human-algorithm interaction online.* Springer Nature. https://doi.org/10.1007/978-3-031-52569-8

Shin, D., & Akhtar, F. (2024). Algorithmic inoculation against misinformation: How to build cognitive immunity against misinformation. *Journal of Broadcasting & Electronic Media, 68*(2), 153–175. https://doi.org/10.1080/08838151.2024.2323712

Spampatti, T., Hahnel, U. J. J., Trutnevyte, E., Brosch, T. (2024). Psychological inoculation strategies to fight climate disinformation across 12 countries. *Nature Human Behavior, 8,* 380–398. https://doi.org/10.1038/s41562-023-01736-0

Tay, L., Hurlstone, M., Kurz, T., & Ecker, H. (2021). A comparison of prebunking and debunking interventions for implied versus explicit misinformation. *British Journal of Psychology, 113*(3), 591–607. https://doi.org/10.1111/bjop.12551

Traberg, C., Roozenbeek, J., & van der Linden, S. (2022). Psychological inoculation against misinformation. *The ANNALS of the American Academy of Political and Social Science, 700*(1), 136–151. https://doi.org/10.1177/00027162221087936

Tully, M., Bode, L., & Vraga, E. (2020). Mobilizing users: Does exposure to misinformation and its correction affect users' responses to a health misinformation post? *Social Media + Society, 6*(4). https://doi.org/10.1177/2056305120978377

van der Linden, S. (2023). *Foolproof: Why misinformation infects our minds and how to build immunity.* W.W. Norton & Company.

van der Linden, S. (2024). Misinformation poses a bigger threat to democracy than you might think. *Nature, 630*(8015), 29–32. https://doi.org/10.1038/d41586-024-01587-3

van der Linden, S., Roozenbeek, J., & Compton, J. (2021). Inoculating against fake news about COVID-19. *Frontiers in Psychology, 12,* 3554. https://doi.org/10.3389/fpsyg.2020.566790

Vivion, M., Anassour Laouan Sidi, E., Betsch, C., Dionne, M., Dubé, E., Driedger, S. M., Gagnon, D., Graham, J., Greyson, D., Hamel, D., Lewandowsky, S., MacDonald, N., Malo, B., Meyer, S. B., Schmid, P., Steenbeek, A., van der Linden, S., Verger, P.,

Witteman, H. O., & Yesilada, M. (2022). Prebunking messaging to inoculate against COVID-19 vaccine misinformation: An effective strategy for public health. *Journal of Communication in Healthcare*, *15*(3), 232–242. https://doi.org/10.1080/17538068.2022.2044606

Weiler, S., Matt, C., & Hess, T. (2022). Immunizing with information – Inoculation messages against conversational agents' response failures. *Electron Markets*, *32*, 239–258. https://doi.org/10.1007/s12525-021-00509-9

Subject Index

A

accountability frameworks 3, 7, 14, 63, 91
accountability heuristics 92
accountability in AI systems 206–220
adaptive algorithms 282
adaptive moral frameworks 264
adoption (AI) 150, 163, 171, 189, 191, 201
adversarial attack 37, 232
adversarial behaviors 210
adversarial debiasing 251, 263
AI acceptance and adoption 171–189
AI autonomy 17–18, 22–23, 31–32, 122–124, 189, 243–244, 283–285
AI bias feedback loop 21, 70, 101, 192
AI-driven bias checking 87–90
AI empowerment 23, 110, 151, 172–174, 192
AI ethics frameworks 5–6, 13
AI for social good 5
AI governance models 229–233, 239–248
AI immunity 109, 125, 270, 272, 275, 277–280
AI in assistive technologies 173
AI in healthcare 60–61, 88, 244
AI in journalism 198–201, 219–220
AI journalism ethics 199, 201–203, 207, 211–212, 217–219, 223
AI trust paradox 23
AI value alignment 16
algocracy 229, 247
algorithmic accountability mechanisms 92, 240
algorithmic attributes 91, 165, 190
algorithmic bias 20–21, 37, 50, 87–93, 105
algorithmic decision-making 263
algorithmic divide 48, 160, 252, 254
algorithmic equity 149
algorithmic effects 60–68
algorithmic governance 119, 229, 247
algorithmic immunization 270, 287
algorithmic manipulation 23, 32, 50, 60, 72, 106–107, 133, 211
algorithmic nudging 49, 57, 105–106, 109, 122
amplification (algorithmic) 87, 88, 92, 116, 220, 254, 268, 280
anonymity heuristic 47
artificial morality 13–15, 30
autonomous moral agents 17
autonomy and AI 6, 17–18, 115

B

bias detection 7, 275
bias detection methods 88–89
bias mitigation 151, 201, 240, 266
bias-resilient AI systems 281, 284–285
black-boxes 16, 37, 51, 88, 94, 237
built-in privacy in AI 48

C

California Consumer Privacy Act 235
California Invasion of Privacy Act (CIPA) 38
ChatGPT 10, 32, 34, 37, 82, 94, 95, 112, 158, 169, 178, 188, 190, 194–197, 225, 271
Choice architecture 59, 107, 108, 109, 115, 119, 123, 124, 265
Coerced 50
cognitive AI models 91–92
cognitive heuristics 95, 103, 127, 129, 137, 140, 171–172, 191, 193
computational algorithmic evaluation 211
control heuristic 45
conversational agents 42, 58, 84, 102–103, 288
credibility 32, 33, 39, 59, 61, 62, 65, 66–70, 72–83, 93–104, 107, 112, 128, 130
cross-cultural AI ethics 252

D

data-driven decision-making 237
data protection and privacy 36, 38, 46, 54, 106, 162, 201, 215–216, 230, 230, 236, 264
debiasing mechanisms 87–90, 138
debunking 4, 91, 271, 275–276, 279, 287
decision readiness 42
decoding 34, 37, 39, 41, 43, 47, 49, 51, 53, 55, 57, 59
deepfakes and misinformation 126–145
deep learning transparency 88, 118, 237–238
default setting heuristics 47
democratization of AI Access 118, 123, 231
deontology 17
diagnosticity 91, 93, 103, 127, 130–142,
discernability 127, 137, 138
diversity-aware 10, 59, 125, 249, 250, 251–269
dual-process 25, 32, 42, 91, 164, 169, 171, 202, 218, 223, 273

E

ecosystem (AI) 42, 79, 234, 236
echo chambers 220, 250, 257, 259, 267, 280
empathy in AI 5, 16, 24, 29, 122, 222, 243
epistemology of AI 8, 9, 147
ethical AI adoption 6–7
ethical AI principles 6–8
ethical dilemmas in AI 27–28
ethical sensemaking 26, 79, 91, 150
ethics by design 201, 239, 246
ethics-centric AI regulation 231
EU AI Act 238, 240, 241, 242
explainability frameworks 18, 37, 46, 62–65, 84,
        94–95, 120, 137, 151, 156, 210–214
explainability in journalism 213
explainability heuristic 46
explanatory cues 113, 114, 129, 132, 133, 135, 138,
        144, 171, 213

F

fact-checking 61, 78, 80, 101, 112, 114, 115, 132,
        142, 162, 200, 211, 217, 275, 279, 281,
        287
fairness heuristics 19, 92
fairness in AI 89, 150, 159, 230, 245
FAT–REAP framework 220
federated learning 48, 269
filter bubble 98, 103, 111, 250, 257, 259
fraud detection by AI 38

G

generative AI (GAI) 34, 35, 43, 61, 84, 91,
        109–114, 121, 141, 144, 169, 175, 181,
        200, 225
generative algorithms 167
Get Inside the Heads 65
governance of algorithms 48, 57, 61, 90, 112, 118,
        201, 229–233, 239

H

hallucination 121, 127, 156–158, 164, 173, 176,
        190
heuristics in AI interaction 19–20
human autonomy and AI control 6–7
human-AI co-creation 120
human-AI collaboration 6, 22, 244
human-AI emotional interaction 16, 24
human-AI feedback loops 21, 70, 101, 192
human-AI trust 22, 33, 45
human-centered AI 6–10
humanity 3, 8, 18, 27, 27–30, 33, 82, 211, 222,
        248–249, 252, 254

I

impact of AI on society 6–7, 18, 22, 30, 57,
        123
impartiality 156, 202, 206–209, 217–218, 221
inclusivity 22, 210, 234, 239, 243, 249, 252, 253,
        254, 255, 264, 266
interaction effects 67, 74, 75, 76, 77, 99
interpretability 63, 119, 159, 166, 210, 213,
        237, 245
immediate gratification heuristic 47

J

journalistic heuristics 202, 207
journalistic values 199, 201, 209, 210, 213, 216,
        220, 258

L

large language model (LLM) 34, 109, 189, 268
labeling 56, 61, 66, 68, 77, 80, 82, 112, 124, 133,
        155, 217
literary (algorithm, AI) 28, 29, 31, 55, 97, 117, 119,
        120, 140, 144, 265

M

machine heuristics 19, 67, 69, 74, 77
machine learning transparency 16, 19, 30, 37
media accountability 211, 221
mediating effects 75, 76, 139
misinformation diffusion 79, 92, 142, 151,
        162, 194
misinformation inoculation 91, 103, 123, 270
model-close approach 63
moderation effect 73, 74, 77
moral agency in AI systems 13, 17–19, 88
moral challenges in AI 14, 115
moral heuristics 171
multimodal interaction 224, 251

N

natural language processing (NLP) 17, 188, 195,
        238, 253
news recommendation by AI 61, 65, 67–70, 72–75,
        77–81
newsroom AI ethics 198
normative heuristic 45
nudging techniques 45, 48–62, 71–84, 105–125,
        256

O

ontology of AI 11, 17

P

pairwise *t*-test 73, 74, 136
paternalism 52, 114
phenomenology of AI 8, 9, 85
polarization 21, 66, 113, 123, 258–259, 267
prebunking 275–279, 285–287
privacy calculus 43, 44, 58, 59, 83, 196
privacy decision-making models 37, 39, 40, 49, 51, 56, 59, 114
privacy ethics 106–107
privacy fatigue 53, 57
privacy-preserving AI 36, 47–50, 55–61, 117, 210, 218, 225, 233, 244, 285
privacy-preserving algorithms 57, 218

R

reciprocity heuristic 45
regulatory compliance in AI 198, 230
responsible AI 23, 29, 31, 34, 38, 110, 160, 195, 198, 200
risk assessment in AI systems 113, 172, 177, 186, 187
risk heuristic 45
risk-benefit heuristics 191

S

self-regulation 236, 242
sensemaking 26, 31, 79, 91, 103, 124, 150–174, 199, 220
skepticism 20, 21, 54, 60, 78, 88, 98, 124, 142, 271, 273, 274, 279, 281–283
social construction of AI ethics 26, 27

social heuristics 21, 163
social responsibility of media 218
South Korea 239, 242
source attribution 69, 130, 133, 139, 144
source confidentiality 215
source reliability 212
sustainability in AI 168, 220
systematic process 26, 91, 93, 102, 128, 135–139, 163–164, 186–191

T

transparency and explainability 18, 48, 101
transparency in AI systems 62, 92, 241
transparency nudges 67–68, 78–80, 114
transparency paradox 62, 81
trolley problem 16
trust effects 70, 78
trust-in-the-brand heuristic 47
two-step process 260–261
Type 1 25, 107, 113–115, 152, 156, 158–159, 202, 207, 208
Type 2 25, 107, 113, 115, 152, 156, 160, 161, 202, 211

U

user cognitive heuristics 78, 95, 103, 107, 127, 129, 137, 140, 171, 191, 193
user trust in AI 6–19

V

value-sensitive AI 28, 120–122, 250

Name Index

A

Acquisti, A. 37, 39, 43, 44, 45, 50, 53, 57
Adadi, A. 63
Anderson, M. 1, 27
Anderson, S. 1, 27
Araujo, T. 58, 131, 142, 252, 257, 266
Arrieta, A. 63
Avnoon, N. 6

B

Bandura, A. 173, 189, 194
Bonnefon, J. F. 17–18, 126
Bryanov, M. 216
Burrell, J. 39

C

Calvo, R. 6–7, 233
Chaiken, S. 22, 25, 31, 91, 101, 128, 140, 142, 163, 168, 172, 194
Coeckelbergh, M. 2, 6, 10, 16, 31, 150, 168, 195
Compton, J. 109, 123, 270, 271, 281, 286
Crawford, K. 251, 267
Cristianini, N. 230

D

Diakopoulos, N. 66, 81, 92, 93, 97, 102, 198, 200, 202, 223, 224
Dignum, V. 230, 245, 246

E

Ecker, H. 88, 94, 96, 102, 132, 222, 270, 275, 280, 286

F

Floridi, L. 10, 14, 22, 23, 31, 229, 230, 246, 247
Formosa, P. 7

H

Hayes, A. 74, 75, 82, 194
Helberger, N. 97, 102, 111, 123, 169, 257, 258, 259, 260, 266, 267

J

Jesse, S. 211

K

Kahneman, D. 42, 58
Knudsen, J. 256–257
Kumar, V. 25, 32, 150, 169, 183, 194, 202, 223

L

Lewandowsky, S. 102, 275, 283, 286, 287

M

Metzger, M. 25, 31, 33, 65, 69, 83, 96, 103, 132, 144, 197, 286

N

Noble, S. 26, 32, 87, 98, 103, 213, 261, 268

P

Peacock, C. 65, 66, 83
Pennycook, G. 78, 83, 91, 94, 103, 112, 124, 130, 144, 271, 280, 283, 286, 287
Prunkl, C. 6–7

R

Roozenbeek, J. 91, 103, 274, 277, 283, 285, 287

S

Schoenherr, J. 149, 150, 169
Shin, D. 1, 6, 17, 19, 88, 106, 126, 198, 207, 208, 270
Shneiderman, B. 2, 10
Sumner, J. 121
Sundar, S. 18, 19, 21, 33, 46, 60, 67, 69, 77, 84, 91, 95, 97, 99, 102, 112, 127, 128, 139, 144, 163, 170, 250, 267, 283
Sunstein, C. 50, 52, 60, 105, 107, 117, 125, 286

T

Taddeo, M. 229, 230, 246, 247
Thaler, R. 50, 52, 55, 60, 105, 107, 117, 125

V

Vallor, S. 247
Van der Linden, S. 103, 109, 125, 271, 272, 275, 280, 283, 285, 286, 287

W

Wallach, W. 13
Wu-Ouyang, Y. 219

Z

Zimmermann, V. 35, 36, 37, 38, 44, 47, 48, 50, 52, 58, 59, 60